DESIGNED TO CRUISE

By ROGER MARSHALL

Designed To Win

Designed To Cruise

Race To Win

Sailor's Guide to Production Sailboats

Yacht Design Details

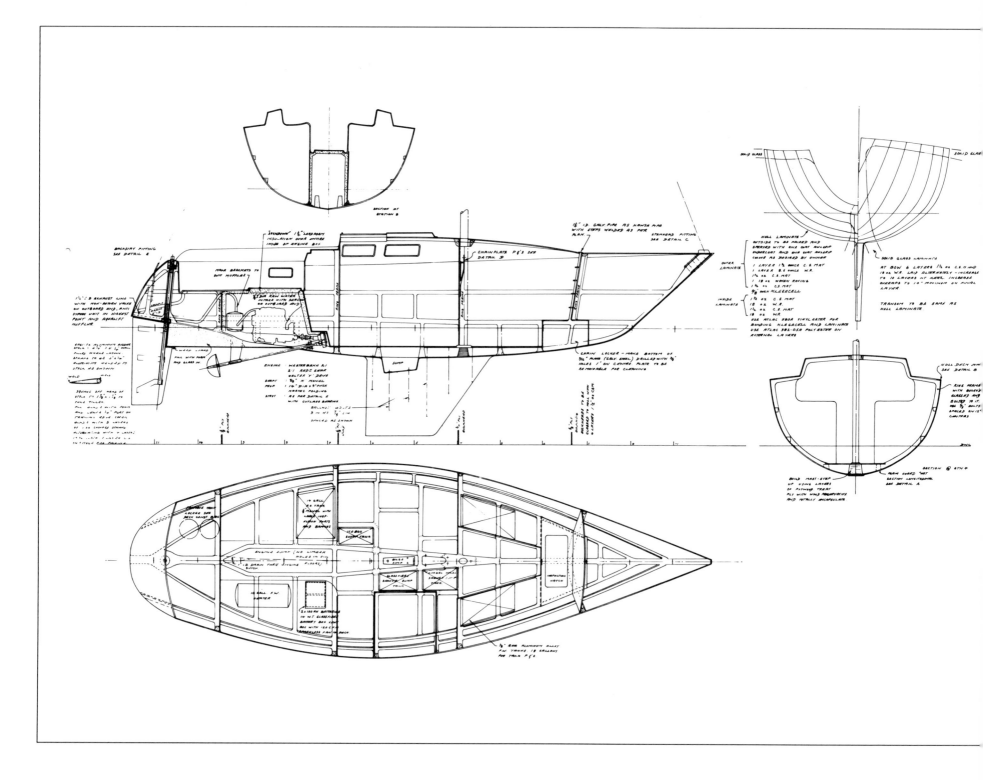

DESIGNED TO CRUISE

ROGER MARSHALL

W·W·NORTON & COMPANY

New York · London

The text of this book is composed in Aster, with the display set in Eras Book.
Composition by Com Com.
Printing by Arcata Graphics/Kingsport.
Binding by Nicholstone Book Bindery.
Book design by Jacques Chazaud.

Marshall, Roger.
    Designed to cruise / Roger Marshall.
        p.   cm.
    Includes bibliographical references and index.
    1. Yachts and yachting.   I. Title.
  VM331.M369   1990
  623.8′223—dc20

ISBN 0-393-03333-3   90-38979

W. W. Norton & Company, Inc., 500 Fifth Avenue, New York, N.Y. 10110
W. W. Norton & Company, Ltd., 37 Great Russell Street, London WC1B 3NU

Contents

CHAPTER 2: CONSTRUCTION   47

CHAPTER 3: SAIL PLANS AND RIGS   85

CHAPTER 4: INSIDE THE HULL   119

CHAPTER 5: THE CRUISING DECK   157

CHAPTER 6: ANCHORS: THEIR USES AND STORAGE   185

CHAPTER 7: A SENSE OF DIRECTION 199

CHAPTER 8: POWERING THE YACHT: THE ENGINE AND THE GENERATOR 219

Chapter 9: PUMPS, COMPRESSORS, AND THE SUPPORTING SYSTEMS *231*

Chapter 10: THE ELECTRICAL SYSTEM *241*

Chapter 11: ELECTRONICS *255*

Chapter 12: THE PUSH-BUTTON BOAT   265

Chapter 13: HAVING A NEW BOAT DESIGNED FOR YOU   269

Introduction

"Designed To Cruise"—the title conjures up visions of a purpose-built yacht sailing off into the sunset with the mountains of a remote island slowly receding in the distance. However, this is a book about the ideal performance cruising boat as seen through the eyes of a designer. There are very few similar ideal boats, though: every sailor has different ideas, ideas developed on many different oceans and in many different parts of the world. The designer's job is to consider all the alternatives and integrate them into the perfect yacht for that sailor—which may not be the perfect yacht for another. For instance, one person may want his boat to be as simple as possible, even down to a hand-pumped fresh water system, a bucket and chuck-it toilet, and two or three hanked on sails; another more modern yachtsman may require all the luxuries of home, right down to the TV, VCR, stereo, and air conditioning.

In this book I've attempted to look at many of the facets of the modern cruising yacht and to eliminate prejudices that may blind a reader to the real value of an item. For instance, a popular misconception is that a yacht must be heavy to be seaworthy. If that were true the ultimate boat would be made of lead! Well-engineered boats can be faster, safer, and more seaworthy than a heavy craft, but lighter yachts have a different motion in the ocean and need to be sailed differently, which often makes them seem less seaworthy.

This book discusses some of the ways of handling a boat, but only from the standpoint of design. It also looks at the huge range of equipment available to a sailor fitting out a yacht today. I have recommended only equipment I have used and, whenever possible, noted comments from fellow sailors on other items they have recommended.

This book, then, is about the modern performance cruising yacht. I make no apologies for including a section on such esoteric items as watermakers. If you are sailing far offshore a watermaker can be a boon. Nevertheless, there are so many more items that could be discussed. Bow thrusters, for instance, are now being installed on large cruising boats. Some large boats have twin engines. How do they handle? Perhaps the success of this book will beget another book on these new and innovative features.

Push-button sail handling is another developing area. Developments in the area of short-handed sailing have created an opening for systems that enable a crew of 2 to do the work of 10. Without roller furling gears, autopilots, and electric or hydraulically operated winches, more crew would be required, necessitating higher costs and bigger boats. Many new designs are being built that use the latest in this technology. How long will it be before the boat depicted in Chapter 12 is sailing?

As much as I would have liked to cover all the ground, the publisher would not be happy with a tome of several thousand pages, so some items are brief summaries of what is available. In those cases I recommend that you talk to your designer, builder, or chandlery manager to help you make up your own mind.

The process of building a boat is a long one. First comes the design, then the discussions with the builder. Then the keel is laid and the boat is built. I hope this book, in some small way, helps you make the right decisions to get you your ideal yacht.

Acknowledgments

It is always hard to put your ideas on paper, and even harder to make a considered opinion about gear and equipment. A reader might select a piece of equipment on my recommendation only to have it fail when he uses it. I sincerely hope such disappointments will be rare. Almost all the gear I mention I have used at one time or another. It has worked for me and I hope it will work for you. When I suggest gear that I haven't used, I do so on recommendation from fellow sailors and professionals in the industry whose opinions I respect and who were kind enough to comment on the manuscript for this book. To them I give sincere thanks for taking time out of their busy schedules to peruse the manuscript and to supply the photos or pictures I needed. They are:

Roger Birdenell, Cetrek Autopilots.
Bob Congdon, Suunto Compasses.
Ben Hall, Hall Spars, Bristol, Rhode Island.

Will Keene, Vice President for Sales, The Edson Corporation, New Bedford, Massachusetts.
Bill Larson, Exmar Inc., Newport, Rhode Island.
James Lippman, for permission to use the ABYC references.
Steve Lirakis, Lirakis Harnesses, Newport, Rhode Island.
Jim Nolan, President, Autohelm America Inc.
Dick Rath, Vice President for Sales and Marketing, IMI Barient.
Humphrey Sullivan, mentor, sailor, and all-around good friend.
David Vietor, Marblehead Associates.
Bob Wallstrom, fellow designer, Blue Hill, Maine.

Roger Marshall
Jamestown, Rhode Island

DESIGNED TO CRUISE

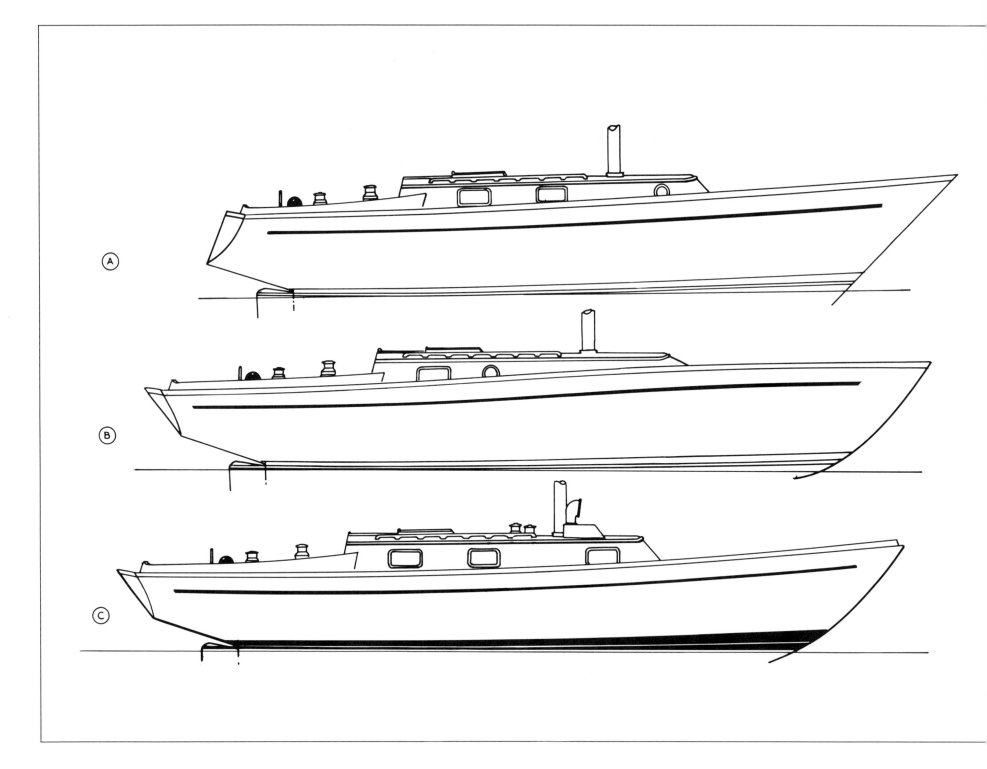

CHAPTER 1
The Cruising Hull

When a designer sets out to design a cruising boat, the shape he draws is based upon the owner's requirements, factors imposed by the ocean, and the designer's own knowledge of how a particular hull form reacts under sail. When that same designer works upon a racing yacht, the hull form is shaped by the particular racing rule and drawn to take maximum advantage of that rule, occasionally to the detriment of good naval architecture.

For example, during the latter part of the last century, beam was taxed excessively under British racing rules and racing yacht hulls evolved into long, extra narrow shapes, which took advantage of the heavy penalty on beam. What is more unfortunate is that, often, cruising yachts are based upon designs drawn up for racing: every sailor harbors a subconscious desire to get there before the next fellow. There is no need for this, however. In fact, a hull designed purely for cruising will often be faster and more seakindly than a similar racing hull, which may be distorted to obtain a lower rating.

WHAT DOES A HULL DO?

Before we get into a discussion of particular hull shapes, it is worthwhile to go back to basics and ask ourselves what the hull of a cruising yacht must do. Should it keep the water out? Should it float lightly over the tops of the waves? Or should it divide the water and smash its way through the ocean? The answer is that it should do all this and more.

A good hull should keep the water out by virtue of its structural integrity. It should appear to float lightly on the waves, and it should be strong enough to resist impacts from waterborne debris and the occasional light collision with a dock. It should also do more. It should have adequate length, beam, and draft to carry the people, stores, and accommodation to faraway places. The hull should have structural strength to carry the loads imposed by the spars, the keel, and the sea. The bow and stern should be shaped so that the water flows smoothly past the hull. There should be enough freeboard to give adequate headroom, and stability to allow the boat to heel without submerging the deck. As you can see, there are many components to the cruising hull.

Length

The speed at which a boat can sail through the water is governed by its length and displacement. If a hull is light enough to use dynamic lift to rise above the surface of the water, it is said to be able to plane and will be able to move very much faster than a displacement hull, which must plow through the water. Almost all cruising boats are of the displacement hull form, and as such there is a direct relationship between the speed at which that boat can sail and the length of the hull.

FIGURE 1.1. *When a boat is sailing in smooth water its speed can be estimated from the number of wave peaks along its side. For instance, if the wave length L is taken from P1 to P2 then wave A has three crests each ⅓ of L. If the distance L is 36 feet then the boat speed is .33 × $\sqrt{36}$ = 2 knots. Now, let's suppose the boat is sailing faster. The wave crests are at P1 and P2, therefore the boat speed is 1 × $\sqrt{36}$ = 6 knots. As boat speed increases so will the wave length until a theoretical maximum is reached. This maximum will be about 1.34 × $\sqrt{36}$ = 8 knots.*

This relationship was first discovered by Froude at the beginning of this century and is known as Froude's Law. It says that the maximum speed a displacement hull can move through the water is 1.34 times the square root of the waterline length, or

$$Vs \text{ (knots)} = 1.34 \times \sqrt{LWL} \text{ (feet)}$$

where Vs is the speed of the boat. Figure 1.1 shows the reasoning behind this theory. If we wanted to be strictly correct we would change "LWL" to read "sailing length," but for comparison purposes LWL is generally used.

For instance, a yacht that is 33 feet (approximately 10 meters) on the LWL will have a maximum speed potential of $1.34 \times \sqrt{33} = 7.70$ knots. In very heavy conditions the boat may exceed this speed as it surges or surfs down a wave, often reaching speeds in excess of 1.5 times the sailing length. A boat with a displacement/length ratio under 75 which has enough sail area may exceed twice the sailing length under planing conditions.

The sailing length will also depend upon the shape of the ends of the yacht. For instance, a boat shaped as in Figure 1.2a will have a much longer sailing length than a boat shaped as in Figure 1.2b.

Beam

A beamy boat is slower in light to moderate winds than a narrow boat of the same length, all else being equal, because with wider beam there is more frontal area and more wetted surface being pushed through the water. But the fatter hull will have more stability and therefore should be able to carry more sail, making it better in heavier winds. So beam is one of the first tradeoffs a designer must make

when laying out the boat. Enough beam for stability but not too much to slow the boat.

Beam also affects the interior accommodation, sheeting angles, the deck platform, and the chainplate position. A comfortable cruising

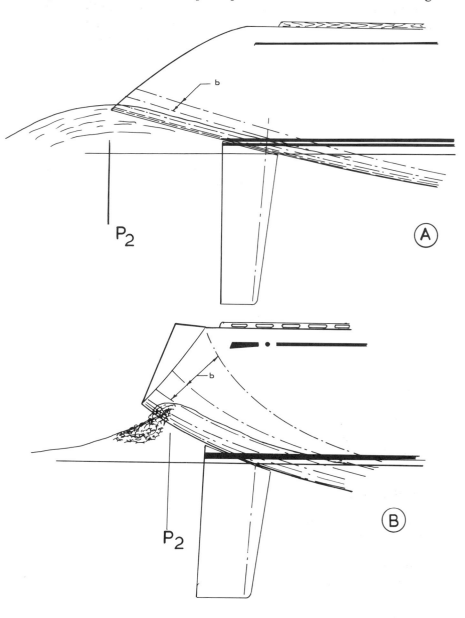

FIGURE 1.2. *If the buttocks (b) sweep upward fairly steeply, then the following wave will tend to try to follow them until gravity makes it collapse. This will happen at point P2 in Figure 1.2b. In 1.2a the bottocks are much lower and the wave crest tends to move aft rather than upward. This will increase the distance between the bow and stern crests and allow the boat to sail faster through the water. Maximum possible boat speed is reached when the buttocks are very flat and the boat "planes." At this speed the boat is fully supported by hydrodynamic lift. However, flat buttocks are no guarantee that a boat can plane. It will need other features, such as light weight and directional stability.*

hull should have good accommodations, but in many older, long, narrow British cruising boats the interior layout is rather like a railway carriage, with berths along each side and not quite enough room to get past the table. Unfortunately, reduced beam was emphasized by early British rating rules, and many older cruising hulls reflect this thinking. Many modern racing hulls, in my opinion, go too far the other way with fat, shallow hulls that have poor stability at very large angles of heel.

Hull Draft

In boats that follow modern racing practice, the hull draft is becoming less as the span or depth of the keel increases. This is good for performance craft, but on cruising hulls it reduces storage under the cabin sole, and any bilge water that gets into the boat will not be contained in the bilge and is sure to get up into lockers and drawers on either side of the boat.

For this reason cruising yachts should have a moderately deep bilge or a fairly large sump situated in the area over the top of the keel. The drawings for the boat should also show plenty of limber holes to allow water to drain into the sump.

Total Draft

While hull draft is the depth of hull from the water surface to the bottom of the hull, the total draft of a boat is the maximum draft including the keel. There has been a tendency in recent years to minimize draft on cruising vessels. Until 1983 this meant you either had to have a centerboard or some other form of lifting keel to be efficient to windward. In 1983 the 12-meter *Australia* showed a winged keel that dramatically improved shallow draft performance. With this feature yachts can cruise in areas previously unreachable, without the encumbrance of a centerboard or lifting keel.

Displacement

Simply put, displacement is a nautical way of saying how heavy a boat is. For instance, a boat that is 12 tons displacement will weigh 12 tons.

What does displacement do for you? According to Uffa Fox, the only place for weight is on a steamroller. Unfortunately, many sailors believe that you need a heavy displacement yacht to sail offshore. This

TABLE 1.1 LIGHT OR HEAVY DISPLACEMENT?	
Light Displacement	Heavy Displacement
Light hull, usually easily driven	Heavy hull, any shape
Usually a small rig	Needs large rig for best light air performance
Accelerates easily in puffy winds	Slow to accelerate, but will coast through flat spots
Smaller, less expensive rig and sails	
Smaller, less expensive engine	
Lower fuel consumption	
All gear is lighter	Heavier, stronger gear
Livelier performance	Better motion and performance in headwinds
Faster reaching and running	
Hull should be carefully engineered	Built in redundancy, with greater margin for error
Large amount of stores affect performance greatly	Large amount of stores has small effect on performance
	Stronger feeling of security in inclement conditions on a well-built hull
Needs less ballast	Needs more ballast for same stability

is in part, I believe, because of misleading advertising, which equates seaworthiness with weight. (If this were true the ultimate yacht would be made of lead!) Light displacement boats are good for offshore cruising providing they are well engineered. Engineering is the key to reducing weight, and a well-built lightweight boat will absorb a tremendous amount of damage before it will come apart.

There are pervasive arguments for lighter offshore cruising boats. They get you there sooner. Thus bad weather at sea can be avoided more easily. Against this must be balanced the quicker, bouncier motion, which will probably be more tiring. Lighter boats also use less material in the hull structure, which has the double benefit of reducing the cost on a per pound basis and allowing the size of other items in the boat, such as the engine, sail plan and mast height, tankage, and ballast weight, to be made smaller. But don't fall into the trap set by many so-called experts, of using expensive hi-tech materials when conventional low-tech materials will do the job equally well. For instance, it was suggested that we use a Kevlar running rigging on a small boat to save weight aloft. We had to increase the diameter of the Kevlar to make it large enough to grip, and the total saving came to about four ounces. Of course, the cost was almost triple that of conventional line. In another instance, the owner of a boat we designed insisted that we use Kevlar as an outer skin on the hull to increase impact resistance. When we showed him a cost-performance analysis of conventional materials against Kevlar and graphite he agreed to go with the cheaper conventional materials at a total weight gain of a few pounds and an appreciable monetary gain. If a light boat is well engineered it can be a good seaboat, without the added expense of exotic materials, which raise the cost often beyond the value they give to the structure.

On the other hand there are people who say that a heavily built hull must be stronger. Usually this is true, but engineering in a heavy hull is less critical and more often likely to be sloppy. I once sailed (not far!) on a very heavily built 45-foot ketch that had layups over 2 inches thick in the bottom of the hull. But in way of the chainplates daylight could be seen because the laminate was improperly built! For the sailor who has to choose between light or heavy displacement, the options are laid out in Table 1.1.

THE SHAPE OF THE ENDS OF THE BOAT

Bow and stern shapes have a tremendous impact on the speed, aesthetics, sales, pitching motion, and sailing ability of the boat. There-fore, it behooves a designer to select the shape most suited for the boat's intended purpose.

The Bow

Looking back through the history of yachting we can see that often the part of a boat that has the most influence on the yachting writer's eye is the bow. In the 1983 America's Cup challenge pundits discussed the "bobbed" bows of 12 meters as they did 50 years ago, when the "spoon" bow first made its appearance. Today most bow profiles are a raked straight line following the effect of the IOR (International Offshore Rule) calculations for forward overhang component. In this calculation designers discovered that the way to get the lowest rating was to make the profile a series of straight lines. Most cruising boats followed suit, and now we see most bow profiles developed from straight lines.

Apart from the shapes that have been around since ships first sailed, most changes in bow profile have usually been dictated by a rating rule and carried over into cruising boat design.

What is the best bow shape for the offshore cruiser? For me it is the shape that best allows the tasks normally done in the bow areas to be performed easily. For instance, sails must be attached to the headstay, mooring lines passed through chocks on the bow, and anchors handled forward, which means not only the anchor, chain, and line but bow rollers, an anchor windlass, and anchor storage must be positioned there. There should also be sufficient freeboard to reduce the amount of green water likely to come aboard and large scuppers to get rid of it when conditions are very rough. Finally, there should be some form of rail, toerail, or bulwark to stop anybody working forward slipping off the deck. All these practical considerations can be applied to many bow profiles. But sailing ability or other desirable features can dictate a bow shape which may compromise practicality. For instance, a bow that is U-shaped in section may be desirable for a lightweight hull that has to beat into a seaway, but there will not be much room to retrieve an anchor or fit a large amount of anchor handling gear. Figure 1.3 shows some of the options for bow shapes.

Stern Shapes

The variety of stern shapes appears to be so large that it would take this entire book to discuss them. However, by looking at how the water flows around the hull and what kind of waves are generated we

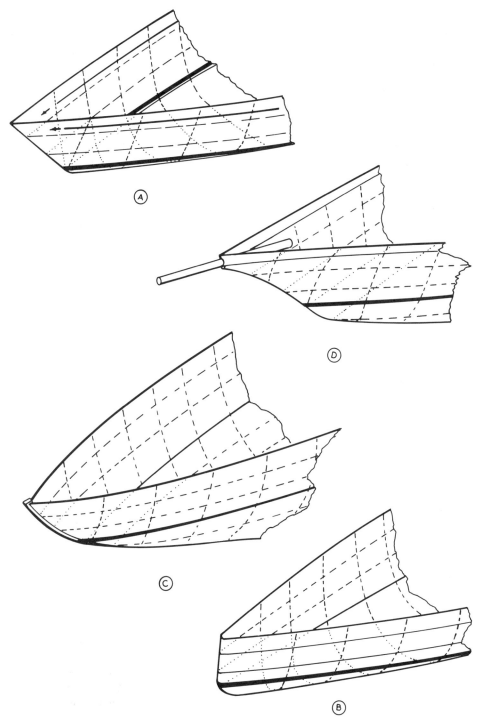

can quickly decide on the most seakindly type of stern for a cruising hull. When we discuss the stern shape we get a better idea of how the water flows if we look at the buttocks and the diagonals, buttocks for downwind sailing and diagonals for beating and reaching.

For instance, on many rounded stern boats the buttock lines tend to sweep upward fairly steeply, as in Figure 1.2b . When the boat is upright and sailing downwind the water wants to follow the buttock line as far as gravity will allow it. As boat speed increases, the water climbs higher up the buttocks, generating a large quarterwave. This effectively locks the stern wave tightly to the stern of the boat, limiting boat speed and spending a large amount of energy generating the stern wave. The opposite type of stern has buttocks that are very flat. In this case, if the boat is light enough the water flow breaks free of the transom, as in Figure 1.2a. As boat speed increases, the water simply keeps flowing out past the boat. The wave formed is simply a pressure wave, which pops up somewhere astern of the boat depending on boat speed. These flat buttocks are typical of a planning craft, where very little energy is spent dragging a large quarterwave. It is the designer's job to select the best slope of the buttocks to suit the displacement and anticipated speed of the new design.

The Diagonals

In the previous discussion we looked at a boat sailing upright and downwind. The picture is complicated by the fact that the boat also has to sail upwind and across the wind. Under these conditions the shape of the diagonals becomes critical. (See Figure 1.4).
If we look at the shape of the hull in Figure 1.4, then the diagonals (solid lines *A, B, C, D*) are fairly straight. This tells us that the water

FIGURE 1.3.   *Various bow shapes. A is the modern shape bred in part from the IOR influence on yacht design. B is the plumb bowed shape often used in racers, where the waterline has to be made as long as possible. Again, it is an influence that has spread into cruising boat design from considerations other than good naval architecture. C is the more traditional bow, which has a reserve of bouyancy as the boat pitches into a seaway. It also has a moderately large area on deck for anchor and sail handling. However, it is perceived, today, as old-fashioned and is not likely to become a regular fixture on new cruising boats. C is the well-known clipper bow that has also been around for many years.*

will flow cleanly past them and the boat will probably have good speed upwind. Now if we modify this shape (dashed lines *A2, B2, C2, D2,*) and round the diagonals off, then the water will act in a similar way to that at the buttocks of our round stern boat. It will be sucked in behind the boat and lock the vessel into a fixed speed. It will also cause a lot of turbulence as it tries to break clean of the back of the boat. This means that a hull with this type of diagonals sailing at moderately high speeds would create a large wave immediately astern.

The ultimate conclusion of this type of stern would be the truncated look we saw in the 12-meter *Mariner* in 1973. People said of this boat that she sailed with a "bone in her stern" because of the amount of water dragged along in the wake.

On the other hand, a boat that has reasonably flat buttocks and nicely curved diagonals can leave the stern wave some distance behind the boat. This increases the "sailing length" and, consequently, the maximum attainable boat speed. Therefore, we can see that the shape of the buttocks and the diagonals at the stern are a good indication of the potential boat speed.

FIGURE 1.4. *While the buttocks tell you about the sailing characteristics of the boat in the upright condition as we saw in Figure 1.2, the diagonals can tell you a lot about how the boat will sail when heeled. In Figure 1.4a, by cutting the sections on lines A, B, C, and D and drawing the cut lines out as in 1.4b, a designer can obtain a feel for the way the water will flow past the stern. The solid lines A, B, C, and D show that the water will leave the hull smoothly, while the dashed lines will suck the water in toward the centerline. This will generate a wave at the stern of the boat that will absorb energy.*

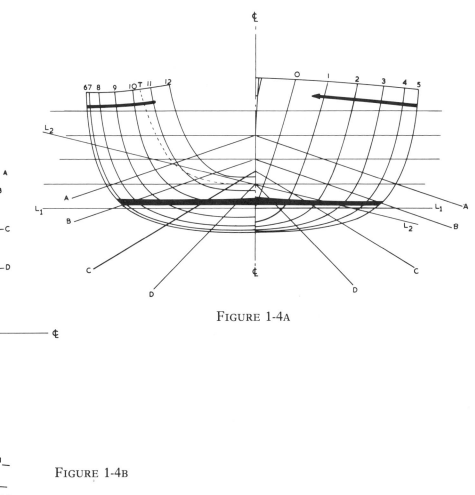

FIGURE 1-4A

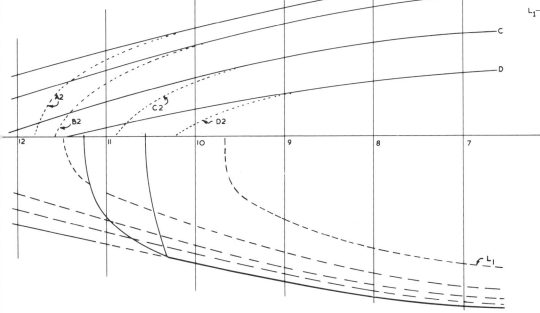

FIGURE 1-4B

Transsoms

While the stern shape can make or mar the appearance of the boat and can affect the steering ability quite considerably, the shape of the transom has small influence on the sailing ability of the boat, but it has a huge influence on the aesthetics. For instance, we can take a boat as in Figure 1.4 and change the transom in a number of ways. Figure 1.5 shows the same boat with the different transom. Both give a different character to the stern and affect the sailing ability of the boat only slightly. So what do you look for?

Only the boat buyer can answer this question. If it looks "right" but doesn't appear to suit the boat, then avoid it.

Does the Stern Shape Affect Steering?

Steering ability is of prime importance, and boats that do not steer well can be dangerous and make sailing unbearable. Unfortunately, there are few indicators to tell you how effective the steering is when the boat is out of the water. The only reliable method of finding bad or unbalanced steering is to sail the boat under strenuous conditions.

FIGURE 1.5. *By varying the position of the buttock lines at the stern the transom shape can easily be changed. Both transoms affect speed and sailing ability only slightly, while one is definitely more attractive than the other.*

A few years ago some racing boats developed a huge "bustle" (shown in Figure 1.6), which created a turbulent area just in front of the rudder. In our 12-meter towing tank work we have seen this turbulent area form just in front of the rudder blade and spread down across the blade, reducing the action of the rudder. In a seaway this turbulence would spread over the entire rudder, causing a very pronounced loss of control, possibly making the boat virtually unsteerable. Once again, this was a feature developed to gain a lower rating and make the boat sail faster and then, unfortunately, carried over into cruising boats.

Stern shapes, then, can vary tremendously. But as long the buttocks and diagonals run smoothly out from the mid-section, the boat should move easily through the water with little turbulence, assuming, of course, that everything else is in good order.

The Influence of the Ends

So far we've looked at both ends of the boat separately, but together they influence the sailing characteristics of the yacht. The shape of the ends has a marked effect on the pitching and sailing ability, especially to windward. A beamy boat that has fine or pinched ends will pitch as it is sailing to windward or reaching in a seaway. This will give it a slow, uncomfortable motion. A boat that has a fine bow and a full or wide stern will reach well but tend to sail bow down going to windward and will be wet forward. However, the wide stern will

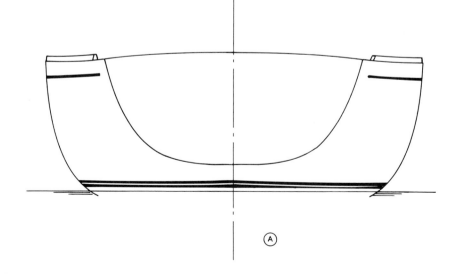

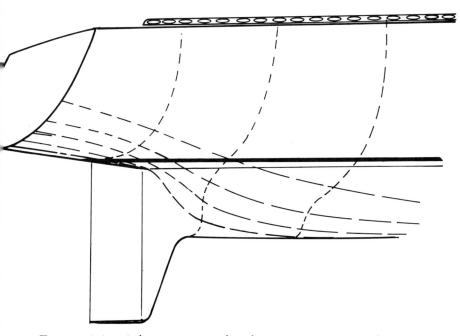

FIGURE 1.6. *A few years ago bustles were a common feature on boats. They made the boat hard to steer, and some cruising boats still have this feature. Sail-test a boat with a large bustle under strenuous conditions before you purchase it.*

quickly dampen any pitching motion, giving an easy motion reaching and off the wind.

The opposite type of hull shape, a full bow with a long, drawn out stern, sometimes called a cod's head, mackeral tail shape, is slightly faster on a reach and a run but much slower to windward.

WHAT ABOUT THE MIDDLE OF THE BOAT?

So far we have looked at each end of the boat, but the middle part is also of critical importance. Designers usually use the midship section as a reference point; Figure 1.7 shows some typical midship sections.

The older shape, the plank-on-edge style, was common in European waters, and there are still a few around today. These type of craft are heavy. They require a lot of ballast. But they have tremendous stability, usually heeling to 25 or 30 degrees and then staying there until the wind reaches gale force. It is almost impossible to capsize this type of

FIGURE 1.7. *Various sectional shapes taken through the middle of the hull. A is the old-fashioned plank-on-edge shape. B is a slightly more modern variation on it. C is definitely tending toward the modern cruising boat hull shape. While D is the latest shallow-hull, high freeboard hull, toward which rating rules have led designers. Although it has plenty of interior accommodation, it is not the ideal seaworthy hull shape for a cruising boat.*

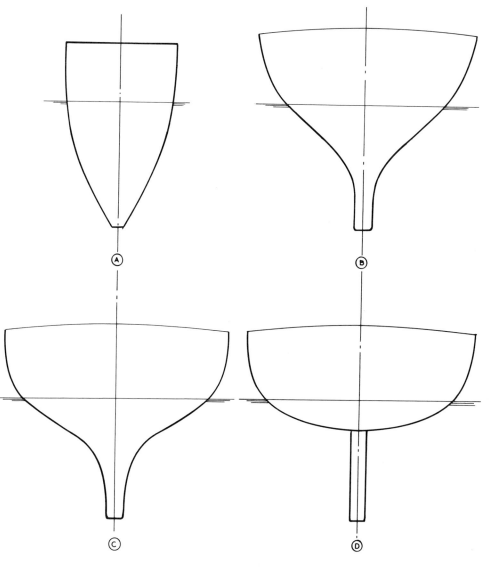

craft because their righting moment only turns negative at about 180 degrees (see "Stability"). The hull has a fairly high wetted surface, making light air speed and acceleration poor compared to modern hulls. But this is usually overcome by giving the boat a large sail plan. The 12-meter shape is a derivation of this type of hull.

On the other hand, the modern midship sectional shape as shown in Figure 1.7d is the complete opposite. The hull is very flat underneath, and the deep keel has a large span (see "Keels"), making it very efficient. This type of hull should not be sailed at more than 22–25 degrees of heel for best performance. Its major problem is the complete lack of anywhere for the bilge water to go and smaller range of stability compared to the boat above. As soon as the boat heels, and it does quite easily, water slops up the side of the boat into lockers and bunks and can make quite a mess.

For me, the best cruising shape is somewhere between Figures 1.7c and 1.7d. The hull is deep enough to keep water in the bilge when the boat is heeled. Some of the keel efficiency is lost, but in return the stability has been improved. On a boat like this a moderate displacement will give a good easy motion.

WETTED SURFACE

When a designer speaks of wetted surface, he means any part of the boat that is in contact with the water. On a racing yacht wetted surface is reduced to a minimum by putting on the smallest keel and rudder possible and making the hull sections as round as possible (see Figure 1.4 or 1.7d). Unfortunately, this has the effect of making the boat more difficult to steer in a straight line. The reason for reducing wetted surface is that it is an easy method of reducing hull resistance. When a boat is sailing in light winds, about 80 percent of the drag is caused by wetted surface friction. This proportion drops as speed increases until frictional drag is only about 15 percent of the whole—wave-making drag now being the culprit.

However, most cruising boats have no particular need to get from A to B in a hurry and also have other requirements that may increase wetted surface. For instance, an owner may want good protection for the propellor and a moderately long keel to enable the boat to stay upright when it dries out. This means the keel could be well over minimum size, which will increase wetted surface tremendously.

If a boat has high wetted surface, the easiest method of overcoming the frictional drag is to increase sail area. In fact, one of the ratios a designer uses to compare boats is the ratio of sail area to wetted surface area. But high sail area is hard for a short-handed cruising crew to handle, and most cruisers want to sail as quickly as the other sailors. What is the answer? An intelligent reduction in wetted surface—enough to keep sail area manageable but not so much that the boat becomes hard to steer.

Freeboard and Sheer

It is essential that a boat have adequate freeboard, because freeboard provides extra stability at larger angles of heel by allowing the angle of heel to increase before the deck edge is immersed, and greater freeboard will give more headroom below deck. High freeboard, though, is detrimental to windward performance and should be kept within moderate limits. Unfortunately, if your boat has inadequate freeboard there isn't much you can do about it. Unless you are prepared to spend quite a large amount of money lifting the entire deck off and extending the hull, bulkheads, and frames, it is usually less expensive to lower the cabin sole or sell the boat and buy another.

Freeboard is also affected by the shape of the sheerline; a lot of curvature as in Figure 1.8a will reduce freeboard in the middle of the boat, where it is most needed, and put it in the ends, where there is not much living space. Reverse sheer, however, does the opposite and is often seen on multihulls. I cannot help but think that here the multihull designers have made a big step forward while monohull afficionados remain hidebound by tradition.

As the hulls of modern boats become shallower underwater, headroom inside the boat is decreasing. In order to maintain standing headroom, many builders are raising freeboard and increasing cabin height. This is leading to many features such as hull stripes, rub rails, and chines at the sheerline, intended to disguise the high sides. Unfortunately, the combination of a shallow, beamy hull, high freeboard,

FIGURE 1.8. *Various sheerlines. A is the modern trend. Very flat, raked bow and bobbed stern. Freeboard looks high and is high to get headroom inside. I wonder whether we'd like the sheer in D if it gave a rating rule advantage. The "S" sheerline is not very common today; however, if the rating rule had given a bonus for this shape, then we'd probably see it as the latest in cruising boat design. C is a traditional sheerline with plenty of curvature to it. Note that all the sheerline curves start and end at the same height.*

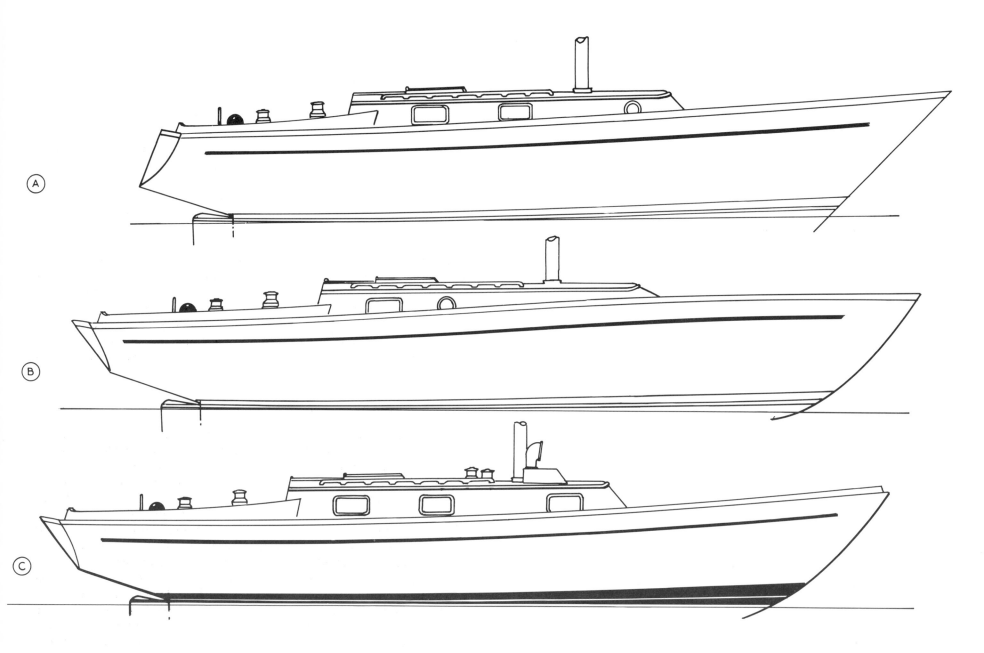

A

B

C

and moderately light displacement is moving toward a naval architecture danger zone. In the 1979 fastnet race several boats of this style were proven to have poor stability at very large angles of heel (60 degrees plus). This leads me to believe that the type of hull outlined above needs more development before it is used for long-distance offshore cruising.

Stability

When the wind blows, it tends to heel the boat. The waterline beam and the vessel's center of gravity combine to resist the heeling force of the wind. The wind forces are called the heeling force, or heeling moment, while the hull forces are known as the restoring force or righting moment. The principle is illustrated in Figure 1.9. Some boats, sailing dinghies, for example, rely totally on beam and crew weight as the restoring force, while others (12 meters, etc.) rely on the center of gravity of the ballast weight to keep the boat upright. Obviously, then, the best cruising boat will be a combination of ballast weight and beam that will enable the boat to sail in all conditions with a moderate heel angle provided the sails are reefed or changed correctly.

To ascertain the best stability the naval architect will make many complex calculations and, if he is working by hand, may even do a complete stability curve. If, like most designers today, he uses a computer, a complete, highly accurate stability curve will take only a few minutes. This curve shows how much force it takes to heel the boat to any angle. As you can see from Figure 1.10, the stability curves for multihulls are much higher than for monohulls, but at a certain angle the multihull restoring moment drops off very quickly and over she goes. The beamy, high freeboard, light hull is also shown and at about 120 degrees turns negative. At this point the boat is more stable upside down! Notice how the narrow heavily ballasted yachts can be heeled to almost 180 degrees before the curve turns negative. This gives this type of craft a much greater range of stability. These stability curves are mostly of academic interest but serve to indicate why certain types of craft are less stable than others.

Keels, Centerboards, and Leeboards

In recent years there have been many sophisticated technical papers written on the effectiveness of keels and centerboards. Almost all of these papers are aimed at finding the most efficient appendage to the hull that will make the boat go fastest to windward. But if you really stop and think about it, how many cruisers beat to windward for any length of time? Do I hear somebody saying, "It's handy to have so that you can beat off a leeshore." This argument has been around since sailing began. It got its foundation when ships were notoriously bad at sailing to windward and before the time of engines.

My philosophy is that the man who gets himself caught on a leeshore is a pretty poor seaman to begin with, and with today's powerful engines, if he cannot power off the shore with some sail assistance he deserves to get wrecked. This may seem like a hard-line philosophy, but after 50,000 miles of racing, where engine use is not allowed, and

FIGURE 1.9. *The force of the wind (W) heels the boat. This force is known as the heeling moment. It is countered by the righting moment (RM) of the waterline beam and the weight of the keel.*

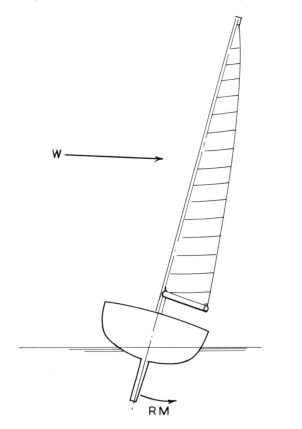

W

RM

FIGURE 1.10. *Various curves of static stability and the hull shapes that fit those curves. If we allow that the catamaran as an example, notice how the trend is toward less stability. The multihull shape A has high initial stability, but when the boat reaches a certain value it will capsize. The point at which the boat starts to capsize is shown here at about 35 degrees. B is a meter-boat type of hull which has a large amount of lead compared to its interior volume. C is a moderate cruising boat of about ten years ago, and D is the more modern shallow-hulled cruiser. It may be that the trend toward lower stability is starting to reverse and boats will begin to have more moderate shapes and stability.*

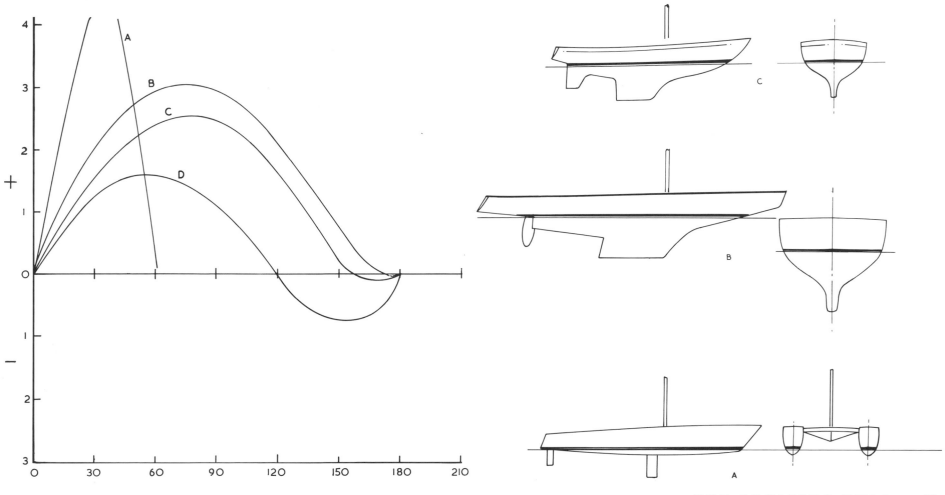

probably an equal amount of cruising, I have yet to be in a desperate leeshore situation.

All this discussion is really leading up to a pitch that says, Don't be restricted to carrying a huge lump of keel around for an event that may never occur in your cruising lifetime. If you keep your engine in good order and a prudent eye on the weather, you should rarely be caught unaware.

Having said all that, let's look at keels, centerboards, and leeboards in a new light. First, a look at what they do, then a discussion of why one is better than another and how they affect the hull and interior design.

The Keel

This is probably the appendage with which everyone is most familiar. At boat shows it is usually at eye level, while the important parts of the boat are so high they are invisible. The keel's function is to help the boat go to windward. In technical terms, it has to generate the maximum amount of lift for the minimum drag, somewhat like the wing of a plane, and to do this it has to have a certain shape. The keel shape has an effect on its performance, and there are certain technical names for the keel shape, which are shown in Figure 1.11.

Tank tests and other studies have shown that the optimum *sweepback angle* is directly related to the *aspect ratio,* and from the graph in Figure 1.12, you can see that, in general, the greater the aspect ratio, the smaller the sweepback ratio. What this means is that smaller, slower boats need longer, more vertical keels to obtain the lifting force, whereas bigger and faster boats have a lower aspect ratio and greater sweepback. This is similar to modern aircraft, in that the slower, smaller aircraft have much less sweepback than the giant delta wing bombers that occasionally fly overhead.

Keel *lateral area* is another important factor. Studies have shown that minimum lateral area is proportional to the square root of the sail area. This seems logical if you realize that the lift and drag from the keel are the forces that oppose the sideforce and driving force from the sails. From this discussion you can see the keel is at its best when it is sailing to windward. How efficient is it downwind? It's not. It's a total drag! The boat would sail better without it, but we have to keep it aboard so it's ready for the next upwind leg.

Keels also restrict the places where you can take a boat. But if you intend to sail on long ocean cruises in deep water, they are the best option. They are very efficient for windward work, providing lift (and

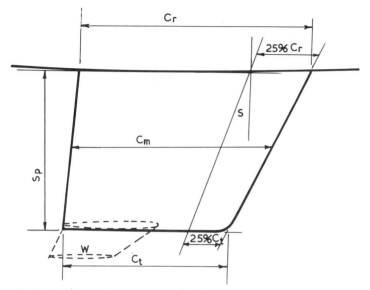

FIGURE 1.11.   *The various parts of a keel.*
   Cr is root chord.
   Cm is mid chord.
   Ct is tip chord.
   Sp is Span.
   S is the sweepback angle taken at the 25% chord line.
   W is a winglet.

some drag) and a place to stow the lead ballast. Positioning the ballast in the keel in a secondary function, but it helps tremendously with stability.

However, if you intend to sail in fairly shallow harbors, or sheltered estuaries, a deep keel can become a major problem. This is when alternatives must be considered. One of those alternatives is the winged keel, others are centerboards, leeboards, and daggerboards.

The Winged Keel

In 1983 *Australia II* won the America's Cup by a combination of superior design and superior sailing. Many critics attributed her success to the radical winged keel; however, that was not the whole story. The winged keel enabled the design team to change many other factors on the boat to produce a winner.

The winged keel concept can be used in cruising boats, but it must be designed to match the hull. Lately I've noticed winged keels on many boats, many of them appendages designed to look like a winged keel without any practical research to back the design.

What can a winged keel do for you? First, it can reduce draft. But draft increases when heeled, is the criticism I hear often. Think about how you go aground. You sail heeled over when the keel hits bottom. The first thing the boat does is come upright. So a winged keel becomes a benefit. It is deeper when the boat is heeled, but as soon as you hit and come upright, draft is reduced and you can get off the mud.

Second, it increases stability. The wings at the bottom of the keel lower the center of gravity of the lead and stability. The alternative could be even better. If a designer wants to maintain the same stability he can use less lead and make the boat lighter. So, in practical terms, a winged keel can make the boat faster simply from increased stability or reducing weight and cost.

FIGURE 1.12. *A graph of aspect ratio versus sweepback angle.*

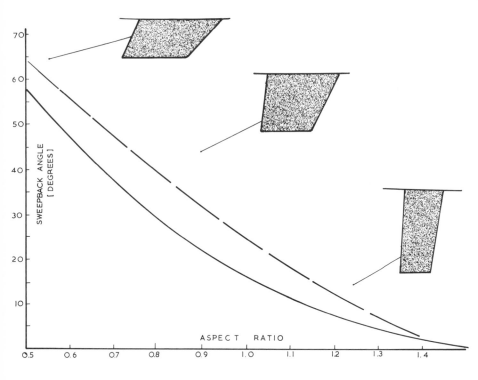

Third, a well-designed winged keel can have the same wetted surface as a conventional keel and a reduced amount of induced drag. So we have a net gain in drag. (Induced drag is caused as the keel moves through the water. Eddies spin off, taking energy from the keel and increasing drag. With a winged keel these eddies tend to be smaller.)

Finally, a winged keel removes the need for a centerboard, with its associated wires and trunks, all of which cause extra drag, noise, and cleaning and painting problems.

Twin Keels

Two wrongs don't make a right, runs the old adage, and two keels are not better than one. But in this case there are good reasons for twin keels.

In favor of them is the fact that a boat can sit on them if it goes aground and will stay upright, provided the rudder skeg is strong enough to act as the third point of the tripod. Also the keels can be "toed in" slightly to make them more efficient for windward sailing. They also give the hull tremendous directional stability. Against this is the large increase in wetted surface, which will slow the boat in lighter winds.

So the decision to have one or two keels is basically a matter of where you keep your craft. If the mooring is shallow or dries out at certain states of the tide, a twin keeler is a reasonably good option. However, you should have as much sail area as possible to help overcome the drag of the extra wetted surface.

The Long- or Full-Keeled Craft

This keel option, sometimes called a traditional keel, is very common on older boats and, in many cases, is an extension of the hull as shown in Figure 1.13. The long-keeled boat does have much more wetted surface than a comparable fin keeler, but it also has better directional stability. One of the other arguments in favor of this type is that it can sit alongside a dockwall and dry out without tipping onto its bow or rudder. Unfortunately, this last point is often neglected by designers, who put a lot of drag (slope to the bottom of the keel), ensuring a bow-down attitude when the boat is allowed to dry out.

Where a boat is likely to be sailed over a long distance by a short-handed crew, a long keel makes a fair amount of sense. This type of hull is slow to tack, stays on course well, will hove to easily because of the damping motion of the keel, and is not troubled by beam seas, as a fin-keeled boat might be.

However, its disadvantage is a very high wetted surface with consequent loss of light air performance. Although the boat tracks well it may be slow to tack—"slow in stays" was the old-fashioned term. And finally, because of the hull shape, it has to be of a moderately heavy displacement, which costs more money.

A point that most of today's sailors seem to be unaware of is the handling capability of the long keel in inclement weather. With a long-keeled boat it is relatively easy to put the jib aback and lash the helm to lie hove to. If you think about the forces involved, the headsail is pinned aback and wants to push the bow down, while the rudder and mainsail want to push the bow up into the wind. As long as the two forces are approximately equal the boat will stay hove to *because the keel is long enough to dampen the oscillations between the forces.*

On a modern short- or fin-keeled boat, heavy weather techniques have to be different simply because the forces acting on the bow and stern are no longer being dampened sufficiently. In fact, the forces can be said to be *pivoting around the keel* and would probably become more extreme. So the fin keel has led to a different method of sailing in extreme conditions. The boat has to be kept moving. In 1972, during a tropical storm on the way to Bermuda, the wind was blowing over 60 knots with seas to match. We found the best way to sail the boat under these conditions was to sail on a close reach, laying the boat off on the backs of the waves and making sure that sail area was reduced so that we didn't sail right off the top of the waves!

FIGURE 1.13. *A typical long-keeled design.*

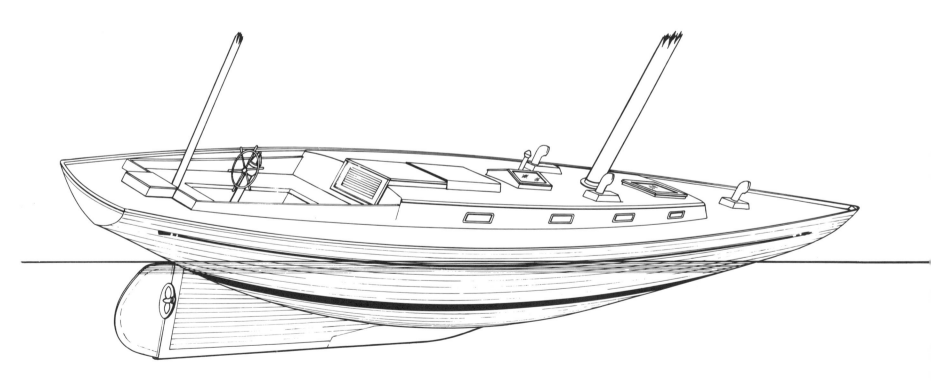

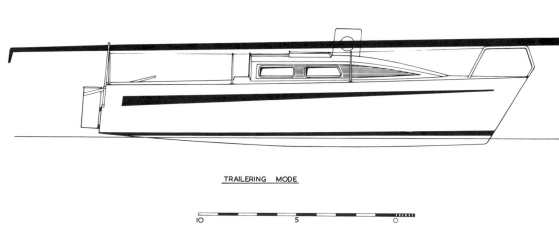

TRAILERING MODE

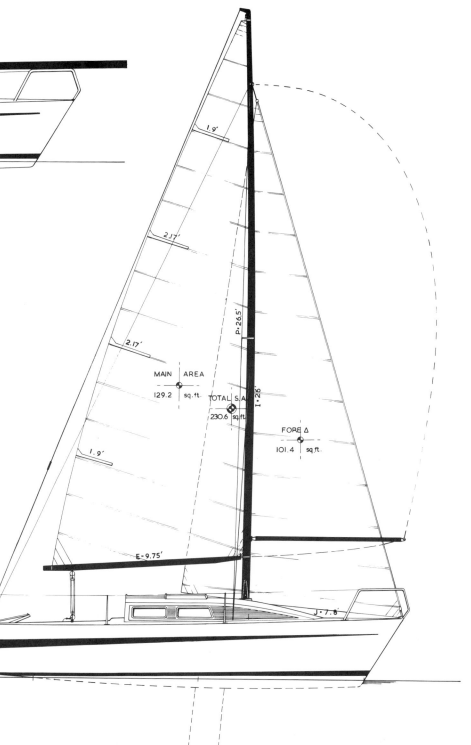

Why Not Shoal Draft?

In his book *Little Ships and Shoal Waters,* published in 1937, Maurice Griffiths advances some very convincing arguments in favor of shoal draft boats. Although not all he says has stood the test of time, there are some real advantages to shallow draft that designers have been aware of for centuries and other advantages that have emerged in recent times. One benefit that has been around awhile is the ease with which these craft can be beached. A shallow draft boat can often sail or power to within a few feet of the shore and occasionally so close that the crew can step ashore dryshod. A more modern adaptation of this benefit is the trailer-sailer, a shallow draft boat that can be launched and retrieved off a trailer. Figure 1.14 shows one designed in my office that draws 6 inches in light ship condition and 10 inches fully laden. As marine congestion increases and the cost of keeping a boat on a mooring increases, this segment of the market will get larger.

FIGURE 1.14. *A daggerboard sloop that draws 6 inches with the board up can be used for trailer sailing to avoid the cost of moorings and haulouts.*

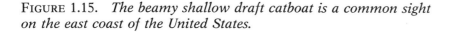

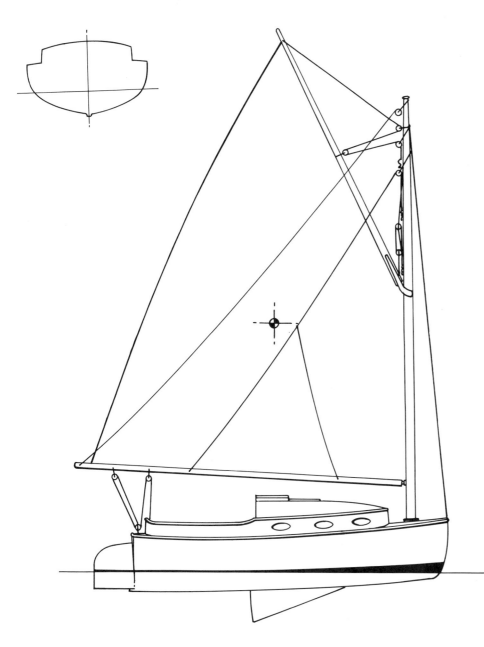

A centerboard design that has been around a long time is the American Catboat. Its gaff mainsail and shallow draft have made it a fixture on the east coast of the United States. Figures 1.15 and 3.1 show a typical catboat. It has some inside ballast, a tremendous beam—often over 10 feet (approximately 3 meters) on an LOA (length overall) of 25 feet (7.62 meters)—and a huge "barn door" rudder.

Many different types of centerboard boats have been around for a long time. In fact, there are so many variations on this theme that one could be forgiven for not knowing them all. In some boats the board is in the hull. In others it's in the keel. Some have a tapered board, others have V-shaped boards. Some have a flat plate for a board, while others have a specially shaped board that will operate efficiently at any depth.

How efficient are they? I can only give an idea from some observations I made while sailing on two boats that had the same configuration above the keel line. Below the hull one had a board in the shallow draft keel and the other had a deep keel.

The keel centerboard boat sailed to windward about 2–3 degrees lower than the deep-keeled boat. But off the wind, the shallow draft boat raised the board and pulled away from the deep-keeled version. As most cruising sailors prefer not to sail to windward, a centerboard is a very viable option if you intend to sail in shallow waters.

VARIOUS BOARDS

Most of the shallow draft hulls discussed above have some form of centerboard. But that is not the only type of board. Daggerboards, bilge boards, and leeboards are a few of the various types. (Bunkboards are discussed in Chapter 4).

Centerboards

Centerboards are the most popular ways of gaining lateral area, and centerboard styles can be as simple as a rectangular steel plate held in place with a pin and raised and lowered by a lanyard. Unfortunately, because of its simplicity, this style is becoming more prevalent in the less expensive cruiser. Its drawbacks are many. Should the pin—which is often totally embedded in fiberglass—or the pennant break, the board is left hanging below the boat. This hanging area will undoubtedly get damaged when the boat is beached or docked for repairs.

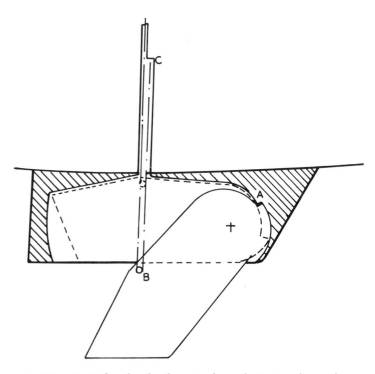

FIGURE 1.16. *Details of a keel centerboard. Notice how the pennant is ended inside the boat for easy changing. Several features make this type of board work efficiently:*

1. The block through which the pennant runs in the board should be positioned so that it is just outside the keel when the board is down.

2. There should be a stop, as shown at A, so that the board will not hang vertically down if the pennant breaks.

3. The pennant should be vertical when the board is either up or down.

A better arrangement is shown in Figure 1.16, where a stop takes the weight of the board when it is fully down. This will relieve strain on the pennant as well as act as a safety feature should the pennant break.

Another type of board is illustrated in Figure 1.17. This type is usually seen in more modern cruising boats, and the board itself may be shaped for good water flow over it.

All of these boards emerge from a slot in the hull of the boat, which can create turbulence and slow the boat. They all need some form of pennant to raise and lower them, and often, when the boat is sitting at the mooring or dock, the board can be heard banging around in its case.

Daggerboards

The daggerboard is a way of getting around the problems outlined above. There is no long slot to create turbulence. The trunk can be made snug enough so the board doesn't rattle. A daggerboard can also be raised and lowered hydraulically, reducing the need for a pennant. But, and it's a big but, a daggerboard has no "give" to it, and if you go aground it could easily be bent or damaged. Also, to get an effective length to it, it has to be housed in a trunk that goes through the middle of the boat. This can negatively affect the accommodation.

FIGURE 1.17. *A slightly different board. This one will need to have the trunk hidden under a table inside the boat. However, it is slightly more efficient than the board in Figure 1.16 and can be designed so that it has good sailing efficiency at any position.*

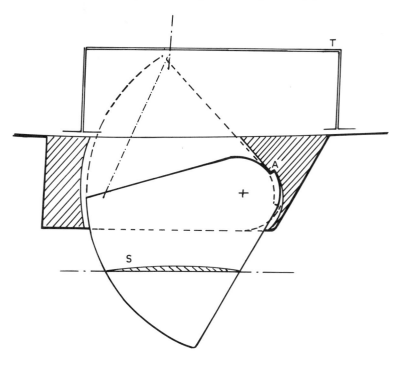

Bilgeboards

Bilgeboards have all the disadvantages of a daggerboard plus the fact that there are two of them going up through the accommodation. Their only advantage is that they can be toed in about 3 or 4 degrees to help reduce leeway. But like the daggerboard above, two bilge boards make a worse mess of the accommodation. However, with clever interior design the trunks can be disguised and placed just at the inside of the berths, making them of interest to people who are looking for the ultimate in up and downwind performance and beachability.

FIGURE 1.18. *Leeboards have been around for many years and provide good lift without intruding into the inside of the boat. They do, however, require a slightly boxier hull shape to get some end plate effect from the hull.*

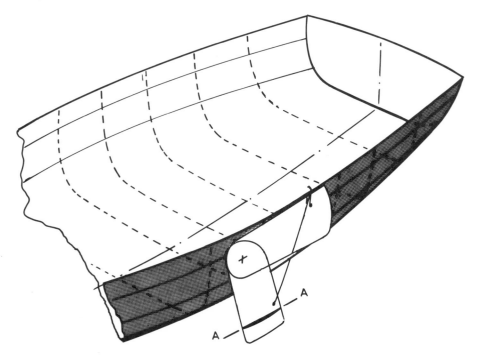

Leeboards

Leeboards are probably the only leeway resisting device that has been around for hundreds of years. Chapman's *Architectura Navalis Mercatoria,* first produced in 1768, shows boats with leeboards. Unfortunately, leeboards are rarely seen today, even though they are simple to build and easy to install and maintain. Leeboards also have the advantage that they can be angled or toed in a few degrees and can be asymmetric to reduce leeway to a minimum. Figure 1.18 shows how a leeboard works. Notice how the hull form is very boxy to give maximum support to the leeboard.

Board Construction

When boats were built of wood, most of the boards were made of wood. Other options were iron, bronze, or even lead. Bronze was favored for corrosion resistance properties, while iron corroded, and lead, although it gave great stability, usually bent.

Nowadays boards may be made of wood, galvanized iron, stainless steel, aluminum, fiberglass, bronze, or any combination of these. Weighted wooden boards are still a prime choice, followed closely by fiberglass and stainless steel. The major construction points you should look for when selecting a boat with any type of board is compatability and minimum friction. By compatability I mean that the metals used should not set up electrolytic corrosion. If the trunk or case is stainless steel, the board should be wood, stainless steel, or fiberglass. Don't put a bronze board in a wooden centerboard case that has been fastened with iron bolts—eventually the bolts will corrode away. Friction is another problem with boards. I have seen a superbly made wooden board fitted perfectly into its housing while the boat was being built, only to jam solid as the board swelled when the boat was put into the water. There should be a gap about 3/16 inches (5 millimeters) on either side of a centerboard to allow for warping or bending.

One of the major problems with all board systems except for leeboards is that of antifouling the inside of the slot. This is a difficult job at best, impossible at worst, and best done with a long-handled, thin brush when the boat is in slings waiting to be launched. Although I have heard of one novel solution: pour antifouling into the trunk while the boat is afloat, letting the motion of the waves move the paint around. I don't think this is a very practical method and I am sure it can be guaranteed to get conservationists up in arms. The antifouling could also gum up the whole works and leak out only to appear on the topsides!

The keel, or centerboard, then, is an essential part of the boat. Its effect is felt best on the windward leg. But for offwind sailing, a centerboard or drop keel has added advantages that for many cruising sailors outweigh its disadvantages.

MULTIHULLS

So far we have discussed many of the features seen in monohulls, but multihulls are a viable alternative for offshore and inshore cruising. They have distinct advantages over monohulls in that they are shallow draft, have lots of deck space, are very fast, and can be quite inexpensive to build. However, there are some disadvantages, probably the best known being their capsizability. But they do float upside down, giving a platform from which rescue is possible.

There are two major types of multihull, the catamaran and the trimaran, plus a number of lesser-known variations such as the proa and outrigger canoes. Interestingly, although catamarans have been commonplace in the Pacific for thousands of years, the first European development took place in England in the 1660s. when Sir William Petty built the *Simon and Jude,* the first European double-hulled sailing ship. This was followed by three other double-hulled ships over the next 20 years. Between the late 1600s and the nineteenth century many catamarans were built in Europe and America. In the late 1870s, N. G. Herreshoff designed and built several catamarans. One went to the west coast, another to England. Later Thomas Fearon of New York built several catamarans for wealthy east coast sailors. These were all fairly heavy and performed poorly in light winds. The modern story really begins when resin glues were discovered during World War II, allowing much lighter boats to be built in the years after the war. Prout Brothers in England, who built shearwater cats during the late 1940s and early 1950s, and Woody Brown, who built *Manu Kai* and later *Waikiki Surf,* were the early pioneers.

The trimaran has a similar story. It was undoubtedly experimented with in the Pacific and was first developed as a pleasure craft by Victor T. Chetchet of Long Island in the early 1940s. Although both types of craft have certain similarities, it is best to look at them separately and allow the discussion to overlap as it will.

The Catamaran

A catamaran should have a definite beam-to-length ratio because if the hulls are put too close together the wave interaction between the hulls tends to reduce the speed of the vessel. Too narrow a boat is also easier to capsize. A beam–length ratio of .4–.5 seems to be about right; in other words, the beam should be just under half of the width. However, even this characteristic is changing. Modern racing cats often have a beam-to-length ratio of .8 or .9, and as racing tends to influence cruising to a great degree, I would expect to see cruising catamarans become much beamier.

Too wide a beam can also lead to problems. If the hulls are too far apart the lateral stability of the boat becomes more than the longitudinal stability. This can lead to a capsize by putting the bow of the leeward float underwater and pitchpoling (stern over bow) rather than simply immersing the leeward hull or flying the weather hull and then recovering.

Because catamarans can be constructed very lightly (they don't need heavy scantlings to carry the keel weight), the hulls can be narrow, light, and of a semicircular shape, to minimize frictional drag. The best beam-to-length ratio for each hull appears to be between 7 and 9 to 1 for cruising craft. This is a critical dimension for best balance between load-carrying ability, speed, and seaworthiness.

Another critical dimension is the height of the bridgedeck above the water. Too low a bridgedeck will give a very noisy ride as the bow wave splashes up and hits the deck. Too high a deck and any headroom in this area is severely reduced. For the sailor who wants full standing headroom on the bridgedeck, the boat has to be fairly large, in the region of 40–45 feet long.

When you are looking at a catamaran hull you can get a very good idea of how the boat will tack or how it will maintain a straight course. A boat that tacks easily will have some "rocker," that is, curvature, to the bottom of the hull. Probably the best example of this is the Hobie Cat, with its conspicuously curved hulls. The boat designed for good course keeping will have almost a straight keel from bow to stern. This will occasionally make such a craft very hard to tack.

One of the different feelings about sailing a catamaran is the motion of the boat. It doesn't heel like a mono or trimaran. A catamaran conforms to the shape of the wave, as shown in Figure 1.19. Because of this the heel angle is generally much less than a mono and slightly less than a trimaran.

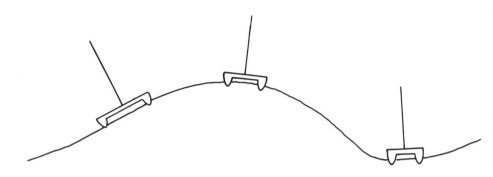

FIGURE 1.19. *A catamaran follows the surface of the wave and can be uncomfortable in a large swell.*

As on a monohull, the shape of the ends of a catamaran also affect the pitching of the boat. A boat that is fine at both ends has nothing to dampen the pitching, whereas a fine-bowed boat with a fat destroyer-type stern uses the stern to dampen pitching. This second type of hull shape tends to sail faster in rough water than a craft that is symmetrical fore and aft.

Because the bows of catamarans are so fine, they often require some form of spray deflectors to reduce the amount of water that comes aboard. These spray rails can also be designed to give lift to the bow and increase buoyancy forward, which will help reduce pitching.

Bridgedeck design is critical for a catamaran and should be completely integrated with both hulls on cruising boats. This will spread the racking loads along the entire hull-bridgedeck joint rather than concentrating these loads on two or three cross-beam joints. The racking and twisting loads are worst when the bow of one hull and the stern of the other hull are both supported on the crest of a wave while the opposite bow and stern are in the wave trough. These loads together with rigging forces have led to many catamarans breaking up when the boats are pushed very hard.

A catamaran, then, can be a stable, comfortable sailing platform with a large amount of cruising accommodation. It can sail very fast but does suffer from some drawbacks. One is the twisting and racking forces, which can be overcome by careful design. The other major disadvantage is its capsizability, which can be minimized by careful seamanship. This type of boat is not for everybody, but for the cruis-

ing sailor who has the necessary seamanship a cat can be a superb, fast, and spacious cruising home.

The Trimaran

If you took the ballast off a monohull it would capsize. If you tried to stop the boat capsizing by putting an outrigger on one side you would end up with a proa, which could only sail in one direction. You would have to put an outrigger on both sides of the boat to enable the boat to be tacked. Both outriggers and the center hull would give you a trimaran.

This type of catamaran with accommodation in the main hull and buoyant outriggers does not have as much interior volume as the twin hulls of a catamaran. In fact, it has only a little more space than a comparably sized monohull. The advantage of a trimaran over a monohull is the smaller heel angle, lighter weight, and greater speed. Also, there is much more area on a trimaran if the deck space between the hulls is closed in. The type of trimaran described here is one of the styles that trimarans have evolved into, what I call a racing type. The large cruising tri (over 50 feet LOA) on the other hand, has a main hull with two outrigger hulls that may have almost as much accommodation as the main hull. When these three hulls are integrated in one boat with a large deck cabin, the boat often has more accommodation than many small homes.

Trimaran hull shape can vary as much as monohull shape, but in general certain types have better characteristics than others. Figure 1.20 shows the four main hull sectional shapes. The "V" is the least expensive to build but lacks space inside the hull. It also has a high wetted surface. This sectional shape is often used in small tris, where it can supplement the leeway resisting ability of the centerboard. Often when this type of main hull is used the amas are made slightly asymmetric and no centerboards are used.

U-shaped hulls, on the other hand, have much less wetted surface and more area at the cabin sole level. This shape is best for a cruising trimaran that is to sail in areas of light wind. Shape C is a combination of A and B and is used more often on racing trimarans, when the interior headroom requirement is subordinate to boat speed. Hull shape D has similar ease of building attributes that a chine monohull hull has. Plus it has good space at the cabin sole level.

The floats or amas of a trimaran should have a fairly high volume depending upon the type of tri. Usually float volume is about 100

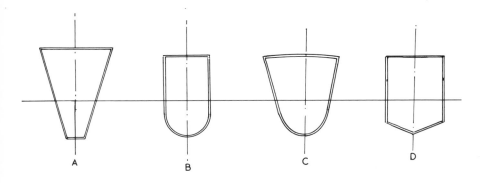

FIGURE 1.20. *The four main types of multihull sectional shapes.*
A is easy to build out of plywood.
B is a minimum wetted surface shape.
C is probably the best compromise between A and B. It has minimum wetted surface, some reserve buoyancy, and more deck room than B.
D is a compromise shape for plywood construction that gives more interior room than A.

percent of the displacement on a cruising tri. The more modern, faster boats have higher float volumes, often in the 150–200 percent range. That means that for a 100 percent float volume the entire float is only submerged when the main hull and weather ama are out of the water.

A few years ago designers used low buoyancy floats with about 30–40 percent of the main hull volume. While some tris are still built with these "small" floats, the trend is toward larger floats set ahead of the longitudinal center of the main hull. The size of the float helps to give the boats stability—a large volume float can be nearer the main hull to get the same amount of stability. Increasing the size of the floats and putting them farther from the main hull makes the boat much more powerful, and consequently it will sail much faster. However, putting the float too far from the hull increases transverse stability. If transverse stability exceeds longitudinal stability, then there is a good possibility the boat will pitch pole rather than capsize. One method of increasing longitudinal stability is to put the longitudinal center of the floats forward of the center of the main hull. This increases the longitudinal stability, allowing more beam and greater speed.

Which Is Better, a Catamaran or a Trimaran?

It depends on what you intend to do. If you want space, then a small catamaran has better accommodation than the same length trimaran. If it's speed you want, then a well-designed tri is likely to be faster than a similar catamaran.

There are some experts who say trimarans have more advantages than catamarans, any way you look at it. For instance, I've heard it said that a tri has better stability than a comparable catamaran. If the boat is designed to be fast then it is likely to have full buoyancy floats. This will make it stiffer. However, if it has, say, 50 percent buoyancy floats (in other words, the floats have 50 percent of the buoyancy of the main hull), then it may be more tender than a similar cat. It has been said that as the volume of the float approaches that of the main hull then the trimaran will act more like a catamaran.

A trimaran does have a simpler steering system. One rudder instead of two. However, if that rudder fails it must be jury rigged. On a cat, on the other hand, the two-rudder system does give a backup when needed.

Tris also have a simpler engine arrangement, one motor in the main hull. A two-engined catamaran has some advantage in that the engines can be smaller, the boat will be more maneuverable, and there is a backup if one fails.

In general it is said that trimarans have less windage than cats. However, that depends to a large extent on the shape of the hulls, bridgedeck, cabintop, and amas. Again depending on the design, there can be more or less clearance under the bridgedeck depending on the type of hull.

These advantages must be weighed one against the other to decide which type of hull arrangement best suits your sailing needs. It is hard to make a blanket statement that covers all design contingencies. For the multihull buyer, it pays to look at all the options and choose one that is right for you and your type of sailing.

The lines plan of Design Number 18. *This 22-foot LOA boat was designed for sailing inside Narraganset Bay. Note how the buttocks and diagonals are very smooth, with no bumps or hollows. This set of lines is shown in three dimensions to help you understand how a lines plan works in real life. The buttocks B, sections S, and waterlines W are clearly shown. (Lines plan copyright Roger Marshall Inc. 1984)*

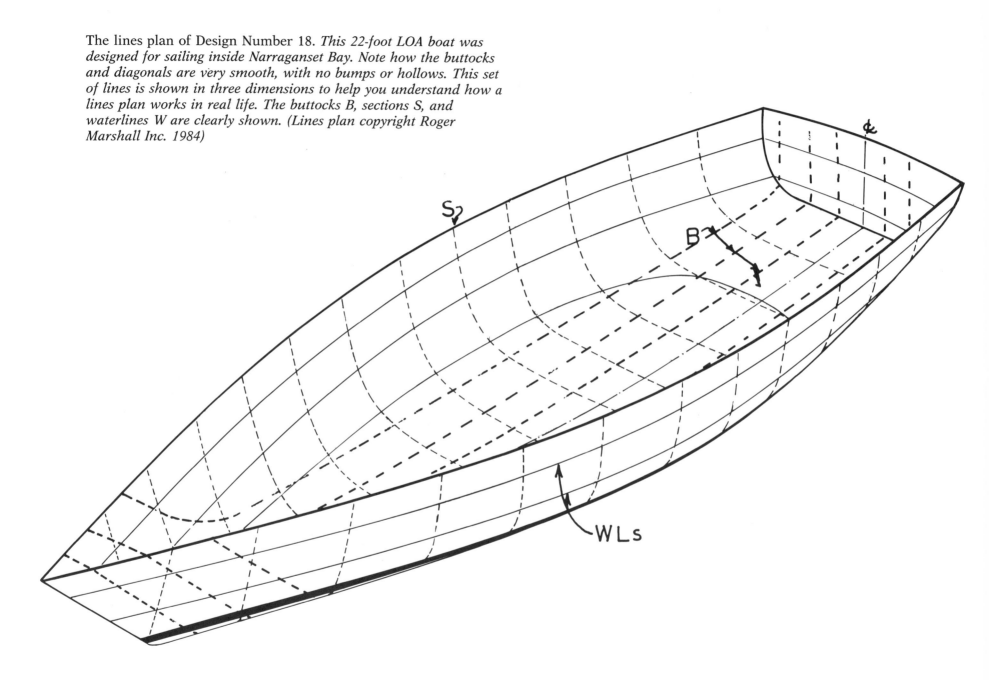

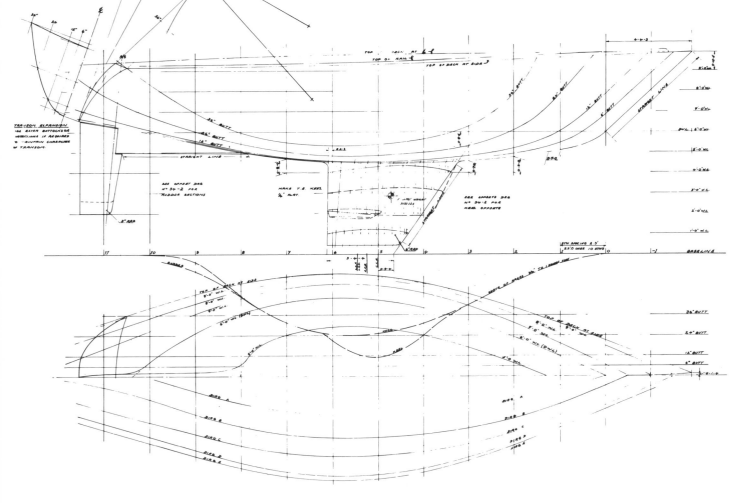

The lines of Design Number 37. *To minimize draft, this boat was designed with a reasonably flat bottom and a winged keel. The skeg is fairly large to give the boat slightly more than usual directional stability, which is helped by the large deep rudder. Note, also, that the diagonals are as smooth as possible with no hollows or bumps. On this boat the transom development was interesting because the transom curved in two directions. (Copyright Roger Marshall Inc. 1986)*

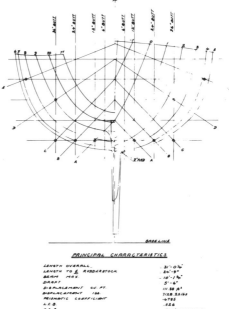

The lines of Design Number 7A. *This 38-foot sloop was designed a few years ago. Figure 2.11a shows this boat under construction. It was intended for reasonable offshore cruising from Maine to the Carolinas and had a keel/centerboard that gave it a fairly shallow draft. (Copyright Roger Marshall Inc. 1985)*

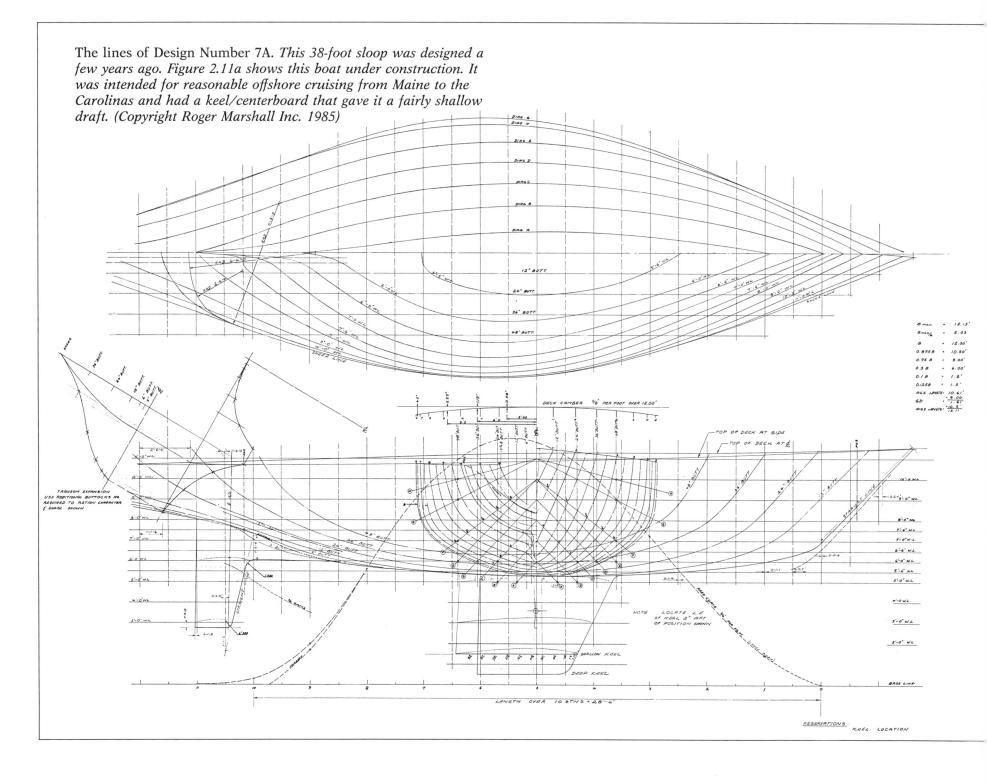

CHAPTER 2

Construction

When sailors buy a boat, the hull material is usually a low priority item. The interior arrangement, the rig, and the deck plan almost always have a higher value. But the purpose for which the boat is intended will often dictate hull construction and material. For instance, a boat that will sail to remote places should have a hull that can be repaired in those places. This rules out a sophisticated lightweight laminate. A better material for this purpose might be steel, which can be repaired with relatively unskilled labor.

Often repair work is the job of the crew. But the forces exerted on the hull by the rig, the sea, the ballast, and the crew can turn a good repair into a disaster if they are not considered. In this chapter we will look at these external forces on the hull. We shall also discuss hull and deck materials, how they are used to construct the hull, and their care and repair.

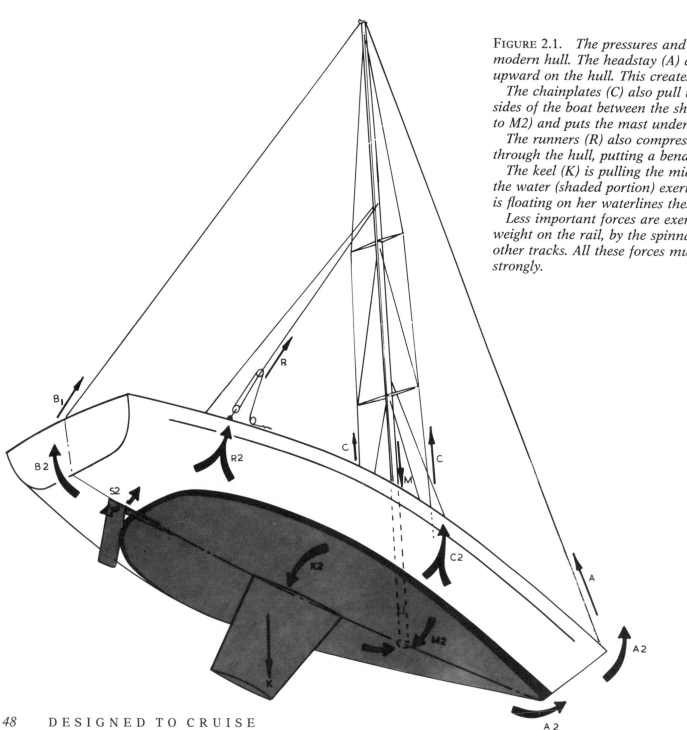

FIGURE 2.1. *The pressures and tensions that are exerted on a modern hull. The headstay (A) and the backstay (B1) both pull upward on the hull. This creates bending forces A2 and B2.*

The chainplates (C) also pull upward on the hull, which puts the sides of the boat between the shrouds and the bottom in tension (C2 to M2) and puts the mast under compression.

The runners (R) also compress the mast and try to force it out through the hull, putting a bending load on the hull.

The keel (K) is pulling the middle of the boat downward while the water (shaded portion) exerts an upward force. When the boat is floating on her waterlines these forces are in equilibrium.

Less important forces are exerted by the rudder (S2), by crew weight on the rail, by the spinnaker pole, and by the mainsheet and other tracks. All these forces must be resisted by building the hull strongly.

THE HULL STRUCTURE

Figure 2.1 shows the various pressures and tensions that work on the hull and deck of a modern cruising boat. The mast is being pushed down into the boat by the tension in the rigging. The fore and aft stays (forestay and backstay) are not only pulling up on the bow and stern but are putting the deck in compression and the hull in tension. The shrouds are also pulling up on the hull and are putting the deck in transverse compression. While these loads are tensioning the hull and compressing the deck, the keel is trying to pull downward, while water pressure is trying to push the hull upward.

The hull has to resist all these loads without plate deformation or longitudinal bending. This is usually done by a complex system of longitudinal and transverse framing. The hull plating forms an I beam with the frames to increase the sectional modulus of the frames. It also keeps the water out.

As an example of the hull structure, think of a shoebox floating on a duckpond. When it is floating, no forces or tensions are trying to distort it. But if you pull the ends inward as the backstay and forestay are trying to do on a boat, the middle of the box will bow outward. Because their lengths of timber were relatively short, the old-time boat builders used transverse frames, which indirectly resisted the bowing action in the middle of the boat. Modern builders tend to use longitudinal frames, which directly resist the fore and aft compression. (Modern glues allow the builder to join short pieces of wood without losing strength.) But this is only part of the story. If the lid is put on the shoebox, then the whole unit resists compression and becomes a fairly rigid beam. This is also what happens when the deck is put on a boat. Figure 2.2 shows how the shoebox-hull structure analogy works.

FIGURE 2.2. *The shoebox squeeze. Take an ordinary shoebox as in A and push inward on the ends. The sides buckle outward. Now put the lid on the box and push it again. This time it takes much more force to make the box deform.*

In older boats the bending of the sides was indirectly resisted by the ribs or frames. They would stop the sides bending outward and consequently enable the backstay and headstay to be tensioned. The deck (shoebox lid) would also help stop the bending but only because it helped stop the sides from bowing. In a modern construction, longitudinal members in the hull and deck directly resist the bending moment.

The keel also hangs off the bottom of this "box beam," and it, too, is trying to pull the middle down while buoyancy forces try to push the hull up. The shrouds are trying to pull the sides of the boat upward and force the mast out through the bottom of the boat.

When we see how these forces are trying to bend the boat, it becomes apparent that the internal structure—the ribs and longitudinals—must be designed to carry the loads and resist deformation.

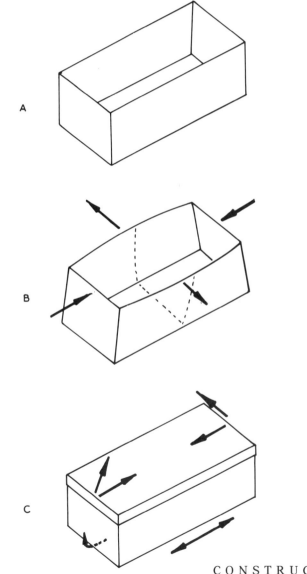

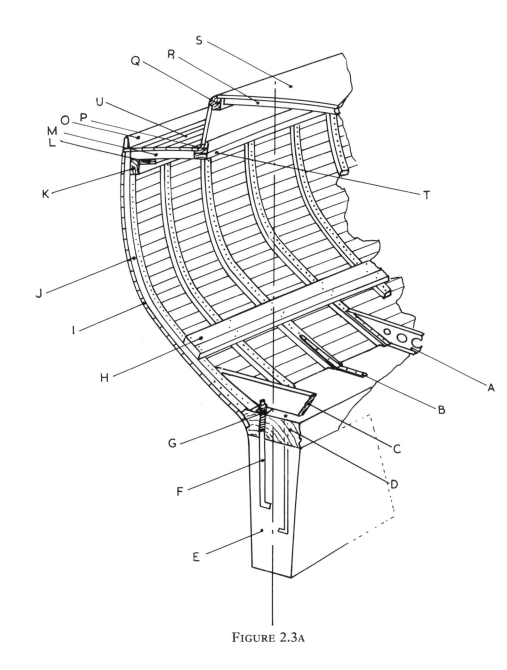

FIGURE 2.3A

FIGURE 2.3A. *The various parts of a traditionally built hull:*

A   A metal floor bolted to the keel and frames.
B   A strap floor.
C   A wooden floor. It is unlikely that a yacht would have all three types of floor. These are included here to show the various types.
D   The keel.
E   The lead ballast.
F   Keel bolts.
G   Oversized large plate washers under the keel bolts.
H   Bilge stringer. This usually runs from one end of the boat to the other.
I   Hull planking. This may be done in several ways.
J   Frames.
K   Clamp.   P   Trim.
L   Beam shelf.   Q   Corner piece.
M   Deck beam.   R   Deck house or cabin top beam.
N   House side.   S   Cabin top.
O   Toerail.   T   Carlin.

FIGURE 2.3B. *Modern WEST system construction is considerably simpler. The parts are as follows:*

A   Laminated floors. Usually, floor will be laminated as part of the frame.
B   Laminated keel.
C   Filler. Usually a mixture of epoxy and either sawdust or microsheres.
D   Limber holes.
E   Ballast keel.
F   Keel bolts.
G   Oversize flat washer.
H   Longitudinals.
I   Hull planking. Notice how the hull planking is carried completely around the hull over the keel. Usually a false keel is added after the planking is complete. This makes it easier to laminate the hull on a round- or reasonably flat-bottomed boat.
J   Frame.   Q   Corner piece or corner post.
K   Clamp.   R   Cabin top beam.
O   Toerail.   S   Cabin top laminate, usually plywood.
P   Subdeck,   U   Deck planking screwed and glued to
    usually plywood.   plywood.

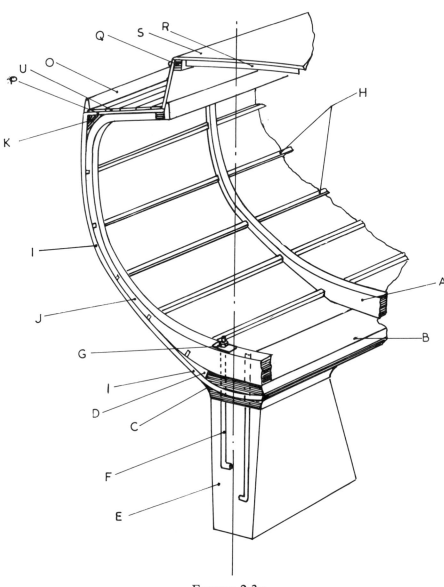

FIGURE 2.3B

In traditional wood, steel, aluminum alloy, and WEST system boats, the loads placed upon the hull are carried by the framing, deck beams, and longitudinals, which are usually spaced at regular distances. The hull plating serves to stiffen the framing and to reduce the buckling effects of loads imposed by the sea, rigging, and keel. In a fiberglass hull the frames and so forth carry the loads, but they are rarely spaced at equal distances. Instead, a careful designer will make much of the structure landing points for bulkheads, bunk flats, and other items of furniture. This reduces the amount of work required during building and ensures that bulkheads do not butt up against the hull, giving a hard spot which can lead to hull distortion.

With careful design the mast loads can be developed to ensure the loads are exerted solely on the mast. For instance, if the shrouds are tied to the mast step, the shroud loads compressing the mast at the chainplate become a simple tension-compression unit. The spreaders act in compression in concert with the deck to keep the shrouds away from the mast. This means that the entire unit can be designed to be dropped into the boat so that it will not put any strain on the hull. On racing boats a pipe frame is often used for this purpose. However, the framing would be impractical for a cruising boat.

The alternative method, where thick hull plating is used with few frames, is also used, but not for structural reasons. For instance, a 40-foot boat built in steel could have frames spaced 12 inches apart and hull plating that is only 0.088 inches thick, but welders who can work with such thin plate are rare. Usually the plating will be increased to enable it to be welded easily and to make a small allowance for corrosion. However, the corrosion allowance has become much smaller with the advent of modern epoxy paints. In this type of construction it is more sensible to use ⅛-inch or ³⁄₁₆-inch plating and space the frames 24 inches apart. When painted with an epoxy-based paint and carefully maintained, this should last a long time.

The Construction Members

Whatever method is used to build the boat, a poor job may be done if the owner or designer describes the item inaccurately. For instance, the clamp, sheer plank, covering board, and beam shelf are all in the same part of the boat. What happens if the owner, returning to a closed yard on a Sunday afternoon, leaves a note saying, Please repair the split in the covering board. The yard man goes out to the boat and finds nothing wrong with the covering board, so nothing is done. The following week the owner is complaining that the split has not been

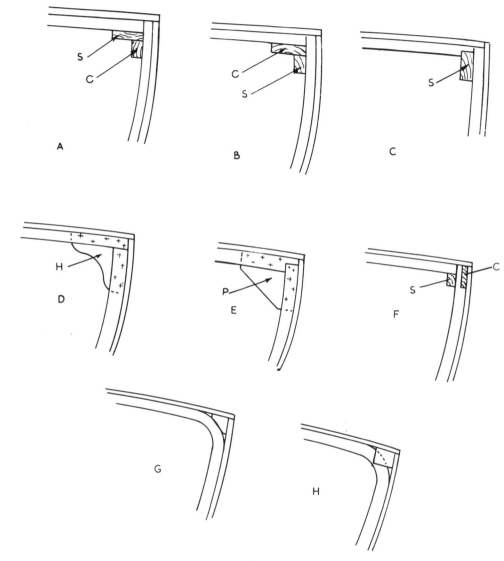

FIGURE 2.4. *The method used to hold the deck onto the hull varies all over the world. Often it varies from builder to builder. This figure shows eight ways of making up the hull deck joint on a wooden hull. The shelf (S) and the clamp (C) are often used interchangeably, depending where you are. Alternatively a hanging knee (H) or a plywood knee (P) could be used on every frame. In laminated construction the clamp is either fitted behind the frame, as in G, or the frame is notched to take the clamp, as in H.*

repaired. When the yard man and the owner get together, they find the split is in the bulwark, not in the covering board.

Unfortunately, this type of mistake is common, especially when one region or country calls a part by a different name. Figures 2.3a and 2.3b show the parts of a wooden boat. Note how many parts have two or even three different names, and some parts have the same or similar names. For instance, according to where you look, Lloyd's shows the clamp and beam shelf as in Figure 2.4a. Another builder shows it as in Figure 2.4b, while yet another builder says the terms are interchangeable.

Metal boats, on the other hand, are slightly more modern, and the terminology is a little less archaic and confusing. Figure 2.5 shows the various parts of a metal-hulled boat. Note that the longitudinal can be installed in several different ways.

With the advent of fiberglass hulls, the building method and terminology has been very much simplified. Nowadays, instead of "floors" one hears the term *interior pan* or *spider,* referring to the entire (in some cases) floors, longitudinals, bunk flats and faces, and shower stall. Instead of the clamp and beam shelf controversy, you now hear discussions of hull-deck joint styles. Figure 2.5 shows a typical production cruiser with an interior pan. Notice how all the openings are exactly the same size. This means that only one template need be made, simplifying both production and fitting time.

Pros and Cons of Building Materials

How do you decide what material you want to build your boat from? Do you go to a boat show and simply say this is the boat for you? Or do you think that fiberglass is the only building material? There are many building materials available and even more methods of using those materials. Table 2.1 lists some of the more popular methods of construction. How do you make a reasoned judgment of what is best for you? Table 2.2 analyzes various materials.

In the building skills section of Table 2.2 an unskilled amateur is assumed to be one who can follow the directions on the label or read a book and do the job with a reasonable amount of success. The special tools that may be required are only listed if they would not be found in a fairly skilled workman's tool box. For instance, a router is very handy for many jobs on a wooden hull, but many home handymen have one, so it is not included in the list. Generally, chine hulls and extremely heavyweight hulls need a special hull design. It would be, for instance, very difficult to build a hull designed for C-flex con-

TABLE 2.1: HULL CONSTRUCTION

Wood
Traditional keel and framing using carvel planking.
Traditional keel and framing with strip planking.
Lightweight frames with lapstrake planking.
WEST system hull and deck.
Cold-molded.
Hot-molded.
Double diagonal planking.
Plywood hull and deck.

Fiberglass
Heavyweight fiberglass laminate with minimum framing.
Moderate weight fiberglass laminate with substantial framing and longitudinals.
Foam- or balsa-cored fiberglass laminate.
Fiberglass-covered wood or plywood construction.
C-flex.
Composite hull using core material, S glass, carbon fibers, etc.

Aluminum Alloy
Thick plating with few frames (plating up to ¾″ [19mm].
Thin plating with many frames.
Cored plating with two layers aluminum each side on closely spaced frames.

Steel
Heel-welded longitudinals under moderately heavy plating, many frames, and longitudinals with thin plating.
Few frames and many longitudinals with thin plating.

Ferro-cement
Simple thick-skinned hull over metal armature.
Prestressed lightweight skin.

FIGURE 2.5. *Two frames are ready to be laminated in this picture. On the left of the drawing the keel lamination has been started. Note the large number of blocks used to get a fair keel laminated.*

TABLE 2.2 BUILDING MATERIALS

Material	Building Skill	Special Tools Needed	Special Design Needed	Material Cost	Labor Intensity	Special Tools To Make Job Easier	Finished Hull Weight Assuming Reasonable Scantlings	Ease of Maintenance	Ease of Repair
Wood									
Traditional carvel planking	expert			moderate	high	Band saw, planer	heavy	high	moderate
Traditional strip planking	moderate	Planer		moderate	high	Band saw, planer	medium	high	moderate
Lightweight lapstrake planking	moderate			moderate	high		medium	high	moderate
WEST system	moderate			high	medium	Staple gun	light	medium	hard
Cold-molded	moderate			high	medium		light	medium	hard
Double diagonal	moderate			high	medium		light to medium	medium	hard
Plywood hull and deck	moderate		yes	reasonable	medium		light to medium	medium	moderate
Fiberglass									
Heavyweight single-skin laminate	unskilled			moderate	medium	Resin spray gun	very heavy	low	easy
Moderate single-skin laminate	moderate			moderate	medium	Resin spray gun	medium	low	easy
C-flex laminate	moderate			moderate	medium	Resin spray gun	medium	medium	hard
Composite high-strength laminate	expert	Vacuum bag		very high	very high		very light	medium	moderate
Sandwich-cored laminate	moderate			moderate	medium		light to medium	medium	moderate
Sandwich-cored vacuum bag laminate	moderate	Vacuum bag		high	medium		light to medium	medium	moderate
Glass-covered wood	moderate			moderate	medium		heavy	medium	moderate
Aluminum Alloy									
Thick plating—few frames	moderate	MIG or TIG		moderate	medium	Plate-handling equipment	heavy	low	moderate
Thin plating—many frames	expert	Welder and plate-bending machine	yes	moderate	low		light to medium	medium	moderate
Cored plating—many frames	high			very high	very high		very light	high	moderate
Steel									
Heel-welded angle bar	unskilled	Welder and plate-bending machine	yes	moderate	low	Plate-handling equipment	heavy	high	easy
Thin plating—many frames	moderate			moderate	medium		heavy	high	easy
Thick plating—few frames	moderate			moderate	medium		very heavy	high	easy
Ferro-cement									
Thick-skinned hull	unskilled		yes	reasonable	very high		very heavy	medium	moderate
Prestressed hull	moderate		yes	reasonable	very high		heavy	medium	moderate

struction in ferro-concrete (ferro-cement in the United Kingdom) because of the extreme difference in weight.

The materials cost is simply the cost of all the materials necessary to build the hull and deck. To obtain the total cost of the hull and deck you should add in the labor cost. In Table 2.2, this is shown as labor intensity and is intended simply as a guide to how much work might go into building the boat. For instance, on a 50 footer for which we recently received bids, the hull material cost was about 6½ percent of the total cost, while labor costs ran about 15 percent. This was a foam-cored boat for which the material and labor costs are shown as about medium. On a ferro-concrete boat of this size, material costs may shrink to about 3 percent, but labor costs would go up to close to 20 percent, assuming that the builder-owner would have to pay for labor.

The finished hull weight affects much of the other gear in the boat. A heavy hull will require more material in the hull and a larger engine to push the boat through the water, which, in turn, means a larger fuel tank. It will also need a taller rig, which means larger, more expensive sails. A lighter hull, on the other hand, will have a smaller engine, smaller mast, and smaller sails, which in this case will translate into lower costs for a new boat.

To find the boat hull for your needs, you should carefully scrutinize Table 2.2. For instance, let's say you want to build it yourself and are an unskilled amateur; your choice of hull material is limited to fiberglass, steel, or ferro-cement. But if you can hire a moderately skilled person, then the building skill levels are very much expanded. Let's assume you don't have any special tools, nor do you want a special hull design. You will accept a moderate level of material expense and a moderate level of labor expense, the final hull weight should be in the light to medium category, and maintenance should be as low as possible, but a moderate amount would be acceptable. By looking through the table we can decide that certain boats are acceptable. They are C-flex, balsa-cored laminate (in fact, any of the cored laminates will do), or WEST system, but that is all.

But there may be other requirements that will modify the type of hull material you want. In the following pages we will look at each type of hull material in some detail and then at methods of maintaining and repairing the various hulls.

WOOD TYPES

Do you use long leaf yellow pine, teak, or Port Oxford cedar for planking? Can you use hackmatack or larch for crook knees? The answer is that any of these woods will do the job. Usually the wood used varies from area to area, even the name varies from area to area. Hackmatack and larch are the same wood, depending on whether you are in New or Old England.

Different woods are used in different places on the boat because some woods have more durability, others have more flexibility or rigidity. Still other woods are used in different countries for the same purpose.

Oak

In England there is simply English oak. Americans have both red and white oak. English oak is used for frames, planking, keels, stems—in fact, almost all the parts of a boat can be made from English oak. However, without adequate care gluing oak with resorcinal glues can pose problems. Lloyd's Register rates English oak as durable. It also rates American white oak as durable but does not rate red oak, which is known to be weaker and less durable. American white oak can be used for frames, keels, stem, and horn timbers. It is slightly denser than English oak and will hold fastenings well. Red oak, on the other hand, is more porous than the other oaks. In fact, one test for red oak is to suck air along the grain through the large pores in the wood. For this reason, red oak should not be used on boats.

Teak

Probably no other wood is so well used by boat builders as teak. It is used for hard-wearing deck planking, for keels, for hull planking. In fact, if you can keep your tools sharp enough, the entire boat can be built of teak. It is the only wood that Lloyd's scantling rules give an "A" for every building job. It is rated as very durable, but because of its slightly oily texture, care must be taken when gluing teak, as the oil film can prevent a good bond. Unfortunately, teak takes a very long time to grow and is in such demand that large quantities are becoming very limited and very expensive. So its use is becoming limited except for boats built in the Far East, near the source of supply.

Mahogany

There are many species of mahogany: Philippine, African, Honduran, and Mexican. Philippine or African mahogany are the types used most often. For instance, the wood known as Khaya (from West Central Africa) is African mahogany. Luan, or Lauan, is another name for Philippine mahogany. Other species often called mahogany are Meranti (from Sarawak, Indonesia, and Malaya) or Seraya (from Borneo). They are both related to the Philippine mahogany but are often coarser than Luan. All these types can be used for planking, interior and exterior trim, and finish. Lloyd's rates the finer-textured African mahogany as moderately durable and the coarse-grained Honduran as durable.

Spruce

The two major types of spruce used in boat construction are sitka spruce and, in North America, northern white spruce. In Britain, where long lengths of sitka spruce are difficult to obtain, Douglas fir is often used instead. Sitka is used for wooden spars. It is rated as nondurable, which means care must be taken to preserve it. It also glues very easily and can usually be obtained in long clear lengths. Northern white spruce, on the other hand, is used for decking and framing when the boat has to be as light as possible. But it, too, is not very durable, so care must be taken to avoid areas where water and rot spores may collect.

Cedar

There are several types of cedar, each with different qualities and uses. Port Oxford cedar is used in planking on its own or as a laminate with mahogany in WEST system or cold-molded boats. It is fairly strong and straight-grained. Western red cedar from the northwest coast of America can be used for deck planking and hull planking above the waterline. It is rated as durable by Lloyd's, but the wood is not strong and may split or check at fastenings. Alaskan cedar is also good for planking because it is straight-grained and moderately durable.

Ash

Well known for oars, frames of small boats, and occasionally for deck beams, this timber is very durable, straight-grained, and easily steam bent.

Larch

Also known in the United States as *hackmatack*. Lloyd's rates this timber as moderately durable. Its most popular use is for grown or crook knees. It can also be used for planking or, according to Lloyd's, for the beam shelf and clamp. They also rate larch as permissible for laminated framing.

These are some of the many timbers used in building boats. There are, of course, many others. Pitch pine, kauri, gaboon, lignum vitae, and iroko are used structurally. Some of the more ornamental types like walnut, birch, cherry, and butternut are not suitable or are too valuable for the structural parts of the boat and are used inside for bulkhead paneling, tables, and trim. Also, with many new cruising boats being built in Central and South America, new species are being introduced to sailors worldwide.

CONSTRUCTION METHODS

If we understand how to put a boat together, then taking that boat apart to repair it or doing maintenance work is simplified because we know where everything goes and where any problems might appear. In this section we look at ways of building wooden boats and where any potential problems for future maintenance and repair may be. It will, of course, touch only lightly many areas of the subject. A comprehensive study of wood building techniques could fill many volumes.

WOOD CONSTRUCTION

In the days when glues were simply melted down animal bones, wooden boats were held together by screws, nails, and trunnels (wooden or tree nails). This meant that a skilled builder knew how to fasten many relatively short pieces of timber together in such a way that water (well, most of the water) was kept out and the hull was able to maintain a relatively high structural integrity. But these short pieces of timber moved about as the boat was sailing, and the movement combined with the effects of fresh water rotting the wood gradually destroyed older wooden craft.

Nowadays boats are built using large amounts of glue. Craftsmanship has suffered, but the all-embracing epoxies make a rigid boat that usually rots before it falls apart. This is especially true when glued boats are built in an environment with no humidity control.

But let's first look at a traditionally built boat. The keel or backbone is the first part set up, then the frames or ribs are notched into the keel. They are fastened to the keel by means of floors, which run across the keel, as shown earlier in Figure 2.3a. If the boat is built upright, the sheer clamp or some ribands are the next items to be installed. These help to keep the frames steady and in place. Other longitudinals such as the bilge stringer or engine beds are usually put in place at this time.

The Keel, Stem Piece, and Horn Timber

At one time these three pieces of timber were built out of solid wood and joined by scarphs backed by knees and thoroughly bolted. In more modern craft the backbone is likely to be built up from a number of laminations. Figure 2.3a shows a typical traditional method of building the backbone of a cruising boat, while Figure 2.3b shows what it would look like if it were laminated.

Note that in each case the rabbet (or rebate) line is clearly shown. Also notice the stopwaters that are installed where a scarph crosses the rabbet line. The stopwaters are installed after the entire keel is joined together.

After it is firmly bolted together, the entire backbone is "set up," that is, placed in position ready to take the frames. On a large boat the hull will probably be built right side up, but smaller hulls are usually built upside down and turned over after the boat is planked. "Setting up" is a critical operation which must be done with absolute accuracy if the boat is to be built true to the designer's intentions.

Fitting the Frames

Frames can be sawn, grown, bent, or laminated. *Sawn frames,* as their name suggests are sawn from straight pieces of wood. They are the easiest and cheapest to make and are also worthy of least consideration, being only really of use on straight-sided, "V," or flat-bottomed craft.

Grown frames are, as their name suggests, cut from trees that have a natural bend to them. They are usually made from tree branches that have curved naturally, and the curve often has to be "helped" by

some judicious steaming or planing. With laminated and steam-bent frames being used more and more, grown frames are rare today.

A person building a traditional wooden boat today would probably *steam-bend* all the frames. This is the most common method for smaller boats, when the cost does not justify laminated frames.

Laminated framing is probably the most common method of building light strong frames, and with today's glues these frames will last a long time. Figure 2.5 shows how a frame is laminated. Many builders save time by making the frame double thick and simply sawing down the center to get a frame for port and starboard sides of the boat. When the boat is reasonably flat-bottomed, the frame can be run from sheer to sheer. This will give great strength and rigidity to the whole structure. Figure 2.6 shows such a frame set up in the boat.

FIGURE 2.6.   *Two laminated frames set up in the boat. The portion of the frame that is curved downward will become the cockpit side framing.*

Floors

Floors are used to join the frames to the keel or backbone of the boat. Several types are used, depending upon availability, cost, and the scantling rules. The most common types of floor are straight-grained wood such as oak, forged steel, bronze, or welded steel. At one time natural crook floors were fairly common, but today they are rare.

Bolts are usually used as fastenings to the frames, but I have seen rivets used. Lloyd's rules recommend various floors depending on the type of frame. For instance, grown frames can have a wood, steel, strap, or angle floor on every frame, but bent frames can have angle floors or strap floors. Lloyd's also insists on more than three fastenings in each arm of the floor, and the throat must be fastened to the keel with at least two bolts. As you can see, a boat built to Lloyd's rules is very substantially built.

Longitudinals

Most traditionally built British boats use a similar longitudinal system to that specified by Lloyd's, even if they aren't built to Lloyd's scantling rules. Lloyd's recommends a bilge stringer on all boats with an "L" of over 30 feet, or under 30 feet if bent frames are used. American practice is to use stringers on almost all round-bottomed boats. The stringers are often composed of several strakes clamped tightly together and screwed or bolted to the frames.

The other major longitudinals are the sheer clamp and beam shelf. These are always placed on the inside of the frames and bolted to the frames and the deckbeams.

When all the frames, floors, and bilge stringers are in place, the hull is planked up. As the planking nears the top of the hull, the clamp and shelf are put in place and the planking continued up over the bolts holding the clamp.

Planking

There are several methods of planking up a hull. The older, straight-forward carvel planking, which gives a nice smooth finish, has given way to strip planking. With carvel planking the plank edges are beveled slightly, and the space between the plank edges may or may not be caulked with cotton or caulking compound. When caulking is used, the bevel is about ¹⁄₁₆ inch per 1 inch (1.5 millimeters per 25 millimeters) of plank thickness, as in Figure 2.7.

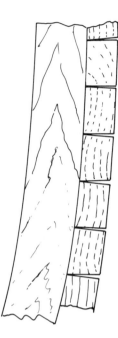

FIGURE 2.7. *Traditional hull planking is often tapered, and the voids are then caulked with cotton and caulking compound.*

FIGURE 2.8. *Butt blocks must be placed behind the ending of every plank. At A the butts are too close; good practice says there should be at least three planks between each butt block.*

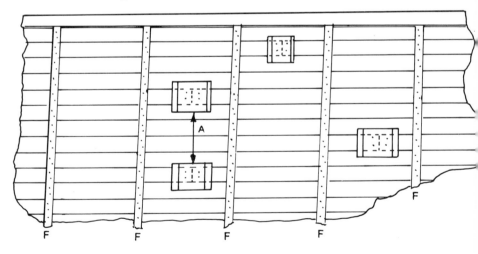

FIGURE 2.9. *A hull planked with strip planking often has planks with a slight concavity on one side and convexity on the other to facilitate easy fitting.*

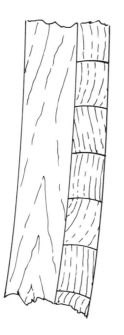

FIGURE 2.10. *Carvel or Lapstrake (clinker in the United Kingdom) planking is an old traditional method rarely seen today. The planks are lapped over each other and riveted through the one below to the frame.*

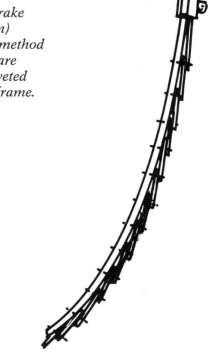

Today, you are more likely to see a strip-planked hull where the 3-inch (75-millimeter) planks have a convex and a concave edge. These edges are laid tightly against each other with no caulking or cotton and glued. This is done by a few yards, and usually the end result, especially if the boat is varnished or "bright" rather than painted, is simply magnificent.

Care must be taken that the ends of the planks or "butts" are properly staggered. It is usual to allow three planks between butts and to back each butt joint with a butt block, as shown in Figure 2.8.

Some older boats had a double-skin construction, where one layer of planks was put on and then a second layer laid over the top. But this is very expensive—almost double the cost—for very little gain.

Another method of planking up a hull is strip planking, using thin (about 1- or 1½-inch wide) planks. Each plank is rounded slightly on both edges, concave on one convex on another, as shown in Figure 2.9. The planks are glued and edge-fastened to each other and to the frames, giving a strong, light hull. This also gives the hull a nice smooth surface.

One method that does not give a smooth surface is clinker or clench-built planking, sometimes called lapstrake planking. With this type of planking each successive plank is lapped over the next, as shown in Figure 2.10. Because such a light, strong hull can be obtained with this method, it is often used for dinghies or yacht tenders that can be hauled out of the water easily.

WEST System

The WEST (wood epoxy saturation technique) system is a method of construction credited to the Gougeon Brothers of Michigan, who developed the principle of totally encapsulating wood in an epoxy solution in order to prevent the wood from rotting by keeping the moisture level in the wood down and sealing the wood from water, rot spores, and oxygen penetration. In addition, because wood has its greatest strength (tensile and compressive) along the grain, it can thus be aligned in the direction best suited to its strength. And because the hull structure is glued together, the forces from the rig, keel, and

FIGURE 2.11A.   *A 38-foot (11.6-M) sloop designed by the author in the initial stages. The temporary frames can be seen between the closely spaced longitudinals. The hull will be laid up over these longitudinal battens. The strips of veneer resting on the hull will be laid over the battens and stapled but not glued. The second layer will be glued to the first.*

FIGURE 2.11B.   *The hull has now been laminated and rolled over and the temporary forms stripped out. The horizontal strips on the left side of the hull form the ceiling, which will be outboard of the bunks. The half-frames run into the floors (bottom right). At the back of the boat you can see the aftermost ring frame.*

FIGURE 2.11C.   *The bulkheads ready to be put in the hull. Note the frames already glued to the bulkheads.*

FIGURE 2.11A

FIGURE 2.11B

FIGURE 2.11C

ocean are carried over a wide area rather than being held at one or two points by screws.

Boats built using this system generally have the planking running at 45 degree diagonals to the centerline of the boat. But if the owner wants to have a varnished or bright finish, the inner and outer layers can be run fore and aft. If an extremely light hull is desired, a core material between two layers of laminate is often used rather than a solid wood laminate.

Because the hull is a monocoque structure instead of many pieces, very little planing need be done to fair the hull up and the hull thickness need not be as thick as for a traditional planking. For instance, a hull for a boat about 35 feet (10.66 meters) long is usually made from five or six layers each ⅛ inch (3 millimeters) thick.

The framing can also be about 10–15 percent lighter than usual. This will ordinarily give a hull that is up to 20 percent lighter than a comparable planked wooden-hulled boat.

However, care has to be taken when building the boat to ensure humidity is tightly controlled and that the hull laminates are completely encased in epoxy resin. Figure 2.11 shows a boat being built using the WEST system.

DuraKore Hull Construction

A relatively new method of constructing the hull of a yacht is to use a new material offered by the Baltek Corporation. It is a balsa-cored strip with wood veneer faces called DuraKore that comes in 8-foot (2.44-meter) planks. The width of each plank is 1.75 times the thickness, and each plank has a number of fingers on the ends to facilitate joining. To construct a boat using the DuraKore method, the short 8-foot planks are joined to make strips the full length of the boat. These are laid over temporary molds and screwed into place using sheetrock screws.

The edges of the planks are coated with a "low density syntactic foam" as they are laid on the mold. When the foam (a mixture of epoxy resin, hardener, "Q" cells, and Aerosil) has hardened, the sheetrock screws are removed. The outside of the laminate is then completed by fairing with epoxy foam, which covers all the screw holes, and then fiberglass or Kevlar layers are added to give a very light, strong hull. When the hull is thoroughly set it can be turned over and the temporary framing stripped out and finished in the conventional way.

An even better way of using the DuraKore method is to build a female mold instead of the conventional male mold. This enables the boat to be constructed right side up and all the interior added before it is taken off the mold. Using this method the hull can be removed from the mold without incurring any of the distortion that might result from using a male mold.

Cold-Molded Wood Hulls

This system is the forerunner of the WEST system and can be thought of as similar but using resorcinal-based glues rather than epoxy. The planking is laid up, generally at a 45 degree angle to the centerline, and the next layer of planking is put on at 90 degrees to the first layer. Each layer of planking is about ¹⁄₁₆–⅛ inch (2–3 millimeters) thick, and up to six layers may be used on a 40 footer. In this type of construction the layers are held together by waterproof glue, and the hull may have one or two layers of fiberglass on the outside for impact and abrasion resistance.

On the inside, however, the hull can be prone to rot unless some care is taken to avoid potential trouble spots. This would mean treating the inside of the hull with wood preservative, varnishing, painting, or otherwise sealing the inside of the hull. Even with these precautions care must be taken when the boat is in use.

In spite of this, a cold-molded hull is one of the least expensive types for a skilled amateur. The hull can be designed so that a minimum number of molds are used with many longitudinals. The planking is then stapled to the longitudinals, which are left in the boat when the molds are ripped out. This method reduces the cost of hull molds because they become part of the hull. Also, because planking is fairly labor intensive, the amateur builder will save money compared to a professional.

Hot-Molded Systems

The construction of hot-molded boats is very similar to cold molding, but the glues are cured by placing the whole boat in an autoclave or giant oven. Because of the efficiency of today's glues and epoxies and the cost of autoclaves, hot-molded wooden boats are rarely built today. Many hot-molded hulls were built in the late 1940s and early 1950s, when Fairey's in England had an autoclave left over from producing the hot-molded Mosquito fighter plane of World War II fame. The early Albacore and Firefly dinghies were typical examples of this technique.

Double Diagonal

This is another hull planking system that has largely died out. In this type of building fairly thick layers of planking were laid up diagonally across the hull and glued and screwed or nailed in place. A waterproof fabric or cloth was then laid over the hull and a second skin at 90 degrees to the first was glued and screwed to the hull. Modern resins and glues have rendered this technique obsolete.

Plywood Hulls

If you want to build a hull using sheet plywood as the plating, you will need a specially designed hull shape. This shape is known as a "developed" shape because it is developed from cylinders and cones. It has to be made this way because plywood will only bend in one plane. However, undeveloped hulls have successfully been built by using two or three thinner sheets of plywood and gluing and screwing them together.

Plywood craft almost always have chines, one each side in the case of a power boat, two or more for sailing craft. Because these chines expose the end of a plywood sheet, care must be taken to ensure there is no water penetration, which can cause delamination. Often this is done by taping the seams with fiberglass tape.

Larger hulls built with plywood are glued and screwed to a conventional framing system, which gives the hull rigidity and strength. These hulls have tremendous longitudinal stiffness and can be an easy way for an amateur to build a light, strong boat.

On smaller craft, quite often, a technique known as stitch and glue is used. This style of building uses copper wire as the stitching "thread" to hold two pieces of plywood together. Fiberglass tape and polyester resin are then laid over each seam to waterproof it and provide some longitudinal stiffness. The Mirror dinghy is built using this type of construction.

Deck Planking

On a traditionally built hull, the best hull planking is a laid teak deck with the teak strips parallel to the side of the hull. When this is combined with a varnished covering board and margin plank, the deck looks extremely attractive. However, laid teak decks are expensive, and it takes an expert builder to make them leakproof. Because of this some variations have been developed.

Plywood is often laid over the deck beams and glued and screwed downward to the beams. The teak is then glued and screwed to the plywood. The screws in this case are put in through the plywood first or upward. This gives a deck free of any bungs or screwheads and is known as back screwing. This method gives a slightly less expensive and more waterproof deck than solid teak while retaining the beauty of teak.

Another method is to use plywood for the deck and either paint it or cover it with fiberglass or canvas to make it waterproof. This is a cheap method of building a deck, but unless the fiberglass or canvas is very carefully bonded to the plywood water can seep in and rot may start.

Tongue and grooved pine boards are also commonly used for decking. However, the thin edge of the groove will often curl upward and split off, leaving a spot for water to penetrate and rot to start.

Straight planks butted together and caulked are yet another way of building a deck. However, the planks tend to warp and curl, and unless special precautions (such as glassing over) are taken, leak can develop.

Many builders of WEST-type hulls use plywood for decking and encapsulate the entire sheet in epoxy. Often, two layers of plywood are used and the joints staggered to minimize any chance of a deck leak. The deck can then be painted, have teak laid over it or simply have sand added to the final layer of epoxy to form a nonskid deck.

FIBERGLASS HULL CONSTRUCTION

Since fiberglass boats were first built in the late 1950s, probably more boats have been built of this material than any other. Today, boats up to 150 feet (about 46 meters) have been built of fiberglass or sandwich laminates. This type of hull construction lends itself easily to almost any shape. You only have to be careful with sharp corners and narrow grooves, where it is difficult to fold the glass in. An infinite variety of colors can be molded in, and by varying the number of laminates or using higher strength materials the hull or deck can be locally reinforced without tremendous cost.

Glass fiber is usually used in two or three ways to build a new boat. It can be used as chopped strands about 1½–2 inches long (35–50 millimeters) and about the thickness of a human hair. Either it can be laid up by being sprayed from a chopper gin and mixed with resin on the way to the mold, or the strands can be formed into a thin mat at the factory and delivered in rolls, rather like curtain material. The mat can be laid up by hand in layers. To lay up mat the mold is wetted with a layer of resin and the mat laid on the resin. Then, by careful rolling the mat is pressed into the resin, or "wetted out." On small boats chopped strand may be used exclusively, while on larger craft the layers of mat are alternated with biaxial or triaxial cloths, woven rovings, or other types of reinforcement.

The most common method is to use alternate layers of woven roving (WR) and chopped strand mat (CSM) both of which can be obtained in various weights. Usually, CSM is expressed in ounces per square foot, while woven rovings are expressed in ounces per square yard. Hence CSM may be called 1-ounce or 1½-ounce mat, while WR may be called 18-ounce WR or, in the lighter weights, 4-ounce cloth. In Europe the weights are in grams per square meter.

Woven rovings are made of many strands of glass fibers woven into a cloth, rather like a bedsheet is woven from cotton fibers. "Biaxial" refers to the two directions the roving is woven in, 0 and 90 degrees. Triaxial roving has an additional layer woven into the cloth at 45 degrees.

Chopped strands are used to reinforce the laminate between layers of woven rovings. This reduces resin absorption and increases the laminate's flexural and impact strength. Some smaller craft, such as dinghies and tenders, are laid up entirely of chopped strand bonded with polyester resin. This is usually done with a chopper gun, which sprays resin out of one nozzle and strands of fiberglass from another. The theory is that the glass becomes coated with the resin on the way to the mold. In this case the boat is often heavier than a comparably hand-laid-up craft due to the greater amount of resin applied with a chopper gun layup.

Some of the latest high-strength materials have two or more layers of unidirectional cloth bonded together at 0 and 90 degrees. This gives a very high-strength laminate with the properties of unidirectional but without the expense of single layers of unidirectional.

We have mentioned some materials briefly without really explaining what they are or what they do. To understand how a modern boat is built it is essential to have a full understanding of the materials. In this section the materials have been divided into three groups: (1) reinforcements: the fiberglass laminates, including special materials intended for use on custom or one-off boats; (2) cores: the section between two laminates used to increase the stiffness of the laminate; and (3) adhesives: the various resins and epoxies that hold the laminate together.

Reinforcements

Before it is used, the reinforcement, be it woven roving, chopped strand, biaxial or triaxial fiberglass, Kevlar, or graphite, is a flexible, easy-to-bend material rather like a bed sheet. It is only the addition of a mixture of resin and hardener that turns the reinforcement into a solid laminate. In fact, if we added a mixture of resin and hardener to a bedsheet we could turn it into a nonflexible material. The reinforcement comes in many different thicknesses, strengths, and costs. The brief discussion that follows of the materials used in modern cruising boats will give you an idea of the potential for innovation and costs of a modern boat.

"E" glass was originally developed as an electrical insulation. In the late 1950s and early 1960s it was used as a boat-building material.

FIGURE 2.12. *Various types of unidirectional tapes as supplied by the Orcon Corporation. Kevlar, S2 glass, and Graphite are shown. Note how they are held together with a scrim backing, which contributes no structural strength.*

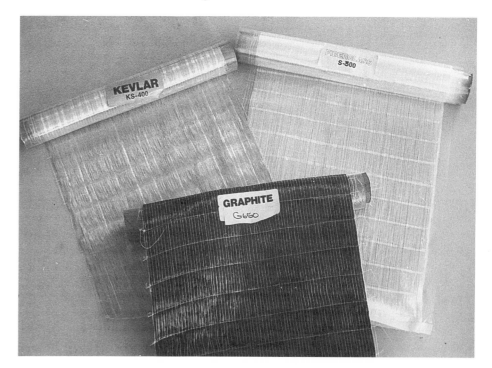

Its physical properties are quite low when compared to some of the modern materials. However, its cost is also relatively low, making it the most commonly used type of glass fiber.

"S" glass. It used to be that if higher strength, lighter weight laminates were required, the only alternative to E glass was aircraft-quality S glass ("R" glass in Europe). This glass was produced specifically for the aircraft industry and was extremely expensive. Because of the high cost it was rarely used in boats.

"S2" glass. Because S glass was so expensive, there was a demand for a lower cost, higher strength glass. S2 glass was developed to meet that demand. It has better tensile strength than E glass with only a slightly higher cost and is the type most commonly used in high-tech laminates for boats.

Carbon fiber is probably the best-known high strength material. Strictly speaking it should be known as graphite fibers, but popularly it is called carbon fiber. It was originally developed for high-speed turbine blades and later found its way into performance boats. It looks like black fiberglass and is much stronger in tension and compression than regular fiberglass. Carbon fibers are used in hulls, masts, booms, and even sails in some ocean racers. In fact, it can be used anywhere high strength, corrosion resistance (although carbon does not corrode, it can cause electrolytic corrosion if improperly bonded to metals like aluminum), fatigue resistance, and light weight are required. Figure 2.12 shows Kevlar, graphite, and S-glass tapes as supplied by the Orcon Corporation.

It is usually supplied in unidirectional or "prepreg" (preimpregnated with resin) tapes up to widths of 12 inches (.3 meters). Bidirectional and tridirectional woven fabrics can be obtained in wider widths, or the material can be ordered as nonwoven mat.

Whereas carbon fiber is used mostly to absorb and distribute tensile and compressive loads, *Kevlar 49* made by Dupont is often used as an impact-absorbing material. It is very strong in tension but not as strong as graphite or even E glass in compression. Weight for weight it is five times as strong as steel and up to three times as stiff as E glass. It is used in bulletproof vests, ropes, cables, and many, many other marine applications. Kevlar is slightly more expensive than S2 glass, but when combined with graphite fibers, and fiber orientation is defined, a laminate can be designed that has the best properties of tensile and compressive strength and impact resistance, something no other single material can offer. For the cruising sailor who wants a lightweight, strong hull that will put up with impacts from floating debris, Kevlar is a material to be incorporated into the hull laminate.

One of the most popular uses for Kevlar is in the form of ropes. It can be used instead of wire for halyards and sheets; the weight saved helps increase the yacht's stability.

C-flex is a form of fiberglass planking that is composed of rods about ½ inch (10–12 millimeters) diameter, held together by a light fiberglass cloth. The material is strictly unidirectional and will require additional glass mat or woven roving to make up the laminate. Each rod has a very high glass content, which means it is possible to obtain a high glass to resin ratio.

C-flex is reasonably inexpensive and can be applied with fairly unskilled labor. It will, however, require an extensive amount of fairing to get a really smooth hull.

Core Materials

Core materials vary depending on the desired workability, weight, and strength of the required laminate. The materials currently in use are Airex, balsa wood, Klegecell (Plasticell in Great Britain), and Nomex. These are the most popular, but in recent years Divinycell (similar to Klegecell and Plasticell) has become popular. There are others, such as the aluminum-cored F-board and Rohacell, but these are not really suited to the marine environment. Each type has distinct properties, advantages, and disadvantages.

Airex is a closed-cell, semi-rigid, polyvinyl chloride (PVC) foam. Airex type R62.80 can be compressed up to 50 percent of its thickness without rupturing and can be bent around a radius without fracturing. It is resistant to water, fuel oils, and so on but does deteriorate slightly when used with acetone or styrene. Airex, because it is a bendable foam, is slightly harder to sand or grind than is Klegecell or balsa.

Balsa. As of now this is the least expensive of the core materials and probably the most widely used in the marine industry. According to most tests, a balsa-cored laminate has the highest stiffness for a given layup. But although it is stiffer, it will fail if overloaded. Balsa, being an organic material, can suffer from wickability (it absorbs resin and moisture along the direction of the grain); however, several coatings have been used to reduce or eliminate this problem in the last few years. While the outer skins are intact, the styrene in the laminate ensures that neither rot nor degradation can start inside the core. But if the outer skin is fractured, then the core can absorb water and may rot if the water is not removed. It is approved by Lloyd's, and some builders of balsa-cored boats guarantee their craft for up to 10 years.

Known as Plasticell in the United Kingdom, *Klegecell* is a closed-cell polyvinyl foam. It comes in various densities (2, 3, 4, 5, 6, and 15 lb/ft²). The 2 and 3 lb/ft² foams are not recommended for structural laminates (i.e. hulls). Klegecell can be formed by bending around a mold and if heated gently will retain the bend. It will not rot and does not absorb moisture. It is also nontoxic when burnt and will not support a flame. However, Klegecell is a brittle foam and will fracture if subjected to high impact loads, although it is stiffer and will fail at a much higher value than a comparable Airex panel.

Nomex is extremely light. Most of the core is air! It is also expensive. Although it is called a paper honeycomb, it is, in fact, made from Aramid, which is a special type of nylon. To ensure a good bond and no "dimpling" of the skins, a "prepreg" laminate should be used. This is a sheet of fiberglass preimpregnated with resin and kept from curing by refrigeration. Nomex does not burn, or rot, and it will resist the action of solvents and chemicals. Its best properties are obtained by curing under high temperature and pressure.

One of the most recent applications is to sandwich the Nomex between two pieces of plywood to produce a light, strong panel. These panels can be used as bulkheads, or to build furniture in a light, strong boat. Figure 2.13 shows various core materials.

Selecting a core material. As these brief descriptions of core materials have suggested, each material has advantages and disadvantages. It is up to the designer or builder to select the core that best suits the given purpose. Several factors should be considered:

1. Is the material readily available, and if not, how long will it take to get it?
2. Is the cost compatible with the cost of the overall project? For instance, a flat out racing yacht may be subject to an almost unlimited budget in the quest for speed. But the buyer of a cruising yacht may prefer to put extra money into more comfortable amenities rather than the unseen core material.
3. Is the hull form suited to the material? For instance, it is not worth using a Nomex-cored hull in a boat designed in the traditional wooden style. Extra weight would have to be added to bring the boat down to its lines.
4. Is the core suited to the type of use envisioned for the craft? For instance, a pilot boat may be subjected to high impact loads as it comes alongside a ship to take the pilot off. In this case the best type of core may be the semi-rigid Airex, which can take some deformation.

5. Does the core complement the type of fiberglass and resin used to bond everything together? For instance, it is poor planning to use a flexible core material and bond it with a brittle epoxy.

You can see that a certain amount of knowledge is required to select the right core for the job. It isn't simply a matter of saying we'll use that and that; the cores, adhesives, and laminates should be carefully selected to complement each other and add to the total structure.

FIGURE 2.13.   *Various types of core material:*
  1. Klegecell.
  2. Contoured balsa core with scrim backing.
  3. Contoured Dyvinicell.
  4. Airex.
  5. Nomex honeycomb.
  6. Aluminum F board with the facing partially stripped.

Adhesives

Without adhesives all the glass fiber in the world would not make a good boat. Polyester, vinylester, and epoxy resins are the glues that hold boats together. Most boats are built using polyester resin, higher tech boats use vinylesters, and the top quality yachts use epoxy. Not many builders use vinylesters for the entire laminate nowadays, as its cost is about 80 percent more expensive than polyester and about 10 percent less expensive than epoxy, and the high styrene content makes it a health hazard. (Note that the cost of resins is also predicated upon how far they have to be shipped. This can artificially inflate the cost well beyond that of the factory price.) However, because of problems with osmosis, the number of American builders using vinylester is growing. It is used in the gel coat and the first laminate to protect against osmosis blisters.

Polyester resin is the "glue" used in most production plants. It is made up of three components: the resin, the catalyst, and the accelerator. The catalyst is the component that makes the resin set, while the accelerator allows this to happen at normal working temperatures. The accelerator is dimethylanaline (DMA), and I'm told it can pose some serious health hazards. Nowadays many resins come with the accelerator already mixed in, needing only the addition of the catalyst to make it harden. The catalyst that is most commonly used is MEKP (methyl ethyl ketone peroxide). When MEKP is added to a resin with the accelerator, the resin, which is a thin syrup, sets up into a solid lump and gives off some heat. Once set it will never again turn into a liquid. Because of this it is known as a thermo-setting resin.

Vinylester resin is simply a vinyl-based polyester that has better tensile and flexural strength than polyester resin.

Epoxy laminating resins are also slightly different from epoxy adhesives in that they have a lower viscosity (they pour easier), which makes them more suitable than the adhesive form for wetting out a laminate. Like the tubes of epoxy you can buy in the store, the resin comes in two parts, and it is necessary to mix the hardener with the resin to get a cure. They are also more expensive than polyester resins. However, they are usually lighter and stronger than comparable poly- or vinylester resins. Cure time can be varied by changing the type and quantity of hardener added to the mix. Often a reasonably fast (up to two-hour) cure time is used.

Usually, only small boats, canoes, rowing shells, and other high performance boats are built using these materials in their single-skin form. Larger craft almost always use a core in the laminate to get higher stiffness and strength. If we make a small canoe using a core material, the skins can be extremely light to get the same stiffness as a solid laminate. Quite often only one layer of material need be used. But with only a single skin over the core material, impact resistance is very poor. If you have ever seen the abuse a canoe gets when it is dragged over the beach or hits a submerged rock, you'll quickly realize that good impact resistance is an essential item in a small boat. Of course, you can increase the skin thickness to improve impact resistance, but the advantage of having a core material would be lost.

Osmosis

We have all heard horror stories of boats with bottoms that have blistered and soaked up water. But what caused it and how is it cured? The process starts when a boat is first laid up. The gel coat is sprayed onto the mold, and then layers of laminate are laid against the gel coat. Between the laminate and the gel coat small air bubbles are often created as a result of the rolling to eliminate larger air pockets. When the boat is immersed in liquid, minute pinholes in the gel coat allow moisture to permeate into these bubbles. This moisture reacts with the chemicals already in the laminate to form a very acidic solution. It is this solution that causes the blisters on the hull.

The minute pinholes can be caused by poor laminating techniques, overenthusiastic sanding when working on the bottom, or sandblasting the bottom. The cure is to put a bottom on the boat that is nonhydroscopic. That is, it must stop any water permeation.

Let's pause for a moment and look at the resin used in the gel coat. It must be a resin that is compatible with the resin used for the other parts of the laminate, which, because of the cost involved, usually means that it must be a polyester resin rather than an epoxy. There are two types of polyester resin: isophthalic- and orthophthalic-based resins. The names "isophthalic" and "orthophthalic" refer to the acid base of the polyester resin. Isophthalic-based resins have better physical and chemical resistance and stop water penetration more effectively, but they were slightly more expensive than orphthalic resins, and builders shied away from them. When problems arose with blistering of hulls that were immersed in water over long periods, builders turned to isophthalic resins. Today, most top quality builders use either isophthalic resins or epoxy in their gel coats to eliminate any potential water permeation and blistering. Quite often, builders who use these materials offer guarantees of several years against hull blistering.

PRODUCTION BOATS

For most people the cruising yacht they own or will own is a production boat, and knowing how it is put together will often help them understand how improvements can be made.

Over 90 percent of the production boats built today use polyester resin and E glass. The glass laminate may be in the form of bi- or triaxial rovings and chopped strand mat, but it's unlikely to be much more sophisticated. About 60 percent of builders build a boat using sandwich construction rather than the single-skin method. Most will also use an interior pan or liner inside the hull and deck to produce a finished appearance inside the hull and to form a foundation for the bulkheads, bunk flats, and other interior furniture.

These methods are reasonably inexpensive and cut down on the amount of labor required. In the next section we'll look at how the modern production cruiser is built, and then we'll see how a custom builder works. Finally, we'll look at some designs and building methods used by amateur builders.

The Production Hull

When a builder decides to build a fiberglass boat he has to construct several parts before the boat can be laid up. First comes the plug. That is, the required hull and deck shapes are built in wood to very precise tolerances and finished very carefully. A good plug builder will make a plug that is almost perfectly smooth. Any protrusions or hollows will be built into the plug. For instance, if a deck plug were being built, all the winch bases, cleat mountings, stanchion base mountings, drain holes, and track positions would be built into it to save time later when the equipment has to be located and bolted in place.

Once the male plug is made a female mold has to be made from it. This entails applying layers of fiberglass over the plug until a thick laminate has been built up. Reinforcing is applied to the laminate to ensure the finished mold will not distort. After the mold has cured it is removed from the plug, which is usually discarded. This mold can now be used for up to 200 new boats before the heat given off by the curing process for each boat wears out the mold. Most builders, though, produce new molds long before the two hundredth hull is produced. With each use the mold deteriorates slightly so that it takes longer to polish it for the next unit.

Now the mold must be cleaned and polished and a layer of mold release wax applied to it. Then comes the first part of the new hull—the gel coat. This is simply a thick layer of resin to protect the boat against minor scratches and polishing. The gel coat can be clear and a design painted on the inside, or it may be of one solid color. Next to the gel coat is placed a layer of chopped strand mat. Woven roving is sometimes used, but unless it is a very lightweight material it may show through the gel coat (a feature known as print through). With the first layer in place the laminate is built up with alternate layers of mat and rovings until the desired thickness is reached. Quite often a layer of Coremat (a special thin foam made by Westpoint Pepperell and Feret in Europe) is placed behind the outer laminates to avoid any chance of print through.

Alternate mat and roving layers are used because when two mats are put next to each other it takes a large amount of resin to fill the voids between the layers. This will lower the density of the laminate and make it substantially weaker. The mat acts as a filler between the layers. On the other hand, many layers of mat placed together have reduced impact and tensile strength, necessitating a thicker laminate.

The strength of the laminate used to be determined by the amount of glass in it. Lloyd's, for instance, requires a glass-to-resin ratio of at least 30 percent, while the American Bureau of Shipping (ABS) expects a 35 percent glass-to-resin ratio. Most manufacturers can get a ratio of about 40 percent, but the industry standard appears to be about 35 percent, although experienced builders can get higher ratios up to about 55 percent. However, the actual ratio will depend upon the type of cloth or weave used. For instance, if the builder were to use unidirectional material the ratio might be as high as 65 percent. It is recognized that without special materials or techniques "resin dryness" can result. That is, the glass is not fully wetted out by the resin and weak, dry spots result, spots that might lead to delamination and failure of the member.

You sometimes hear of boat hulls laid up using a "chopper gun." This is a gun with two nozzles: resin is sprayed out of one nozzle, while short glass threads are fired out of the other.

In theory the glass is coated with resin on its way to the hull mold. Because of the reduction in the strength of the laminate it must be thicker, which means a heavier hull. A hull laid up with this method can also have variable laminate thickness, which could easily lead to local failure spots.

These, then, are the basic techniques used for building or laying up a simple fiberglass hull. They are best suited for the production builder who uses a female mold to lay up the boat. Because the mold is expensive and necessitates several steps, producing a single-skin fiberglass hull is not the technique for the amateur builder. Figure 2.14 shows various stages in the production of the O'Day 302.

A better method of making a production hull is to use a sandwich core between two exterior laminates. (See page 71 for more on sandwich construction.) In a production boat the gel coat and exterior laminate are hand laid in the mold and then a layer of core material is laminated on top. Once the core has set up the interior laminate is added. Most production builders today use sandwich cores, making their hulls stronger and stiffer without increasing weight. However, some builders, such as Boston Whaler, make a sandwich hull by laminating the hull, adding the deck, and filling the space between them with sprayed-in foam.

FIGURE 2.14B

FIGURE 2.14A. *The hull mold for the O'Day 302. Note the strong reinforcing around it and the circular rollers. The rollers allow the mold to be turned for ease of laminating the hull. (Photo by author.)*

FIGURE 2.14C

FIGURE 2.14B. *The interior pan of the O'Day 302 ready to go into the boat. Note the wiring pigtails already in place. (This series of photos by author courtesy of Starcraft.)*

FIGURE 2.14C. *Workers glassing the interior pan into the boat.*

FIGURE 2.14D. *Bulkheads have been fitted, and the rest of the interior is about to go inside the hull.*

FIGURE 2.14E. *The deck being worked on upside down.*

FIGURE 2.14F. *Decks ready to be fitted onto a hull. Note that all the deck gear is in place.*

The Interior Liner

While the hull is being built, the interior pan is being laid up in another part of the plant, together with the deck mold, the deck mold liner, and several small fiberglass parts. Each part will become a piece of the completed hull.

The interior pan in probably the second largest piece of the boat to be built out of fiberglass. At its most comprehensive this pan will cover the entire interior of the hull, from sheer to sheer, and will have the bunk flats, counters, bulkhead positions, and smaller foundations and flats all molded in. All that remains is to drop the premade furniture modules into their designated positions.

The interior liner is usually built upside down, and quite often wiring harnesses, plumbing lines, and other details are fitted before turning over. In some plants the liner is turned over and more items are added. For instance, the entire head unit may be fitted into the liner, all the galley equipment, ice box, and sinks may be added, and often the engine is mounted before the liner is dropped into the hull.

When the liner with all its prefitted equipment is put in place, it is bonded to the hull with resin or epoxy and the fittings are connected up. Sometimes all the small voids are filled with foam, but in general the bonding is expected to serve to integrate both parts.

The Deck Mold and Liner

The deck is assembled in yet another part of the plant. It, too, is usually made in two parts, the actual deck and a deck liner. When the deck has cured it is popped out of its mold and placed on trestles. Next, all the deck fittings are bolted in place. Winches get bolted around the cockpit, cleats are fitted with backing plates and bolted down. Sheet tracks have backing plates or oversize washers fitted and are bolted in place. Windows are inserted and screwed down. Deck openings are trimmed up and hatches fitted until all the deck gear is in place.

While this is being done the deck liner has been made and is removed from the mold. It is usually fitted with the wiring harness and any lights that have to be installed. Voids are filled with foam, and the liner is trimmed up.

Then it is time to marry the liner and the deck mold. Usually the liner is wetted out with epoxy or resin and the the two are tightly clamped together. This gives a finished appearance on both sides of the deck unit. The bonding process that joins both the hull and its liner and the deck with its liner often make it difficult or impossible to add gear or replace gear. Unless the design is very carefully thought out, repair costs on a production cruiser can be extremely expensive. For instance, I knew an owner who wanted to add another winch on deck. Simple, he thought, you just buy a winch, drill a few holes, and bolt it down. He drilled a few holes, one of which went right through the wiring harness, shorting out his cabin lights. Having spent several hours repairing that job—by cutting away the liner and splicing new wires—he bolted the winch down. Only to crush the foam core and severely weaken the deck. The expert that repaired the boat had to remove the core, add reinforcement, adjust the wiring, and reglass the liner. Total cost was in the hundreds of dollars, just to add a single winch.

The Hull-Deck Joint

The hull-deck joint becomes one of the most important parts of the boat. When the hull and the deck units are finished they have to be joined. This is where a carefully designed hull-deck joint is of major importance. Figure 2.15 shows a series of hull-deck joints.

While these production methods reduce the cost of a new boat, they do have some drawbacks. For instance, while many builders test their boats for leakage before the vessel leaves the factory, quite often a leak will develop after the boat has been sailed for some time. Because there is an interior liner, the water may appear at some distance from the actual deck leak, which could make it an extensive chore to find the leak.

Adding more deck gear can also be fairly risky. In our earlier example we saw how expensive it could become.

A reputable builder will usually help you eliminate both problems. They often have had experience with deck leaks and will usually have a good idea of its position. If you need to add more deck equipment, unless it is on the coaming, it pays to ask your dealer or builder if there is any likelihood of damaging interior fittings *before* you drill.

CUSTOM BOATS

Many sailors have to settle for a production boat, but an increasing number of people are finding it difficult to find exactly the boat they want. These are the experienced owners who want a boat designed to suit their needs. They may want a beautifully varnished hull, or an interior designed specifically to their requirements. For them, the choice of hull materials is much wider, the potential for large gains in performance and cruisability much greater.

In this section we look at sandwich construction methods. Even though many builders use a sandwich core in their production boats, I have included it here because it is a building technique that can be used for both production and one-off custom boats. Another building method is C-flex, a material mentioned earlier whose use we'll examine here. Finally, we'll look at a few of the more revolutionary methods of building a boat.

Sandwich Construction

You may think this section is about fitting a piece of ham between two slices of bread. It's not, it's about fitting a core material, balsa wood or one of the various foams, between two layers of fiberglass.

A relatively easy method to build a custom boat is to make some molds and sew a core material (usually sheets of Airex or Klegecell foam are best) over them. Fiberglass laminates are laid up over the core until an outer skin has been built up. Then the whole thing is turned over, the mold stripped out, and the interior laminate added. Another, more popular method today is to build an entire male mold, lay up the inside laminate on it (and vacuum-bag if desired), add the sandwich core, and then lay up the outside laminate (now vacuum-bagging is required). This is a very brief explanation of the process. To look at the first method in more detail, consider the boat shown in Figure 2.16a, a small 22 footer I designed and built as a cruiser/racer. It uses a Klegecell core with two layers of Orcon S2 glass on either side. The whole laminate was bonded with Atlac 580A vinylester resin from ICI. The hull and deck of this boat weighed just over 400 pounds and the all-up weight was 1,500 pounds.

To construct this boat molds were cut for each station. The molds were set up on a strongback, and longitudinal battens were nailed to the longitudinal molds. Klegecell foam was laid over the mold and sewn around the longitudinals. Where necessary the joints were faired up and puttied over to make the whole thing smooth and true. Then the Orcon S2 glass was draped over the hull and wetted out as in Figure 2.16a. After two layers of glass had been applied at 0 and 90 degrees, the hull was given a fairing layer of ¾-ounce chopped strand and faired up. Any hollows were filled and bumps smoothed down until a nice fair surface emerged.

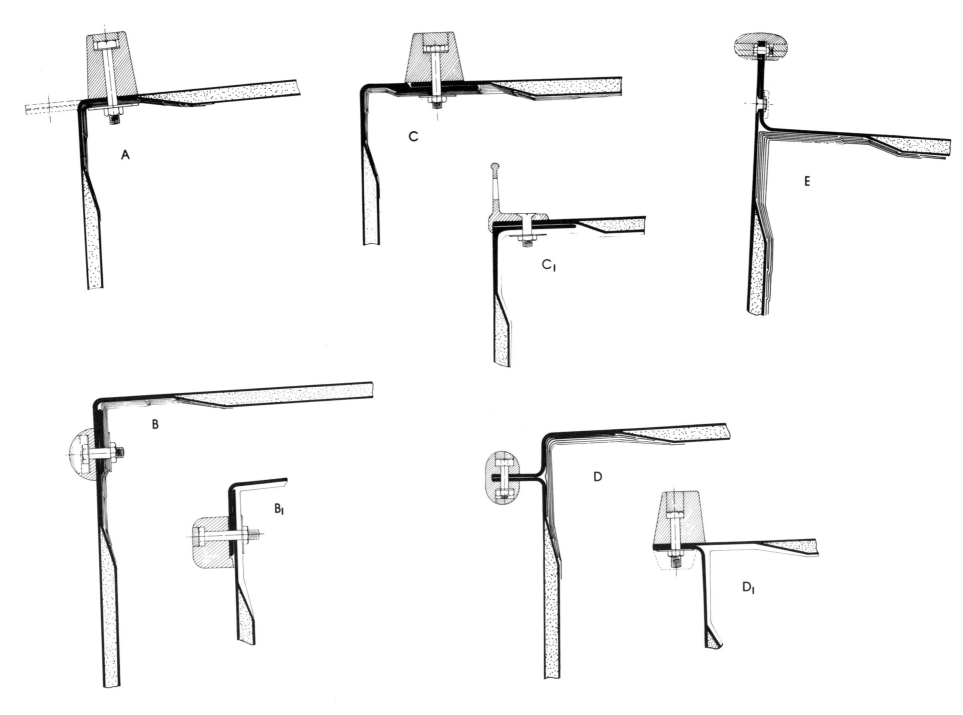

A cradle was then made to fit the bottom of the boat and the whole unit turned over. When the hull was right side up the sewing holding the Klegecell to the mold was cut and the mold removed from the hull. At this point the hull was very wobbly, but it firmed up as soon as the interior layers of S2 glass were laid up inside and wetted out.

With work on the hull temporarily finished, the deck was made up. Again a mold was made. But because the deck had many large flat areas, the deck mold was finished with a layer of thin plywood and all the corners and joints filled as in Figure 2.16b. The outside fiberglass laminate was then laid up on the mold. Figure 2.16b shows the initial stages. Next, the Klegecell was laid on the laminate. In places of high loads the deck was reinforced with pieces of plywood. For example, the winch bases and cleat mounting all had pieces of plywood as a core rather than the Klegecel.

Next, the inside layer of Orcon glass was laminated into place and the whole thing left to cure. When it had cured sufficiently, the deck was popped off the mold and rolled over. Now it could be faired and nonskid gel coat rolled on in the appropriate areas.

At this point the boat was moved over to Merrifield-Roberts, Inc., of Bristol, Rhode Island, for finishing. (They built the 12-meter *Heart of America* and several other well-known boats.) They fitted out the interior and glassed the hull and deck together. The boat was painted and the deck gear and other equipment added.

Although many of the materials seem high tech, they have many advantages for the custom cruising boat. They are relatively easy to use, have a reasonable cost, have sound- and heat-insulating qualities, produce a relatively lightweight structure, and can be cut or bent before laminating to suit almost any shape.

FIGURE 2.15. *A series of hull deck joints. A shows the joint used on the 22-foot cruiser in Figure 2.16. The deck was laid over the outward-turning flange and glassed inside. The flange (shown dashed) was trimmed off and the outer sides glassed. B is known a a coffee can hull deck joint, where the deck fits neatly over the hull and the two are bolted and glassed together. C is another common method of joining the hull and deck. An inward turning flange is laid up and the deck sits on it. They are glassed and bolted together. D shows two outward-turning flanges. This type of construction serves as a rubrail base but also can get wedged on or under a dock wall or piling. If a bulwark is desired, the hull-deck joint as shown in E is very strong.*

This is only one method of building a cored hull. Production manufacturers lay the boat up inside a female hull mold. The outer skin goes down on the gel coat, then the core is added, finally the inner skin is laid up. Most custom builders build a complete male hull plug, which enables them to lay up the interior lamination before applying the core and the outer laminate. This makes it easier to remove the plug afterward and makes for a stiffer hull when the plug is removed. However, it is more expensive and the hull will still need to be faired and painted while it is upside down.

C-Flex Hull Construction

Like the construction method for the sandwich hull, building a boat using C-flex requires a male mold. The mold can be very simple, merely a number of frames set up on a strongback and fastened securely in place. The C-flex is laid over the molds cut to size and stapled in place. When the hull is reasonably fair, the C-flex is wetted out and extra layers of fiberglass added to maintain the required shape.

After the hull has cured it is completely faired; often the fairing will be taken to where the hull is undercoated ready for the final topcoat. Then it is turned over, the mold stripped out, and extra glass (usually woven roving but occasionally chopped strand) is added if required. At this point frames and bulkheads are added and taped in place and the remainder of the structural items are glassed in place.

When all the structure is in, the interior furniture is fitted. Usually the deck will be built of the same material, and after the interior is fitted the hull and deck will be joined.

The advantage of C-flex is that it is very simple to work with. It is reasonably labor intensive, but the labor need not be highly skilled. The hull molds, which are usually disposed of after use, are not very expensive to build.

Some Novel Construction Techniques

There are some interesting experimental methods of fiberglass boat construction now entering the marketplace. One I received a flyer on a few weeks ago makes use of extruded plastic beams. Each beam has a hollow groove in one side and a bead on the other side that fits into the groove. To build a boat using this method one simply fits the bead into the groove to form the hull plating. The beams are cut with a V slot down the middle to taper them, and the whole thing assembled

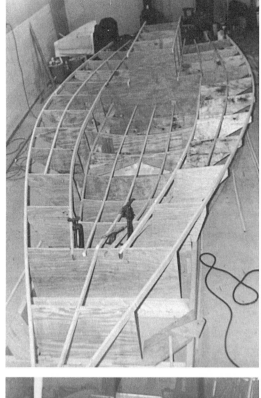

FIGURE 2.16B. *The deck was built using a mold as shown. Because most of the surfaces were only slightly curved, not many longitudinals were used. The cockpit is the box in the background.*

FIGURE 2.16A. *The hull of a 22-footer designed by the author. It was built of Klegecell over a male mold using Orcon "S2" Glass and ICI Atlac 580A Vinylester resin.*

At this stage it has the first layer of "S2" glass laminated in place. The diagonal stripes are the edges of the glass, and the small light marks are where the edges of the Klegecell were bonded together. Note the open garage door. This boat was built almost entirely in a two-car garage. (Photo by Bill Medeiros.)

FIGURE 2.16C. *The gel coat has been laid on the deck mold, and the first layer of fiberglass has been laid out on the right of the mold.*

on a set of frames. Once the plating is set up it is epoxied in place and there's a boat!

I'm not sure that this will catch on, but it shows someone is thinking about the challenge of building a boat using different techniques.

Another method of building a glass boat is to lay up a laminate on a flat surface and then use the flat panels to build the boat in a manner similar to a plywood boat. The only advantage I can see to this method is that a hull mold is not required and the finished hull is easier to maintain than a similar plywood hull would be.

These, then, are some of the ways fiberglass boats can be built. No doubt somebody will think up other methods, but for the cruising sailor tried and tested methods are usually the simplest and best. No matter what type of boat you want, be it a production cruiser or a one-off custom design, fiberglass offers many options and an infinite number of ways of achieving those options.

METAL HULLS

Metal hulls can be divided into two types: steel and aluminum alloy. Both are very strong and have good impact resistance. But there the similarity ends. Aluminum is light, while steel is heavy. Steel will rust, while aluminum protects itself by forming an oxide layer on its surface. Steel is also fairly inexpensive, aluminum is not. Steel is easy to weld, aluminum is more difficult. In the next section we will look at each material and discuss its suitability as a boat-building material.

Aluminum Boat Building

Of all the hull-building materials, fiberglass is the least difficult to maintain. But close to it in ease of maintenance comes aluminum alloy. It is also very easy to form into compound shapes and easy to work—even with woodworking tools. It is relatively simple to build in tanks, seats, and hatches, and with an alloy deck, deck leaks can be almost eliminated. In fact, the only disadvantages of aluminum are its cost and the difficulty of welding.

Aluminum itself is a pure metal electrolytically refined from bauxite. The pure metal is very soft and weak, so to improve its mechanical properties various elements are added to it. For marine use these elements are usually small amounts of chromium, iron, magnesium, silicon, manganese, and less than .1 percent copper. Too much copper would ruin the alloy, as copper corrodes in sea water.

The modern marine alloy has very high corrosion resistance and good strength combined with good weldability. The corrosion resistance is aided by aluminum's affinity for oxygen. The outer layer of any aluminum surface combines with oxygen to form an oxide layer, which resists any further degradation of the metal. This oxide layer also creates problems for welders, who have to use a flux to initially remove the oxide layer. The heat of the torch will then melt the oxide as the flame progresses. To prevent any reforming of the oxide layer an inert gas is injected around the flame. The welding technique takes its name from the method used, tungsten-inert gas (TIG) and metal-inert gas (MIG). A good MIG or TIG welder using modern pulsed-arc equipment can weld plates under ⅛ inch (2 millimeters) thick.

On the debit side, electrolysis can corrode a boat very quickly, but this should not happen unless the electrical system is badly designed or incompatible metals are used next to each other.

There appear to be two major schools of thought in aluminum boat building. The first says a thick skin with minimal framing is best, while the other says many frames and longitudinals should be used. Most other builders are somewhere in the middle. The thick-skinned cruiser has some merit, but the builder at the other end of the scale is probably only interested in building racing boats.

The *thick-skinned hull* was developed by META in France and uses plating about 15 millimeters (⅝ inch) thick on a chine hull. The chines serve as stiffeners. Interior bulkheads together with a few frames give transverse support. This method is heavy on materials but light on labor. The boat is also fairly heavy, but its impact resistance must be phenomenal. So if you are going to ram harbor walls and pound on coral heads, this could be the boat hull for you.

In *normal aluminum hull construction*, depending on the boat and the scantling rule being used, normal frame spacing is about 18–22 inches (.5–.6 meters) with longitudinals about 14–18 inches (.4–.5 meters) apart. This takes a reasonable amount of material and man-hours to build. Its advantage is that the hull shape can be anything desired, and a fairly thick, ⅛–¼-inch (3–6 millimeters), plating will give good impact resistance combined with a moderate to light displacement.

As for *lightweight aluminum hulls*, in the racing fraternity sandwich-cored aluminum hulls have been built over many closely spaced frames and longitudinals. The theory behind this says that if you can reduce the panel size, that is, the area of hull bounded by two frames and two longitudinals, you can make the plating thinner. I suppose the ultimate would be to space the frames and longitudinals so close

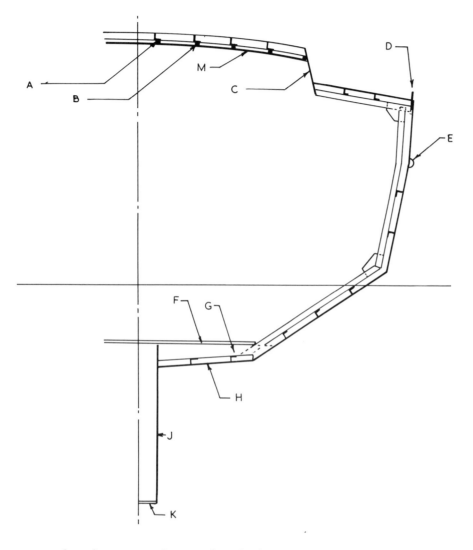

FIGURE 2.17. *A relatively simple method of building a steel hull. The angle bars are welded to the frames and the plating welded to the angle bars. The various parts are as follows:*

A   *1.25 × 1.25 inch (30 × 30 mm) angle bar on 10 inch (250 mm) center.*
B   *.4 × 1.5 inch (10 × 38 mm) wooden deck beams.*
C   *.4 inch (10 mm) plate.*
D   *.5 × 6 inch (12 × 150 mm) toerail, drilled for shackles as shown on deck plan.*
E   *2 inch (50 mm) split pipe rubrail.*
F   *.75 inch (20 mm) cabin sole boards.*
G   *.25 inch (6 mm) steel plate floor.*
H   *Hull plating .25 inch (6 mm) plate.*
J   *.4 inch (10 mm) keel plating.*
K   *Keel shoe 1 inch (25 mm) plate.*
M   *Ceiling.*

Steel Boat Building

Why steel? you may ask. Steel has distinct cost advantages over aluminum. It is very strong, easy to weld, and almost an ideal material for extensive worldwide offshore cruising. Everywhere in the world where commercial ships go somebody can repair, weld, or supply steel. Its only major drawback is that steel corrodes in a marine atmosphere, but with the modern epoxy paints this problem can be significantly reduced. For instance, Chay Blyth sailed around the world in *British Steel,* and when he returned there was very little sign of any corrosion on the boat.

Unfortunately, many stock plans for steel craft still specify large scantlings and very heavy plating. They are designed to empirical scantling rules derived from existing boats. These rules developed in the days when a big allowance had to be made for plating or framing that would eventually corrode away. Such a large allowance is no longer needed, however. Today's modern coatings so greatly reduce corrosion that steel boats can be made lighter, thus saving materials, time, and money.

For instance, a 35-foot LWL hull (about 42–45 feet LOA) designed using empirical scantlings might have a displacement/length ratio $\Delta_T/(0.01L)^3$ (displacement in tons divided by LWL/100 cubed) of 320 and would weigh about 30,700 pounds, of which approximately 35–40

together that you end up with a thick-skinned hull once more.

This method is labor intensive, expensive, and not entirely successful. However, it is another path on the long road to the ultimate boat-building method.

So the extremes are a thick hull plating, which is material intensive, low on labor and of moderate cost, to a very thin-cored hull where the plating must be epoxied together because it is too light to be welded, which is very light, labor intensive, and expensive.

FIGURE 2.18. *A section through the hull, in way of the engine room, of a 49-foot steel ketch we designed. This hull uses flat bar longitudinals and requires slightly more work than the hull in Figure 2.17. The parts are as follows:*

A *1.25 inch (30 mm) wooden half round.*
B *2 × 1 inch (50 × 25 mm) wooden oval rail capping.*
C *1.25 × .2 inch (30 × 5 mm) longitudinals.*
D *Icebox. Note the insulation around the box: 3 inches (75 mm) against the hull and 2 inches (50 mm) on the inside faces.*
E *Hull plating .2 inch (5 mm).*
F *Floors .2 inch (5 mm).*
G *Lead-filled keel with .4 inch (10 mm) external plating.*
H *1 inch (25 mm) keel plate.*
J *Main engine.*
K *Westerbeke 7 kw generator.*
L *Lightening holes.*
M *Engine compartment insulation 2 inch (50 mm) lead/foam.*

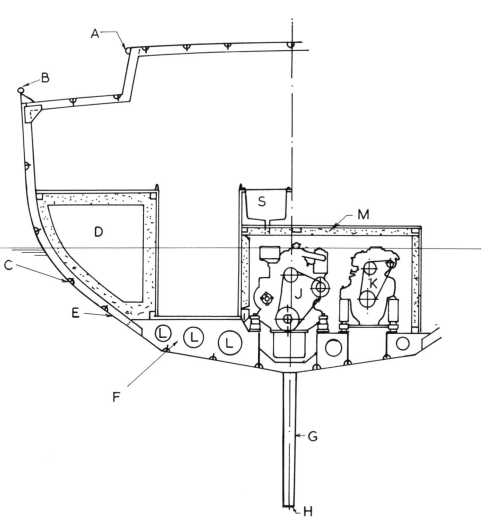

percent would be the weight of the steel. In contrast, by carefully calculating the scantlings given the durability of today's coated steel, the same-sized boat could weigh about 25,000 pounds. This tremendous saving in weight would not come out of the steel hull alone. The boat would also have a smaller engine, less tankage, less ballast, and a smaller rig—all made possible by the now lighter hull.

Virtually anyone who can weld has the skill needed to build a steel hull. But the specific construction method recommended will vary somewhat depending upon exactly who is doing the building and the size of the boat being built. For the inexperienced amateur builder, I usually specify a quick and simple method that eliminates much of the notching of frames. This method is best for craft up to about 40 feet LOA. The frames are spaced well apart (there may only be five or six in the whole boat), and angle bars are welded to the frames. The plating is then welded to the angle bar, as shown in Figure 2.17. Although this method is quick, easy, and fairly inexpensive, it does require careful placement of mouseholes and other corrosion-inhibiting details.

A method for more experienced amateur builders or for professionals again uses a small number of frames, but this time flat bar longitudinals. The longitudinals are notched into each frame and tack welded at the bow and stern, after which the plating is welded to the longitudinals and usually to the frames. Finally, the longitudinals are welded to the frames (although the longitudinal-to-frame weld may be eliminated with no ill effects). This method gives a strong, light, and fair hull but takes more work than the first method. Figure 2.18 shows a section using this type of construction.

The most conventional style of steel building, and the one used for large craft, involves many frames spaced closely together. (The frame spacing will depend on the boat's size and weight and on the thickness of the material used.) The longitudinals are then placed at fairly wide intervals along the frame. The longitudinals and frames may be either

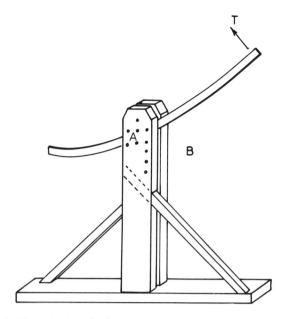

FIGURE 2.19. *A simple frame bending jig. The frames are inserted between two posts and pins placed in the posts at A. Force can be exerted at T to bend the frame.*

FIGURE 2.20. *A plate can be leaned against the hull, tack-welded at A, and gently bent. As it is bent it can be tack-welded at B and C until the entire plate is bent to fit the hull. E is the centerpost to which the block and tackle are attached.*

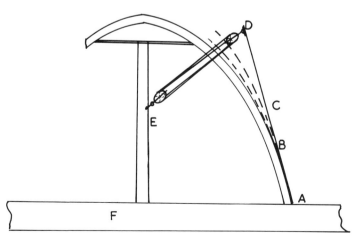

angle or flat bar. Usually, professional skills and equipment are required to cut and bend them to the required shape.

Regardless of the basic method of construction, there are certain techniques that make building in steel easier. For instance, most steel yacht hulls are built upside down and turned over for outfitting. When the hull is upside down, all welding can be done "downhand"—that is, the welder is over the top or to the side of his work so that any sparks or weld splatter will fall away from him. When the hull is built the right way up, some of the welding will be overhead, and a piece of hot welding rod falling down inside coveralls can be extremely painful!

There are times, however, when a hull must be built upright, and those who intend to work in this manner should know how to make this job as safe as possible. The welder can protect himself by putting elastic bands around his sleeve ends and by buttoning his collar up to the neck. A scarf or bandanna worn around the neck can also help prevent hot weldment from getting inside clothing. Finally, try to wear loose-fitting clothes without a belt, so that hot metal entering at the neck can fall out of a leg rather than getting trapped where it can burn. Loose-fitting workman's overalls are best.

Another way of making it easier to build a boat upright is to put the keel into a hole in the ground. The keel of most steel boats is built as an integral part of the hull rather than being bolted on afterward. The keel box is filled with lead shot, boiler punchings, or scrap metal, which is either concreted in place or covered with pitch. Molten lead can also be poured directly into the keel box as long as it is very dry. A plate is then welded over the top. The advantage of building the keel first and placing it in a hole is that the hull of the boat will be lowered 4 or 5 feet nearer ground level. This reduces the need for scaffolding and the distance that the builder must climb to get inside the boat.

The plating schedule for a steel boat must be carefully worked out. You cannot plate one side and then the other. Heat distortion from welding will actually bend the keel toward the side that is plated. When putting the plates on the framing, start on one side and put on one plate. Tack weld it in place with three or four welds about ½ inch (12 millimeters) long. Next apply the plating to the corresponding place on the other side of the hull and tack weld it in place. Work steadily down the hull, tack welding each plate in place and applying the plate first on one side, then on the other. When all the plating is tack welded on, check the keel for straightness. If all is well, you can start welding up the plating. Again, work first on one side, then the other, until the entire hull is closed in.

There are several methods of bending steel for hull construction. If you want to bend flat bar frames, a simple bending jig can be constructed using pipes and lumber. Such a jig is shown in Figure 2.19. Angle bar can also be bent using this jig, but extreme care must be taken to ensure that the angle is not twisted. Larger thicknesses of flat bar will have to be bent with a much more powerful machine. If you intend to build in steel, you should find out if such a machine is available in your area.

Large flat plates can be bent in one direction either on the boat or with a bending machine. A bending machine is essential if you need to bend the plate in two planes. This machine works by passing the plate back and forth through a set of rollers. If you have access to such a machine your work will be considerably easier. However, you can still do a good job of single-plane bending using a come-along or wedges. Figure 2.20 shows how to bend a plate using a come-along. One end of the plate is tack welded to the job, while the other has one or two eyebolts welded to it. A block and tackle is then used to bend the plate around the frames. Care should be taken that you do not distort the frames or strongback when bending plate in this way. Where the plate has to be bent locally, a U-shaped piece of scrap metal can be welded over a strongback and wedges used to pull the plating into place. This technique is shown in Figure 2.21.

The deck of a steel-hulled boat can be built of almost any conventional material, such as steel, aluminum, or wood. Each has advantages and disadvantages that the builder should carefully consider.

Steel is the heaviest and least expensive deck material. The only reason for using it is that the hull and deck structures can be made thoroughly watertight. There will be no hull-deck joint to give you trouble. And because chainplates can be welded at the deck, any leaks that often accompany deck fittings can be almost totally eliminated. Unfortunely, however, a steel deck is heavy, and if the yacht has a large amount of superstructure all the weight aloft will reduce stability. Steel must also be painted with nonskid paint to make it a safe surface to walk on.

This last point is also true of aluminum. But aluminum has the big advantage of being light in weight and therefore ideal for decking and superstructure. It creates none of the loss in stability that a steel deck does. The liner *Queen Elizabeth II* and all British RNLI lifeboats have aluminum alloy superstructure for this reason. Unfortunately, aluminum is only practical for the amateur builder who has the facilities needed to weld it. For those who do, care must be taken when bonding steel to aluminum. The two must be electrically separated to prevent

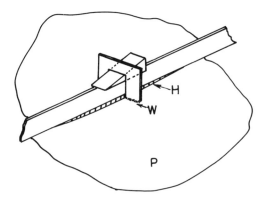

FIGURE 2.21. *Where there are local hollows in the hull or deck, as at P, they can be pulled out by tack-welding an inverted U-shaped piece over the hollow H. A wedge can then be hammered through the opening and the hollow pulled out so that the frame or longitudinal can be accurately welded.*

FIGURE 2.22. *If two dissimilar metals are fitted they must be insulated from each other to prevent corrosion. In the section shown, S is the steel hull plate and A the aluminum alloy plate. I is insulation, C the bushing, and B a bolt holding the materials together. In section B the two materials are epoxied (E) together. In this case the epoxy is the insulation.*

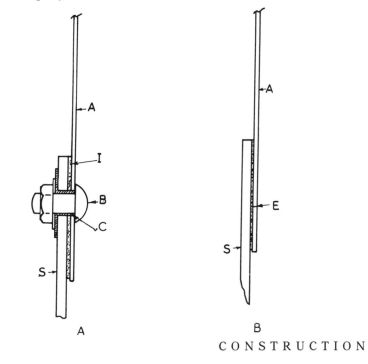

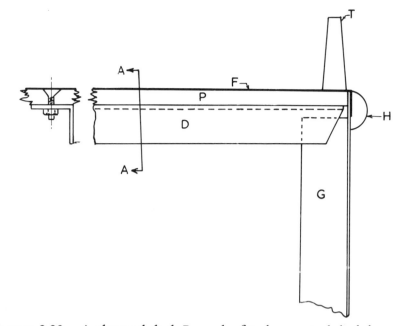

FIGURE 2.23. *A plywood deck P can be fitted over steel deck beams D by using the method shown. A layer of fiberglass F is laid over the deck and turned down at the edge to prevent water ingress. The half round H covers the fiberglass edge and stops water seepage behind it. G is the hull frame, and the section at AA shows how the plywood is bolted to the beam.*

electrolytic corrosion. Figure 2.22 shows two methods of doing this.

In terms of weight considerations, wood falls between steel and aluminum. But a wood deck has much greater aesthetic appeal then either of the other two materials. One of the simplest methods of wood decking is to bolt plywood to steel deck beams and fiberglass over the plywood. However, the hull-deck joint has to be done extremely carefully to avoid any leaks. Figure 2.23 shows one technique. I would prefer to see plywood fastened to wooden deck beams. The beams can be bolted to steel hanging knees for maximum strength. If a laid teak deck is desired it can be laid on plywood or steel, although laying teak on plywood is easier. Again, the hull-deck joint will require extra care to make it watertight.

A steel boat, then, can look as attractive as any modern wood or fiberglass boat can. And frequently it can also save you money. Anyone who is a good welder can probably handle the job. All that is needed is time, adequate work space, and care over the finer points of construction.

FERRO-CEMENT HULLS

When ferro-cement boats were first built they used conduit pipe, concrete reinforcing rods, and chicken wire to form the armature, which then had a mixture of Portland cement forced into the voids. The cement encapsulated and protected the metal. Unfortunately, this method gave a very heavy hull, which was often badly finished and soon deteriorated. However, some builders persisted, and out of the many, many amateur efforts came one or two professional companies who have upgraded their methods and materials to produce a reasonably competitive hull weight.

The modern theory behind ferro-cement is similar to fiberglass building. Whereas in fiberglass the idea is to get as much glass into the layup as possible and use the minimum amount of resin, ferro boat-builders try to get as much steel into the armature and use the cement as a binder and protection for the steel.

This means that a modern hull will be made from cement reinforcing rods probably on 3–4-inch (75–100 millimeter) centers welded at each joint. This wire armature is then covered with a cement-polyester resin mix that is about one-third the weight of regular cement.

To my way of thinking, if the objective is to get as much steel in the laminate as possible, why not build a steel hull to begin with and remove the plastering and curing problem associated with the cement hull?

No matter what type of hull material you choose, the following points should be kept in mind. The hull only comprises about 20–25 percent of the cost of the boat, and you should try to select the most suitable hull material for your budget and the type of sailing you want. In some instances special hull shapes are required for certain types of boats. If you are going to build the hull yourself, make sure you have the time and knowledge or can hire an experienced person to do the job. Unfinished or badly finished hulls are as costly or often more costly than a well-executed job. Finally, make sure you get a set of drawings from an architect who is familiar with the materials and can give advice on the pitfalls and problems of that material. Often, the best architects are those who have actually built boats and know the problems.

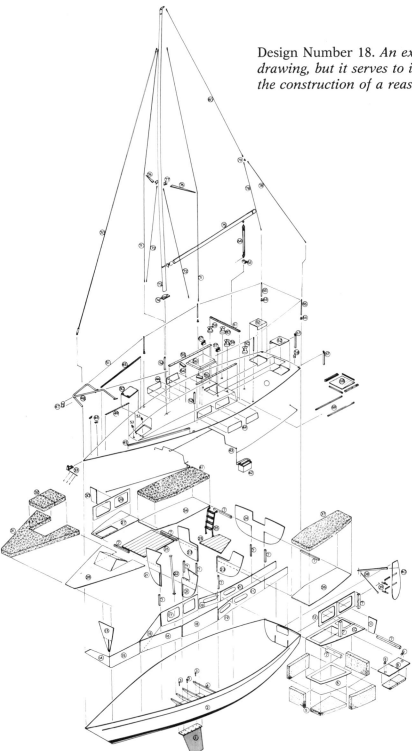

Design Number 18. *An exploded view is not quite a construction drawing, but it serves to indicate the number of pieces that go into the construction of a reasonably small boat.*

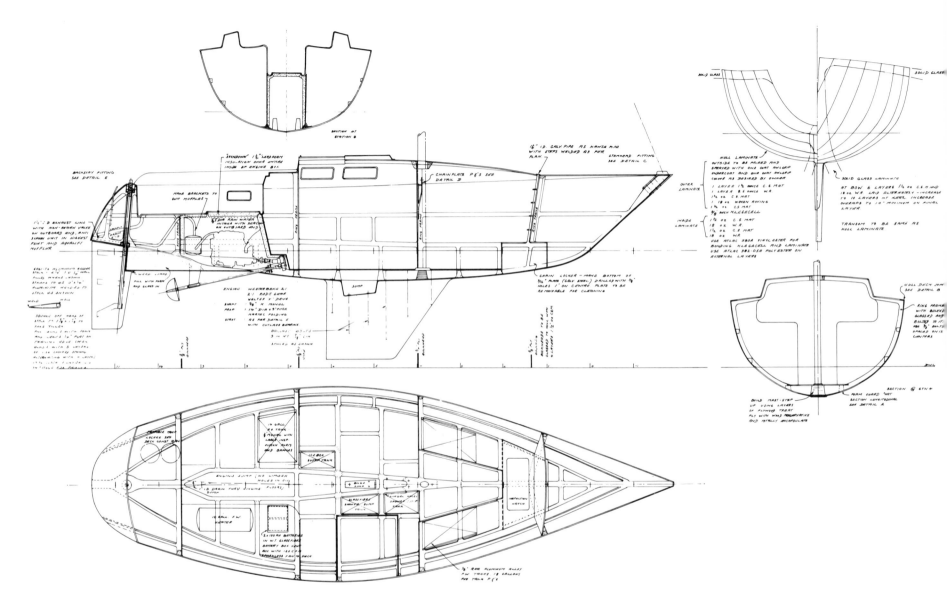

Design Number 37. *Part of the construction drawing for this foam-cored fiberglass-laminated cruiser. This plan shows the longitudinal reinforcing members and major components. On the right of the plan are the sections of the hull showing the laminate schedule and a section in way of the ring frame at the mast.*

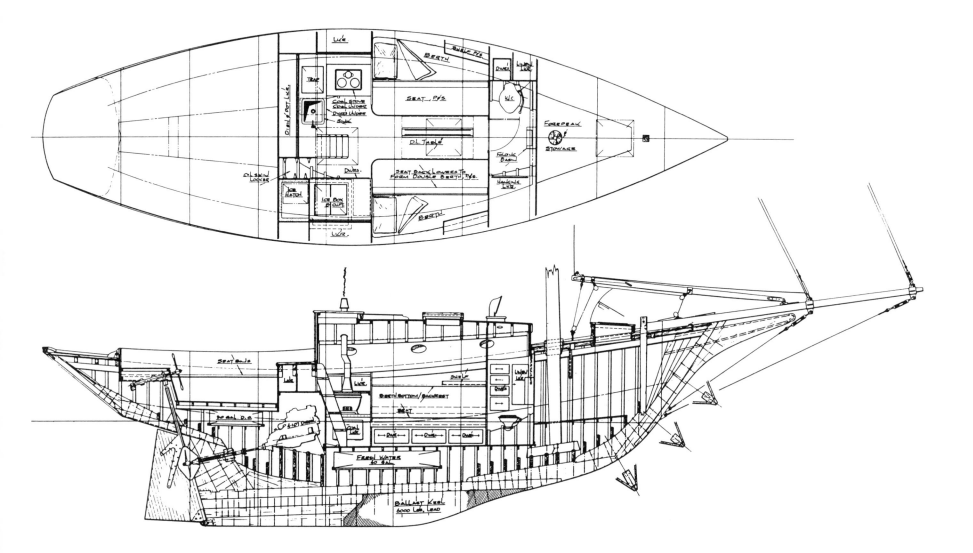

Design Number 58. *By Brewer and Wallstrom. This boat is included because it shows a well-built friendship sloop using traditional wood construction. (Plan courtesy Bob Wallstrom)*

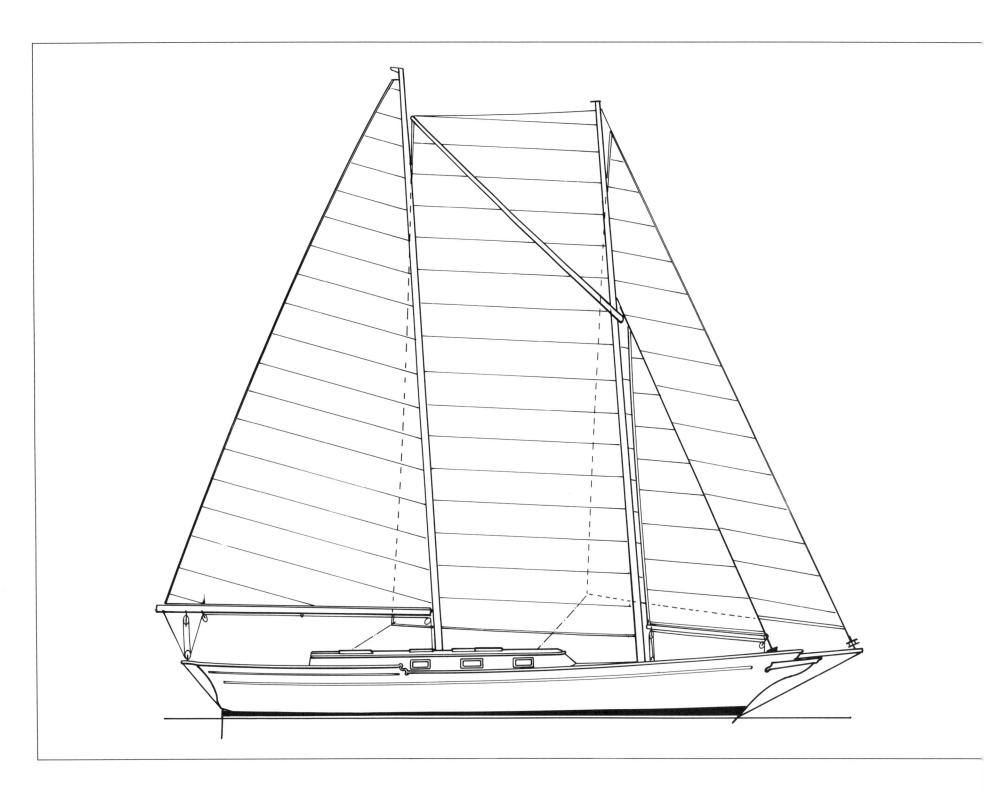

CHAPTER 3
Sail Plans and Rigs

In 1895 Captain Joshua Slocum made one of the first recorded single-handed crossings of the Atlantic Ocean. This feat has been repeated many times since with the elapsed times getting faster and faster. Slocum's west-to-east trip took 65 days. Sir Francis Chichester, in the first single-handed race going east to west in 1960, took 40 days, and in 1905 the schooner *Atlantic* set a time of just over 12 days from Ambrose light to the Lizard. Since then times of 7 days have been set by big multihulls trying specifically to beat the record.

A cruising sailor might ask, Why go faster? The answer is complex. Some sailors will want to cross slowly and enjoy the trip. For others the pressures of modern businesses and the need to get back to a busy office might prevail, especially when vacation time is limited. Even so, there are definite benefits in sailing a little faster over long distances.

First, the shorter time at sea can allow you to avoid a following storm. Because you are at sea for a shorter time, fewer provisions need be carried. There is less wear and tear on the boat between overhauls and less mental strain on the skipper and crew.

Let's face it. Many skippers are not professional seamen like Slocum was, and for many people being at sea on a long trip can be quite trying. Jumping from the relative safety of the office onto a boat and going to sea for three of four weeks can be quite an experience for the busy executive who is not used to being out of touch for so long.

How can an efficient sail plan help make it easier for a cruising sailor to sail long distances? Answering that question is a lot easier than the previous one we posed.

A modern, efficient rig can reduce the number of sail changes the crew has to make, make the few changes that need to be made easier and quicker, and allow the crew to handle larger sails than ever before.

Slocum in his early crossing used a gaff sloop rig, which he later converted to a yawl to make sail handling easier. Chichester's *Gipsy Moth* was a ketch to split the sail area up into easily handled segments and to make the boat self-steer as easily as possible. The trimaran *Moxie* used a sloop rig to set as much sail as efficiently as possible. In a relatively short span of time boats have changed dramatically, and nowhere have they changed more than in sails, rigs, and sail-handling systems.

In days of yore rigs evolved the way they did because the trees used for spars were of limited length. For instance, the gaff rig used three fairly short spars to project the maximum amount of sail area aloft. Its efficiency was not very high when sailing to windward, but neither was the efficiency of the hull. Off the wind both the hull and sail plan worked extremely well.

The gaff rig has largely died out today, but there are ideas to be culled from the basic principles. For instance, let's say we lived in an area where windward performance didn't matter. Could a gaff rig be used and would it be efficient?

Yes. Assuming we don't want to fuss with setting a spinnaker, the gaff rig would project more sail area than any other sail plan. The rig could be made more efficient by using modern materials in the spars. In the old days, if you wanted a mast 30 feet long, you went into the forest, like Slocum did, and cut down a suitable tree. The diameter of the spar was a gentle taper of about 8 inches down to about 4 inches, which suited your purposes well. You would never have cut down a 50-foot tree with the thought of reducing the thickness by planing it. That would be too much work and effort.

Today we can go to a spar maker and say, "I want a 3 inch tube with these fittings on the end," and have ourselves the spar we need. This means that the spar can be any length and any diameter.

With lighter weight aluminum spars, wire rigging, and winches the gaff rig can be made much more efficient. However, its efficiency is still restricted to offwind sailing. Today everyone seems to want to go to windward like a 12 meter. Unfortunately, that just isn't possible with the fat beamy hulls that have evolved into the modern production cruiser. The modern cruising boat has succumbed to the trend toward simplicity and efficiency and has become a sloop that uses a spinnaker to improve offwind performance.

But we can learn from earlier sail plans, and in the following pages we'll look briefly at some of the ideas that might be culled from older rig configurations.

THE CAT OR UNA RIG

One of the simplest of all rigs, the catboat rig has undergone a revolution in recent years. Although certain types of boats have been called catboats for hundreds of years (Chapman's *Architectura Navalis Mercatoria*, originally published in Sweden in 1700, shows various catboat rigs), the beamy, single-masted rig as we know it today derives from the New Jersey-New England coast, where it was developed as a work boat. In 1852 the Marquis of Conyngham purchased a boat called *Una* and took it back to Cowes, where it sailed so well many others were built like it. Since that time the cat rig has been known in Britain as the Una rig.

The traditional catboat rig is not often seen today; however, Marshall Marine of South Dartmouth, Massachusetts, makes a very traditional one, as shown in Figure 3.1a. A modern derivation has made its way into the sailing arena. The catboat from Nonsuch designed by

FIGURE 3.1A: *A traditional catboat under full sail. This boat is out of Padanaram, Massachusetts, and is built by Marshall Marine of South Dartmouth, Massachusetts. (Photo by Norman Fortier courtesy of Marshall Marine.)*

FIGURE 3.1B. *The Nonsuch rig designed by Mark Ellis and built by Hinterholler Yachts of Canada. (Photo courtesy of Mark Ellis.)*

FIGURE 3.1A

FIGURE 3.1B

FIGURE 3.1C. *The cat ketch rig of the Freedom 40 showing the wishbone clearly.*

Mark Ellis in Canada utilizes a wishbone boom and an unstayed spar, while the Freedom catboat has a fully battened mainsail set on an unstayed mast. Figure 3.1b shows the Nonsuch under full sail. Both the Nonsuch and the Freedom are more efficient versions of the older catboat, and both use the latest in modern materials to achieve easy sail handling and top-notch performance.

FREESTANDING OR UNSTAYED MASTS

On all except the smallest boats, masts were either extremely thick or they were supported by many stays and shrouds. It was not until the advent of Freedom yachts, with their sophisticated carbon fiber spars, that unstayed spars became a practical alternative on larger craft. Nowadays, many builders use aluminum or carbon unstayed spars.

This type of spar has many good points. Because there is no rigging, many potential failure points are eliminated; also eliminated is the windage of the rigging. However, the thicker spar has more frontal area than a stayed mast and is likely to be less aerodynamically efficient.

A mast held up by shrouds and stays is somewhat like a bowstring: the compression exerted by the rigging is countered by the stiffness of the mast and the strength of the hull around the mast. On a freestanding spar these loads are largely eliminated, simplifying tuning and construction. However, the deck will need to be reinforced in way of the mast with extra frames or a bulkhead to carry the loads imposed when the boat heels. An unstayed mast can also be tapered from the deck to the masthead as the sail weight and loading decreases, thus cutting down on weight aloft.

In spite of all these positive qualities, the freestanding spar has a few drawbacks. It is difficult to set a second sail on the spar. For instance, a jib or genoa will tend to compress the spar and to pull the top of the mast forward, requiring some form of running backstay to hold the masthead in place.

Another problem is the reefing system, which varies from builder to builder depending on the type of boom used. One of the easiest types of reefing system for most sailors is the jiffy or slab reefing system. This is the system used on many freestanding rigs with a wishbone boom.

The boom has several clew lines, similar to a regular mainsail. Each line is taken to a point on the leach like a conventional reefing line. When reefing the loads on the sail must be eased and the reefing line taken in. It should be cranked in hard to make the sail as flat as possible. Once this is done the reefed portion can be gathered up and tied in with conventional reefing lines. The reefed sail has a large sausage of sailcloth hanging at the bottom.

The Freedom concept allows the battens to be lowered to the boom, where they are secured in a similar fashion to the battens on a junk rig. By using lazyjacks the sail is guided onto the boom in all but the worst of conditions.

Another slightly more sophisticated method is for the freestanding mast to be rotatable. When it comes time to reef, the mast is rotated and the sail rolls up around the spar. This method is simple and foolproof. (Until the mast jams!)

THE SLOOP RIG

In today's sailing world this is the most common rig. On older boats, sail area had to be split up into smaller portions to make the sails easy to handle by a short-handed crew. With modern hydraulic systems and computer consoles today's rigs can be any size, and a two- or three-man crew can handle a sail plan that a few years ago would have been worked by a fully crewed yacht. For instance, most 60–70-foot cruising yachts built in the late 1960s and the 1970s would have had a split rig to break up the sail area. Look at any boat built during the 1950s and 1960s: many of them had split rigs to simplify sail handling. It is not unreasonable to suppose that if they were to be built today they would be sloop rigged.

Developments in hydraulic systems and self-tailing winches have made it easy to handle large areas of sail. *Amazon,* a boat built by Camper & Nicholson of Gosport, England, in the early 1970s, had two small pedestal grinders—I believe they were both Barient no. 90. The same boat built today might have self-tailing primary winches, either electrically or hydraulically driven. Most of the other winches would probably be electrically driven and could be controlled from a master panel mounted near the helm position.

On the headstay there would be a roller furling unit, probably the hydraulically operated Lewmar Commander or the Barient equivalent. The mainsail would be a stowaway system, furled and reefed hydraulically by another unit set inside the mast. Not only would this boat have a large electrical panel, but she'd also have a comprehensive hydraulic panel showing where all the units are connected and whether they are open or closed.

There is a definite trend toward the sloop rig, so let's look at why this sail plan is currently most favored. First, the sloop rig is the most efficient for sailing upwind, and although it is not as efficient across the wind or downwind, supplemented with a reaching headsail and a spinnaker for offwind work, the sloop rig becomes one of the most efficient all-around sail plans.

The sloop rig has several advantages over the single-sailed cat rig in that the foresail or headsail complements the mainsail. The foresail or headsail helps to accelerate the airflow through the slot and over the lee side of the main, making the mainsail more efficient. Also, breaking the sail area into two easily handled segments allows the crew to adjust helm balance without major sail changes, thus reducing crew and helmsman fatigue.

Sloops can have either a masthead rig or a fractional rig; however, in America in recent years cruising boats have departed from the racing fleet and moved away from the fractional rig toward a large headsail masthead rig. In Europe, where most cruisers are both raced and cruised and tend to be smaller, the fractional rig dominates on boats up to 35 feet (10.67 meters). More recently the American trend has been toward a larger mainsail and a better-balanced rig. Some builders are working hard to make cruisers easier to sail by making the headsail smaller, often roller furled and self-tacking, and the mainsail fully battered.

Even so, there are many reasons why a fractional rig is suitable for a cruising yacht. One major one is that it reduces the size of the sails in the foretriangle; hence sails are less expensive, are easier to handle, and take up less room when stowed. Another is the large mainsail, which, when used alone, is often satisfactory for sailing the boat short distances.

However, many American sailors have little or no experience with the fractional sail plan and prefer to stick with the easier-to-use masthead sailplan.

THE CUTTER

A decade ago it was easy to tell a cutter from a sloop. A cutter had a mast stepped much further aft than the sloop. But with the advent of large foretriangles, the distinction has become somewhat blurred. Now it is generally accepted that a cutter has a second stay set well back from the headstay on which a staysail can be set. The cutter, then, is basically a two-headsail rig: a topsail or Yankee set above a staysail. The sailor who wants a cutter rig, in my opinion, is neglecting the advantages gained from modern equipment. Increasing the number of sails rather than simplifying things. Now, if we introduce a bowsprit and set a flying jib from it . . .

Usually the staysail stay or inner forestay is removable and the rig can be converted into a sloop, using large genoas, quite easily. Often the staysail stay, like the headstay, has roller reefing gear and the staysail can be rolled up and stowed. If this arrangement is coupled

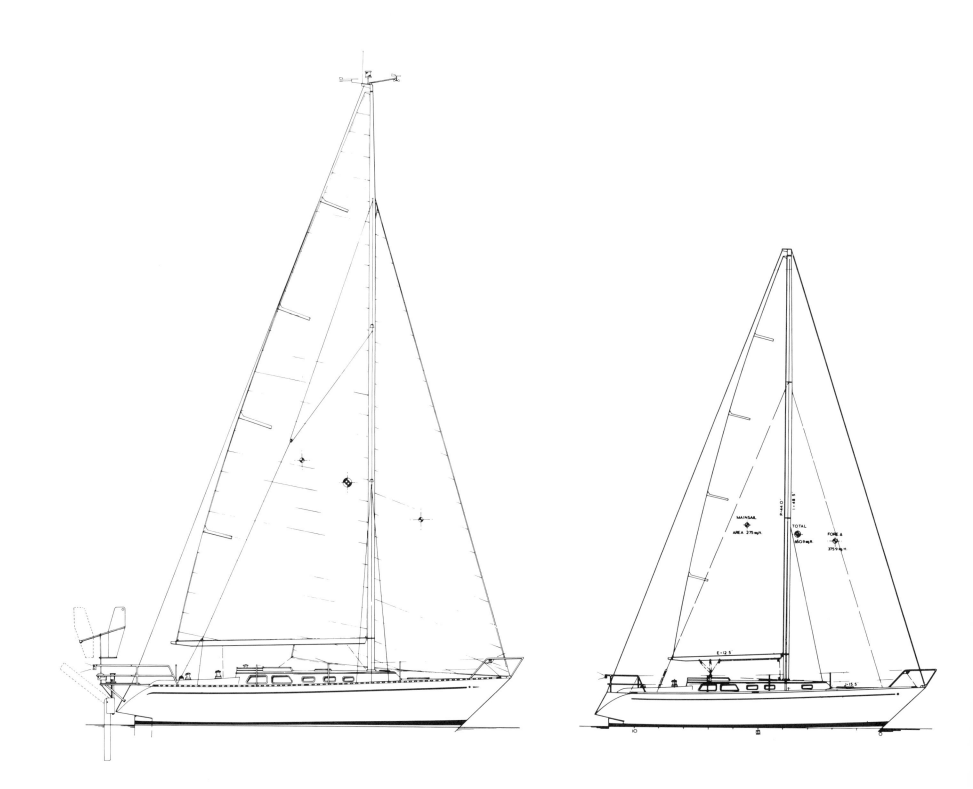

with either a transverse track just forward of the mast or a club foot on the staysail, the entire sail can become self-tending, making the boat that much easier to handle.

KETCHES AND YAWLS

Both ketches and yawls can be thought of as sloops with a mizzen mast. As to whether a boat is a ketch or a yawl, the difference is in the position of the mizzen mast. On a yawl the mizzen is always *aft* of the rudder post; in a ketch it is *forward* of the rudderstock.

For reaching and offwind sailing, the ketch and the yawl are much handier than the sloop. On a sloop the only extra sail that can be set is a spinnaker or one of the poleless spinnakers developed for cruising sailors. The two-masted rigs, however, can set a mizzen staysail and a spinnaker, dramatically increasing sail area. And what is more fun than creaming along at maximum hull speed on a broad reach with all sail set and drawing?

In Figure 3.3 you can see typical yawl and ketch rigs. Notice that the mizzen on the yawl is much smaller than the mizzen on the ketch. If we go back to basic design for a moment we will see why they are different. In a simple sloop rig the center of effort (CE) of the sailplan is a certain distance away from the center of lateral resistance of the hull. The sail forces can be said to act through the center of effort, while the hull forces can be said to act through the center of lateral resistance (CLR). Each force operates at the end of a lever arm (assumed to be half the distance of the length between the forces) giving a moment. When these moments balance each other out the boat is in perfect balance and the boat is easy to steer. If the sail forces are too far forward, the force times the lever arm will form a larger moment than that working against it and the boat will have a tendency toward lee helm, or, conversely, if the sail forces are too far aft the boat will have weather helm. Now, if we add another sail aft of the sloop's sail plan, its effect can be found by multiplying the distance of its CE from the sail plan CE by its area and adding the moments.

FIGURE 3.2. *Fractional and masthead rigs on the same hull. Both rigs have approximately the same sail area. However, the fractional rig has a much smaller foretriangle. Its sails cost about a third less than the masthead rig. Notice also the height of the masts and their relative positions.*

This has the effect of increasing weather helm. (In practice, the designer assumes the mizzen is up 50 percent of the time and adds only 50 percent of its value.) To eliminate weather helm the entire sail plan must be moved forward slightly when a mizzen is added. If we add a large mizzen, the moment it exerts on the helm is very great, but its moment can be reduced by putting it as close to the mainsail as possible. A small mizzen can be placed farther away from the mainsail because its moment is smaller.

For the cruising sailor, then, the extra mast has a number of advantages. It reduces the sails into smaller, more easily handled segments. It can also be used to balance the helm. Francis Chichester used his as a self-steering vane, and on yawls the mizzen can be used as a weathervane to keep the head of the boat into the wind in heavier conditions when at a mooring, but because the mizzen of a ketch is farther forward, this latter technique is more difficult and maybe impossible.

THE SCHOONER

Somebody once described a schooner as a ketch going backward. This almost derogatory description describes the sail plan fairly accurately but fails to do duty to the beauty of a large schooner reaching along under full sail. Technically, on a schooner the foremast is shorter than the aftermasts, and a schooner can have any number of masts. The *Thomas W. Lawson* had seven; more usual are two masters with an occasional three master to be seen.

There are many different types of schooner. For instance, a staysail schooner has staysails between the masts rather than a boomed foresail. A wishbone schooner uses wishbones, as in Figure 3.4, rather than booms.

While they look beautiful reaching along under sail, schooners do have a drawback: they don't go to windward that well. Where reaching is of primary importance the schooner rig has no peer, but to windward they can easily be outpointed by a sloop, or even yawls and ketches. However, as most cruising sailors spend most of their time sailing on a reach, I believe the schooner rig should be looked at in light of the advances made with modern equipment.

This poses an interesting question. Would some of the older rigs be better if they were upgraded to use the equipment that has been developed for the modern cruiser? What would a schooner look like with self-tacking, roller furling sails?

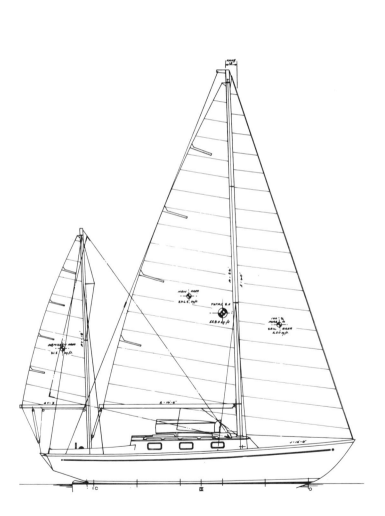

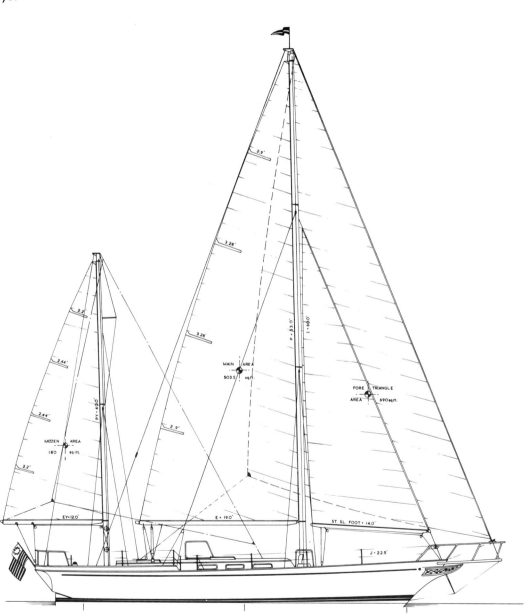

FIGURE 3.3. *A yawl and a ketch. Both boats were designed in my office. The larger ketch was designed to be built out of steel for long-distance cruising, while the 34-foot yawl was intended for coastal cruising.*

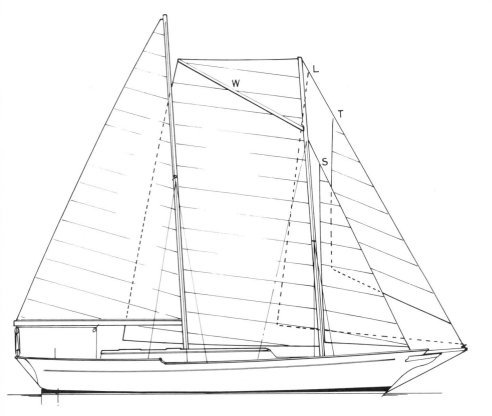

FIGURE 3.4A: *A wishbone schooner. W is the wishbone being used to project the maximum amount of sail area. S is a staysail and T the topsail.*

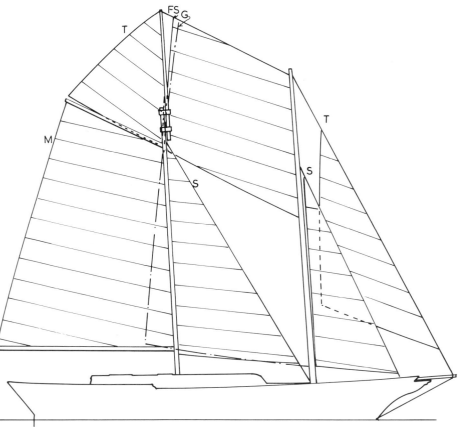

FIGURE 3.4B. *A staysail schooner uses staysails between the mast. In light winds it might set a gollywobbler G to project as much area as possible. M is the mainsail.*

Let's assume we could fit a twin headsail rig on the foremast, both with roller furling gear and the staysail on its own self-tacking track. The foresail would have a wishbone staysail sheeted to a self-tacking track, and the mainsail would be a conventional boomed main. Figure 3.5 shows such a sail plan. All the sails except for the topsail are self-tending, like any sloop or ketch. The staysails are all roller furled, and the mainsail rolls inside the mast. This entire rig could be tended by one or two people quite easily, and on a larger boat the furling gear and winches could be electric or hydraulic, making the whole sail-handling chore a matter of pushing buttons.

With one of the modern keel configurations it could be reasonably close winded and very comfortable in a seaway. I see this boat as being built of steel, which could use the extra sail area, and designed as a world cruiser.

GAFFERS, SPRITS, AND JUNKS

Throughout this book we have been discussing cruisers with good performance—boats that the average sailor could assume are often derived from racing designs.

Although racing boats are fast, they are designed to a rule, and their rigs are selected largely on the basis of what is efficient for both sailing fast and rating low. Pure cruising boats should have no preconceptions and should use the rig that will most suitably do the desired job.

This means that a cruising sailor need not be satisfied with a simple single-masted rig, but should have a working knowledge of other rigs. In this section we will look at some of these older and often more versatile rigs.

From a historical standpoint the evolution of sail plans gives us an idea why rigs evolved to where they are today. First came a log boat with a branch or bush sticking up. An ancient sailor probably noticed that the boat sailed faster downwind when the wind caught the branch. His contribution to sailing technology was to find a bigger branch with more leaves on it to catch more wind.

Next, probably several hundred years later, a sailor fell off his log and hung his loincloth on the branch to dry. He noticed that the boat sailed faster with the hanging cloth, and so he made a crude cloth or

FIGURE 3.4c. *A traditional schooner,* The Bill of Rights, *under full sail.*

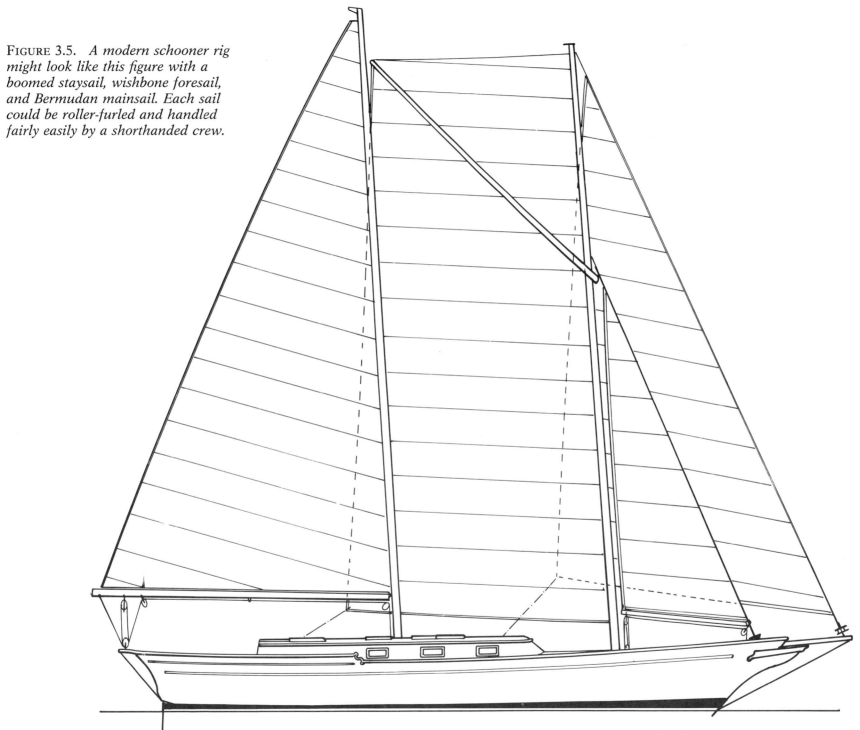

FIGURE 3.5. *A modern schooner rig might look like this figure with a boomed staysail, wishbone foresail, and Bermudan mainsail. Each sail could be roller-furled and handled fairly easily by a shorthanded crew.*

skin sail, which enabled him to get there faster than his rival. His rivals made bigger skin sails and hung them on bigger branches. However, technology halted when a huge branch with a huge sail capsized the boat and the designer drowned.

The sail plan didn't progress again until another intelligent sailor launched a particularly wide log and used a brace to hold the sail up. That brace eventually evolved into a square sail. In order to go to windward more efficiently, the square sail was tilted and trimmed fore and aft, whereupon it became a gaff rig.

From this point on there was no turning back. More and more people sailed. It became a way of life. People sailed to work. They sailed for a living, even though sailing was hard, demanding work. Every sailor tried to make his job easier and tuned his sail plan to suit the conditions under which he sailed. So rigs evolved, the gaff gave way to a sprit, which in another part of the world became a gunter rig. Thousands of miles away weather conditions indicated a different direction of evolution. The gaff became a lateen rig, and so rigs evolved. While the actual evolution of sails is lost in the mists of time, it is fairly easy to see how one rig developed from or into another.

One of the drawbacks to the early rigs was that they matched the performance of the hull shapes. By that I mean that the hulls were not designed to sail to windward as well as they are today so there was no requirement for sails to drive the boat to windward overly efficiently. Consequently, almost all the following rig configurations are very efficient for offwind sailing and sacrifice some windward ability.

Gaffs, Lugsails, Topsails, and Watersails

In the days of wooden ships and iron men, the height of the mast was dictated by economics and the length of a tree. Trees of the right diameter were often very short, and it was not economically feasible to take a large tree and mill it to a smaller diameter. The alternative, then, was to design a rig that projected sail area aloft using relatively short spars. There were several alternative solutions. Figure 3.6 shows some of them.

The *lugsail* may be either a standing or dipping lug. A standing lugsail stays or stands on the same side of the mast on each tack, whereas the dipping lug boom is pushed aft around the mast on each tack. This sail appears to be derived from an effort to make square sails work more efficiently to windward.

This is another rig that projects a lot of sail area on relatively short spars. Unfortunately, in the old days the spars were heavy and detracted from the stability of the boat. Think of what you could do today if the spar holding the lug in place were made of carbon fiber. Set on a freestanding carbon-fiber mast, this rig would project a huge amount of sail area on a simple, easily handled sail plan.

The name *gaff rig* comes from the boom at the top of the sail—the gaff boom. Raising the peak of this boom until the spar is parallel to the mast results in the slightly more efficient gunter rig. It would be easy to suppose that the Bermudan mainsail evolved from this rig.

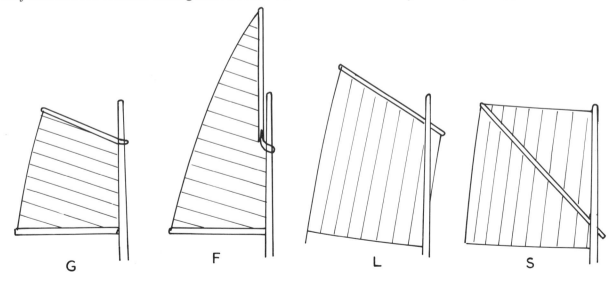

FIGURE 3.6. *Rigs that project the maximum amount of sail area on short spars are shown here. G is a simple gaff, F is a gunter rig, L a lugsail, and S a spritsail.*

G   F   L   S

FIGURE 3.8. *A watersail hangs down under the boom to enclose the space between the boom and the water. A modern equivalent might look like the one shown here, which is sheeted to the quarter.*

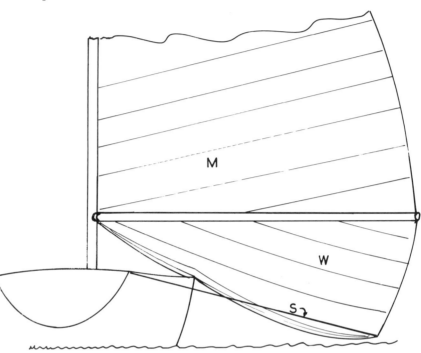

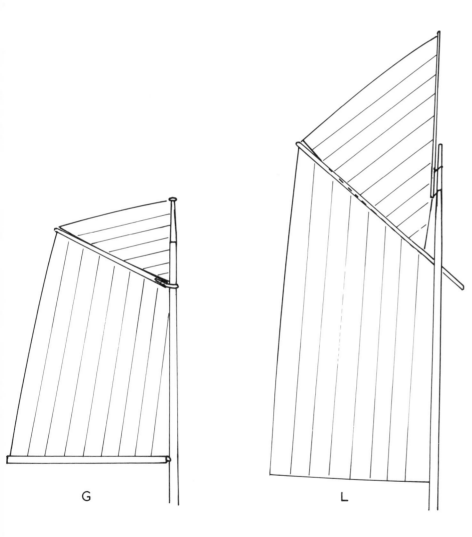

FIGURE 3.7. *Additional topsails were used to project extra sail area. G shows a gaff topsail and L a jackyard topsail.*

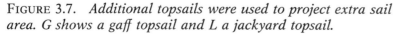

The gaff is controlled by throat and peak halyards. The throat halyard raises the boom, tensioning the luff of the sail, and the peak halyard controls the tension in the leach of the sail. Unfortunately, this isn't a good rig for windward work because the peak of the sail tends to fall off to leeward, giving the sail undesirable twist. However, for offwind sailing gaff rigs project a lot of area and are very efficient.

Both the lugsail and gaff rigs could easily increase sail area by setting a *topsail*. On a lugger the topsail was of a similar shape to the lugsail, whereas on the gaffer the sail merely filled the space between the mast and the gaff boom. Later a jackyard topsail was used to project more sail area aloft. Figure 3.7 shows the various extra sails.

Although they are banned by the racing fraternity and consequently are rarely seen today, *watersails* were another method of increasing projected sail area when sailing off the wind. The sail was suspended from the boom out over the water and filled any gap between the boom and the water. Figure 3.8 shows such a watersail.

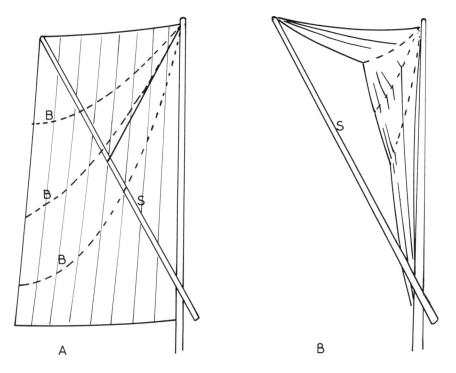

FIGURE 3.9. *A sprit rig is like a curtain with one corner held up by the spirit boom. The spirit S is held up by a halyard, while the brails B serve to reef the sail. In B the sail is brailed up, leaving the spirit in position.*

Sprits, Bowsprits, and Sprityards

In the sprit rig the gaff boom and the main boom have been replaced by a single sprit, as shown in Figure 3.9. This type of rig is fairly rare in the United States, but in Britain it is a characteristic of Thames sailing barges, which were usually handled by a man and a boy.

Imagine, if you will, an 80-foot boat with a huge load of hay, piled so high that the helmsman had no idea what was in front of him, sailed up the narrow, winding River Thames by a man, a boy, and, often, a dog. Very few modern sailors would attempt to make a trip like that, loaded to the gunwhales, in an ancient barge. Yet in those days it was routine.

On a *bowsprit,* The relationship between the center of effort (CE) and the center of lateral resistance (CLR) must be maintained regardless of the amount of sail area or the shape and length of the hull.

As sail area moves aft—using either a long boom or a mizzen mast—so either the main mast must be moved forward or sail area increased in the foretriangle to keep the CE in its optimum position. When the foretriangle area base exceeds the distance from the stemhead to the mast, then a bowsprit must be used to tack the headsail on. Bowsprits can vary in length, style, and thickness. For instance, the Friendship sloop has a 14-foot bowsprit on a 30-foot LOA hull, whereas one 84 footer has only a 2-foot bowsprit. Figure 3.10 shows a sail plan of a Friendship sloop designed by Bob Wallstrom.

The dangers of a long bowsprit are that the crew might fall off when taking in sail in heavy conditions, or that the helmsman might poke it through somebody else's boat, window, rigging, or dock when maneuvering in confined waters!

To supplement offwind speed sailing ships often used an extra yard slung under the bowsprit, called a *bowsprit yard.* If a boat is intended to be sailed offwind, then the designer might want to consider extra sail area in the form of a bowsprit yard.

The Junk Rig

Yet another rig that should be included in the repertoire of a good cruising boat designer is the junk rig. For ease of handling, reefing, and simplicity this rig is hard to improve upon. It is basically a fully battened lugsail rig but with some distinct differences. To the uneducated Western eye, all junk rigs look alike, but, in fact, they vary considerably in details.

Although it has been around forever in the Far East, the rig was pioneered in Britain by H. G. (Blondie) Haslar in 1960, and in the United States by Thomas E. Colvin in about 1965. It consists of a yard, which takes the weight of the sail, and, at intervals below the yard, the battens.

The Chinese use sails of various shapes that often have different length battens, but for practical purposes and to solve stowage problems, a design using battens of the same length would be best. The sail is held to the mast on one tack with parels; on the other tack the sail simply rests against the spar. Just as gaff riggers use lazy jacks to gather the sail, the junk rig uses multiple lazy jacks or topping lifts to form a cradle into which the sail drops when it is furled. The sail is sheeted at almost all batten ends, thus there is no need to tie down the

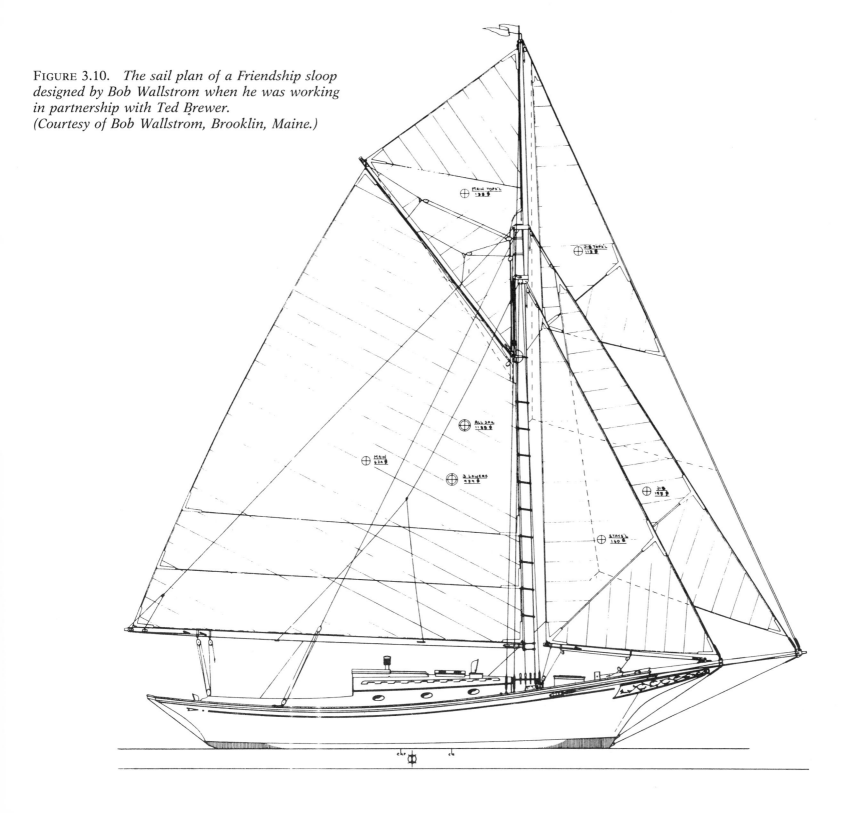

FIGURE 3.10. *The sail plan of a Friendship sloop designed by Bob Wallstrom when he was working in partnership with Ted Brewer.*
(Courtesy of Bob Wallstrom, Brooklin, Maine.)

clew every time the sail is reefed. One of the major advantages of this rig is the ease of reefing compared to conventional rigs. To reef, one man simply eases out the halyard and then trims in the mainsheet, a job that takes but a few minutes. The sail can be reefed to any batten, and the reefs can be shaken out as fast as they are put in. When the sail is reefed it is unnecessary to tie in reef points or to handle sail, as the weight of the sail gathers itself in the lazy jacks. Another advantage is that there is only one sail per mast, so the changing of huge, wet, heavy jibs is eliminated.

Because of the way the sail is set up on the mast, masts are usually stepped unstayed, so compression loading, spreaders, and expensive rigging are also all eliminated. With all these advantages it is surprising there aren't many more junk rigs about.

In the previous section some of the controls used to raise and trim the sail were discussed. Rather than review the sail control devices used on soft sail rigs (soft sails are sails made of cloth, i.e., synthetic fibers, nylon, and use battens merely to support the roach; hard sails are solid rigid structures, such as wing sails), I would refer the interested reader to my earlier book, *Designed To Win*.

Modern Cruising Sails

What type of sails should you have on your boat? Should they be Kevlar reinforced? Roller furling? Fully battened? Should you use lazy jacks, or will they cause too much chafe? These questions and others are continually being asked. To find out the answers I asked several sailmakers. I asked them what sails they'd put on a masthead cruising boat about 26 feet long—the type of craft you might purchase at a boat show—and what sails they'd put on a masthead cruising boat about 38–40 feet long.

Bill Shore of Shore Sails, Newport, Rhode Island, suggested that the smaller boat have a working jib about 95 percent LP for easy headsail handling. This sail would be made of Dacron (terylene) and would be cut radially to minimize stretch in the middle of the panel as the wind increased. For a mainsail he suggested a radially cut Dacron sail with battens conforming to IOR batten lengths. Again, the radially cut mainsail would minimize stretch in the middle of the sail and reduce the probability of having to reef when the wind increased. He felt that this outfit would give the best compromise where cost and size are major considerations. For a spinnaker he recommended a poleless cruising sail for easy handling by a typical cruising couple. The larger boat should have a fully battened mainsail, even though small prob-

lems still exist with the inboard end fittings of the batten pockets. Here Bill thought the sail could be radially cut and made with selective Kevlar reinforcement. This would cut down on stretch and keep down the weight aloft. The sail should be cut reasonably full and mastbend used to flatten it. It would be furled by dropping it into lazy jacks. He commented that a great deal of racing technology is now filtering down into the performance cruising end of the market, and cruising sailors should take advantage of it. The headsail should be a roller-furled 150 percent high-cut genoa with a second, smaller jib as an option. The small jib would be used in heavier (force 3 and up) conditions and could have a boom attached to a small track just forward of the mast, which would eliminate flying sheets and a lot of hard work when the boat was tacked.

The spinnaker could either be a cruising chute without a pole or, if the owner's level of skill were up to it, then a conventional spinnaker should be aboard.

David Vietor, now with Doyle Sails in Marblehead, Massachusetts, suggested that the small boat sailor use a Dacron mainsail with conventional battens; however, he also thought that a fully battened mainsail could be fitted on this boat if the owner wanted it. It would last longer, but as it is a relatively small sail it should only have three battens rather than the usual four. The headsail should be roller furling with a maximum LP of 150 percent and should be constructed from one of the new laminated fabrics. This has better tear resistance, while the film reduces ultraviolet degradation. A smaller 95 percent working jib/heavy air sail would complete the inventory. For a spinnaker, David recommended a cruising chute that could be used either with or without a pole.

For sails on the larger boat, David would use a fully battened mainsail, again with a laminated cloth. The headsail would be a 150 percent genoa roller furled on the headstay. In addition, he'd have a 110 percent working jib or number 3 and a storm jib. The spinnaker would be a ¾-ounce asymmetrical sail that could be used with or without a pole.

Formerly president of Hood Sails and now running his own small sail loft, Chris Bouzaid recommended that the small boat sailor look for a 135 percent roller furling genoa made out of Dacron. The mainsail should be fully battened, again made from Dacron, while the spinnaker should be a cruising MPS that can be used either with or without a pole.

On the large boat Chris offered two options, one for offshore use and the other for close-to-shore cruising. The offshore option is to split the headsail into a Yankee or jib topsail and use a staysail under it. Both sails would have roller furling for ease of handling. The mainsail would be fully battened with Kevlar in areas of high loading. For inshore use he'd put a 150 percent genoa aboard on a roller furling unit with a fully battened mainsail. For a 50-footer he'd eliminate the fully battened mainsail and use a stowaway mast with a roller furling jib.

There you have three opinions from three highly regarded sailmakers who have been involved with the sport from cruising to America's Cup levels. While they all agree on a fully battened mainsail for the larger boat, they offer different options depending upon the ability of the owner and the area where the boat is likely to be sailed, demonstrating that every owner should discuss their abilities and desires with a good sailmaker before plunking down money for sails.

Fully Battened Sails

One of the features that has been around since sailing began is the fully battened mainsail. Chinese junks have used it for hundreds of years. Today it is seeing a revival on the masthead sloop. By why is it good for the cruising sailor? Is it the ease of reefing? Better sail shape? Better sail control?

The answer is some of all of the above and a little more, but like other new developments it has some drawbacks. It is certainly more aerodynamically efficient. The battens enable a consistent sail shape to be built into the sail. More sail area can be projected when sailing off the wind because of the large reach that can be built into the sail. Sail shape is easier to control, and like the junk rig the battens allow the sail to be reefed much more quickly and easily.

Should you have one on your boat? In answering this question I would have to ask if you intend to sail offshore for long periods. If the answer is yes, then you would have to be cognizant of chafing at the inboard ends of the battens and the problem of changing a batten should it break while underway.

Which Rig Is Best?

To answer this question the designer or owner must ask himself where the boat is going to sail, how many crew it will have, and what their level of competence is. For instance, an owner may want a masthead sloop rig for canal cruising. There are usually many bridges on canals, some of which cannot be opened, so a deck-stepped mast in a tabernacle is the most logical arrangement. A mast stepped through the deck would have to be lifted out of the boat and carried on deck in order for the boat to negotiate low bridges with ease. This is a simple example of designing a rig to suit the intended purpose, but there are many more considerations that should be taken into account.

One of the first considerations is whether the rig should be fractional or masthead. While fractional rigs are more common in Europe on boats under 35 feet, they are not as common in America on the smaller-sized vessels. Cruising boats over 35 feet are almost all masthead unless the owner has a specific desire for a fractional arrangement. We often hear that the fractional rig is easier to control. That power can be spilled out of the mainsail to bring the boat back under control more easily than a masthead rig can is the argument used most. If you analyze this statement you'll find that it has to be true because the larger mainsail loads up to a greater extent than a smaller sail, consequently letting the sheet out will bring the boat under control more quickly, but because the sail loads up more quickly the boat nears the edge of control faster! On a masthead rig, letting the mainsail out brings the boat back under control, but it doesn't happen so quickly because the sail is not so large. (Nor does the boat near the edge of uncontrollability as fast.)

That the fractional rig reduces the number of headsail changes required is another argument often used. While headsail changes are reduced, the fractional rigs I have sailed with all required much more mainsail adjustment and trimming than any masthead mains. One of the most critical adjustments is mastbend, which at the top level of racing needs almost as much control as the mainsheet. On a fractionally rigged cruising boat the mainsail still needs to be adjusted more, and to a higher degree of sophistication, to get the best out of it. This means that the backstay and running backstays used to control mastbend must often be incorporated into the rig of a fractional rigged boat, adding extra controls and complications.

Another argument used in favor of the fractional rig for cruising is the lower cost of sails. This is a very valid argument. We designed a boat with both masthead and fractional rigs and the fractional configuration was about 28 percent less expensive.

However, the type of hull shape and the style of cruising you do are the real items that dictate the rig style. If you prefer a fast, light boat and will keep it light, the fractional configuration is the better rig. If you prefer a moderately heavy boat and don't want to bother with constant sail adjustment, then the masthead rig is more suitable.

These are very simple conclusions, and you may have other reasons why you want one or the other, but don't jump in because a so-called expert said one was best for you. Try both and see which you prefer.

Some rigs are much more efficient on certain points of sailing than others, although some of the inefficient rigs can be improved with the addition of other sails. The owner must decide whether he is to spend time changing sails or to accept the inefficiency inherent in certain sail plans. Other considerations for a cruising sail plan are chafe, simplicity, and strength and rigidity.

One of the major problems with using a junk rig for long-distance sailing is the continual chafing of the various pieces of gear. More and more today the gear used on boats is designed for the weekend sailor who doesn't worry about chafe as an offshore sailor might. If you intend sailing offshore you should check the equipment you intend to use. It may look old-fashioned, but it probably handles chafe better than a lot of the latest streamlined stuff.

FIGURE 3.11. *The Forespar quick attachment fitting clips onto the headstay for easy fitting of a boomed staysail. (Photo courtesy of Forespar.)*

In addition, the ideal rig may be so complex to control that its benefits are lost, or if it breaks in the middle of the ocean complexity may make the rig impossible to repair and much less efficient than a simpler compromise. For instance, I sailed a few months ago on a Freedom 21 that had been fitted with a gun mount spinnaker. There were 11 lines leading back to the cockpit! I found it slightly intimidating and wondered what the novice sailor thought, especially when the Freedom rig was touted as hasslefree and simple to use.

Finally, rigs should be both strong and rigid, which means they should be stayed and tuned properly, unless there is an unstayed mast. There is no point having a strong mast waving in the breeze because it isn't stayed or set up properly.

From the foregoing it should be obvious that not many experienced owners want exactly the same thing. Often it is the job of the designer to cajole the owner to accept, not the rig the owner wants, but a rig that is practical for the intended purpose.

Self-Tacking Jibs; Tracks and Fittings

Self-tacking jibs are another option for the short-handed sailor. They make tacking as simple as putting the helm over. The beauty of a self-tacking jib is that it can be retrofitted or designed as part of the original specifications. In my design business we've specified several types of boomed self-tacking rigs.

One of the simplest was for a client who wanted to be able to cruise and race. On his boat we recommended a Forespar quick attachment fitting, part no. 315000, as shown in Figure 3.11. This consists of an aluminum slider that fits over the headstay. Into this slider another solid piece of metal is fastened, to which the pole is clipped. The whole unit takes a few minutes to set up and remove from the headstay. At the other end of the pole the sail clew is clipped into a fitting. The sheet is shackled to the underside of the pole, and the whole unit is ready to go. We fitted the unit on the bare headstay just above the rail and just below the headstay luff groove unit. This enabled us to set a 100 percent jib that filled the foretriangle and gave the boat reasonable performance in light winds. However, it made a former 40-foot (12.2-meter) cruiser/racer into a cruiser easily handled by the owner and his wife.

We have also specified the Forespar 300 series fitting. Instead of fitting on the headstay, the forward end of the pole is pinned to a base, which has to be bolted onto the foredeck. If this is what you want to do, then you should make sure the deck is strong enough to take any

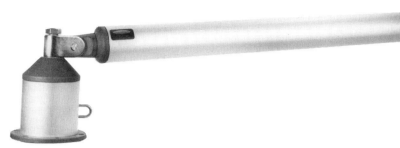

FIGURE 3.12. *The Forespar 300 series boomed staysail fitting. This fitting can be bolted to the foredeck to carry the boom. (Photo courtesy of Forespar.)*

extra loads you might impose on it. Figure 3.12 shows the Forespar 300 series fitting.

To make both these systems as easy as possible to use, we fitted a transverse track across the boat just forward of the mast. This tack track allowed the sail to trim itself to either tack as required. With a short piece of track the staysail became totally self-tending.

SPARS

In the previous pages we looked at some of the rigs that seem to be disappearing into the past and some other rigs that are becoming the wave of the future. In this section we'll look at the spars that support the sails, wires that hold the spars up, and some of the more advanced applications that could become part of the future of sail plans.

Masts: Wood, Alloy, or Carbon Fiber?

Once or twice during a sailing season you see a truly unforgettable sight, and a few days ago I saw a varnished ketch reaching out through Narragansett Bay. The hull sparkled as the little ketch raced by. The wooden masts were exactly the same shade as the hull and were set off perfectly against the snowy white of the sails. As the water boiled away from her transom I realized I was seeing one of the last of her type. No longer are many boats built with such care, with matching wood planking. No longer are there many skilled mastmakers to make such beautiful wooden spars, and, sadly, it seems that very few

young craftsmen are worthy of the name. Traditionally planked wooden-hulled boats and their builders, but for a few old craftsmen in various parts of the world, seem to be going the same way as Stockholm tar and copper tingles.

Wooden mast builders, too, are almost impossible to find. I know of many woodworkers who say they can build a mast, but not many actually try it. It seems that wooden mast building is about to become another lost art.

The few builders that do produce wooden masts usually see their entire production placed on "character" boats, usually replicas of traditional craft that are now being built in fiberglass. The result is often interesting, but I have yet to see a plastic hull that could hold a candle to a varnished wooden hull with wooden spars.

This is not to advocate we all go back to wooden masts. In fact, aluminum offers so many advantages over wood that it would be foolish even to think about replacing alloy masts with wooden ones.

Wooden Masts

Although wooden masts are becoming more and more uncommon, they offer a certain aesthetic value, especially on a replica of an older, traditional craft. Wooden spars are usually made from spruce, as straight and knot free as possible.

Usually the mast is made in four pieces, but six or eight pieces can easily be used. The more pieces there are, the lighter and more circular the mast will be. One very attractive method I have seen is to make the mast round up to just above the gaff jaws and taper the spar above that, leaving the top part hexagonal or octagonal, depending on the number of pieces used in the building.

FIGURE 3.13. *The old-fashioned masthead had straps running across the top.*

When I first learned to sail, the shrouds were attached to a wooden mast by splicing a loop in the upper end and dropping the loop over the mast, where it rested on a cleat fastened to the spar at the appropriate height. The shroud was then fastened to the chainplate at its lower end by a lanyard and seizing. This style of rigging was old then and rapidly gave way to tangs screwed or bolted through the mast wall with metal bottlescrews or turnbuckles at the chainplates. At the masthead the tangs often took the form of a plate screwed to the top of the mast with strapping running over it. The spinnaker bale genoa and main halyard were also attached to this plate. Figure 3.13 shows a typical setup. But even while tangs were replacing loops over the spar and epoxies were replacing the animal bone glues, aluminum was being extruded to form the first of the modern masts.

Aluminum Spars

Aluminum must surely qualify as one of the first exotic materials to be used on a boat. In the 1860s, when it was first refined, it cost almost $600 per pound. Fortunately, these costs had dropped to pennies per pound by 1900, and they have stayed relatively low ever since. In the 1960s extruded aluminum masts were tried on racing boats for the first time and proved a success.

The step to alloy masts coincided with the first fiberglass hulls, and quite soon it was possible to reproduce hulls and rigs accurately and quickly, which gave rise to the boating boom of the late 1960s that is only now starting to show signs of subsiding.

Most aluminum spars today are made out of 6061-T6 alloy, which has a minimum ultimate tensile strength of 45,000 lbs/in²2. The number 6061-T6 tells a knowledgeable person about the alloy. The first digit, 6xxx, tells you that the major alloying elements are magnesium and silicon. The second digit, x0xx, indicates any alloy modifications, in this case none, and the xx61 indicates the minor alloys in the group. The "T6" after the number serves to indicate a specific heat treatment process. In this case the alloy is heat treated and then artificially aged.

Reynolds Metal Company in the United States has recently announced a new "superstrong" mast alloy rumored to be 7129-T5 type. Zinc is one of the major elements in the 7000 series alloys, and as most sailors know zinc corrodes very quickly in sea water. However, the 7000 series alloys do have a very high strength and have been used on 12 meters for the American Cup. It remains to be seen whether the

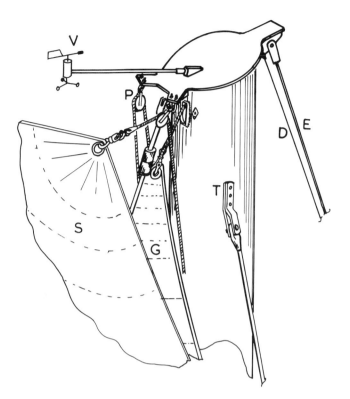

FIGURE 3.14. *A typical masthead for offshore cruising. Note how all the fittings are easily accessible and set up so that chaff is minimized:*

E	*Backstay.*	S	*Spinnaker.*
D	*Topping lift.*	P	*Spare spinnaker halyard.*
T	*Tang.*	V	*Wind instruments.*
G	*Genoa.*		

7129-T5 alloy will be stronger and corrode less than 6061-T6, or whether it will be used on cruising yachts.

Alloy 6061-T6 can easily be welded by gas or arc welding, but welding destroys its heat treatment and much of the alloy's strength. After welding it needs to be heat treated once again. It has good resistance to corrosion, which is improved when anodized and painted. It is, however, sensitive to machining or cold working, which can reduce its tensile properties.

One of the benefits of an aluminum mast is the ease with which tangs, sheave boxes, and spreaders can be attached. Ideally they

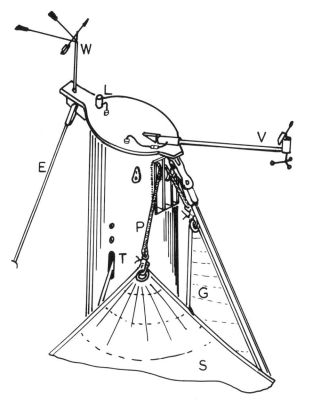

FIGURE 3.15. *A modern racing masthead where chaff is not considered. Note the internal tang T, windex W, and light L for the windex.*

The *spreaders* also need careful consideration. Unlike a mast on land, where the staying base is extended over a large area, the staying base of a mast on a boat can only be extended as far as the edge of the deck (or channels if fitted). If we took the shrouds or stays directly from the deck to the masthead we would have a very small angle between the mast and the shroud at the connection. While this would most likely support the mast, it would put a tremendous compression load on the spar and would not stop the masthead from swaying. Using spreaders increases the angle between the mast and the shroud and exerts more control over the movement of the masthead. In general, the wider the spreaders are, the less compression on the spar and the more rigidly the masthead is fixed. However, there are practical limits to the spreader lengths. If the sails are to be trimmed efficiently, the spreader lengths should be just long enough to hold the shroud but not so long that they interfere with the sail. Usually the minimum angle between the mast and the shroud at the masthead is considered to be 8 degrees, although 10 degrees is more common. The number of spreaders also influences these angles. In general, more spreaders means larger angles.

The spreaders are another area where modern "racing" sections are of little use to the blue water cruiser. The style popular today, shown in Figure 3.16a, can lead to splitting along the trailing edge. For long-distance cruising the type shown in Figure 3.16b is more rigid and a lot more secure.

Incidentally, if your boat has wooden spreaders, one area can reduce the life of the spreader considerably, and you won't even notice the loss of performance until the mast falls down. I'm referring to the upper surface of the spreader, which gets baked by sunshine all summer and dries out rapidly. I once took a spreader off a boat where the upper surface had deteriorated so badly the only solution was to have new spreaders made. I would recommend the upper surface of wooden spreaders be painted with white paint to ward off the damaging effect of summer sun and to protect the spreader.

What is the tang? It is the fitting that joins the rigging to the mast wall. The modern trend is to make a fitting that is inserted into the mast, located by two screws, and given its strength by bearing on the mast wall, as shown in Figure 3.17a. Unfortunately, this type of fitting is almost impossible to repair, but it does have the advantage of low windage and relatively easy installation. A more expensive type of tang to install but a better one from the maintenance point of view is the one shown in Figure 3.17b. On this type all the "workings" are outside the mast and for the offshore sailor are much more repairable.

should all be bolted to the mast, but many spreader bases are welded onto the spar, generally not a good idea, as doing so destroys the heat treatment of the alloy and weakens the mast. The long-distance blue water sailor should try to have all mast attachments bolted on to reduce the effects of welding and to make any repairs easier.

The *masthead* of many racing boats is designed for minimum windage and low cost without much thought about wear and chafe. On a cruising boat this arrangement is adequate if the boat is only intended for local cruising. But the blue water cruiser should be extremely wary of this setup. For long-distance sailing I would prefer to minimize chafe and wear by using the masthead detail shown in Figure 3.14, rather than the racing type in Figure 3.15.

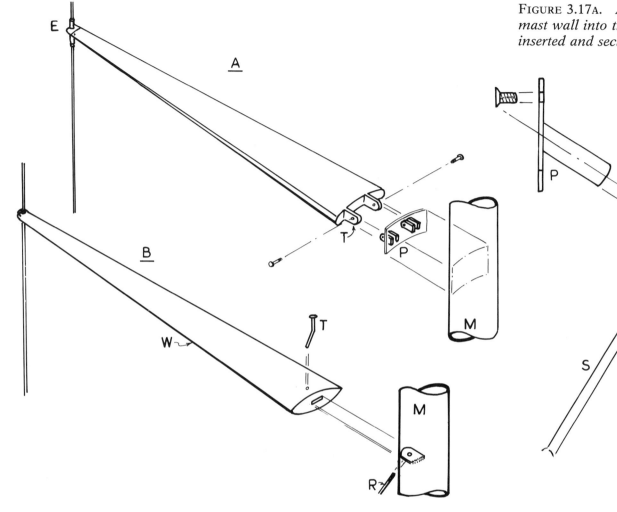

FIGURE 3.17A. *An internal tang. The shroud S is fitted through the mast wall into the socket T. When it is securely in place, a pin P is inserted and secured to the mast wall with a small screw.*

FIGURE 3.16. *A shows a spreader for offshore use where all the parts are easily accessible. The tangs T fit into the plate P, which is bolted to the mast. B shows a production-oriented spreader where the two edges W are welded together. Halyards can rub against these edges and cause considerable wear. The spreader fits over the tang welded to the mast and is held in place by the pin T, which also serves as the diagonal shroud terminal. Welding the tang to the mast wall can cause heat distortion of the mast wall, leading to failure.*

FIGURE 3.17B. *An external tang. This type of tang is better for offshore use because all the parts are external and can be easily changed or repaired.*

Although it may seem like a very minor detail, the tang fitting can make the difference between the mast going over the side or staying in the boat. I remember a fastnet race when a sistership to the boat I was on lost the bolt holding the shroud to the tang. Because the tang was fitted externally, the crew was able to replace the bolt and successfully complete the course. With an internal tang this would have been impossible and the boat would have had to motor to the nearest port or, worse still, may have lost the rig. This example illustrates that accessibility to a minor item such as a tang pin can mean the difference between getting to port without mishap and losing the mast and being towed home.

From these examples we can see that the type of sailing you intend to do will affect almost everything on the boat, even down to a small mast tang.

The Mainsail Track

Should it have slugs, slides, or should the bolt rope run in a groove? Once again it comes back to the type of sailing you want to do. If you are like most sailors and sail most weekends, then any of the tracks will suit your needs. Most likely you will have no decision to make as the builder will have already designed and built the mast with whichever type of track suits his budget for the boat.

But if you cruise offshore, once again, you need to consider chafe. You will also want to look at methods of changing the main at sea, reefing, and setting a storm trisail in bad weather.

All the tracks will work on an offshore cruiser. The slides and slugs will need to be protected so that they don't chafe through the sail, and if you go the more modern route and use a bolt rope then you will have to protect the sail over its length to reduce chafe in the rope guide.

If you intend to sail long distances it will pay to have a storm trisail and extra track; however, such a track is not essential. The mainsail can be reefed a long way in severe conditions before a trisail is needed.

To fit a trisail track you will need either slugs or slides to match the existing mainsail slugs or slides and have an extra portion of track fitted below and next to the main track. (Although some designers recommend an entire separate track, I do not. It adds extra weight aloft and can chafe the mainsail when sailing downwind.) A gate will enable you to switch tracks and fit the stormsail. Points to remember are:

1. The gate should be high enough so that the main can be dropped onto the boom and stowed and still have some track between the mainsail and the gate. But it must be within easy reach of the crew. If it is too high the crew might try standing on the boom, a precarious perch in moderate weather and certainly no place to be in a storm.
2. Ideally the storm trisail track should extend down to the deck so that the trisail can be fitted to the track and remain stowed when not in use.
3. Whatever type of track you use should be smooth enough to affect the changeover without hanging up either sail.
4. If you are retrofitting, make sure that the track is strong enough to carry a storm trisail.

Figure 3.18 shows a storm trisail track on the back of a mast.

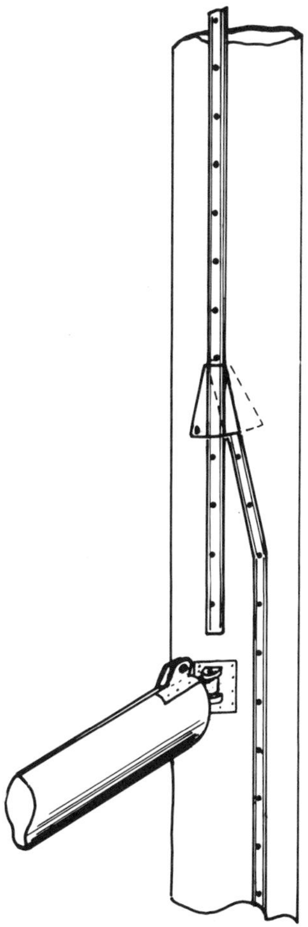

FIGURE 3.18. *A storm trisail track. Its use has largely faded out, but if you intend going on long offshore trips it may be advisable to have one. The trisail is bent on the lower portion of the track until needed. When it is required the mainsail is dropped and the gate is switched to allow the trisail to be hoisted. A point to note is to ensure the gate is high enough to allow all the mainsail slides to sit below the gate.*

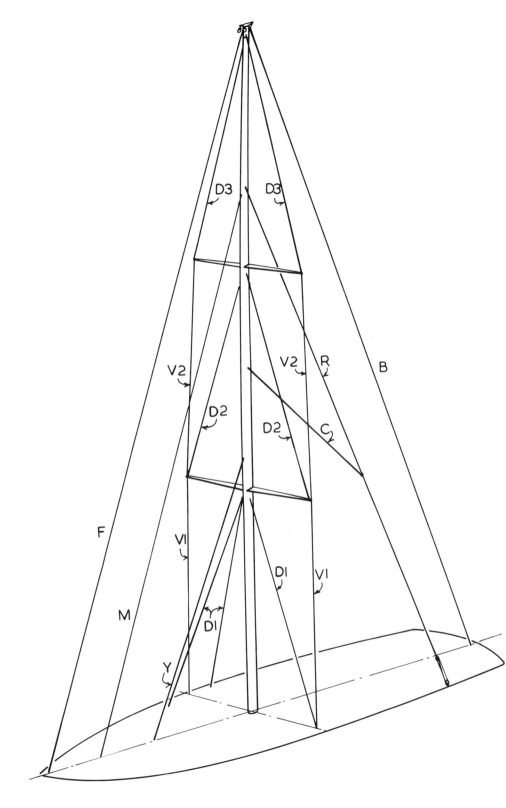

STANDING RIGGING

At one time all masts except the very smallest used standing rigging to hold up the spar. But with the advances in today's technology the freestanding mast is eliminating the need for standing rigging. In this section we are concerned with spars that need some form of rigging—dare we say, conventional systems. The standing rigging comes in several forms: wire, rod, and Kevlar, which at one time was highly touted for standing rigging, but I don't see this material becoming available for cruising boats for many years. Even then it is subject to sudden breakages and doesn't hold up well.

Standing Rigging Configurations

When a single short spar was the entire mast of a yacht there was no need for spreaders because the staying base was wide enough to support the mast easily. But as rigs grew higher, the angle between the top of the mast and the vertical shroud grew smaller, putting the mast in compression and reducing the control at the top of the spar. This led to the introduction of the first spreader.

Single spreader rigs were and still are the least expensive to produce. But they have distinct disadvantages. The mast must be very

FIGURE 3.19. *The stays and shrouds of the modern rigged are named as follows:*
  B   Backstay.
  R   Running backstay or runner.
  F   Forestay or headstay.
  M   Midstay.
  Y   Babystay.
  C   Checkstay.
All the vertical shrouds are designated with a V and a number dependent upon their height up the mast. For instance, the lowest vertical is called the V1; that between the lower and upper spreader becomes the V2. Diagonal shrouds are designated with a D, hence we have a D1 as the lower shroud, D2 between the lower and upper spreader, and D3 from the top spreader to the mast. If a third spreader were fitted, then the top shrouds would be the V3 and D4 shrouds. The D1 shrouds are designated the same way whether they are single (to port on this drawing) or double shrouds (as shown on the starboard side.

large and heavy because the unsupported length (distance between the partners and lower shroud attachment points) is so great.

The double spreader came next and with it a reduction in the mast diameter. Now many racing boats use three or even four spreader rigs. Fortunately, I don't think there is any desire for these multi-spreader spars to make it into cruising boats. The practical cruising boat limit appears to be two spreaders.

Fore and aft staying also affects the thickness and stability of the mast. The more stays there are the better control you, as a sailor, have over the mast. Figure 3.19 shows the correct nomenclature for longitudinal stays and transverse shrouds.

Wire or Rod: Which Is Better?

Once again, the type of sailing you do will affect the type of equipment you should select for your boat. The choices for standing rigging on cruising boats are wire and rod. Each has different characteristics and different applications.

Wire rope is made up from many strands of round metal wire and is expressed as the number of strands in a wire and the number of wires in a strand. For instance, the most commonly used wire on boats is 1×19, which means there are 19 single stranded wires in the wire rope; "7×19" has 19 strands, each made from 7 individual wires. Usually 1×19 is used for standing rigging, while the more flexible 7×19 or 7×7 is used for running rigging.

Either 7×19 or 1×19 can be galvanized, that is, a coating of zinc plating electrically deposited on the wire, or it can be stainless steel type 316. However, galvanized does not appear to last better than stainless steel when used for halyards. Type 304 is sometimes used. This has less susceptibility to crevice corrosion. Note that all 300 series stainless steels are nonmagnetic.

The early *rod rigging* was made from type 316 stainless steel, which, although fairly resistent to corrosion, suffered from a fairly low cold-worked tensile strength. The standard rod rigging for cruising boats is made from VMB 24/Nitronic 50, which is an alloy of 22 percent chromium, 13 percent nickel, and 5 percent manganese. The next level of strength is given by cobalt rods made of MP35N, a nickel cobalt alloy. This has higher strength but is rarely seen on cruising boats. The top racing craft use titanium, but this is extremely expensive.

Rod rigging can be obtained as round rod or in lenticular. Its biggest advantage over wire is that rod stretches about 35–40 percent less.

Thus a mast with solid rod rigging will hold its tune longer than a mast set up with wire standing rigging. However, there can be drawbacks to rod rigging. For example, on one trip to Bermuda we ran into a tropical storm with winds over 60 knots. The rig was set up very tightly with very little "give" in the system, so when we sailed off the top of some very large waves the main bulkhead broke. As the mast was whipped forward or sideways by the huge waves, the only place the boat had any "give" was in the hull. The result was structural damage rather than slightly stretched shrouds.

For this reason, on a boat intended for offshore cruising I prefer a mix of rod and 1×19 wire. Upper shrouds D3, D2, V2, and V1 (See Figure 3.19) should be rod, while the D1 shroud can be wire. The rod rigging should be discontinuous. That is, the rod should terminate at link plates at the end of each spreader. This has several advantages. It reduces fatigue on the spreader ends, it allows the designer to specify lighter rod as the loads become smaller nearer the top of the spat, and the shorter lengths of rod hold their tune longer and stretch less than long lengths.

The headstay can be rod, wire, a roller furling system over wire, a solid roller furling, or a luff groove device. The options here are entirely up to the owner. On an offshore cruiser the backstay should be 1×19 wire. Coastal cruisers and production craft need not be quite so specific about the type of rigging, which can be either 1×19 wire or rod. Character craft will no doubt use wire or, occasionally, galvanized wire with bull's-eyes and whipping.

Kevlar offers stronger, lighter rigging than either wire or rod, but it is extremely expensive. While it has been used as running rigging, its use as standing rigging has been limited to a few small boats. It is susceptible to chafe, and end fittings are not at the state of reliability that rod and wire end fittings are. However, there is a considerable reduction in weight, which makes it worth looking into for one or two special projects.

Shroud End Fittings

Cold-formed headed rod, screw fittings, Norseman, crimped, swaged, or Castloc—which is which, and which is best? There are so many methods of attaching fittings to the end of shrouds that few people other than qualified riggers can tell them apart.

For rod rigging several types of end fittings can be used: cold-formed ball head, developed by Navtec, a swaged end fitting, or a screw end fitting. Wire fittings range from screw-on ends to compres-

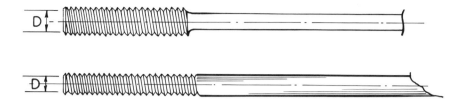

FIGURE 3.20. *Early rod end fittings had the thread cut into the rod, leading to weaknesses as in the lower fitting. Later fittings had expanded ends and larger threads cut into them. Compare the diameters D of both fittings.*

sion fittings that actually flow around the wire. There are even glued fittings, but reports on their reliability vary.

End fittings on rod rigging have varying rates of reliability and strength. The best are the cold-formed head and screw fitting. The cold-formed head developed by Navtec, Inc., does not weaken the rod at all. In fact, it can often increase the rod's strength. The cold-formed head is usually inserted in a machined ball and the whole unit fitted into specially made terminals.

Some manufacturers cut a screw thread into the end of a piece of rod to attach fittings. When this was first done the screw threads were simply cut into the rod, but that significantly reduced the available diameter and led to many failures. Today the rod diameter is increased in way of the threaded part, so as not to reduce tensile strength. Figure 3.20 shows both arrangements.

The strength of a fitting swaged onto the end of a piece or rod is highly variable. The best practice is to rough up the rod end by knurling or threading and thoroughly clean both pieces of the work. Applying the swaging pressure will usually result in good adhesion. But the diameter of the rod is often reduced, or the swaging pressure may be slightly uneven, leading to a slight bend in the swage. Both of these flaws can lead to early failure of the rigging.

Wire end fittings are numerous. Some have stood the test of time. Others have been continually modified until acceptable levels of performance have been reached. Here we'll look at some of the best ones: swaging wire, the Norsemen fitting, the Castloc terminal, and the crimped sleeve. Swaging end fittings onto wire is a slightly more predictable method than swaging onto rod. In this method the wire is cleaned and then pushed into the correct size of swage fitting. When pressure is applied to the end fitting the metal literally flows into the crevices into the wire, forming a very strong joint. This joint is usually

about 80–90 percent of the breaking strain of the wire. But care must be taken that the swage fitting is not bent or cracked during installation, as this reduces the tensile strength considerably.

The Norseman fitting is probably one of the best known end fittings. It is used extensively in Europe and America. A Norseman terminal is one of the easiest to install, requiring only a pair of pliers, a pair of suitably sized wrenches, and thread-locking sealant. It works by placing a small cone in the center core of the wire and clamping that cone in place with the external body of the terminals. For the long-distance offshore cruiser, Norseman terminals and a pair of wire clamps will solve almost any rigging difficulty.

The Castloc terminal is similar to the Norseman in that the cable end must be unlaid slightly. The unlaid section is then pulled into the terminal sleeve, which is then filled with epoxy resin. The terminal stud is screwed into the sleeve, forcing the resin into the voids in the cable. When the resin has set up the terminal is ready to use. As the properties of epoxy resin can vary with temperature and humidity, I have to wonder how long this end fitting will last.

A crimped sleeve (Talurit in Europe) is probably the least expensive method of all. The cable is simply bent around a thimble and the sleeves are swaged or crimped onto the cable. However carefully this technique is used it always leaves the end of the cable visible and ready to tear clothing or fingers unless carefully taped over.

FURLING GEAR

It used to be that only the hardiest cruising sailor had furling gear on his boat. That gear worked intermittently, if at all. Today roller furling is so easy that it is almost *de rigueur* for every cruiser, whether he's a serious sailor or a weekend yachtsman.

The very best gear can be used to reef the sail as well as a place to store the jib between cruises. In my opinion one of the best roller furling gears available is the Furlex system from Seldén Mast of Sweden. It has several advantages over many other units on the market, the most important being that it works easily under load. Many other systems bind up unless all the load is let off the sheet before reefing. When all the load is off the sail they tend to furl with large creases, giving an ungainly, baggy look at the mooring.

I also like the way the Furlex system assembles. It can literally be snapped together in under two hours—and it can be disassembled. Many of the other types are epoxied after fitting and cannot be dismantled for repair or maintenance. The Furlex system appears to be designed very carefully so that it can be maintained, oiled or greased, and assembled or dismantled very easily. It also comes as a complete boxed unit, even down to the six screws for holding the halyard fairleads in place. Usually the rigger has to make up a headstay and then assemble all the missing pieces before he can assemble the unit. Not with this one.

If a lighter unit is desired the Harken unit should be specified. It is about two pounds lighter than the Furlex. I like the design of the drum basket at the bottom of the unit. Where others use what looks like a plastic tube with a lump cut out, which often binds on the revolving furling drum, the Harken unit has a specially made basket to prevent binding. Figure 3.21 shows the Harken roller furling gear.

Both of these systems are a far cry from earlier furling units and can easily be converted to racing units, for that club-level race, simply by removing the drum and basket. I've used both systems and like them.

When you install a furling system there are a few simple steps that will make it easier for you to use. First, when reefing or taking the sail in, it is easier to slacken the jib sheet enough to allow the sail to be furled, but don't let it go completely or else the sail will flog.

Second, if you intend to use the furling unit as a jib-reefing system, you should spend some time on a calm day and work out the position of the jib fairlead when the jib is partially rolled. For instance, take the jib up two or three rolls and locate the new position of the fairlead. Do this for three rolls and then again for six or eight. When you get into conditions where the jib needs to be furled you'll know exactly where to position the fairlead for best performance.

Third, keep the furling unit lubricated and maintained. The easiest route to disaster is to ignore routine maintenance. And, finally, when you hoist the sail make sure the halyard is in its proper position, not twisted around the headstay or furling gear. This happened to a friend of mine and eventually the halyard sawed through the furling unit. The ensuing crash as the unit landed on deck cost him several thousand in repairs and a new unit.

SHROUD ROLLERS

How often have you heard someone say, "I don't need them, they don't work, and they look so old-fashioned."

I was out sailing a few weeks ago on a boat that had been sailed for

FIGURE 3.21. *The Harken roller furling gear. An ideal gear for the offshore cruiser. I like the way it is made and the backup that Harken provides for their equipment. (Photo courtesy of Harken Yacht Fittings.)*

less than a hundred miles. In fact, it was so new that the paint hadn't burned off the engine yet. But the genoa sheets looked like they had been in use for two or three seasons. I asked the owner if he was using the sheets from his old boat. The answer was an indignant no! When I went forward to see what was causing the problem I saw well-taped turnbuckles and carefully padded fittings around the mast. It was only close inspection that revealed the rolled fittings at the end of the shrouds had a razor-sharp edge at the top, which was shredding the sheet every time it passed over it. A simple shroud roller would have saved these sheets and protected the lower portion of the jib that had been lacerated.

I think shroud rollers have their place on a comfortable cruiser and do their bit toward preventing chafe and wear. Even if they do look a little old-fashioned and overly protective.

CARBON OR GRAPHITE FIBER SPARS

On a traditional mast with spreaders and rigging, most of the load on the mast tube is a compressive load exerted by the rigging and halyards. Aluminum is as strong in compression as it is in tension, but carbon fibers are about 65 percent as strong in compression than they are in tension in a typical unidirectional laminate. Consequently, carbon fiber is best for a spar that does not have high compressive loads. The freestanding spar, which is in tension on the windward side most of the time and has low compressive loads, is an ideal candidate for carbon fiber. In fact, most high-performance freestanding masts are made of carbon or graphite fibers and are now produced in various stock lengths.

The major advantage of carbon fiber over aluminum for masts is that it is stiffer and lighter. A carbon fiber mast can also be locally reinforced in high stress areas.

Carbon fiber, or strictly speaking, graphite fiber, starts out as a very fine acrylic yarn, which is then passed through a series of oxygenless ovens. At the end of this processing it is wound on bobbins in the form of a bundle of single strands. Each strand is about 0.003 inches in diameter, and there may be from 1,000 to 24,000 in a bundle. Each bundle or two is treated or "sized" with a thin layer of epoxy to hold it together. The two can then be woven into cloth or made up in "prepreg" form, that is impregnated with resin needing only heat to cure, or it can be obtained as a unidirectional layer.

A mast is made up by winding the carbon fiber onto a mandrel in various directions. Some of the strands are wound around the mast, others up and down, while some are wound on a 45 degree or 65 degree bias. A well-designed carbon fiber mast can have a weight saving of up to 30 percent and be up to 80 percent stiffer than a comparable aluminum mast.

Carbon fiber booms and spinnaker poles are now appearing on 12 meters and IOR-type racing boats. They offer many advantages over aluminum spars, mainly light weight and localized strengthening, but they are very expensive, about two and a half times as much as an aluminum equivalent, and it will be a while before this material appears on standard production craft, other than those with freestanding spars, or on even the most expensive cruising boats.

BOOMS AND OTHER SPARS

Like masts, booms can be made of wood, and again, like masts, the same parameters apply. On new boats almost all the booms, bearing out spars, and spinnaker poles are made of aluminum.

The new boom must be carefully laid out if it is to work efficiently. For instance, putting the sheeting point for the first reef point too far forward will make the sail quite full when a reef is put in. This in turn will slow the boat and give it more heel. Another area of contention on a boom is the types of tack and clew fittings. A simple tack hook, as is often installed on a racing boat, will chafe and wear the sail if it is fitted on a long-distance blue water cruiser.

The clew fitting can also be a problem. Ideally, for best sail adjustment it should have an outhaul fitted. Many production cruisers skip this type of detail and fit a simple pin, which does the job but not very efficiently.

THE MAINSHEET

There appears to be a trend toward mid-boom sheeting, with the traveler mounted on the cabintop for production cruisers. I believe that this trend is a product of the "boat show" sailor, who wants to be able to walk directly down below from the cockpit and does not want anything in his way. (Any green water in the cockpit will also go directly below if nothing is put in its way!)

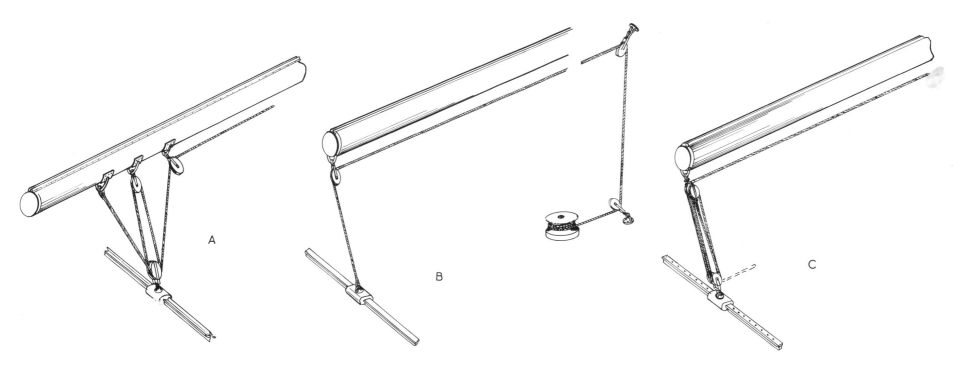

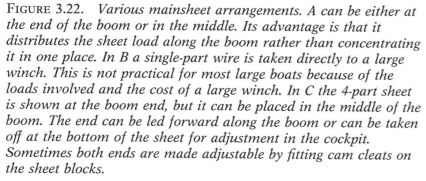

FIGURE 3.22. *Various mainsheet arrangements. A can be either at the end of the boom or in the middle. Its advantage is that it distributes the sheet load along the boom rather than concentrating it in one place. In B a single-part wire is taken directly to a large winch. This is not practical for most large boats because of the loads involved and the cost of a large winch. In C the 4-part sheet is shown at the boom end, but it can be placed in the middle of the boom. The end can be led forward along the boom or can be taken off at the bottom of the sheet for adjustment in the cockpit. Sometimes both ends are made adjustable by fitting cam cleats on the sheet blocks.*

The mid-boom sheeting position is relatively inefficient because of the way the sail is loaded. The maximum loads on a mainsail are generally along the leach from the clew to about 2–4 feet (.6–1.2 meters) in from the leach, and this is where the sheet should be positioned for maximum efficiency. Unfortunately, the mid-boom sheeting position is often well forward of this point, and the boom ends up unduly stressed. I have even seen a boom with a permanent downward bow after having been highly loaded for a long time!

One of the best positions is to put the sheet either at the end or slightly inboard of the end of the boom. This ensures that the sheet is directly opposing the leach load. It also gives the best control over the sail shape and reduces the compressive load on the boom. Unfortunately, the best sheet position for the boom is often the worst for the cockpit. It divides the cockpit in two, making it difficult to walk forward.

On center cockpit boats this problem is solved by placing the entire cockpit forward of the traveler, but there is still a problem for the conventional aft cockpit design.

The mainsheet can be of several parts with no winch or one part and a large winch. The least expensive method is to use a multipart sheet—up to six or eight parts—and no winch. But if you've ever had to jibe using an eight-part sheet you will realize that miles of line have to be pulled in and released quickly. An impossibility for most of us. For that reason most builders use a four-part sheet taken to a small winch. When this arrangement is hooked onto the boom about a foot (0.3 meters) from the leach of the main, the cruising sailor has an efficient and relatively low-cost system.

However, in my opinion the simplest sheeting arrangement is the best, that is, a single-part mainsheet taken to a big self-tailing winch. But big self-tailing winches are expensive, and this arrangement is only seen on 12 meters. Figure 3.22 shows various mainsheet arrangements.

FIGURE 3.23. *The Hall spars vang will support the boom and allow the mainsheet to be tensioned quickly. (Photo courtesy of Hall Spars.)*

VANG, BOOM GALLOWS, OR TOPPING LIFT?

For me, the boom gallows is a thing of the past. A solid rod or spring-loaded vang like Hall Spars' Quickvang is just so much more efficient. It can be used to hold the boom up or lower the boom to tension the leach of the sail. Figure 3.23 shows the Hall Spars Quickvang. The vang is aerodynamically more efficient and will not allow the boom to come crashing into the cockpit unless the gooseneck breaks. Its only drawback is that it is more expensive than a simple rope topping lift. But it doesn't chafe the mainsail leach as the rope topping lift can, nor will it get tangled around the backstay. For my money the air-spring or coiled-spring vang is worth the extra cost.

The ultimate refinement is the hydraulic vang, but although it is easily adjustable it can leak or be released accidently and is not the best option for an offshore cruiser, especially if the boat will be sailing to remote areas.

RUNNING RIGGING

How much running rigging does a boat need? How long should new jib sheets be? Why are wire halyards better than rope? As a designer, I am often asked questions like this. Quite often these questions are hard to answer without knowing or occasionally sailing on the boat, but we will attempt here to formulate some answers to these and other questions.

Halyards

There is to some extent large variation in the possible halyard combinations. Many boats have two genoa, two spinnaker, a mainsail, one or two staysail halyards, and a topping lift, while others get by with just a main and jib halyard.

You *can* get by with just a main and genoa halyard, but I would hate to sail very far offshore with this setup. My philosophy is that the more halyards you have the better off you are. I have been to the masthead too many times replacing broken halyards to be confident that a single genoa and a mainsail halyard are sufficient.

Almost all the halyards I have replaced have broken in one of three places, at the shackles, at the thimble splice, or just in front of the rope-to-wire splice. The most common break is at the masthead near the thimble splice, where the wire passes over the halyard sheave. This is an area rarely checked, and the sheave edges often wear until they are razor sharp. From here it is a simple matter for the sheave to cut through the halyard. Another area of wear is when the halyard bears on the edge of the sheave box. The box edge can cut the halyard very quickly. It often pays to ensure the edges are nicely rounded or protected with replaceable chafing strips.

Another area of failure is the rope-to-wire splice. If the boat is to be fitted out with wire halyards, most sailors prefer to have the wire spliced to rope so that the tail can be easily handled. The wire should run from the head of the sail down the mast with three or four turns on the winch. This will put the splice just behind the winch or between the winch and the cleat, where there is less strain on it. The splice should not be forward of the winch, where it is subject to the full load of the halyard, nor should it be on the winch drum. It also means that you will have to specify stainless steel winch drums, so that the wire will not groove aluminum drums.

Spinnaker halyards, on the other hand, have to have a little give, so that when the sail collapses and fills again the shock loads are taken by the halyard rather than pulling the head out of the sail. For this reason they should be all rope.

The mainsail halyard depends on the type of winches used. If the winches are of the reel type, then the halyard will be all wire. However, reel winches can be dangerous, and I would not put them on a new boat. If the boat has a conventional main halyard winch, then the wire-to-rope halyard is the best.

Those are the conventional choices. A much more up-to-date choice is Kevlar- or Spectra-cored halyards throughout. Kevlar has better tensile strength than steel wire and is comfortable to handle because of the braided covering, which also serves to reduce ultraviolet degradation and chafe of the Kevlar. It does stretch slightly more than wire, but much less than Dacron (terylene). Spectra is not generally liked in the high performance fleet. I've been told that it gives no indication when it is likely to fail. You can be sailing along one minute and the next minute the Spectra line has broken. However, modern blended ropes using a combination of Spectra, Kevlar, and Dacron have virtually solved this problem, and the rope should be sufficient for cruising sailors.

Another feature becoming more prevalent on cruising boats is the use of lock-offs or sheet jammers to secure halyards. I am very ambivalent about this practice. On the one hand, it reduces the number and cost of the winches required; on the other hand the lock-offs work best on rope. This means that either an all-rope halyard must be used or the wire-to-rope splice must be put between the lock-off and the genoa, an area of great strain. I have seen a rope-to-wire splice break in this situation.

If a boat is to be built at reasonable cost and for limited coastal cruising lock-offs are useful. But on a boat intended for long-distance offshore sailing I prefer to see an extra winch or two.

Sheets and Guys

Genoa sheets on cruising boats should always be 16- or 32-plait braided line. There is no reason at all to use 3-stranded rope or wire. If the extra performance of wire is desired I suggest using a Kevlar-cored line, but it is expensive and can get chewed up fairly quickly.

genoa sheets should be tied into the sail clew. It is the least expensive and easiest method, and if you are hit by a flapping genoa sheet it will simply sting a little. If you are hit by one of the metal tack shackles, on the other hand, they will make a good bruise, if they don't break a bone.

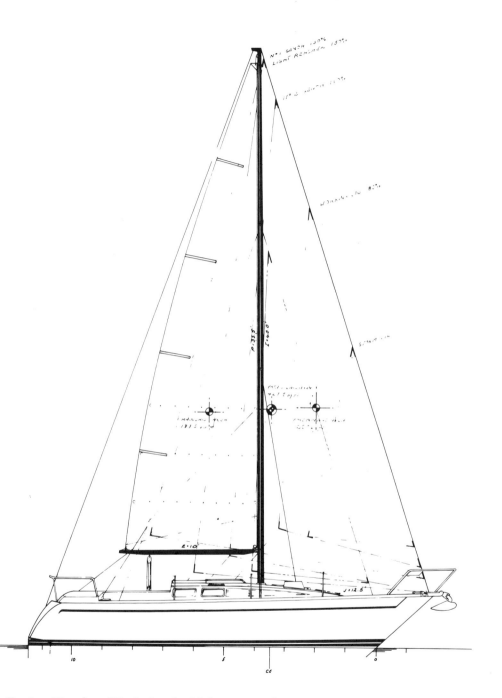

Design Number 37. *A simple 31-foot LOA sloop ideally suited for inshore cruising.*

How long should a new genoa sheet be? I use a figure of one and a half times the length of the boat, but this will vary depending where the primary winches are sited.

The spinnaker sheets should also be 16- or 32-plait braided line, but spinnaker guys are subjected to much higher loadings. Dacron (terylene) lines tend to stretch a lot, rendering control over the pole end unstable at best. However, the last iota of performance is not required on a cruiser, and Dacron lines can be used on boats up to about 40 feet. Over this length, I would prefer to use Kevlar guys.

As you can see, we've looked at a mixture of old and new, but the final decision always depends upon the owner and the type of sailing he will do. If you are like most modern weekend sailors, then the production cruiser will suffice for your needs. But if you want to wander further afield, particular attention should be paid to the sail plan and the amazing number of details that go into fitting out an offshore cruising boat.

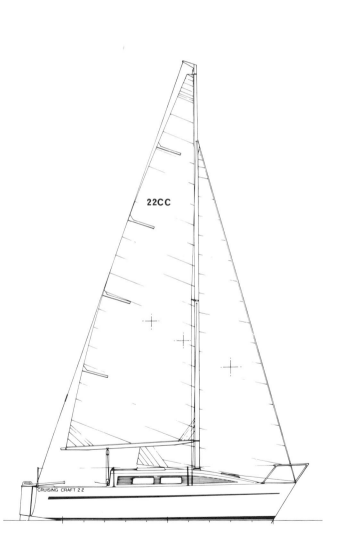

Design Number 18. *The sail plan of a 22-foot LOA sloop with swept back spreaders for easy mast tuning. This boat has a deck-stepped mast so that the spar can be stepped by the crew.*

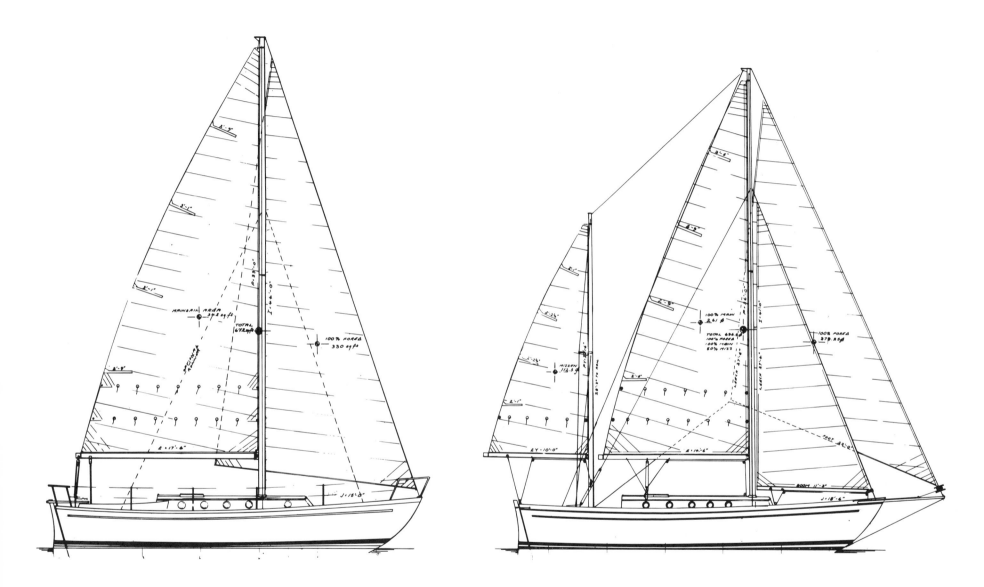

Andromeda. *Another design for Cruising Craft Inc. comes as a sloop or a ketch with a bowsprit. This one is 35-feet overall without the bowsprit.*

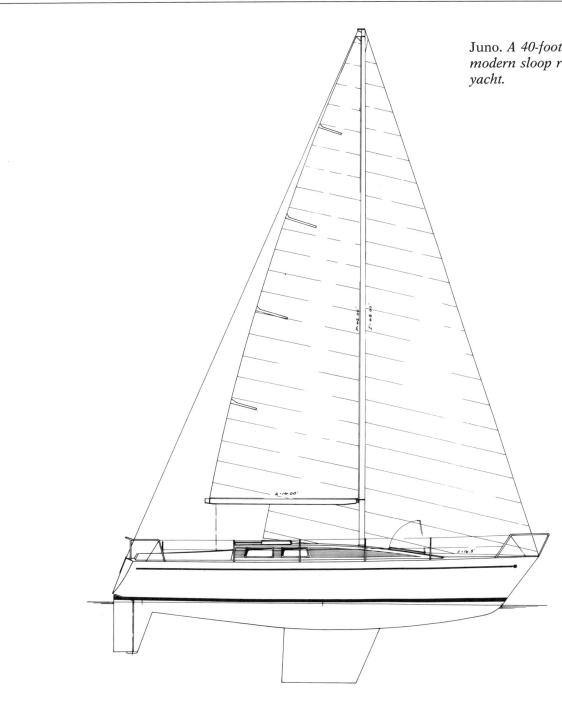

Juno. *A 40-foot LOA design done for Cruising Craft Inc. The modern sloop rig drives an attractive wooden-decked steel-hulled yacht.*

CHAPTER 4

Inside the Hull

S ailor's tastes vary. That is why there are so many interior layouts. Like most businesses, the production boat industry tends to sell what the customer wants. Unfortunately, there are many aspects to a comfortable cruising interior, and many customers who buy production boats are not experienced sailors and often desire features that reduce the safety of their boat. For instance, bridgedecks between the cockpit and the interior used to be considered an essential part of the design. However, a bridgedeck adds two more steps to the ladder leading to the interior, and many customers want to be able to walk directly from the cockpit to the interior, so bridgedecks are going the way of the brontosaurus. Without a bridgedeck, though, if the cockpit fills, the water goes directly below, not back over the side where it belongs.

This trend is showing up in interior design. I once went on a 30-foot production cruiser by a well-known designer and inspected the layout. It had an opening door in the transom and no bridgedeck, and the cabin sole level was only one step down from the cockpit sole. The icebox-nav station was to port and the main dining area to starboard. Forward of the mast and dining area was the owner's stateroom with a large double berth. The head was in the forepeak. Taking this boat to sea would have exposed its problems. What if you had anchored off a beach and opened the transom door to go swimming? Suppose a power boat drove by before the transom door could be shut? The wave would have swept into the cockpit into the interior and all the way to the forepeak. There was nothing to stop it!

Sailing the boat offshore for one night would have revealed that the double bunk forward of the mast was untenable in any seaway. How about using the head in the forepeak as you pounded to windward? You would be better off sitting on the transom and holding the backstay. In my opinion this type of boat should come with big red warning stickers telling the buyer the vessel is only suitable for sailing in enclosed waters and should not be used for offshore sailing. Nor should one attempt to sleep aboard without being securely tied to a marina. Fortunately, it went out of production very quickly. But it serves as a good example of how a boat can be designed for a single purpose and the practice of good seamanship almost completely ignored.

So the first job when laying out an interior is to decide what the boat will be used for. Is it going offshore? Will it only be sailed in sheltered waters and put into a marina every night? Has the owner any desire to sail to Bermuda or trans-Atlantic? How much detail is required? All these questions affect the layout and the budget, and they must be answered before a good design can be said to have fulfilled its design specifications.

In the following pages we'll look at each part of the boat separately and then integrate each part into a complete layout. We'll see how each part can be considered to be a unit unto itself and how it must interact with all the other parts, which may mean compromises before the interior design works efficiently.

THE GALLEY

Cruising at sea presents all the ingredients for a major disaster. Galley size is limited, which means that work space is often crowded. On some boats counters get piled so high with food and utensils that the cook can barely find a spot to slice a vegetable or place a pot. Add to this the ingredient of constant motion and the potential for disaster becomes even greater. Open flames, hot liquids, and sharp knives are much more dangerous in a galley than in a kitchen because of the cook's unsteady surroundings.

On one smooth trip we took to Bermuda the cook placed a nice hot lasagna on the counter top and went on deck to help with a sail change. Unfortunately, the sail change coincided with the wash of a ship and the lasagna upended itself onto the owners' comfortable settee, ruining a very attractive decor and leaving us with sandwiches for dinner. In a tiny galley in rough weather the cook needs the mind of an efficiency expert and the agility of an acrobat. In the absence of either, anything can happen.

Fortunately, a well laid out galley can make a potential disaster area far more safe and efficient. What constitutes a well-designed galley? First, the galley must be laid out with careful consideration of work flow. The extent to which food preparation, serving, and cleanup progress smoothly is much more important than galley size. This means the size and position of the stove relative to the other components must be carefully considered. Second, the galley must incorporate a number of important safety features and other details. Third, the galley must be positioned sensibly in relation to other areas below deck and to the boat's motion. Last, the galley must suit the needs of the owner and his crew. It isn't much use putting a four-burner stove with oven in the boat if the owner and his crew live on sandwiches.

Breaking all these points down into individual components, we find there are many more decisions to be made. For instance, we mentioned the galley stove. Should it be gas, alcohol (methylated spirits in Britain), diesel, kerosene (paraffin in Britain), or electrically powered? Should it be gimbaled? A four-, three-, or two-burner unit, with or without an oven? All these questions will need answering during the design process.

In the following pages we'll look at these questions and try to come to a logical decision on which stove is best for a particular purpose. Then we'll look at the other components of the galley, and finally we'll look at making the galley layout as efficient as possible. Having dealt with the galley, we'll see how the rest of the boat goes together and what the component parts are of each part of the interior.

SELECTING A STOVE

If you had a choice of any stove on the market, which one would you select? What would you look for? The following pages discuss the features of various stoves so that you can make an intelligent decision when the time comes to decide which stove you want.

First, decide what you intend to do with the boat. Are you going to make roast beef regularly, or will you make do with store-bought roast beef sandwiches? If you are going to roast a piece of meat, then you will need an oven.

The first step when selecting a stove is to decide on the type of fuel you want for the stove. Is gas best? Can you live with the inherent danger of heavier-than-air liquified petroleum gas (LPG), or would lighter-than-air compressed natural gas (CNG) suit you better? Do you know which one burns hotter?

Propane, Butane, or Liquified Petroleum Gas

In general, any product containing a mixture of propane, butanes, or butylenes should be known as liquified petroleum gas (LPG). Because these gases are heavier than air and explosive, they pose certain problems for a boat builder. However, the LPG's heat value is much higher than any other fuel, and as long as adequate precautions are taken, there is no better fuel.

LPG is odorless, colorless, and nontoxic, but commercially dispensed gases do have an odorant added to aid in detecting leaks. Because the gas is heavier than air, a leak-detecting system should be installed and turned on at least 10 minutes before the stove is lit. There are two good marine systems that I have found to be excellent, the Ximtex unit from Fireboy Systems and the Newtec Nose from Newtec Industries Ltd. Both have reasonable power drain, the Newtec system has .2 amps on a 12-volt system, and both sense very small amounts of gas. When the Newtec system is used with the Margas marine propane system, you have an almost foolproof system, which reduces the risk of explosion to a very low level.

Any LPG system should be installed so that the gas tanks are stored in a sealed compartment that is vented at the bottom, either over the side or into the air. In fact, several organizations recommend various standards to which the marine industry adheres. They are, in America, the U.S. Coast Guard, the National Fire Protection Association, and the American Boat and Yacht Council (ABYC), in Europe, the International Council of Marine Industry Associations (ICOMIA), and in Britain, the British Standards Institution and the Inland Waterways Authority. However, there are certain precautions every boat owner should take when using an LPG system:

1. Turn the sniffer on before the gas is turned on.
2. Always turn off the gas at the cylinder before leaving the boat.
3. Never enter the boat with a lighted cigarette in your hand or mouth. If gas has leaked into the bilge the cigarette may set it off. (That'd make your eyes water!)
4. Do not put anything other than the gas cylinder in the gas locker. I have seen lifejackets, lines, and tools stored in this locker, and a large wrench could knock the top off the gas cylinder or damage it and cause a leak.
5. Make sure the locker vent is never plugged.
6. Make sure the gas cylinder is securely fastened in its locker.
7. There should be a sign at the stove that says *Turn off gas at cylinder after use and before leaving the boat.* This should ensure you a safe trip every time you use your boat.
8. Finally, if you intend to sail abroad, you should make sure you have various adapters to get your gas cylinder filled in any of the countries you intend to visit.

Compressed Natural Gas (CNG)

CNG is naturally occurring methane gas stored under pressure. It has a lower heat value than LPG, but it is lighter than air and will vent itself out of a boat if allowed to do so. It too is invisible, odorless, and nontoxic and has an odorant added. It also takes a larger percentage of CNG in air before an explosion will occur. Unfortunately, CNG is not available all over the world. Its use is slowly spreading, but if you intend to sail around the world using a CNG system you'd better have some form of backup.

As I was writing this I received a brochure from GSI (Gas Systems Inc.) describing their SAFGAS products. These products are intended for use with CNG and include two- and three-burner stainless steel ranges and a two-burner cooktop, plus an impressive array of accessories. They also provide a list of CNG dealers in various countries. Antigua, Australia, Canada, New Zealand, and the United States are the countries listed, so the CNG system has yet to spread worldwide.

Alcohol (Methylated Spirits)

Quite often some sailors who are most afraid of a gas system will have an alcohol or methylated spirit stove on board. Yet this type of fuel has a much lower flashpoint than any other fuel—a mere 70 degrees—and even when lit the fuel does not give off a very high heat.

FIGURE 4.1. *The Balmar stove is one of the few diesel stoves on the market. However, it is not gimbaled and is best on a boat where the stove will be left on for a long period of time. (Photo courtesy of Balmar.)*

It also uses a lot of fuel. I have seen alcohol stoves run out of fuel and flare up when refilled as fuel lands on the cooking surface and ignites. If you try to put the fire out with water, as some authorities recommend, the fuel can float on top of the water and carry a flame to some very strange places. Either a blanket thrown over the fire or a foam fire extinguisher is the best method of extinguishing it. Note that some authorities recommend a fire blanket be kept near the galley.

For me the final strike against alcohol as a fuel is its cost in various parts of the world, often eight or ten times more than in Britain or America.

Diesel as a Stove Fuel

You probably carry diesel for your engine, so why not use it as a fuel? It's available worldwide, its cost is reasonable, and it gives off a reasonable heat.

However, it has drawbacks. It can often burn with a sooty flame, especially when first lit. Also, a back draft can fill the cabin with smoke. To eliminate any chance of back draft you may have to fit a blower, with the consequent power drain. It also has an odor some people find unpleasant.

Finding a diesel stove may also be a job. There seem to be few, if any on the market, and those that are are not gimbaled. It is usually the boat builder who adapts the stove to be gimbaled. The Balmar stove seems to be the best diesel stove around. Figure 4.1 shows one of these stoves.

For sailing in colder Arctic regions, where gas fuels are not readily available and where the stove may run for a day or two at a time, a diesel stove is a good bet. But if you are going to sail in the tropics you will probably be better off using a gas or alcohol unit.

Kerosene (Paraffin)

Kerosene or paraffin stoves are the old standby of cruising sailors everywhere. Kerosene can be used to fuel the stove or the hurricane lamps. It is usually available almost everywhere, burns with a hot flame, and has a flashpoint of about 160 degrees. However, it too has its drawbacks.

In order to get it to burn it needs to be vaporized. This in turn means the stove must be primed and pressurized. I remember the job it was starting a single-burner Primus stove a few years ago. First a small amount of alcohol kept in a separate bottle was dripped onto a rag.

This was placed under the vaporizing ring just beneath the burner. Then the rag was lit. As soon as the stove was judged to be hot enough, the tank was enthusiastically pumped to pressurize the kerosene. If you judged it right and cracked the pressure valve at the right moment you were rewarded with a beautiful blue-white flame. If you opened the pressure valve too soon unvaporized kerosene flooded the stove and sometimes ignited, causing a huge flareup, or it would put the fire out and you'd have to start all over again. Those were the days; in one easy stroke you could burn the boat to the waterline. Actually the modern kerosene stoves are not that bad. A self-priming version is available, reducing the possibility of burning the boat. They just need work and planning to make a simple cup of coffee or tea.

Electricity

Like the electric stove at home in your kitchen, the marine electric stove is clean and easy to operate. Its use, however, is limited to larger boats that have their own generators or to boats that will be alongside the marina at mealtimes. The smallest boat I have seen an electric stove on was the new 1987 Pearson 37, which had its own small generator hidden in the cockpit locker. The power consumption of an electric stove can be prodigious; nevertheless, some people prefer the ease and convenience of electric cooking. On many boats the generator may also power the air conditioning, TV, stereo, and other electrical appliances.

It can also power the microwave. In the future, when sailing boats have small electrical generators aboard, microwave ovens will become the cooking source of choice. They are already commonplace on larger boats. But they do require a power source, albeit not as large as for an electric stove.

Wood or Coal

Wood- and coal-burning stoves can be quite inexpensive to fuel. Driftwood, in fact, can often be collected along the shore. (That is, if you sail close to shorelines.) But these stoves must be kept burning; they are not the "instant heat" variety. This can be unbearable in the tropics, but for sailing in Arctic or Antarctic zones they are an interesting alternative. They have some risks; coals may fall out, causing a fire hazard. If the boat is closed up tight, there is a possibility that the stove could use all the oxygen inside the boat. And as a final drawback, these stoves cannot be gimbaled; the chimney prevents it.

Which Stove Is Best for You?

Obviously the type of sailing you do influences every detail on the boat, even down to the best stove. For instance, one year we sailed from Newport to Bermuda and the first night out the cook made a superb dinner. Soup first, followed by roast beef with Yorkshire pudding, broccoli, baked potatoes, and all the trimmings, including a bottle of wine. On another yacht the crew ate TV dinners heated in the microwave. Both boats were on the same trip, but the cook of the boat I was on had thought more about the inner man than had the other cook.

									TABLE 4.1
Type of Cooking	Type of Appliance Required	Alcohol (Meths)	Compressed Natural Gas	Propane or Butane Gas	Diesel	Wood or Coal	Kerosene (Paraffin)	Electricity	Remarks
Baking	Oven		x	x	x	x	x	x	
Barbeque	Grill or broiler					x		x	Electric broilers are available but are inefficient. Charcoal or briquettes may be used for barbeque or hibachi.
Boiling	Stovetop burner	x	x	x	x	x	x	x	
Braising	Stovetop or oven	x	x	x	x	x	x	x	Stovetop only
Frying	Stovetop burner	x	x	x	x	x	x	x	Depending on the burner the alcohol stove may have difficulty getting hot enough to heat oil to high temp.
Roasting	Oven		x	x	x	x	x	x	
Gimbaling		Easy	Fair	Fair			x	x	
Flue required					x	x			
Special requirements								x	Needs generator

TABLE 4.2.   HEAT VALUE OF FUELS

	Heat Value BTU per lb.	Burner Output BTU per hour	Fuel Used by TypicaL Burner
Alcohol (Meths)	12,810	2,800	1 qt. per 8 hours
Kerosene (Paraffin)	19,810	4,500	1 qt. per 8 hours
Propane	21,070	5,000	1.9 lbs. per 8 hours
LNG	8,600	5,000	37 cu.ft. per 8 hours
CNG	1,020 BTUs per cubic foot		
Butane	2,350 BTUs per cubic foot		
Electricity (1000 w element)		3,400	

Note: A 5,000 BTU per hour burner will boil a cup of water in approximately 4 minutes. *Courtesy of Kenyon Co.*

It takes some careful analysis to define what you want in the galley. You have to think about the type of crew you will have. Whether they eat the way you do. The size of the galley and the storage facility in the galley. For instance, if you are going to use a microwave for TV dinners you will have to find a place to store the frozen meals, and you will need a generator to power the microwave. Each decision influences something else. Table 4.1 lists the various types of cooking and its requirements. Note that this does not include a microwave, which can be used for heating or cooking almost all types of food. It does require a generator, but because of its versatility it could be a useful item to have aboard if you already have a method of generating sufficient power.

Also note that barbequing is usually done on a transom grill and rarely inside the boat. The grill is not included in this list, as I don't consider it the prime cooking unit on the boat.

Let's suppose we want to do a fair amount of cruising worldwide and that we intend to have a crew of three plus the skipper aboard under normal conditions. The fuels available worldwide are propane (LPG), diesel, alcohol, kerosene, and wood. Wood is out because the boat will sail extensively in the tropics and the stove must be gim-

baled. Kerosene is out because it takes too long to get the unit working. Diesel smells terrible, and alcohol is both expensive and not really hot enough. So that leaves us with the LPG system or electricity. Unfortunately the boat isn't big enough to carry a generator and all the other features we want, so we are left with the LPG system. It must be installed with a leak detection system, and extra connectors will have to be purchased so that we can fill the tank anywhere in the world. Table 4.2 lists the heat value of the various fuels, and Table 4.3 lists the pros and cons of the different types of stove fuel.

The stove will be gimbaled, either transverse or fore and aft. Frankly, I prefer a transversely gimbaled stove. Many times have I taken something out of the oven and found that the remaining contents have upset the balance of the unit. Usually hasty action with oven mitts have prevented a disaster as the stove has swung forward *toward the cook.* In my opinion, the extra cost of a transversely gimbaled stove is well worth it. As of this time I know of one transversely gimbaled stove manufacturer. That is Paul Luke of Boothbay Harbor, Maine. I specified one of his stoves in a boat I designed a few years ago. The unit is a two-part stove where the worktop gimbals separately from the oven. As this stove is very expensive, most of us are forced to settle for a unit that gimbals fore and aft. In this case I would recommend the Mariner series from Balmar or the Shipmate series from Richmond Ring Company. These stoves are substantially constructed out of stainless steel and have many interesting features. They are designed for LPG and CNG systems. The Mariner series also has a kerosene option and a cabinet liner for additional safety and protection. Figure 4.2 shows a Mariner stove. Shipmate, on the other hand makes a wood- or coal-burning range and various ranges for alcohol, gas, or kerosene.

For owners of small boats who do not want to go to the expense of a propane system, the Origo alcohol stoves are about the best of that type. They even have a two-burner/oven alcohol stove.

If you have electricity when the boat is alongside but do not have a generator aboard, the Kenyon 406T is a useful unit. It has alcohol burners set in the middle of electrical rings. When alongside you simply switch on the electricity; at sea you use the alcohol burners. The 406BG is an ultra-modern unit that has an easy-to-maintain black glass lid to complement the galley decor. Figure 4.3 shows a Kenyon model 406 stove.

Stoves, then, are sized and suited to the cooking, sailing, and crew requirements of your boat. They should be carefully installed and should have several safety features already built in.

TABLE 4.3 PROS AND CONS OF DIFFERENT STOVES

Type of Stove	Advantages	Disadvantages	Notes
Liquified petroleum gas (propane, butane)	hottest flame clean available everywhere any number of burners can be used	heavier than air not permitted aboard boats for hire in U.S.A. incompatibility of U.S. and European fittings	ABYC requires that: LPG systems have a rated working pressure of at least 250 lbs. per sq. mi., a manual shut-off valve at each container, and containers located above the waterline so that any escaping gas is vented overboard.
Alcohol	relatively safe fire can be extinguished with water if properly doused	can flare up if improperly used must have drip pan under stove stove must be cool before filling fumes may be unpleasant low flashpoint	To meet ABYC specifications, burners must be wickless and situated so that tank cannot be filled when burners are lighted.
Diesel	available everywhere only one fuel tank needed for engine and stove	odor may be unpleasant flame often sooty stove not gimbaled	
Electric	clean easy to use	requires expensive auxiliary power unit water, heat, and electricity may lead to corrosion stove not gimbaled	
Wood or coal	can be used to warm cabin relatively inexpensive	stove not gimbaled requires large fuel storage danger of hot coals falling out	
Gasoline	available everywhere	highly explosive	

General Stove Safety Features

Once you have picked your stove, the next step is to position it in the galley. When the stove is positioned several safety features should be incorporated:

1. A protection bar should be fitted in front of the stove to keep the cook from falling onto the hot surface should he slip or fall. There should also be a strap or harness to keep the cook in the galley in inclement conditions.

2. The stove should be supplied or fitted with a guard rail about 1¼–2 inches (35–50 millimeters) above the perimeter of the stove to prevent pots and pans from sliding off. Indentations should be provided for pot handles in the higher guard rails. Also, stoves with more than two burners should also have locking fiddles or clamps for each pot for the same purpose.

3. All burner controls should be on the top or front of the stove so that the cook does not have to reach over the unit to get at them. The gas turn-off control should also be to the side of the stove, not at the back or over the top. Ideally, another gas control should be situated in the gas tank locker.

all countertops, sides, and lockers surrounding the stove must be protected from heat. I would recommend placing a fireproof material against the woodwork and a stainless steel stove aperture liner over the fireproofing.

7. Since the fastnet disaster of 1979, the Offshore Racing Council has called for stoves to be securely installed against capsize and to have a safe, accessible fuel shut-off valve operable in a seaway. The ABYC recommends that stoves be properly secured in position. In my book this means the boat should be able to roll through 360 degrees without the stove coming off its gimbals. I would hate to be in a boat where the stove could jump its mountings under any conditions.

FIGURE 4.3. *A Kenyon model 406 stove. This stove has dual heating elements, one for gas and one for electricity. On a smaller boat where shore supply or a generator is available this would be a good unit to install. (Photo courtesy of IMI Kenyon.)*

FIGURE 4.2. *The Mariner stove by Balmar is made out of stainless steel and is suitable for most gas installations. (Photo courtesy of Balmar.)*

4. The gas detector unit controls should be well away from the stove. Ideally they should be situated so that the cook has to go past them to get at the stove on-off control.
5. All edges of the stove, and all other galley furniture, should have rounded edges.
6. The American Boat and Yacht Council recommends that surfaces near a stove should not be raised more than 90 degrees Fahrenheit above the temperature of the galley. To achieve this,

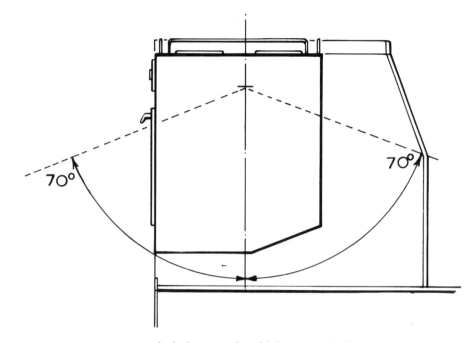

70°   70°

FIGURE 4.4. *A gimbaled stove should be securely fastened and able to swing through an arc of at least 70 degrees. It should also have a lock to fix the stove on centerline.*

8. All stoves should be able to swing through a minimum arc of 140 degrees (70 degrees either side of centerline), as shown in Figure 4.4. There should also be a mechanism that enables the stove to be locked securely in the vertical position.

9. The ABYC recommends that alcohol stoves be of the wickless type so that they are unaffected by the motion of the boat. Also, the tanks on alcohol stoves should be removable or remote from the burners to reduce the risk of fire when refueling.

10. The area over the stove should be adequately ventilated, both to remove cooking odors and to reduce the heat in the galley.

11. Finally, I like to see a damper or friction clutch on the stove gimbals so that the unit is less liable to swing to its limits in bad weather.

ICEBOXES, REFRIGERATORS, AND FREEZERS

These days it is a rare boat that does not carry some form of icebox or refrigerator. The units can vary from the simple portable ice chest sold in various sizes and used on many small (under 25-feet [7.5-meter]) cruisers to the more elaborate freezer-refrigeration on a large power yacht. Once again the type of unit you install is governed by the type of sailing you do and the size of your boat. Nonetheless, there are certain general features you should look for. We'll look here at the features seen by the cook in the galley rather than at the engineering features, which will be dealt with in Chapter 10.

The Icebox

The simplest type of refrigeration device. It has no mechanical means of lowering the temperature and relies on ice, dry ice, or prefrozen items to keep the temperature low. Its simplicity is its major advantage over other systems.

When an icebox is built-in it should have a certain construction to ensure reasonable efficiency. The outermost layer of your icebox will be the plywood cabinet that surrounds the unit. Inside that will be a vapor barrier, usually a plastic sheet or mylar. Any joints in the vapor barrier should be carefully sealed to minimize air leakage.

Inside the vapor barrier is the foam, a minimum of 2 inches (50 millimeters) thick. If possible it should be thicker on the bottom and next to the hull. The rate at which the box loses cooling depends on the thickness of the foam and the number of leaks in the corners. The foam should not be styrofoam, which allows air penetration. Polyurethane foam is the most commonly used material, with a density of greater than 2.5 pounds per cubic foot. All joints in the foam should be tightly sealed with a spray-type foam. Figure 4.5 shows a section through a typical icebox.

Inside the foam is a layer of reflective foil and then the icebox liner. The liner is generally made of fiberglass, but on older boats I have seen stainless steel liners. However, these are expensive and crumbs tend to collect in the corners, where they are difficult to clean. When the liner is made of fiberglass the interior corners are usually rounded, making it cleanable with a simple wipe.

The lid and its position on the box are also of critical importance. First, the opening should be large enough to permit a full bag of ice or an unbroken 25-pound (10–12-kilogram) block of ice. The lid should be as well insulated as the sides. I prefer a top-opening icebox,

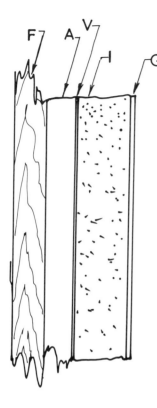

FIGURE 4.5. *A section through a typical icebox, showing:*

A *Air gap between the furniture and the vapor barrier.*
F *Built-in furniture.*
V *Vapor barrier.*
I *Insulation. Ideally this is a polyurethane foam with a density of greater than 2.5 lbs. per cubic foot (.03 kg per M²3).*
G *Fiberglass liner.*

To minimize the number of times your main icebox is opened you may want to use an additional portable box. In the United States, Igloo coolers are the best. They can be stored on the cabin sole, under a table, or in the cockpit. They are substantially constructed and come in various sizes (from 12-quart up to 60-quart). When filled with canned drinks and ice they provide a simple and effective solution to the problem of providing cool drinks for the crew without unfreezing the main icebox.

Do You Need a Freezer-Refrigerator?

This is probably a question you never asked yourself. But first let me qualify it a little. It presumes that your boat is large enough to have a freezer on board. That usually means the boat is over 35 feet LOA.

It is surprising the number of sailors who have a freezer on board and use it once or twice a year. Unless you are going to do some serious cruising or live on the boat, I would venture to suggest that a freezer is no more efficient than a much less expensive icebox and a few bags of ice.

Of course every freezer manufacturer will now be asking how I make ice cubes. The simple answer is I buy them. A few bags at the beginning of the weekend will usually last all weekend. Most sailors buy ice anyway. A freezer can only make enough for about three drinks.

If you've decided you definitely want a freezer, let's look briefly at the possibilities, its size and style, and the powering system it will use.

Size and Style

Once you've decided you definitely need a refrigerator, size is the next most important decision. Size will affect its placement in the boat and its access from the galley. For instance, suppose you've decided on an 9-cubic-foot freezer. With insulation around it and paneling the box will measure about 3' 6" × 3' 0" × 1' 6". While that isn't too large a box to fit into an average galley, add in the cold plates and a few shelves and the size is decreasing rapidly. Put in two 25-pound blocks of ice and you'll be left with about 5–6 cubic feet of volume. Add in two six-packs of beer and a bottle or two of wine and there's barely enough room for the lunchtime sandwiches.

As you can see, it pays to select the largest refrigerator you can possibly fit into the boat, even if it means locating it outside the immediate galley area.

which tends to hold its cooling best, but many people prefer side-opening units because they find it difficult to dig down into the top opening and find the item they are looking for. However, if you open a side-opening icebox or freezer on the wrong tack you are likely to find all your food strewn over the galley sole. To prevent accidental openings, side-opening units should have strong commercial-type closures. One catch is adequate in a heavy seaway but two are ideal.

Whichever type you choose, they both should have shelves. I think the best shelves are those made of clear plexiglass (Perspex in UK) with 1-inch (25-millimeter) holes drilled in to allow the cold air to circulate. The simple metal racks found in home refrigerators seem to rust out in a very short time on a boat.

The box should also have a drain, which ideally will lead to a sump tank from which it can be pumped over the side. The sump tank should be large enough to hold at least one melted block of ice. For me a drain that goes into the bilge is totally unacceptable. It will eventually smell and make the inside of the boat unlivable.

Freezers, too, should be as large as possible. However, the freezer will have more insulation than a refrigerator and for the same size exterior the interior volume will be smaller. The plates will also take up more room, which leaves you with a very small freezer if it is situated in the galley alongside the refrigerator.

Powering the Unit

This subject is covered in more detail in Chapter 9; however, a brief overview will serve to illustrate why certain decisions are made with regard to the size and type of fittings that go in the unit. Many are driven by the main engine; others use a battery-driven electric motor. One older type is powered by liquified petroleum gas. After all we've seen about the hazards of this fuel it seems unusual to find it being used to drive a refrigerator. This system requires a pilot light, which has been known to be extremely dangerous.

I was once walking away from a dock where a boat was being filled with fuel. It was a hot humid day, and the petroleum vapors reached the pilot light. Fortunately, the owner had just stepped ashore to pay his bill when the ensuing explosion blew the deck and cabin top off his boat. Since that time I have been extremely wary of systems that require pilot lights. It is hard enough to keep a pilot light lit ashore without having to cope with it onboard.

A safer way to power a marine refrigerator-freezer is off a compressor driven by the main engine, or by a battery-driven electric motor. With either of these systems a compressor is connected to a holdover eutectic evaporator ("eutectic" means that the ingredients in the refrigerant are combined to give the lowest possible temperatures) in the refrigerator, or to the plates in the freezer. When the compressor is run the temperature inside the cabinet drops until the desired level is reached. The unit stays cold for many hours without operating the compressor. The exact amount of time before the engine or motor must be switched on again largely depends on the number of times the cabinet is opened and the amount of insulation in the walls.

When making a choice between an engine-driven system and a battery-driven refrigerator-freezer, several factors should be taken into account. Compressors require a great deal of power, so boats with electrical refrigeration must have either large, heavy storage batteries or an auxiliary generator. Engine-driven systems, with their direct drive, require neither of these, but you may have to run the engine for a long time to get the temperature down far enough. At the dock, however, electrical systems have the advantage of being able to run off shore power. In an effort to get the best out of both systems many manufacturers are building refrigerator-freezer motors that can be either engine or battery driven.

CHOOSING A GALLEY SINK AND WATER SYSTEM

Most seagoing cooks will tell you that there never seems to be enough room in the galley and the sink becomes a repository for almost everything. During meal preparation the sink is used for washing vegetables and storing pots about to be placed on the stove. After a meal it must hold the dirty dishes and be large enough to make washing up reasonable efficient. A good-sized sink, then, is virtually essential.

Some cooks prefer one large and another smaller sink, while others like two of equal size. Both do the same job so the choice should be left to the individual cook. In any case, make sure that your galley sink is as deep as possible, up to a maximum of about 10 inches (250 millimeters).

The placement of a sink in the galley also affects its efficiency. It should be situated as near as possible to the boat's centerline. If this is not practical, then the sink drain line should be fitted with a nonreturn valve to prevent sea water being forced back up into the sink when the boat heels. Figure 4.6 shows the principle.

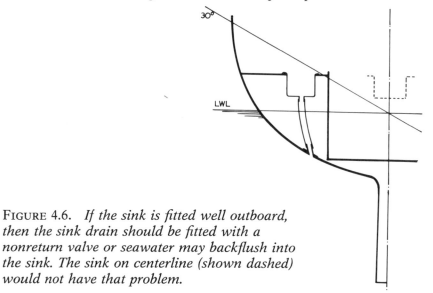

FIGURE 4.6. *If the sink is fitted well outboard, then the sink drain should be fitted with a nonreturn valve or seawater may backflush into the sink. The sink on centerline (shown dashed) would not have that problem.*

The water supply to the galley should also be carefully considered. The real blue water sailor will have a sea water tap in addition to the hot and cold water ones. However, if you don't go very far offshore a sea water tap is a waste. There's no way I would pump sea water from some of our harbors into my galley sink. A salt water tap will help conserve your water supply by allowing you to wash and rinse clothes and dishes in salt water before you rinse them in fresh water.

The next decision to be made is whether to have hot and cold pressure water. This really sorts itself into two decisions. First, should you have hot and cold water, and second, should you have a pressure water system? I say *yes* to both systems as long as there is a manual backup. Even though they add mechanical complexities and drain power, the feeling of being able to shower and get into clean clothes after a particularly cold and messy sail change is well worth it. However, like most luxuries, the decision must be tempered with the extra power drain.

Permit me to digress for a moment and explain my reasoning. It appears that the modern cruising sailor belongs to one of two schools. The first school says sailing is arduous and should be treated as such. If you intend to wander off into unexplored parts of the world then your boat should be as simple as possible. This type of sailor lives on canned foods and enjoys roughing it. Having done my share of camping and roughing it, I belong to the second school, which says, if the boat is large enough, why not cram it with all the luxuries that make cruising simpler and easier, allowing you more time to enjoy the cruise? This, then, is my reasoning for having hot and cold running water. If it leads to too much water being used then I'll fit a reverse osmosis watermaker and a larger generator.

Having said that, the next decision is to select the system and the compressor. (The mechanics of the installation are dealt with in Chapter 9.) I generally specify Paragon pumps, but recently one of my clients asked my opinion of the Balmar line of pumps. After talking to the manufacturer and inspecting a pump I'm very impressed with the unit. It is self-priming and will run dry without damage. The manufacturer says it is designed for low maintenance, and, above all, it is quiet. I have yet to see an installed unit, but the display model I looked at certainly seems to perform well.

Hot water systems need a water tank and some method of heating water. Once again Balmar comes to the fore. It has a number of models, upright or horizontal, from 6- to 30-gallon capacity. The heating unit can be run from shore supply, ship's generator, or the engine cooling system via a heat exchanger. This last is essential; after all, if you are going to run the engine to charge batteries, pull down the refrigerator or freezer temperature, or even get from one port to another, why not use the waste heat to heat the hot water?

We mentioned sink drains very briefly earlier but did not consider whether they drained overside or into a sump tank. The simplest arrangement is an overside drain, but on some boats where the sink is low in the boat the drains are often run into a sump tank and pumped over the side. Sink drains should have through-hull fittings on every drain, and it is good practice to tie a bung suitable for the drain size near the through-hull. Should anything happen such as a hose clamp coming undone or a through-hull corroding, the bung can be hammered into the hole as a temporary measure.

The sink and water system are an essential part of the performance of the galley and should not be passed over lightly. Selection of good, reliable compressors, good installation, and good maintenance procedure will make your cruising virtually hassle-free.

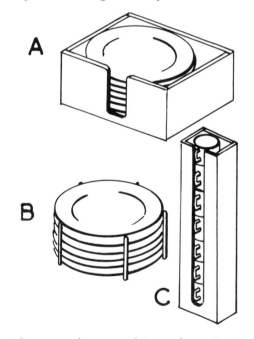

FIGURE 4.7. *Plates can be stowed in racks as in A. Small posts inserted in the bottom of the locker will also hold them in place as in B. Cups can be hung on hooks, but they bounce around and can smash against each other. C illustrates a better method of storing cups.*

The stove, icebox-refrigerator-freezer, and water system are the three main systems in the galley. As such they should command top place in the galley layout scheme. The other parts of the galley are based on these three systems, and careful design is required to get the entire galley unit integrated. The stove requires ventilation and fire extinguishers. Other parts of the galley won't work without pots and pans. Nonfrozen food must be stored somewhere, and even the garbage has to be hidden out of sight until it can be disposed of ashore. So storage is a major consideration in the well-designed galley.

DESIGNING GALLEY STORAGE SPACE

Because a boat heels up to 30 degrees, poorly designed stowage can result in broken plates or a pile of shattered utensils and food jars that have fallen from poorly designed lockers. Fortunately, it is not difficult to think up ways to store most things safely.

Dishes, for instance, can be stored in racks, as shown in Figure 4.7a, or they can be held with dowels fitted into the shelf, as in Figure 4.7b. Hanging cups on hooks is fine if your sailing is limited to fair weather. However, in rough sea, cups stored this way can bounce and break. An alternative means of stowing cups is in a rack as in Figure 4.7c. Finally, one of the better ideas I've seen is a cupboard with a draining rack over the sink in which the dishes are allowed to drip into the sink. Figure 4.8 illustrates this rack.

Kitchen equipment other than dishes also needs proper stowage. Silverware or cutlery should have its own drawer, ideally with compartments for forks, knives, soup spoons, and teaspoons. The cook's knives should occupy their own rack in some convenient location. The rack should be designed so that the knives cannot be dislodged should the boat capsize. If they are stored in a drawer, make sure each knife has its own space and that the drawer is large enough to hold everything.

Similarly, pots and pans usually need lots of room for neat storage, but good planning can help minimize the space required. A set of nesting pots with removable handles, for example, can help solve the problem of limited space on a smaller boat.

Well-designed galley stowage does not end when when all the dishes, pots, pans, and other utensils are safely tucked away. Nonperishable food and kitchen supplies must also be conveniently stowed. A good general rule is to store the foods and supplies most often used in the most easily accessible lockers. Less frequently used items can

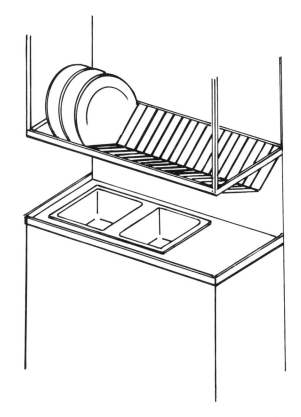

FIGURE 4.8. *Plates can be stored in a rack and allowed to drain into the sink. If desired the entire rack can be enclosed in a locker.*

then be relegated to the more difficult-to-reach places. Remember, too, to take advantage of storage areas outside the galley. For example, if you remove the labels from canned goods and mark them with a felt-tip pen, they can be stowed in the bilge. Extra paper goods, such as paper towels or napkins, can often be kept in spare lockers in the head. Vegetables that don't need refrigeration can live in the lazarette. Any empty space can become a valuable storage area if you think of how to use it intelligently.

Finally we come to the more onerous chore of stowing the nonbiodegradable garbage. I firmly believe that sailors, who are in more direct contact with the ocean, should not dump their nondegradable garbage into the ocean. Nevertheless, I've sailed on yachts where the cook regularly dumped everything over the side.

Unfortunately this attitude is all too prevalent among many sailors and marks, for me at least, the sailor who has no appreciation of his environment. I put him in a class with the people who throw their empty beer cans out the car window for someone else to clean up.

Stowing the garbage is not difficult in a well-equipped galley. A lift-out garbage pail with a plastic liner is all that is required. Figure 4.9 shows a typical example. When the pail is filled the liner can be removed, sealed, and stowed in the lazarette. It is always a good idea to place the individual bags in a larger bag. Then, if the liner breaks open the garbage is still contained.

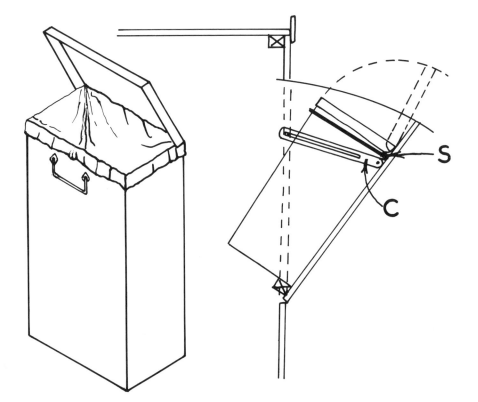

FIGURE 4.9. *A liftout pail is the best way of storing garbage. Note how a plastic garbage bag fits easily inside and the tight-fitting lid keeps smells down. In B the same unit has been installed in a hinge-out locker. S is shock cord holding the pail against the door, and C is the slider that prevents the locker from opening too far and dumping the contents on the cabin sole.*

GALLEY WORKTOPS

The need for galley worktops may seem relatively unimportant and all too often is given low priority. On many boats the only work space in the galley is on top of the refrigerator-freezer, making access to frozen food extremely difficult when a meal is being prepared. Slide-out surfaces and sink lids can help reduce this problem. But awareness of the need for adequate counterspace at the design stage can avoid it completely.

Making sure there are enough worktops in the galley is only half the problem of good counter design. A counter, after all, is more than just a flat surface on which to spread out food and utensils. A well-designed counter incorporates several essential features. First, counters must be easy to clean, so they should be made of stainless steel or a plastic laminate. Second, there should be deep, removable fiddles around the edges of all counters, as well as fiddles down counter centers. Fiddle corners should, ideally, be rounded, and a gap should be left near the corners to allow crumbs to be swept off. Third, proper counter height is essential. The ideal height for the average person is between 33 and 36 inches (.84–.91 meters), although a tall person may feel more comfortable with 38 inches (.98 meters).

If the sinks are a separate unit, the countertop may be slightly higher than the rest of the counter so the cook does not have to stoop to reach the bottom of the sink. Finally, a helpful item to include in your galley layout is a good-sized cutting board.

Having reviewed the many decisions to be made when fitting out the modern galley, it is clear how multifaceted the task of good galley design is. Selecting equipment that meets the needs and style of a particular owner and crew is critical. Carefully matching of galley equipment to individual requirements can transform almost any galley from a merely adequate arrangement into an extremely efficient area that is a pleasure to work in either alongside or at sea. Figure 4.10 shows the galley layout on a small cruiser and shows the compromises that must be made to fit everything in. Figure 4.11 details the galley in a larger vessel. Note the huge amount of space available and the carefully laid out working areas. Figure 4.12 specifies the most useful dimensions for a galley.

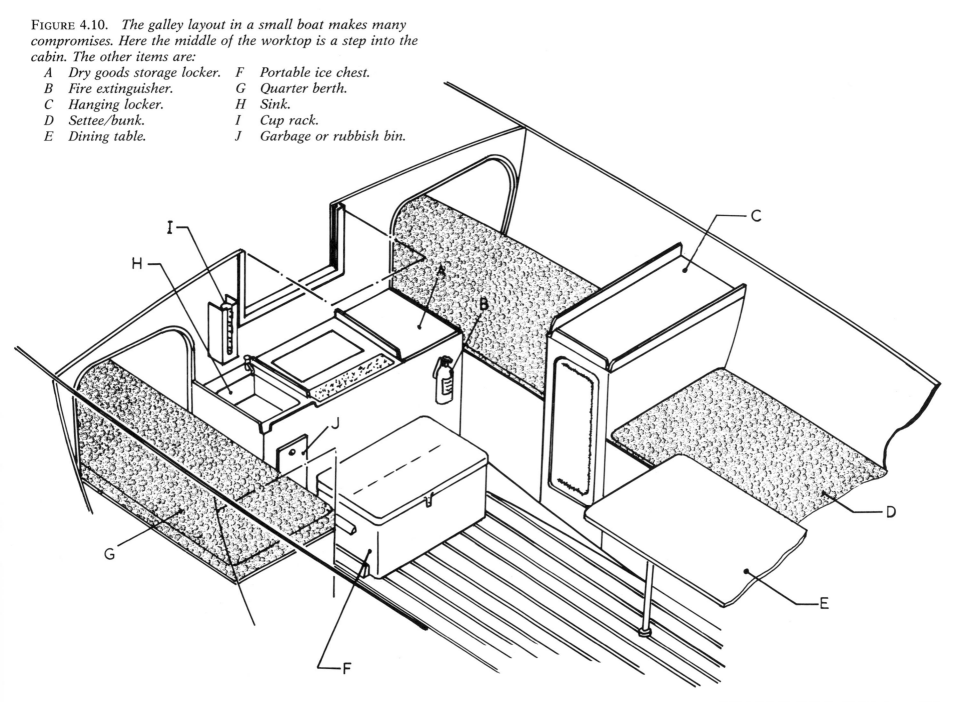

FIGURE 4.10. *The galley layout in a small boat makes many compromises. Here the middle of the worktop is a step into the cabin. The other items are:*

A   Dry goods storage locker. F   Portable ice chest.
B   Fire extinguisher.   G   Quarter berth.
C   Hanging locker.   H   Sink.
D   Settee/bunk.   I   Cup rack.
E   Dining table.   J   Garbage or rubbish bin.

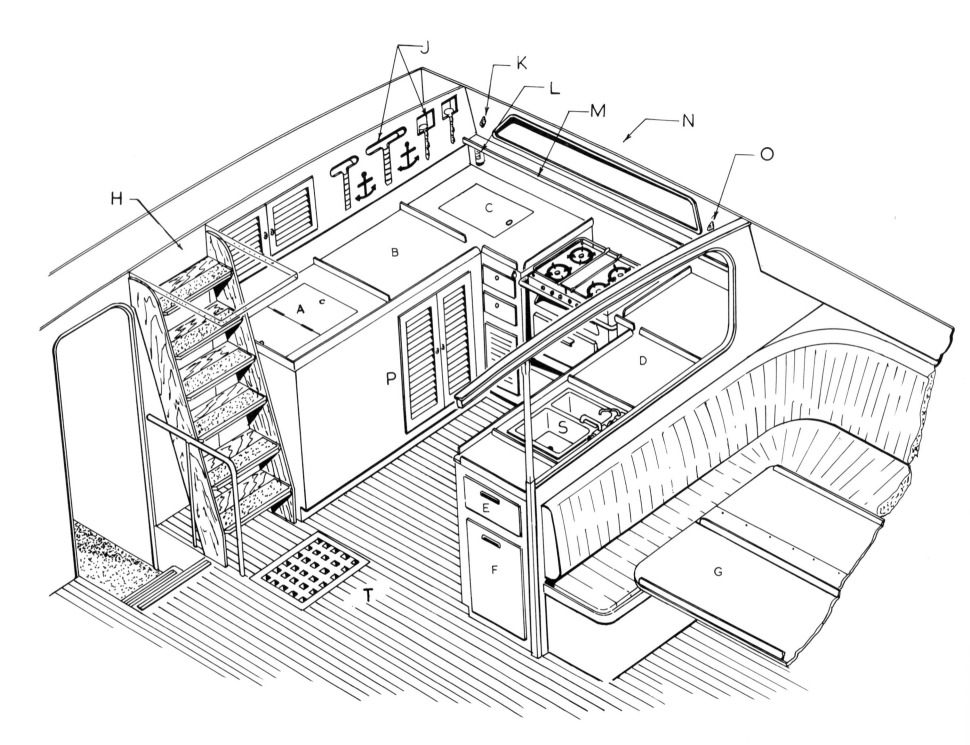

FIGURE 4.11. *The galley layout on a larger yacht features many more comforts and increased space. Here the main companionway hatch is at H. The other items are:*

A   Refrigerator/freezer.
B   Worktop.
C   Dry goods stowage.
D   Worktop.
E   Cutlery drawer.
F   Garbage pail.
G   Dining table.
J   Plate and cup stowage.
K   Padeye for cook's safety harness.
L   Fire extinguisher.
M   Shelf for herbs and small items. Shelf has fluorescent light
       under for maximum galley lighting.
N   Large port for plenty of light.
O   Second padeye for cook's harness.
P   Storage lockers for pots and pans.
T   Grating at bottom of ladder to drain excess water.
       Not obvious is the nonslip floor in the galley and the kick
space under the cabinets to allow the cook to stand close to
the worktops. A knife rack is an omission from this drawing.
I think knives are better off in a drawer, where they cannot
fly around the boat as it jumps off a wave.

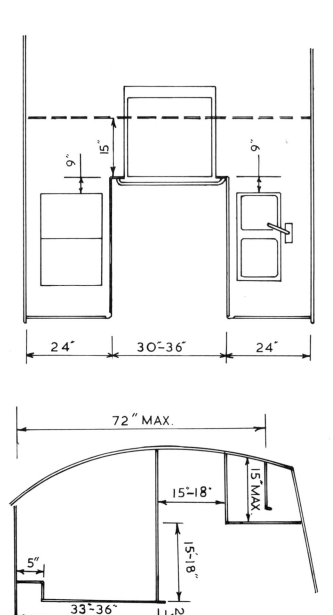

FIGURE 4.12. *Usefull dimensions for an average galley.*

THE DINING AREA

Some of my most pleasant memories of a good cruise have been formed while sitting around the dinner table. On other evenings I have sat in the cockpit or on the afterdeck of a large boat and enjoyed the evening meal with convivial companions. The dining area need not be restricted to just one part of the boat. But whatever the part of the hull that is the dining area, be it in the cockpit, near the mast, or in an aft great cabin, should be comfortable. You will be sitting there for at least 30 minutes and maybe much longer for a good repast.

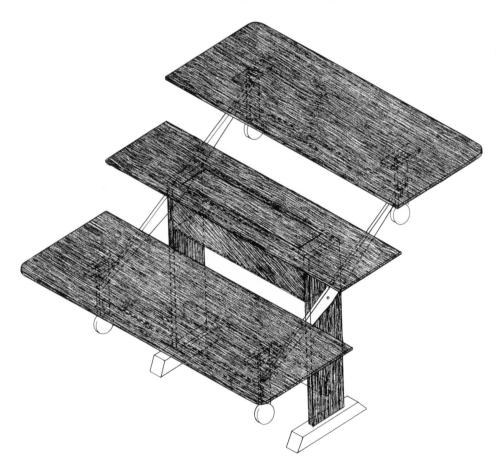

FIGURE 4.13. *A gimbaled table where each side gimbals separately is often better than a table where the whole top gimbals.*

Seats and Tables

The seat must be of a good height (usually 16–18 inches (.4–.5 meters) to the top of the cushion). The seat can be lower, but leg room will have to be increased. It should also be deep enough for you to sit back in, have a comfortable backrest, and plenty of space for each diner. I generally allow a minimum of 20 inches (.5 meters) for each diner around the table, but 24 inches (.61 meters) is better. If the boat has six bunks and potentially six crew, there should be a minimum of 120 inches of dining space around the perimeter of the table.

For use at sea the table should have sea rails (an old-time sailor once told me that fiddles were permanently fitted and sea rails could be removed), but in harbor I find they always get in the way. So they should be removable. If you have a choice of fixed or none I would choose to have none at all, because eating at sea is rather like a picnic. If you don't eat on deck, you usually sit around the table with the food in your lap to prevent it spilling, especially if there is any kind of sea running.

The armchair pundit may ask, but what about a gimbaled table? All of the types I have sailed with are heavy—it took two of us to lift *Lutine's* gimbaled table—and they don't work very well. If you sit on the weather side the table usually bangs on your knees, dumping the food in your lap on each bounce. On the leeside the table is usually about chest high, and as it hits the knees of the diners opposite your food "walks" to the other side. A better arrangement is shown in Figure 4.13, where each side of the table gimbals independently.

There are several other methods of making tables operate at more nearly horizontal levels. One is to make the height of one leg variable. Another solution is to make a table with holes in it for cups and deep bowls. If all of the above don't work you can try some of the modern nonslip cups and plates, and if they don't work simply do as I do; put the bowl of food in your lap!

The shape of the dining table and seats makes a difference to the comfort of the diners, especially in a seaway. Most boats have a settee on each side of the table. This settee can often be turned into a berth. If the table is accessible from both ends of the settee then it will be easy for people to get in and out, but often the dining area is set against a bulkhead. This requires all the occupants to get out of the seat every time the person against the bulkhead wants to move.

This also happens when the dining area is circular and the inside person wants to get out, but a circular table and seating area does have certain advantages. For instance, it is easy to find a comfortable position in a circular seat, but don't try to sleep there!

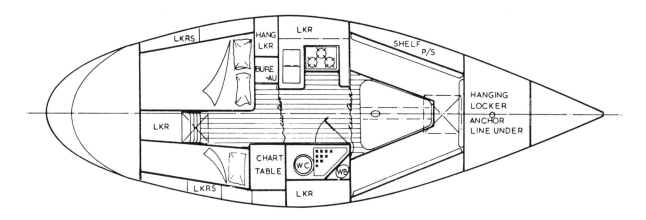

FIGURE 4.14. *The interior layout of a 32-footer showing how two cabins can be obtained by positioning the dining area well forward in the boat.*

Positioning the Dining Area

To obtain the maximum speed through the water, racing sailors try to concentrate the heaviest weights in the middle of the boat. There is no reason why the cruising sailor cannot do the same, although it need not be to the same extent. For instance, if the galley and the navigation area are put near the center of pitch, and lighter items such as the head, dining area, and berths are put further away, then pitching will be reduced. Thus, if the galley is just aft of the middle of the boat, the dining area should be positioned on one side or the other. If it is forward of the galley—the conventional position—then it is near the middle of the hull in the widest part of the boat. This gives plenty of room for a berth or locker outboard of the settee. (An outboard berth on both sides of the yacht is only practical on boats with a beam of over 12 feet (3.66 meters). That means a boat about 40 feet (12.2 meters) overall.

If the dining area is placed forward then the galley, to be near the table, must be forward of the center of the hull. This will give a bouncy ride in anything of a seaway, but on a coastal cruiser it is a way of breaking up the interior to get two "cabins." Figure 4.14 shows a 32 footer using this concept. However, the arrangement is not one I would recommend for offshore cruising, when you would have to eat while sailing.

My own preference is for a conventional type of dining area, the seating running fore and aft on both sides of the table. A boat that has seating running across the hull will usually only seat two people when the boat is heeled, both of them at the leeward end of the table, and for this reason should be avoided.

THE HEAD

All cruising boats should have a fully enclosed head with at least a W.C. and a wash basin. These are fairly common on boats as small as 24 feet (7.3 meters) today. For me these are the absolute basic requirements. I suppose the lonesome cruiser who visits faraway places will be able to make do with a bucket instead of a W.C., but have you ever tried to dump a full bucket over the side when you are anchored in the middle of a crowded harbor?

Currently, in the United States, there are legal requirements that ban you from pumping untreated sewage overboard. On inland lakes you must have a holding tank, while offshore craft must have some form of treatment (chemical or electric) between the W.C. and the seacock. These regulations make good sense for lake sailors but are almost totally unenforced and generally ignored on offshore yachts.

Who makes the best head unit? There are four manufacturers that I would rate as providing the best unit: Wilcox-Crittenden and Raritan in the United States, Simpson Lawrence and Blake in Great Britain. While Raritan offers both electric and hand-operated units, Wilcox-Crittenden offers a variety of sizes. The S.L. and Blake units are all hand operated and can be obtained in a variety of sizes.

Installation

The usual method of installation is to have a Y valve on the discharge line, which can be adjusted to pump the waste into a holding tank or overboard. There should be a vented loop on the overboard discharge to prevent the head back-filling. Also the discharge through-hull should be well aft of the intake through-hull. If it isn't, you risk recycling the waste through the head unit again.

On smaller boats, usually below 30 feet (9 meters), a portable head is often installed. The Porta Potti is probably the best known of these systems and is available from the Thetford Corporation in America. It is a two-piece, self-contained, portable unit that comes with its own fresh water tank and waste-holding tank. Its only drawback is that it has to be dragged ashore to be emptied.

If the W.C. is gimbaled, using it is fairly simple, but for most of us the unit is firmly fixed, and we must gimbal to suit it. This means the head compartment should be fairly small and have a number of strong grab rails fitted at strategic points. I also think the head should be fitted so that the user should face either inboard or fore and aft. A head fitted at an angle means you have to brace yourself against both transverse and longitudinal movement, and who can do this and strain at the same time!

The Wash Basin

The wash basin should always be fitted as far inboard as possible, or fitted with a nonreturn valve. If not it may back-fill, as shown in Figure 4.6. I also think that a foot pump should be required to pump the water into the sink. This can be in addition to pressure fresh water. If a hand pump is fitted, you either have to fill the basin—a difficult task at 30 degrees of heel—or wash one hand at a time while pumping with the other—another fairly difficult task!

The Shower

Many head compartments are fitted with a shower unit. Usually it is mounted on the wash basin and uses a long flexible cord often called a telephone shower. In many boats using the shower ensures that everything in the head gets soaked. The alternative is to have a plastic shower curtain enclosing a small area of the head. This means you must shower in a plastic tube. However, the best option is an entirely separate shower still, which can double as a place to hang wet foul weather gear. This separate compartment should also have plenty of handholds and grab rails.

Because the shape of the hull curves inward as it gets lower, the W.C. must be set well inboard, and as we saw, the wash basin is well inboard. This gives room for plenty of lockers and cabinets against the hull. If the shower unit is in the same compartment the locker doors

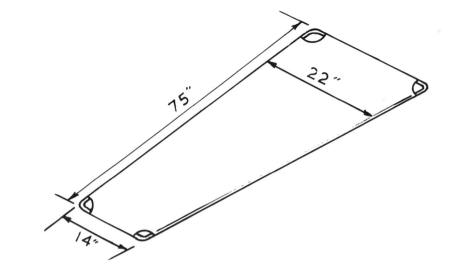

FIGURE 4.15. *The minimum dimensions of a pipe cot.*

FIGURE 4.16. *A canvas-bottomed pipe cot can have a roll-up tube on one side, which can tighten the bunk for using as a seat (solid line) or make the bunk deeper (dashed line) for use as a berth. The pin P holds the canvas at the correct position.*

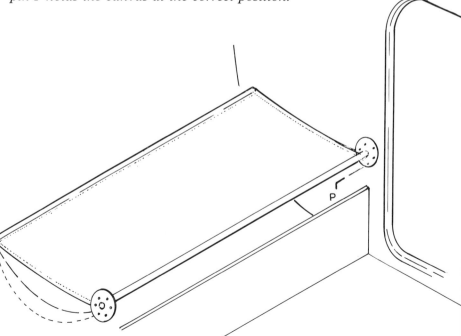

should be made as watertight as possible because it is customary to stow towels and other linens there.

Finally, because the W.C. and wash basin usually discharge through a seacock, all the plumbing should be easily accessed. The shower should drain into a sump tank. If it drains into the bilge there will soon be a greasy scum over everything and obnoxious smells coming from the bilge.

BERTHS

Nothing is quite so nice as snuggling down into a warm dry bunk after spending a wet or cold watch on deck. But if the boat's designer has not done his work properly, the bunk may be too narrow, or it might have a chainplate knee set into one side of it. Even worse, as I once saw in a production cruiser, the rod rigging might pass through the deck and through the middle of the berth. You sleep with a leg on each side of the wire, I was told. But few people actually sleep lying on their back. Also, most people, when they sleep flat on their back, snore—another feature you can do without in the confines of a small boat. So a sleeper must have room to lie comfortably in the bunk, but not so much room as to be thrown around in a seaway. I like to make the bunk about 6½ feet (2 meters) long and about 30 inches (.76 meters) wide. This is the ideal for one person. The minimum can be 22 inches (.56 meters), but 27 inches (.69 meters) wide is preferable at shoulder level and 14–16 inches (.36–.40 meters) at the foot. Minimum length is about 75 inches (1.9 meters), but only if the bunk is wider than the minimum. Figure 4.15 shows the minimum dimensions. Only very small people can be comfortable in a bunk built to the minimum size in all directions.

Bunk Construction

Bunk construction can also affect the comfort of the occupant. How often have you slept in a bunk that has bunk boards that are not quite high enough and dig into your back, or have a mattress that is so thin you can feel the bumps where the builder dripped resin on the bunk face?

There are several types of bunks available, but most production builders use a simple piece of plywood on which the mattress is placed. This is the cheapest method and works well if the mattress is at least 4 inches (100 millimeters) thick. Another style, which I think

is more comfortable, is the pipe cot, where a piece of canvas is securely lashed to the outer pipe, as in Figure 4.15. This type of bunk face can be dropped into the surrounding furniture to make a deep, comfortable berth, as shown.

Another type of bunk with a lot of appeal for the offshore cruiser is the adjustable type illustrated in Figure 4.16. This berth has a canvas bottom, which is rolled up on the tube, as shown, when in use as a seat. When the canvas is rolled up tightly the seat is flat, but when needed as a berth the canvas is unrolled and the seat makes a deep hollow which can be slept in at any angle of heel. This type together with any other canvas-bottomed berth only needs a 3-inch-thick mattress, although I have seen them used without any mattress.

One of the most comfortable berths I ever saw was on a racing boat. Each bunk had its own rail around it and was fully gimbaled. All it took was a small tackle on either side to enable the system to be adjusted to any heel angle. This style berth is illustrated in Figure 4.17.

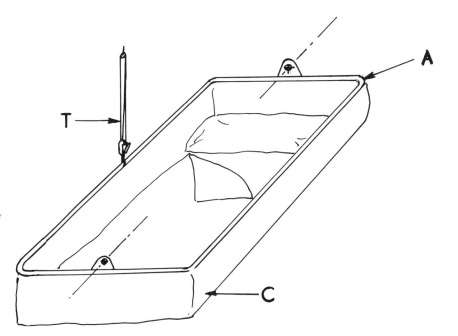

FIGURE 4.17. *By making the bunk as shown with a small tackle on either side, it can be tilted to suit the angle of heel of the boat. A is the pipe frame around the bunk. C is the canvas bunk and T is the tackle (shown on one side only).*

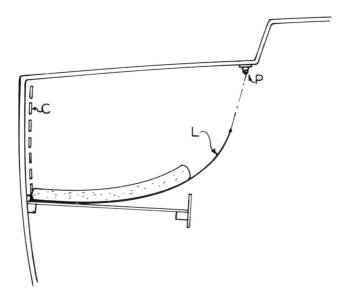

FIGURE 4.18. *If a leecloth is attached to the outboard side of the berth, pulling the leecloth tight will tip the bunk slightly, making it more comfortable for sleeping in. C is the bunk ceiling, P is a padeye, and L is the leecloth.*

FIGURE 4.19. *Cutouts in the face of a bunkboard can be very uncomfortable. The points P can dig into the occupant's back.*

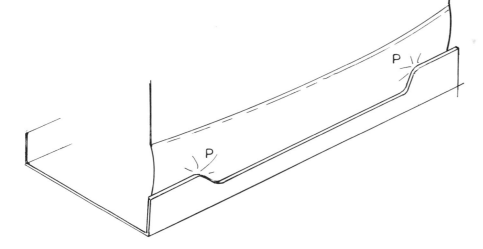

On boats without this gimbal feature the only other method to adjust for heel angle, apart from a hammock, is to use a leeboard or leecloth. I prefer leecloths that are attached on the outboard side of the berth, as in Figure 4.18. This allows you to adjust the level of the whole berth, rather than simply providing a barrier to keep you in the berth. If you intend to use leecloths, then the bunk coaming should be lower than the mattress for its entire length. Coamings with cutouts in them, as in Figure 4.19, are very uncomfortable in a seaway.

Another undesirable feature that is very prevalent is the bunk that slopes outboard, as shown in Figure 4.20. This is perfectly good while the boat is level, but when the boat is heeled 20 degrees the occupant assumes a head-down attitude, which is more likely to make them seasick. Also, after the boat bashes into a few good head seas the occupant slides into the furniture at the low end, emerging several inches shorter after a few hours off watch! The other major problem, amply demonstrated on my last wet trip to Bermuda on Bob James's *Carronade,* is that all the water drains to the low spot, which, coincidently is where your head and pillow usually are. That was the first time I ever thought it was possible to drown in the comfort of the off watch!

You may think that I have forgotten the ubiquitous "V" berth. It is not that it is forgotten, more that I chose to ignore it. Its only use is in harbor, where it is fine for the kids. But at sea it suffers from the disadvantages outlined above, plus the motion that far forward in the boat is usually bouncy and occasionally quite violent, rendering the berth untenable in anything of a seaway.

Bedding

Having slept in everything from conventional beds and bedding to a bathtub wrapped in a spinnaker, I think I could qualify as an expert in what is comfortable bedding. My personal preference even on a boat is cotton sheets and woolen blankets. But these are not often available. Next best thing is a sleeping bag with a cotton liner. I don't recommend a nylon or polyester sleeping bag, as they seem to hold moisture and you wake up feeling like you have been sleeping in a sauna.

Sometimes there isn't enough bedding. For instance, you've had friends to dinner aboard and they've drunk too much to drive home. The best, and most comfortable, sleeping place I ever found was in the spinnaker, as long as the swivel at the top of the sail is carefully placed at the bottom of the bunk.

I like to have a pillow, but pillows stuffed with feathers and boats do not get along. I have seen a crew looking like he lived in a henhouse when he exuberantly jumped into his bunk and landed on the down-stuffed pillow. Finally, there should be somewhere to store pillows when they are not in use. They seem to be the first item to fall off an unused bunk. Next to a bunk there should also be some form of storage space for small personal items, such as a watch, loose change, or a wallet. Quite often this can be a small plastic bag with a loop to hang on the bunk light or netting fastened against the hull side or under the bunk over head.

NAVIGATION AREAS

Ask any navigator what he wants in a navigation area and his requirements will probably be few—a place large enough to lay out a chart, plus space to stow the tools and books of his trade. The problem is that the modest needs a navigator might list off the top of his head are seldom all he really requires. When it comes to laying out a navigation area, a designer must consider much more. The final list looks something like this:

1. An adequate-size chart table.
2. A place to keep charts, preferably unrolled.
3. Stowage for small tools, such as pencils, dividers, parallel rules, so that they will be easy to locate.
4. Stowage for flags and the sextant.
5. A comfortable and safe place to sit.
6. Ample book stowage.
7. Places for the depth sounder, Loran or RDF, speedometer, log, radio telephone, and other electronic gear.
8. Good ventilation, easy access to the cockpit, and good lighting.

Here we'll consider each of these needs and how they might be met on different-sized boats.

The Chart Table

Most navigators would like a chart table big enough to lay out an unfolded chart. But the majority of boats do not have this kind of space, unless the dining table is also used as a chart table. A compro-

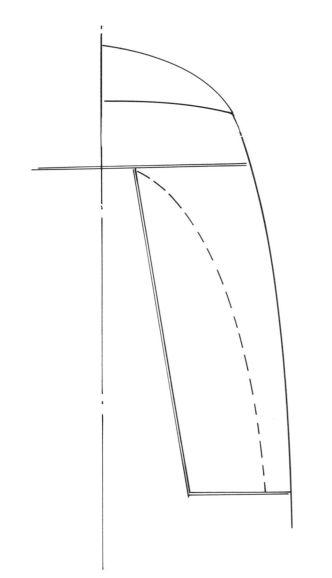

FIGURE 4.20. *When a bunk is tucked into the quarter of the boat, it generally slopes with the head end outboard. When the bunk heels to leeward this end pitches downward, resulting in an uncomfortable sleeping position. It would be better to make this bumk parallel to the centerline of the boat.*

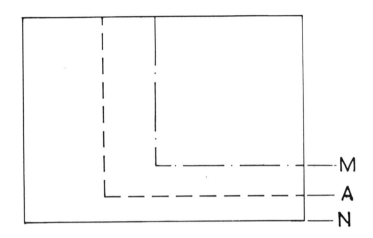

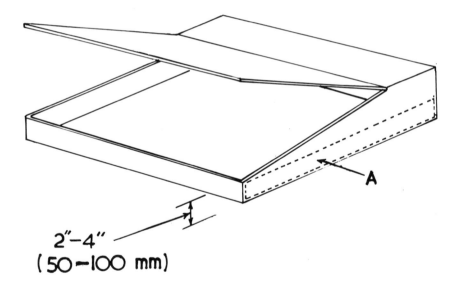

mise must, therefore, be made, which usually means folding the chart to fit the table.

Since the largest charts are approximately 42 × 30 inches, a reasonably sized chart table would be 24 × 30 inches (.6 × .76 meters). The minimum-sized table would be 20 × 20 inches (.5 × .5 meters), but this makes for cramped navigation, which could lead to errors. Figure 4.21 shows these dimensions. Remember that a good navigation table should have a little extra space to put tools, coffee cups, and so on, so that they are not on top of the chart. (Navigating through a coffee stain can be chancey at best!) Note also that a good-sized fiddle—2 inches (50 millimeters) on the sides of the table and ¾ inch (19–20 millimeters) on the front—will keep the navigator's pencils on the table.

FIGURE 4.22.   *Where extra drawers are needed they could be positioned under the nav area, as in this sketch.*

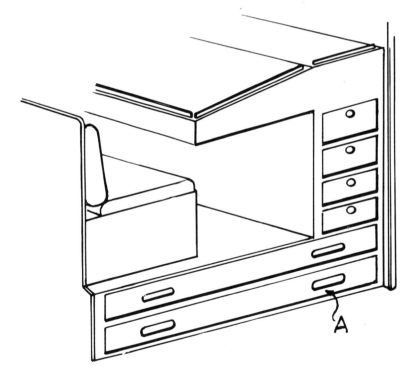

FIGURE 4.21.   *The dimensions of a navigator's table. M is the minimum at 20 × 20 inches (508 × 508 mm). A the average table size 30 × 24 inches (760 × 610 mm), and N the maximum table size 36 × 30 inches (914 × 760 mm). The maximum depth of the table should not be more than 2–4 inches (50–100 mm) to allow the navigator to get his knees under the bunk. If there is no room to allow the table to open as shown, a drawer could be fitted at A.*

FIGURE 4.23. *A picture or deckhead rack can serve as an extra storage space for charts. D is the deck and C is the retaining chain.*

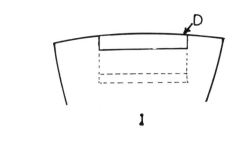

1

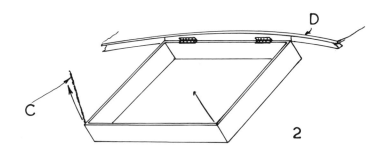

2

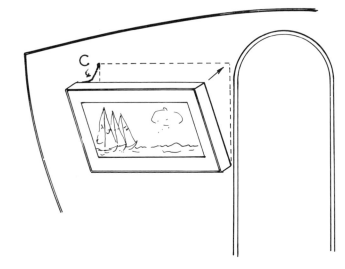

3

Chart Stowage

Most chart tables are made with a lifting lid so that the charts can be stowed in the compartment below. Such a stowage area should be at least 2 inches (50 millimeters) deep, but no more than 4 inches (100 millimeters) (any deeper makes it impossible to get one's knees under the table comfortably). Figure 4.21 shows a typical arrangement. Where space permits, special drawers can be designed as part of the chart table stand or under a berth, as in Figure 4.22. If chart stowage space is extremely limited, then the designer could be called upon to design a wall-mounted rack, or even a deckhead rack in the forepeak. Figure 4.23 illustrates some of these options.

Stowage for Small Tools

A rack for pencils, dividers, triangles, parallel rules, and the like neatly solves the problem of stowing small tools. When designing the bulkhead cutout in front of the chart table, make sure enough space is left to fit such a rack, as shown in Figure 4.24.

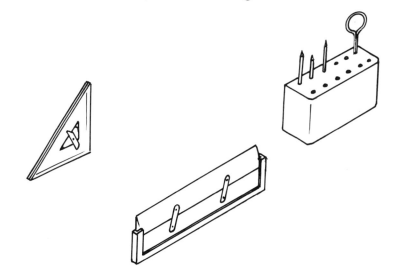

FIGURE 4.24. *Stowage for small items of equipment is essential for the navigator. Pencils can be stowed in a rack. The parallel rules should have a special place to stop their edges being damaged. If you use triangles they could be stowed on a small block on the underside of the nav table lid.*

Stowage for Flags, Sextant, Foghorn, and Larger Tools

Unfortunately, many designers seem to forget that larger pieces of navigation equipment must also be stowed. Others simply assume that the navigator's seat will accommodate everything. It is much better for an owner to give the designer a list of the large items he intends to have aboard and have stowage compartments specially designed to suit them.

A Place To Sit

A comfortable seat for the navigator is one of the most frequently neglected aspects of a navigation area. Usually, the navigator's seat is hard and perfectly flat. Comfort can be greatly enhanced simply by adding some cushions, and it can be further enhanced by giving the seat some radius, so that as the boat heels the navigator can sit on the high part.

Of course, this design idea is impractical if the navigator's seat is the top part of the berth. On smaller boats, where space is at a premium, this type of seating arrangement often works well. There is a problem, however, for the sleeper—his pillow usually slides off the seat! A simple flap, as shown in Figure 4.25, can eliminate this aggravation.

On larger boats the navigator's seat can be a specially built, deep, comfortable chair that reclines, swivels, and gimbals. With this type of seat the navigator will often sleep or doze at his table. On long, hazardous voyages this extra dimension of comfort might make a big difference to the navigator's performance.

A final requirement to remember when designing a seat for the navigator is safety. A harness should always be fitted so that the navigator can work in comfort without having to wedge himself in place.

Book Stowage

All navigators have a library, and some of the books are quite large. *Playboy,* for instance, is almost 12 inches high, and some tidal atlases are even larger. A rack for navigation books should be a minimum of 8 inches (200 millimeters) deep, if possible 12 inches (300 millimeters), and it should be at least 10 inches (250 millimeters) and up to 15 inches (380 millimeters) high, if space allows. A book stowage area should also have some form of removable retaining bar across the front to hold the books in place. And of course, it should be within reach of the navigator.

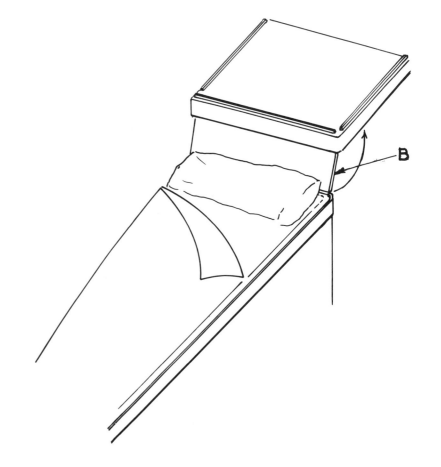

FIGURE 4.25. *A simple board hinging down from under the nav table can stop the navigator's pillow from falling on the cabin sole.*

Places for Electronic Instruments

Once again, the owner should provide the designer with a list of instruments he intends to have aboard. It is then up to the designer to ensure that the locker he designates for electronics is deep enough not only to fit the instruments but also to allow for the connections that often plug into the back of Loran or radio telephone sets. As with everything else in a navigation area, easy access is important. All the instruments the navigator must operate should be positioned so that he can reach them while seated.

When positioning the electronic navigation instruments, try to put the most used ones, or sets with a readout, for instance the Loran or log, directly in front of the navigator with backup, or sets with a dial—RDF, radio, and so forth—off to one side. Remember, though, that the navigator's compass should be placed well away from any instruments that might generate a magnetic field.

Power supplies to electronic equipment are sometimes not considered when designing this area, with the result that at about 3:30 A.M. the engine has to be started to charge the batteries. Obviously battery size should be determined at the design stage, not at sea! This is another reason why an owner should provide the designer with a comprehensive list of electronic equipment.

Ventilation, Access to the Cockpit, and Lighting

Because the navigator spends so much of his time below deck, the navigation area must have good ventilation. A stuffy navigatorium can lead to headaches and nausea, with detrimental effect on performance. I like to allow a 5- or 6-inch (125- or 150-millimeter) dorade-type vent for the navigation area. Another form of ventilation that can be put to good use is an opening port. If this is designed to open into the cockpit, then the navigator can also use it for communication with the helmsman.

Lighting is another detail that is often left to the builder. Consequently, usually the navigators end up with flexi-light and an overhead dome. But a good set of specifications should call for at least one overhead red light and, if possible, a red light over the instrument console. Another not often thought of light is a red light inside the navigation table. All too often the navigator has to put the overhead white light on because the interior of the nav table is shaded by the lifting top. The light can easily be installed so that lifting the nav table lid turns it on.

Positioning the Navigatorium

All the previous points must be carefully considered if the navigator is to work efficiently. Yet even the most careful attention to the details of storage, seating, lighting, and so forth will be of little benefit if the navigatorium is poorly positioned in the boat or gets a large dollop of spray over it every time the hatch is opened. For instance, a navigation station in the forepeak is uninhabitable in a seaway and makes for difficult communications at any time. In my experience, good

access to the navigator's area from above deck and easy communication with the people in the cockpit are major considerations. These argue for positioning the navigation area toward the stern of the boat. Furthermore, if the navigation area is opposite the galley, it can provide structural advantages. For instance, the galley and navigation station bulkheads can be spaced symmetrically on either side of the boat, thus increasing structural rigidity.

Another consideration when positioning a navigation area is the direction in which it faces. This is really up to the individual navigator. Some like to look outboard, while others prefer to face forward or aft. Nevertheless, the choice made can influence the rest of the interior arrangement. Figure 4.26 shows a typical navigation station facing the cockpit.

It is from a series of small and large decisions like these that the navigation area gets its special character. By carefully considering each item, an efficient, workable station can be designed that will greatly speed the navigator's work and allow him to enjoy the cruise.

STORAGE AREAS

It always seems that the smallest boats need the most storage, but in practice, as the boat shrinks so the storage areas get even smaller. Tanks fill the lockers under the settee. The bilge vanishes under the weight of hoses and floors, and the lazarette and bow lockers become even more minute as accommodation is pushed farther and farther into the ends of the boat.

There are, however, many unusual places that can enhance existing storage in the boat. Let's look first at some of the more often used areas and then see how odd spaces can be put to work.

The Lazarette

This is usually the area in the extreme aft of the boat. Access is usually via hatch, either aft of the cockpit or sometimes part of the helmsman's seat.

In many boats the steering gear quadrant is only reachable through the lazarette. This means that the hatch must be large enough to allow a man through—16 × 16 inches (400 × 400 millimeters) is the bare minimum, with 18 × 18 inches (460 × 460 millimeters) a better solution. If other gear, such as warps and fenders, are to be stowed

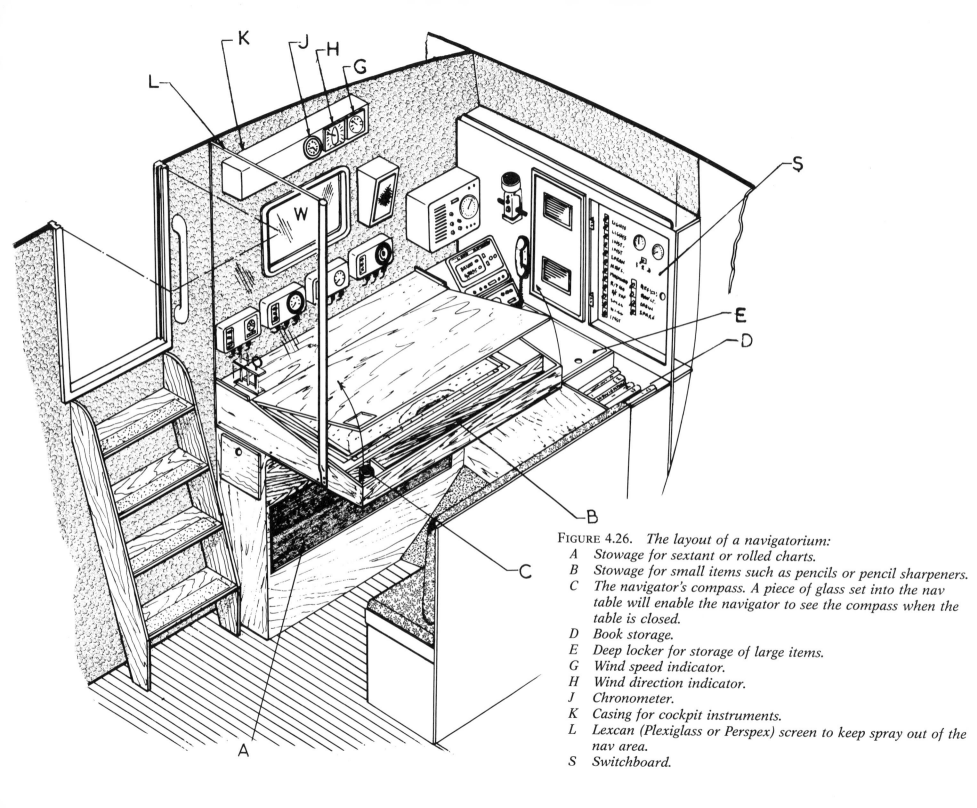

FIGURE 4.26. *The layout of a navigatorium:*
A   *Stowage for sextant or rolled charts.*
B   *Stowage for small items such as pencils or pencil sharpeners.*
C   *The navigator's compass. A piece of glass set into the nav table will enable the navigator to see the compass when the table is closed.*
D   *Book storage.*
E   *Deep locker for storage of large items.*
G   *Wind speed indicator.*
H   *Wind direction indicator.*
J   *Chronometer.*
K   *Casing for cockpit instruments.*
L   *Lexcan (Plexiglass or Perspex) screen to keep spray out of the nav area.*
S   *Switchboard.*

in the lazarette, then there must be some partition or guard to keep the stored gear out of the steering mechanism.

Often running through the lazarette are exhaust lines—from the engine and the battery. These must be insulated as needed.

Cockpit Lockers

To my mind one of the most important features of a cruising boat is a good set of cockpit lockers. These should be large enough to stow sails in, yet small enough to take winch handles, shackles, and spare blocks. There are several places for them—under the coaming, under the seats, in a winch base, and more. When designing the cockpit it can pay to think out carefully where an extra locker can be fitted— even if it only holds one winch handle.

Hanging Lockers

As their name implies, hanging lockers are used to hang clothes, but so often clothes must be squashed in on an angle because the locker simply isn't large enough. The average clothes hanger is 16 inches (400 millimeters) long. This means that the locker must be at least 18 inches (460 millimeters) wide, although 20 inches (510 millimeters) is a better size. Another detail in hanging lockers is that the clothes rod is often run fore and aft, when athwartship may be better. Figure 4.27 shows a typical detail.

Foul Weather Gear Lockers

Hanging lockers and foul weather gear lockers are often interchangeable. But a good wet locker has features not found in a hanging locker. When designing a wet locker, the following points should be taken into account:

1. The locker is going to be full of wet oilskins. Therefore, allow plenty of space.
2. Try to position the locker near the engine, so that the heat, when the motor is run, will help dry the clothes.
3. There should be a grating in the bottom of the locker to allow the oilskins to drain into the bilge.

4. In the specifications, call for plenty of hooks around inside the locker so that wet clothes do not have to be placed on top of one another, or on top of dry clothes.
5. The locker should have plenty of ventilation.
6. It should have a boot rack in the bottom of the locker if boots are not stored anywhere else.

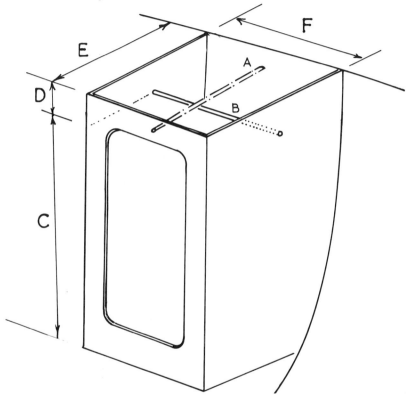

FIGURE 4.27. *The minimum hanging locker sizes:*
C   35 inches (890 mm) for jackets, 55 inches (1.4 M) for long dresses or coats.
D   2 inches (50 mm) minimum, but is better at 4 inches (100 mm).
E and F—As hangers are 16 inches (406 mm) long, this should be 17 inches (430 mm) minimum, but 18 or 20 inches (457 or 508 mm) is better. The locker should be as long as possible in the direction the hanging rod runs to ensure storage for the maximum number of clothes.

Chain Lockers

Storing chain and anchor line is always a problem. A large amount of chain in the bow of the boat can give excessive bow-down trim, especially if the anchors and a windlass are also positioned forward. An owner desiring this equipment should tell the designer early enough for this extra weight to be incorporated into the hull design and keel position.

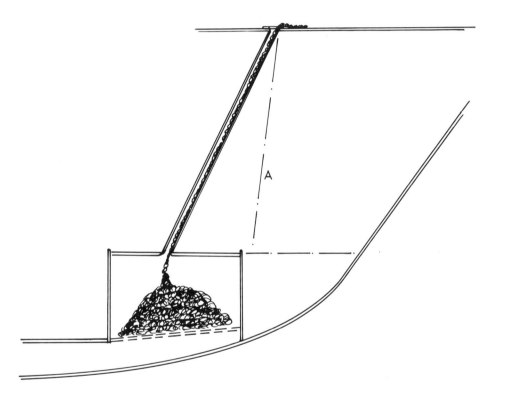

FIGURE 4.28. *The anchor locker can be quite heavy when it is full of chain. This weight up in the bow at position A (shown dashed) is not good for the performance of the boat; by sloping the hawse pipe aft, the locker can be pushed further aft.*

Because of this potential for a trim problem the anchor locker should be pushed as far aft as possible; around the mast is ideal. Figure 4.28 shows how the locker can be pushed aft.

When designing the chain locker, remember that it must be large enough! Many of the chain and cable manufacturers have booklets or leaflets that tell you how much space a given amount of chain will take up. Also remember that this chain is coming down a hawse pipe and will pile up below the pipe. Some facility for access to the locker to distribute the chain should be provided. When designing a hawse pipe make sure it is wide enough to take the chain *plus* any shackles or thimbles that join the anchor line and chain. Even the bottom of the locker should be carefully designed with a slight slope to help redistribute the chain. It should also have enough holes to allow the chain to drain either into the bilge or overside.

The following formulae can be used to approximate the size of the anchor locker:

$$\text{Non-self-stowing chain } D^2 2 \times 35.6 \times 100 = V \text{ in ft}^3 \text{ fathoms}$$
$$\text{Self-stowing chain } (L \times D^2 \times 1.7)/2 = V \text{ in ft}^3, \text{ where}$$
$$L = \text{fathoms}$$
$$D = \text{diameter of chain in inches.}$$

The Bilge

The lowest part of the boat naturally has everything draining into it. But it can be used as a storage area for heavy items such as engine oil cans, spare chain, larger cans of food, and even bottles if they are protected against breakage. If a designer intends this area to be used for storage, he should ensure that the storage areas and limber holes are large enough so that the flow of water to the bilge pump is not inhibited.

Under-Bunk Stowage Areas

Almost all boats utilize the areas under bunks for storage. Unfortunately, access to these areas is often designed with very little thought. On a settee/berth, for instance, access is usually through the top of the locker by removing the cushion. If the berth is occupied, the sleeper has to be turned out until the required gear is found. A better solution is for a flap or drawer to be designed into the front of the structure, as in Figure 4.29d.

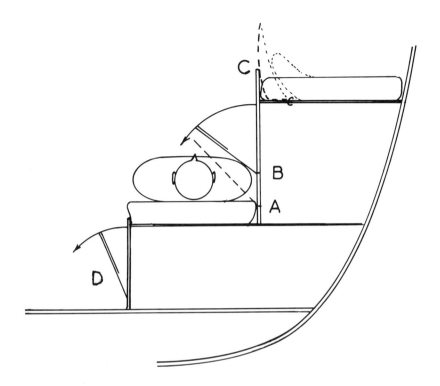

FIGURE 4.29. *Access to lockers under berths is best from the side as shown at D. If access has to be gained into the upper locker, then the opening will be better at B rather than at A, where it would disturb the offwatch sleeper. C shows how a leeboard can be used to raise the corner of the berth for easier sleeping.*

In the upper berth the problem is somewhat more complex. The locker doors are usually in the front of the structure, but the sleeper in the lower berth is still disturbed when a crewman wants to get into a locker. Figure 4.29 shows one possible solution.

In the quarter berths, often the only access is through the top of the locker. Therefore, it is up to the owner to put items that are not often used here. After all, this is usually his berth!

There are other areas large enough for lockers—around the chainplates for instance. A good designer will try to use as many of these places as possible without intruding on the remainder of the interior.

INTERIOR TRIM, LIGHTING, AND VENTILATION

Although the final interior colors and finishes are not usually part of the designer's decisions, he is sometimes asked to advise on these details. A good designer will know what finishes and fabrics will create the interior style the owner is looking for.

Fabrics

When selecting a fabric, there are a few points that should be kept in mind:

1. Select a fabric that is mildew and rot resistant unless you intend the owner to wash them a lot.
2. Try to get a stain-resistant material.
3. The fabric should also be flame-retardant.
4. Heavy fabrics hold water longer and stay wet longer than light.
5. For mattresses, a smooth-surfaced material is more comfortable than a knobbly one.
6. Pick something that is hard-wearing if possible. Many of the manmade fibers fulfill these requirements. Others, such as cotton-based materials, may not meet all the requirements, but their drawbacks are not enough to prevent using them.

Trim and Wood Finishes

Wooden bulkheads and trim can have a major influence on whether the interior is dark and dismal or bright and cheery. The design stage is the time to take a look at the available alternatives.

Mahogany and teak are the usual finishes, but birch, cedar, or oak can give a lighter more airy look, while cherry, walnut, butternut, mahogany, and teak all give a darker look. These darker woods can also be used to highlight a lighter wood. For instance, a birch or cedar bulhead can be trimmed with teak if the designer wants to accent the edges. An alternative is to use a mahogany bulkhead with birch or ash as edge trim. This achieves a lightly trimmed effect. With a little thought a very different look can be obtained at a cost equal to or less than a similar teak unit. Interior trim should be the owner's decision, and he may choose to use any of these woods. In this case, the more unusual ones may have to be specially veneered for use on bulkheads. Alternatively, a lighter, less expensive wood could be used and stained to obtain a darker finish.

There are many ways of finishing wood. The more usual is either oil or a gloss or satin varnish, but paint, melamine, polymer coatings, and glued-on cloth finish have also been used successfully.

Countertops and even tabletops should be made of some form of heat- and scratch-resistant materials. The usual is a plastic laminate, but various resins and epoxies give an adequate surface. They are not very heat resistant, but they do allow the beauty of the wood grain to show. I have seen earthenware tiles used, but for me they have a heavy, slightly ungainly appearance. Even so, a few tiles in the right place could provide a unique accent to the galley.

Surfaces, such as the insides of lockers, wooden floors, and the hidden parts of bulkheads, should be treated with a wood preservative. This will reduce the chances of mildew and rot.

None of these items—fabrics, finishes, and preservatives—are shown on the plans. This is why a good set of specifications is a necessity if the boat is to be built the way it was intended.

The Use of Color

Colors, when carefully matched with attractive wood, can make the interior of even the worst-built boat look attractive. Once again, there are some basic rules that should be followed for the best effect.

First, use colors in a restrained manner unless you intend covering vast areas of white plastic.

Lighter colors generally make the interior seem spacious and airy. So if you are working on the interior of a small boat, use light colors. Conversely, dark colors will visually reduce the size of a compartment.

When using colors try to use the wood grain, white, and one or two other basic colors. More than two basic colors will start to make the interior look uncoordinated. If you, as the designer, actually have to specify colors, remember that colors from the red side of the spectrum tend to complement natural wood colors and will make the interior look warm and cheery. These are probably good colors to use on boats intended to sail in northern, colder waters.

Blues, greens, and colors from that side of the spectrum make interiors look cooler and must be used carefully; they would be best suited to interiors where the boat will sail mostly in the tropics.

Often the exterior of boats with high freeboard is disguised by longitudinal stripes. This same technique can be used successfully inside the boat. For example, stripes running along a berth can make that berth appear longer—until a tall person gets in! If stripes are run vertically, they will make the object appear taller, while horizontal stripes make it appear shorter.

By using these simple rules a designer can specify the products that will display the interior of the boat to its best advantage.

Lighting and Ventilation

Boats that are badly ventilated and poorly lit usually have a short life because rot, mildew, and odors all thrive in this type of environment and detract from the charm of what might be an extremely good sailing boat.

Both light and ventilation can be provided in various ways—by opening ports, by clear, plastic-topped dorade boxes, or by tannoy-type vents. Light can be admitted by clear or smoked glass fixed ports, deck prisms, or simple plexiglass panels set into the deck. Where privacy and light are required, tinted plexiglass or perspex can be used. At the design stage, the designer should consider natural, passive ventilation as well as the better-known dorade-type vents. Carefully sited bow vents, hatches, and louvered doors can give a natural through-flow even when nobody is aboard.

How much ventilation is good? This decision must rest with the individual designer. A boat that sails in a cold area will probably have less than a boat in a hot area. Mechanical ventilation should be provided in the head and in the galley, and the fan should be of the reversible type.

It is by paying careful attention to the small details that make up the interior arrangement that a boat becomes a warm, comfortable environment rather than a cold, damp place in which to crawl when darkness falls.

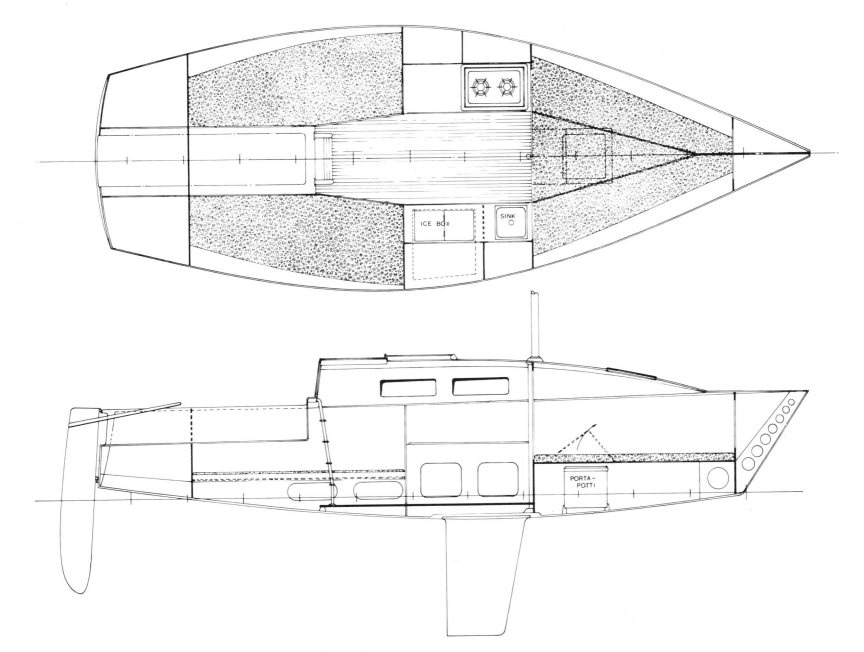

Design Number 18. *The accommodation plan for this hull is very basic and designed around the longitudinal members, which give the hull additional stiffness.*

ICE BOX

SINK

PORTA-
POTTI

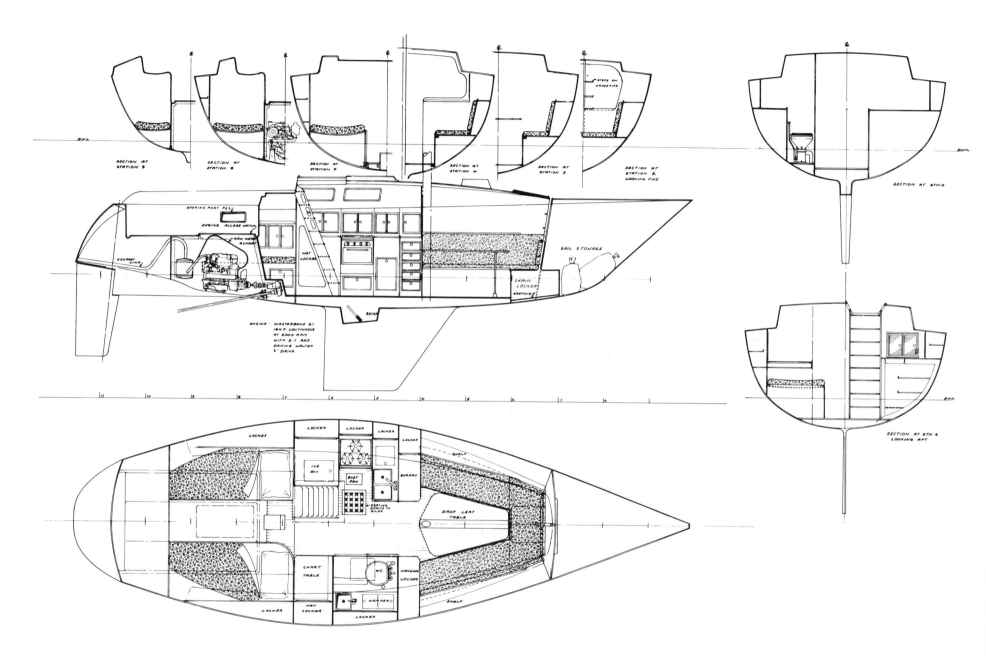

Design Number 37. *The interior layout of this boat has the dining area well forward in order to divide the boat into two cabins.*

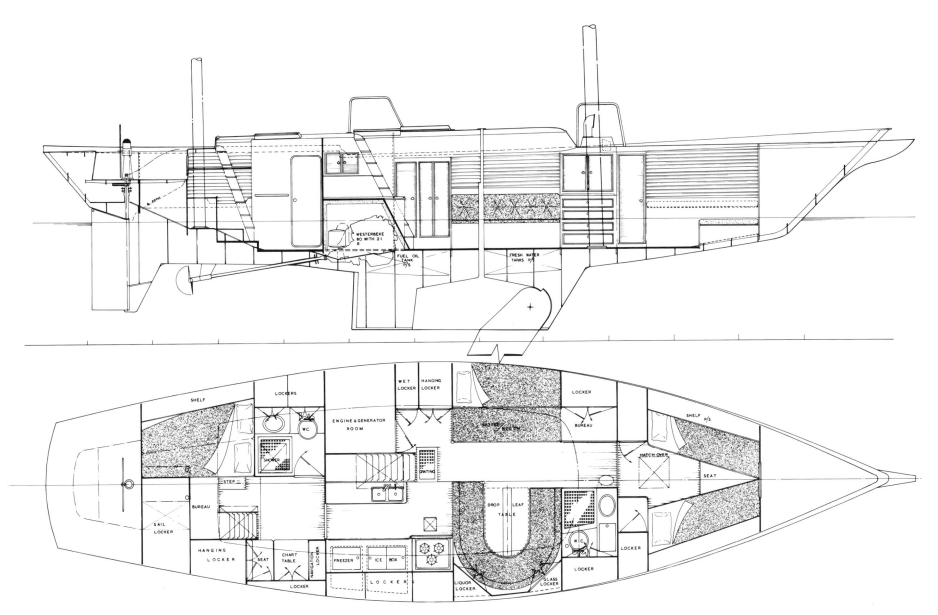

Design Number 26. *The accommodation plan of a 49-foot ketch intended for shorthanded offshore cruising and for entertaining a number of people when in port. The unique features of this arrangement are the large aft cabin with the chart table to starboard. Forward of this is the galley, which opens onto a large U-shaped dining area.*

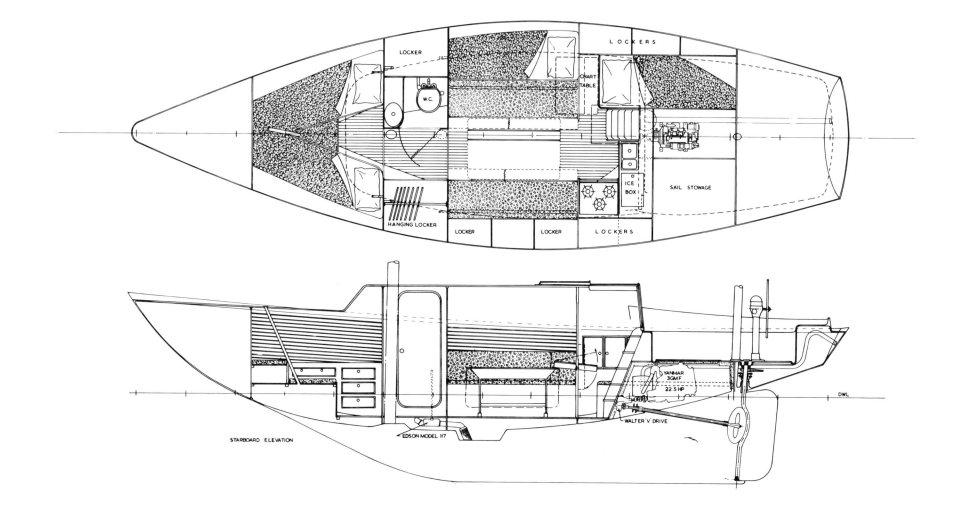

LOCKER

LOCKERS

CHART
TABLE

W.C.

ICE
BOX

SAIL STOWAGE

HANGING LOCKER

LOCKER

LOCKER

LOCKERS

YANMAR
3GMF
22.5 HP

WALTER 'V' DRIVE

DWL

STARBOARD ELEVATION

EDSON MODEL 117

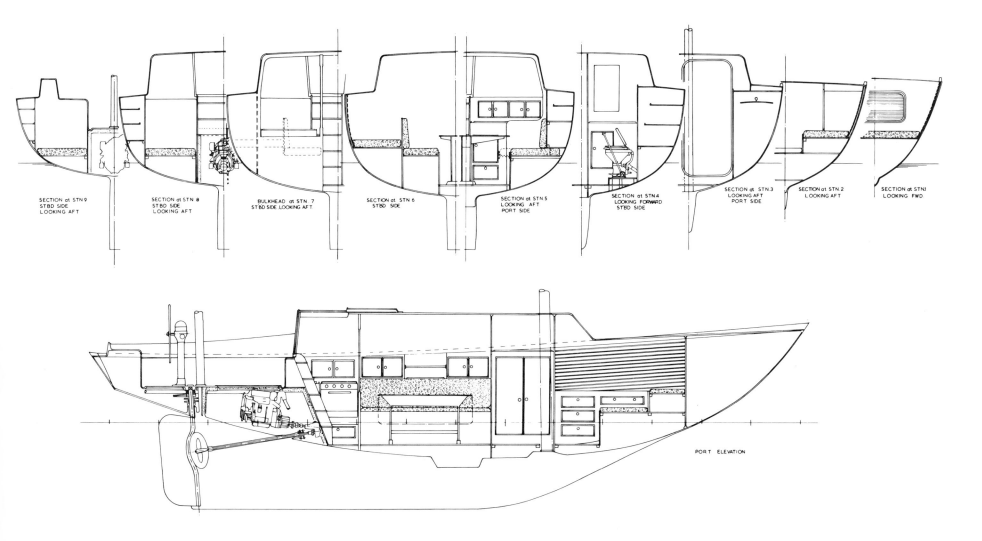

SECTION at STN 9
ST'BD SIDE
LOOKING AFT

SECTION at STN 8
ST'BD SIDE
LOOKING AFT

BULKHEAD at STN 7
ST'BD SIDE LOOKING AFT

SECTION at STN 6
ST'BD SIDE

SECTION at STN 5
LOOKING AFT
PORT SIDE

SECTION at STN 4
LOOKING FORWARD
ST'BD SIDE

SECTION at STN 3
LOOKING AFT
PORT SIDE

SECTION at STN 2
LOOKING AFT

SECTION at STN 1
LOOKING FWD

PORT ELEVATION

Design Number 39. *The left and right sides of the interior of this design give the builder very accurate information for preparing the interior fittings. The arrangement is reasonably simple and can sleep four people. The sections show how each side fits together and adds additional accuracy to the drawing.*

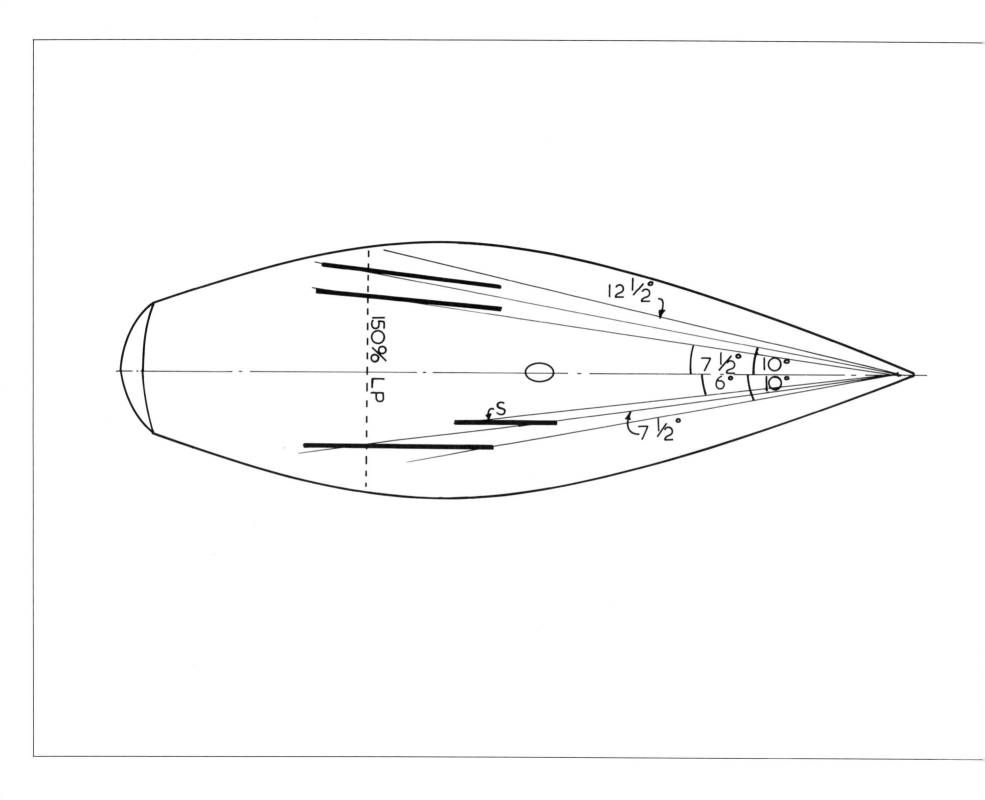

CHAPTER 5

The Cruising Deck

On a cruising boat the deck layout has a lower priority than the deck of an ocean racer. According to one cruising friend the deck is a place to sunbathe. He's right—to some extent—but the deck should be capable of much more.

The deck is the top of the main cabin and, therefore, should be watertight and provide headroom below. It will carry the sheet tracks, winches, and other gear used to trim the sails. It should provide a place to stow the dinghy, to sunbathe, a place for the crew to have a meal in good weather or to take shelter from the elements in bad weather.

In sum, it has to do many things, all of them well, and all without compromising other features of the yacht. Consequently, many decks are poorly laid out. This is unfortunate because it leads to poor performance in many areas, and poor performance can lead to frustration on the part of the crew. There is no reason why a cruising deck cannot be laid out efficiently. All it requires is some attention to detail and a knowledge of how sails, rig, and deck gear interact.

The jobs a deck must be capable of performing can be thought of as different pieces that will later be integrated into a complete deck, somewhat like we did with the interior layout. An obvious primary feature is the basic deck. This covers the position of the cockpits and how they are laid out, the position of the mast and edges of the cabin. All the features that are positioned by the interior of the boat. Chain lockers, the lazarette, and the position of the rudder stock are all parts of what I call the basic deck. All these items are set by other features on the boat and are unalterable, or alterable only with some difficulty.

Next would be the functions performed on the deck. For instance, one of the primary jobs done on deck is sail trim. To make the sails work as efficiently as possible requires the use of various tracks, travelers, and winches. In this section we should also look at how sails work and any special equipment needed for each sail.

Then we should consider other functions of the deck—as an anchor-handling platform, as a place for the dinghy and liferaft—and how the boat is moored when not in use.

Having looked at the functions that need to be performed on deck, we should see how they can be done with maximum safety and comfort. Other features of lesser importance, but those that could be considered an essential part of cruising, are large open spaces to sunbathe, a sheltered cockpit for temperate climes, a dodger or a Bimini top for tropical areas, and comfortable side decks to make the walk forward easy and safe.

THE BASIC DECK

The basic deck unit is the area above the sheerline that encompasses the cockpit, coamings, bulwarks, handrails, hatch recesses, and the host of other foundations that make it easier to position sail-handling gear. It can even be considered to encompass the transom and any steps or stowage that might be molded into it.

The Cockpit

The cockpit on a long-distance offshore cruiser will be completely different from the cockpit designed for a comfortable inshore day sailor. The first type should be small, in case it gets filled during a storm, whereas the second can be very large because its main function is to hold as many people as possible and let them spread out to enjoy the sail. There can also be other uses and types of cockpit. Let's look at some of them and see which is best for your sailing.

Mid or Aft Cockpit: Which Is Better?

I've noticed that, in general, sailors who've done some serious ocean racing prefer aft cockpit layouts, while those who look at their boat as a place for fun and pleasure—their floating condominium—prefer the center cockpit craft. This is only a general observation, but it tends to illustrate the seaworthiness of the aft cockpit boat, where the crew feel as if they are "down in the hull" rather than being perched on top.

In spite of this, center cockpits do have some nice features. I recently sailed on a Bristol 41 where the mid-deck cockpit was superbly integrated with the rest of the design. But even then, when I was steering I found myself reaching to catch hold of the lifelines, which were, of course, out of reach. I also felt slightly exposed perched high up in the middle of the boat.

In general, however, mid cockpits are very spacious and comfortable. With a dodger and side screens they can easily be enclosed to add an extra dimension to living aboard, but note that a mid-cockpit layout requires a boat over 32 feet to work well. When the companionway is in the middle of the boat the center cockpit makes it easier to get up and down the companionway ladder, plus they naturally break up the interior, allowing the designer to fit a comfortable private stateroom aft of the cockpit. The back end of the boat is made much more spacious by a center cockpit. If you don't want a comfortable aft cabin, then a large dining area can be designed in or even two smaller cabins.

But this type of cockpit is high, raising the center of gravity of the boat, and while it provides good all-around visibility, there is still the feeling of being perched high up on top of the boat. With the trend toward high freeboard and a high center cockpit, stability has to be examined carefully.

The Aft Cockpit

Most sailors like to feel that they are protected in some way from the elements by a reasonably deep cockpit in which they can cower when the tops are whipped off the waves and the rain is almost horizontal.

Aft cockpits provide some of this protection, but they spoil the accommodation in the aft end of the boat. Usually only a quarter berth or sail locker can be fitted in the area of an aft cockpit, although the latest trend is to fit a double berth under the cockpit. To make it fit comfortably, the cockpit must be raised slightly so that headroom is limited. Many don't even have room for your mistress to sit up, and sex is possible only if you are a contortionist. Also, a number of builders are using this feature to rejuvenate old tooling. By adjusting the cockpit sole level they are rearranging the cabin layout to get an additional berth, usually a double, under the cockpit. Quite often the only headroom possible is on the extreme outboard side of the bunk. In any case, most cabins on boats under 40 feet tend to be small and cramped, but they do provide some privacy and separation from the remainder of the crew.

So, once again, we find that the type of sailing you do restricts the options available. In this case, where the cockpit is sited. Offshore sailors generally like it to be reasonably small and aft, while inshore cruisers like a larger cockpit area and are willing to accept a mid-deck position if it gives them a better arrangement.

The Offshore Cockpit

The offshore cockpit should be small and comfortable. It may need to be drained quickly and should have large drains. The offshore racing fleet has a rule it might be worth following. It restricts the total cockpit volume to 6 percent of L × B × FA, where L, B, and FA are the IOR approximations for length, beam, and freeboard at the aft corner of the transom. For cruising boats, the LWL, beam, and freeboard aft can easily be substituted. This would give a slightly smaller cockpit than the racers, but usually a cruising boat will have less crew. For boats that stay reasonably close to shore, this volume could be increased to about 10 percent, but I would hesitate to go much larger unless there were some special reason.

The seat length of a cockpit should be a minimum of 6½ feet (approximately 2 meters) to enable a crew to sleep in the cockpit. The maximum width of the well should not be more than 2 feet (.61 meters), to allow crew sitting on the windward side to brace their legs against the leeward seat. The seatbacks should be a minimum of 1½ feet (about .5 meters) high. In general, the lower they are the more uncomfortable they are. The smart designer will slope the seatbacks outboard and ensure that the seats have a distinct slope to them. This is one of the beauties of fiberglass, in that it can be molded to make a comfortable seat as part of the deck design. But remember, if the seats slope outboard then you should specify drains at the back of the seat to remove excess sea water.

The Inshore Cockpit

Strictly speaking, there is no such thing as an inshore cockpit; however, I use the term to define cockpits that are intended for coastal cruising rather than sailing long distances offshore. These cockpits tend to be much larger than a similar offshore cockpit and are intended to accommodate many more crew. They often have a table, with comfortable seats around it, and have a much wider well than usual. The well can be up to 3 feet wide, which makes it difficult to brace yourself against when the boat is heeled.

This type of cockpit can be a mid-deck version or an after-deck type and are often characterized by easy access into the interior of the boat. No bridgedeck is fitted to prevent water going below. While they aren't suitable for offshore sailing, they make a superb platform for lazy evenings in the marina or in some secluded cove.

FIGURE 5.1. *A sail locker should have a large lip around the edge to prevent water getting into the locker. In this sketch the groove serves as a seat drain as well as sealing the locker.*

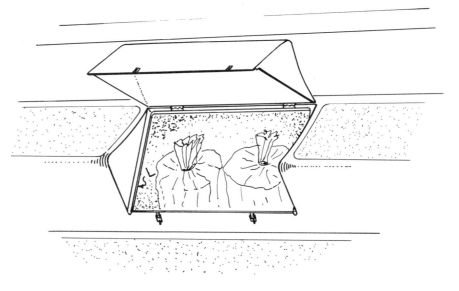

Cockpit Drains

Drains should also be provided in the well so that that cockpit can be emptied quickly if it were to fill in bad weather. Generally, I like to specify 3-inch (75-millimeter) drains at each corner of the well. The drains at the seat back can be joined into them to minimize holes in the hull.

Another cockpit feature that should be carefully designed are any hatches. Sail and other hatches should have a large lip around the inside to minimize the chances of water getting into the hatch. However, many builders use hatches bought directly from the manufacturer which incorporate features that are the best compromise between cost and the needs of production. Figure 5.1 shows how I like to do it.

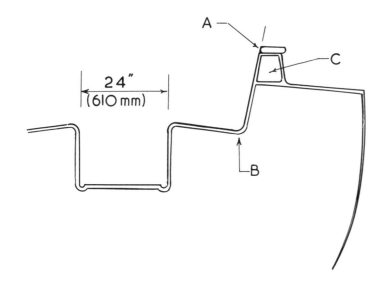

FIGURE 5.2. *Details that make a cockpit comfortable are:*

1. No lip on the inside edge of the teak capping around the coaming. The coaming should also be high enough to make leaning back against it comfortable.

2. Contoured seats for comfortable seating.

3. A small locker in the coaming for winch handles and small items.

We should also consider the width of the cockpit well: 24 inches (610 mm) is about ideal. The cockpit should also have drains at the bottom of the seat and at the bottom of the well.

Coamings and Bulwarks

On a well-designed boat a coaming does several things. A high coaming can be used as a comfortable seatback provided care is taken to avoid protrusions, which always seem to be positioned so they hit you in the small of the back. Figure 5.2 shows some of the details that make the coaming comfortable. Notice how it is sloped slightly and has no sharp edges.

Another important point is to carry the coaming up over the cabintop and around the companionway hatch. While this styling looks old-fashioned, if you sail offshore it is still the best way of fitting a dodger. It also makes it easier to fit a dodger groove and provides a place for the dodger bars when they are not in use. Any lines coming aft can be led through the coaming with a hole just large enough to take the line. This is yet another reason to keep the mainsheet track away from the companionway. If it is too close, then fitting a dodger may be impossible. Figure 5.3 shows a typical coaming dodger layout. Note also that any winches on the cabintop should be easy to operate whether the dodger is up or down.

Another kind of coaming is the bulwark. In the days when work boats first went to sea, every boat had a high coaming around the edge of the deck to keep crew aboard. Today bulwarks are only seen on character boats. Almost all other craft have stanchions and wire lines running around the deck. There are several reasons for this. Bulwarks are expensive, they raise the center of gravity of the boat, and they use more material in the construction process. They also cause more windage when sailing to windward.

In spite of this, many boats have low molded-in bulwarks or toerails around the edge of the working deck to stop the crew from sliding off. The problem then becomes one of getting rid of the water. In older boats freeing ports were used. Today a simple gap in the toerail usually suffices. However, this gap must be positioned at the low point of the sheer when the boat is upright and another at the low point of the deck when the boat is heeled so that the water can be drained most effectively. Figure 5.4 shows some typical arrangements.

Sail Hatches

Sail hatches can be either forward or aft. Usually they are in the cockpit or just aft of it, using up vacant space behind or beside the quarter berths. However, an aft sail hatch means that the sail has to be carried forward before it can be used. If there is room forward,

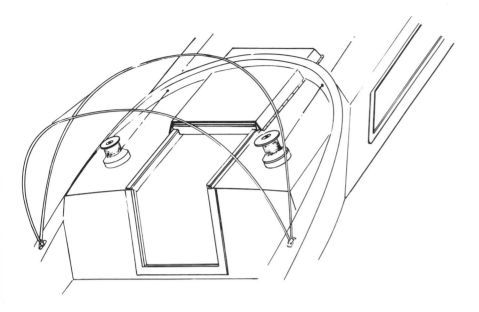

FIGURE 5.3. *A coaming should be shaped so that the dodger bars can lie flat on it easily. The sketch in 5.3a shows a typical layout and the photo in 5.3b shows a practical application.*

FIGURE 5.4. *Various different types of coaming and water drains. A is a typical fiberglass gap in the rail, which should be at the low point when the boat is upright (at A) and at the low point when the boat is heeled (at B). C is a drain fitted inside the toerail. The drain exits at the boottop. I don't like this arrangement because it makes too many holes in the hull. However, if the tubing for this arrangement were to be molded into the hull laminate, the fitting would be much safer and much more watertight. D is a bulwark with a slot or port cut in the bottom. This allows water to drain without any obstructions.*

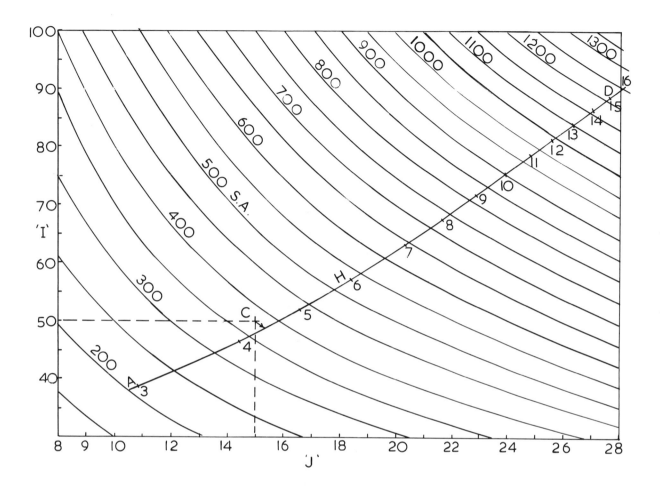

FIGURE 5.5. *A graph of hatch size versus sail area. The I dimension or mast height is the vertical axis, and the J dimension or distance from mast to stemhead is the horizontal axis. SA, or sail area, is calculated by I × J ÷ 2 and is shown by the lines on the graph. To find the hatch area find the mast height (50 feet in the example) and the J dimension (15 feet in the example) and use that to get to position C. Project along parallel to the sail area contours until you hit the hatch size line. In this example the hatch size is 4.4 square feet. So a 2-by-2.5-foot hatch would allow the sails for this boat to pass through.*

then a forward sail hatch makes for less effort on the part of the crew. Even so, the trend toward keeping sails on the spars and on the roller furling headstay has reduced the importance of sail stowage and sail hatches.

The sail hatches should be large enough to allow any sail on the boat to be passed through it when the sail is in its bag. There is no point in having a hatch and a nice sail storage area if the sails cannot fit into it. It should also have rounded edges and no catches or handles for the sail bag to snag on. Figure 5.5 shows a graph of the approximate hatch size for various boats.

Storage areas should be carefully laid out so that every piece of gear is to hand when needed. In Figure 5.6 you can see how hooks have been provided for lines and halyards. Sails drop into bins specially sized to hold them, blocks are snapped over the bar inside the hatch, while winch handles are stowed in the holders on the forward bulkhead.

SAIL TRIM

There is no need for bad sail trim aboard a cruising yacht. But how often do see a boat sailing along with the leach of the sails flapping like a pigeon headed for food? All that is required to stop this noisy commotion, which will eventually flap the sail apart, is a little tension on the leach line. This is not to say that every cruising sailor should set optimum sails, but a little attention now and then will save wear and tear on the sails, get you there just a little quicker, and make cruising much more pleasurable for you and your crew. But what is good sail trim, and how do you apply it to your boat?

Trimming the Jib

On racing boats the jib trim is changed every time the wind puffs or lulls a little. For a cruising sailor to attempt to do this would not only be absurd, but would mean carrying a huge crew and removing much of the fun from cruising. The jib will work quite well if it is trimmed and cleated until there is a major wind shift or course change.

To set the jib properly there must be sufficient tension on the halyard and sheet. This tension serves to change the shape of the sail.

Halyard tension is used not only to hold the sail up but to change the shape of the sail. If you over-tension the halyard you will notice vertical lines appearing up and down the luff of the sail next to the headstay. When the sail is sheeted in those lines should disappear. If they don't, then ease the halyard off until the lines just vanish. If horizontal lines appear, then the halyard has been eased too much.

As the wind increases, the draft in the sail moves aft and requires more halyard tension to pull the draft forward. This can go on until the halyard is as tight as possible and then a Cunningham line in the luff of the sail is tensioned to keep the draft forward. However, modern sails with their much more stable fabrics and laminates do not need as much adjustment as the older, simple Dacron (terylene) sails. Modern sails will be better for cruising sailors who will not want to bother with changing the sail draft every time the wind changes. They are looking for gross settings.

The genoa sheet is used to trim the sail in or out, depending on the angle the boat is sailing to the apparent wind. Sailing closehauled is where the genoa is at its best, but setting the sail up properly is often difficult if you are not an experienced sailor. The position of the fairlead is critical in obtaining the best work out of the sail. To find the best position, bisect the angle at the clew of the sail, as in Figure 5.7, and put the fairlead at this point. Now, trim the sail fully in and look at the foot and the leach. They should have approximately the same curvature. If there is more round in the leach and the foot is tight, the fairlead is too far aft and should be moved forward. The opposite says the lead should move aft.

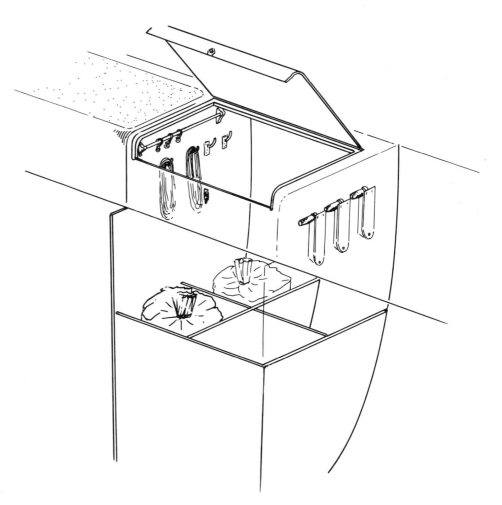

FIGURE 5.6. *Much more can be stored in the locker if it is well organized. Here a bar on the upper left is handy for snap shackles. Hooks under the bar make sheet stowage easy. Sails are stowed in bins made to suit the sail, and winch handles are stowed in holders on the front face of the locker.*

If you have telltales along the luff of the jib then, after bisecting the angles and checking the sail shape, look at the telltales. They should all lift together as the boat moves through the waves. If the lower ones lift before the top ones, move the fairlead aft a hole or two. Conversely, move it forward if the top ones lift first. As the wind increases you may want to move the sheeting point aft as racing sailors do, but this is not an essential for cruising.

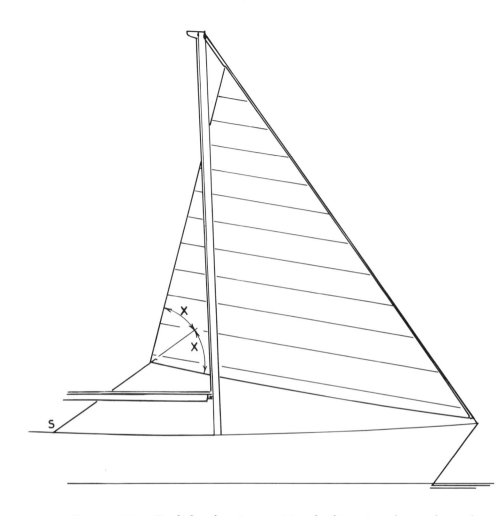

FIGURE 5.7. *Find the sheeting position by bisecting the angle at the clew of the sail. Then check the telltales: if they all lift together the sail is set correctly. If the top lifts first, move the sheet lead forward. Do the opposite if the bottom lifts first.*

Once the best sheeting position has been found, it can be marked on the deck with tape, paint, or magic marker. All the sails in your inventory should be set and their leads marked. Remember also to mark the position of a block on the rail for reaching. This will wait to be forward of the sheeting position on the genoa track. Usually your sailmaker will be only too happy to come out sailing and help you find the best sheeting position for all the sails.

Mainsail Trim

If you were to buy an old racing boat and convert it to a cruiser you would probably be amazed at the number of mainsail controls there are. There would be a mainsheet, traveler, vang (or kicker in Great Britain), outhaul, Cunningham, topping lift, flattening reef, and slab reefs. Even the halyard and mast bend are used to control sail shape. Fortunately, most of these refinements are not needed by the cruiser to set the mainsail up for comfortable sailing. The rest of the features are used to get the last 1–2 percent out of the sail performance. The mainsheet, traveler, vang/boom support outhaul, reeflines, and halyard are usually all the average sailor need concern himself about.

The *mainsheet* is used to position the sail and to keep a little tension on the leach. Imagine, if you will, setting the sail up perfectly using the vang (for leach tension), the halyard (for luff tension), and outhaul (for foot tension). The mainsheet should be thought of as a device for moving the sail to its best position relative to the apparent wind.

The easiest method of checking the alignment is to tie a few telltales on the batten pockets of the main. Easing the mainsheet will let the sail move to leeward and the telltales will stream out behind the sail.

Should the top telltales fold in behind the sail while the bottom ones stream out behind, the tension on the leach is too tight. Easing the vang and the mainsheet slightly will soon remedy the problem by giving the leach slightly more curvature. If you want to keep the boom on centerline, simply move the traveler to windward a little.

The *main traveler* is simply the block at the bottom of the mainsheet. It moves along the mainsheet track, usually positioned in the cockpit. Moving the traveler moves the mainsheet and positions the sail at its best angle of incidence to the wind. The position of the traveler, when sailing upwind, can be controlled with taglines or with stops at intervals along the track. While taglines give more accurate control, stops can be equally effective as long as sail trim is not intended to be perfect.

Self-Tacking Jibs; Tracks and Fittings

We mentioned self-tacking jibs and tacking tracks in Chapter 3. In this section we'll look at them in more detail and discuss how best to use them. The trick is to situate the track so that the boom or sail will not hit either the mast or the forward lower shrouds. It should also be easy to set up and to adjust if desired later. In my design business

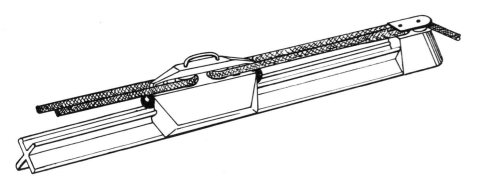

FIGURE 5.8. *The track for a self-tacking jib is often similar to the mainsheet track.*

we've specified several types of boomed self-tacking rigs, as discussed in Chapter 3.

The tack tracks for self-tacking jibs are usually a smaller version of the mainsheet track, as shown in Figure 5.8. Lewmar, Harken, and Nicro-fico all make units we've specified.

Halyard and Sheet Leads

Nobody really wants to be continually moving to adjust a sheet or to jury-rig a halyard to reach a suitable winch. The crew spend most of their time in the cockpit, so why shouldn't all the leads be led to the cockpit? The halyards can be led aft from the mast to winches or cleats placed at the forward end of the cockpit, while sheets and guys could be taken to winches placed on the coaming. Unfortunately, these suggestions are often impractical, as the short-handed sailor will quickly appreciate. If the halyard winches are near the cockpit it would take a man with 11-foot (3.3-meter) arms to raise the mainsail and feed the sail into the luff groove. It is usually much more efficient to place the halyard winches near or on the mast. If desired, some bracing bars, "Granny bars," can be placed about 30–36 inches (750–910 millimeters) away from the spar.

Another solution is to put the halyard winches on deck or on a pedestal aft of the mast. Neither of these positions is ideal because an operator usually has to bend or kneel to operate the winch, and get-

ting a good purchase is often difficult from a kneeling position. But the lead from the mast to a winch is reasonably short and can be close to ideal.

If the lead has to pass through a lock-off before being taken to the winch, it will have to pass along the deck or parallel the mast in order to be locked off. This affects the placement of winches and other gear.

For instance, suppose we wanted to run the main halyard through a lock-off. Because of the nature of the unit, our options are to put the lock-off on the mast or on deck. On the mast is usually out of the question because of the difficulty of leading the halyard to the winch after it has passed through the lock-off, and, because main halyards are usually wire, there will be a problem finding a lock-off that will work.

So that leaves us with the only alternative of putting the lock-off on deck, which makes the winch placement critical. If we put the winch close to the mast so the sail can easily be fed to the winch, the ergonomics of operating the winch are bad, and if we put the winch on the cabintop at the front of the cockpit we will need a second person to feed the mainsail into the groove.

This is the type of decision the designer faces all the way through the design process. It is not easily solved and is one of the major reasons why you should try out every boat before you buy it. You should also check to see that all the leads are fair and that they will not chafe, or bear on surfaces that may chafe them. Chafe will shorten the life of a sheet quite considerably—sometimes reduce it to a matter of hours—and should be avoided wherever possible.

Sheet leads, on the other hand, pose their own set of problems. How do you design a sheet lead that will adjust as the sail is furled or unfurled? Suppose we have a roller furling jib. When the sail is used in light winds it is totally unrolled. The sheet lead will be at the aft end of the track. If the wind gets up we'll have to reef the jib by furling it. The jib lead will also have to be moved forward. Trying to move a jib lead under load is not an easy job, requiring either brute strength or a tack, reset the lead, and tack back. Harken makes a continuously adjustable sheet lead that makes it easy to adjust the track under load. While this was originally developed for the racing sailor, it is ideal for the cruising man, saving time, effort, and frustration.

If you purchase a production boat, quite often there are not enough track leads for efficient sailing. Adding another track is a job that may be worth doing. But where should the track be positioned? Figure 5.12 shows the positions for most genoa tracks, and the section on tracks discusses it in more detail.

If you look at the deck of any modern boat there often seems to be a winch for every line, or banks of lock-offs and a single large winch. Neither of them are essential or necessarily good. Blocks and tackles can often do a faster and more efficient job. For instance, the mainsheet can be a four- or five-part tackle rather than a two-part tackle lead to a winch. There will, of course, be more line to handle, but a properly organized box will easily take care of that.

Another way to reduce the number of winches is to look carefully at work done by each winch and see which ones can do two jobs. For instance, if you fly a spinnaker you don't really need extra winches for the sheet and guy. The haste that goes with racing is not present, so you can take your time and use other means to set the sail. With a well-positioned lock-off, the genoa sheet can be locked and the spinnaker set; when the spinnaker is up and the genoa lowered the sheet can be taken to a winch and the lock-off opened.

Another example is the use of winches on runners. I remember not so long ago using Highfield levers to tension the runners. Cruising sailors don't need to vary the tension in the runners as the racer does, so why use a winch? It wouldn't be difficult to design a better Highfield lever. Then it's a simple one-time action to tension or ease the runner. Some designers use swept spreaders to eliminate the Highfield lever. This, too, reduces the lines needed to control the rig, but must be set up and tuned carefully when the rig is installed. Figure 5.9 shows the action of the Highfield lever on the runner.

Winches, then, are not that important. A block and tackle, lock-offs, and clever design can reduce the number you have on board and give you more money to spend on other, more essential features, like a good bottle of wine. However, in many places winches are essential, and in the following pages we'll see how important they are.

Before we get into using winches it is useful to know what types there are and how they are maintained and repaired.

Single-Speed Winches

In this winch the drum usually moves at the same speed as the handle. In other words, one revolution of the handle gives you one revolution of the drum. It is the simplest form of winch, having only a center spindle around which is a cage or two of roller bearings. At the top of the winch is a pair of pawls, which stop it rotating in the wrong direction. These winches are usually used to pull down the

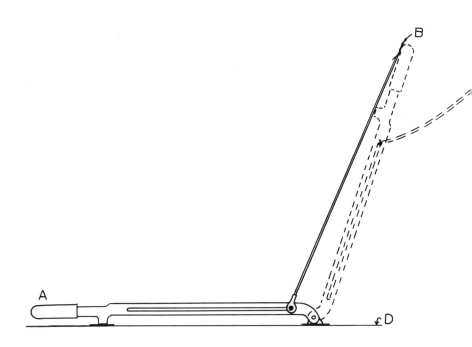

FIGURE 5.9. *A highfield lever tightens the runner in one simple movement. When the runner is at A the runner is tight; at B it is slack. When using a runner lever like this you should make sure your fingers are well clear of the moving parts.*

reefing line on larger boats and are often mounted on the boom. They would only be used as the primary winch on a very small, below 22-foot (approximately 7-meter) cruiser.

Multi-Speed Winches

Probably the most common type of winch in use today. Two- and three-speed winches are found on almost every offshore yacht. They operate by turning the handle one way, usually clockwise, to get the first speed and then turning the handle counterclockwise to get the second speed. Where a third speed is fitted there is usually a button to push, either before operating the winch or during the winding cycle; when it is set, the winch is wound clockwise again to get the third speed.

Most cruising boats have two-speed winches. The first speed is to get the halyard in quickly, the second speed to pull the last few feet in without undue strain. Boats with a lot of sail or a lightweight crew may want a winch with a third speed. This will pull a higher load but at a much slower speed. Figure 5.10 shows an exploded view of a Barient two-speed self-tailing winch, and Figure 5.11 shows an exploded view of a three-speed winch.

Multi-speed winches are used for any job on the boat that may have too high a load on the line for a single-speed winch, or to make it easier to wind in a heavily loaded line. This means that they will be used for primary and secondary winches and for genoa or spinnaker halyard winches.

Self-Tailing Winches

Self-tailing winches are probably the biggest single advance in winch technology for the cruising sailor in many years. This is the perfect example of getting two things done for the price of one. Not only can a self-tailing winch hold the line while it is being reeled in, but it can hold that line indefinitely. Self-tailers are used almost anywhere on a boat; however, I don't like to specify them as halyard winches because crew tend to leave the halyards on the self-tailer, rather than cleating the line securely.

Because of their extra expense they should only be used for sheets and guys with halyards taken to normal winches. Self-tailing winches can be obtained in multi-speed versions and electric versions. To my knowledge none of the major manufacturers makes a winch that can be converted from self-tailing to normal operation and back again.

The electric versions make it possible to sail a huge boat simply by pushing buttons. I once sailed as part of a crew of three (one of us had to fetch the drinks!) on an 80 footer that had electric winches. We pushed buttons to make the Lewmar Commander system unroll the genoa. We unrolled the mainsail the same way and then sheeted the sails by pushing the button controls next to the winch. After that it was simply a matter of sitting back and enjoying the sail. The only danger on a trip of this nature is wearing your fingers out pushing buttons!

Gear and Power Ratios

When you listen to a winch maker or salesman talking about winches, they talk in terms of gear ratios and power ratios. A gear ratio is simply the number of times you must turn the handle in order to rotate the drum once. You must know the gear ratio to find the power ratio. The power ratio is the winch maker's way of defining mechanical advantage. It depends on three factors: the gear ratio, the handle diameter, and the drum diameter. The following formulae will explain both ratios:

$$\text{Gear ratio} = \frac{\text{Number of handle revolutions}}{\text{Number of drum revolutions}}$$

$$\text{Power ratio} = \frac{\text{Gear ratio} \times \text{handle length}}{\text{Drum radius}}$$

For instance, let's say a 200-pound (91-kilogram) man exerts a load of about 100 pounds on a winch handle. Say, the winch has a gear ratio of 20 and the man uses a 10-inch handle in a winch that has a drum diameter of 5 inches. The power the man can exert on the sheet is:

$$\text{Power ratio} = \frac{20 \times 10}{5} = 40$$

Thus, the pull on the sheet is

$$40 \times 100 = 4000 \text{ lbs}$$

Hydraulic Winches

There are a number of technical problems with hydraulic winches that prevented development of satisfactory models for many years. But recently, using higher pressures, often over 1000 psi, winch manufacturers have been able to marry a hydraulic pump to a winch to produce a hydraulic winch. This could lead to exciting new developments in sailing technology (see Chapter 12, The Push-Button Boat). Barient and Lewmar are the leaders in this type of technology, but they are being closely followed by others.

Winch Maintenance

Quite often the winches on a cruiser are ignored until something fails. This is unfortunate because breakdowns can be prevented simply by checking the winch every few months. Here's how to do it. (You can also use the exploded views in Figures 5.10 and 5.11 to help reassemble the unit.)

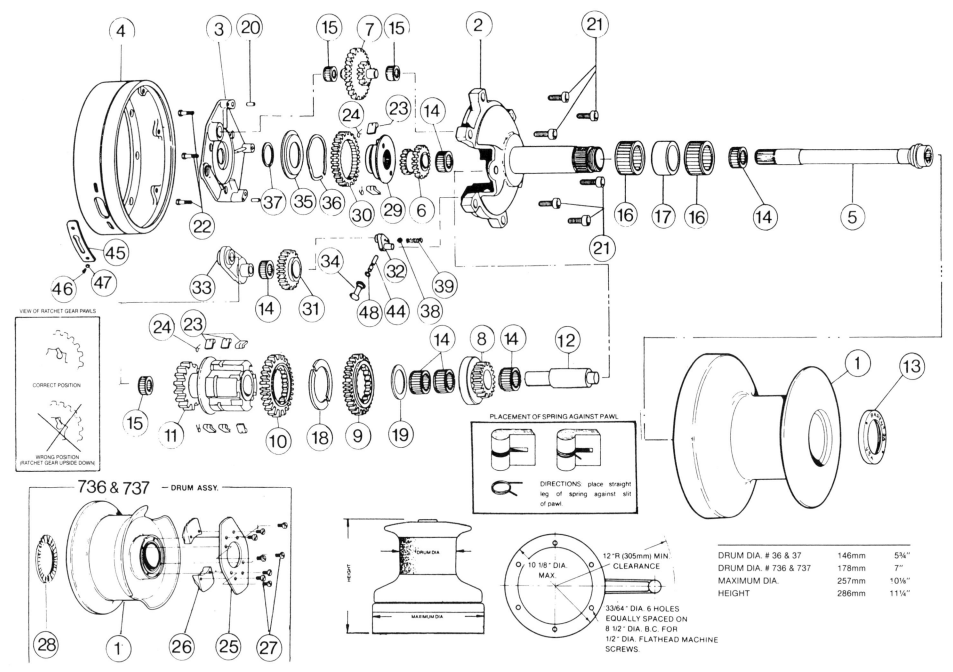

VIEW OF RATCHET GEAR PAWLS

CORRECT POSITION

WRONG POSITION
(RATCHET GEAR UPSIDE DOWN)

736 & 737 — DRUM ASSY.

PLACEMENT OF SPRING AGAINST PAWL

DIRECTIONS: place straight leg of spring against slit of pawl.

DRUM DIA
HEIGHT
MAXIMUM DIA

12"R (305mm) MIN CLEARANCE

10 1/8" DIA. MAX.

33/64" DIA. 6 HOLES EQUALLY SPACED ON 8 1/2" DIA. B.C. FOR 1/2" DIA. FLATHEAD MACHINE SCREWS.

DRUM DIA. # 36 & 37	146mm	5¾"
DRUM DIA. # 736 & 737	178mm	7"
MAXIMUM DIA.	257mm	10⅛"
HEIGHT	286mm	11¼"

FIGURE 5.10. *An exploded view of the Barient model 36 three speed winch. (Drawing courtesy of IMI Barient.)*

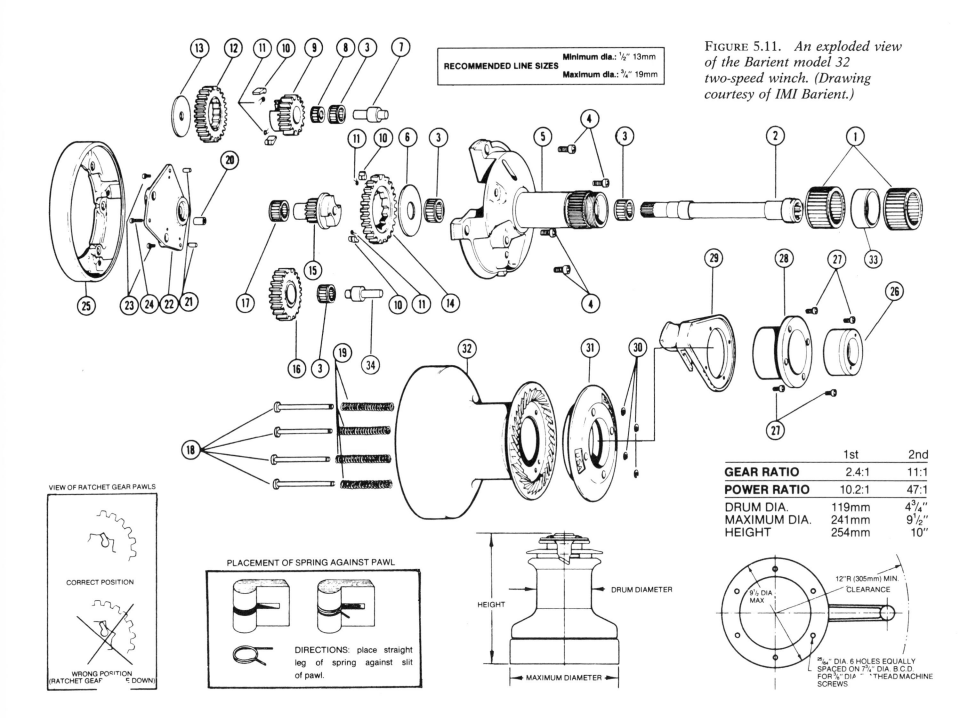

RECOMMENDED LINE SIZES

Minimum dia.: ½" 13mm

Maximum dia.: ¾" 19mm

VIEW OF RATCHET GEAR PAWLS

CORRECT POSITION

WRONG POSITION
(RATCHET GEAR _ DOWN)

PLACEMENT OF SPRING AGAINST PAWL

DIRECTIONS: place straight leg of spring against slit of pawl.

HEIGHT

DRUM DIAMETER

MAXIMUM DIAMETER

12"R (305mm) MIN. CLEARANCE

9½ DIA MAX

²⁵⁄₆₄" DIA. 6 HOLES EQUALLY SPACED ON 7¾" DIA. B.C.D. FOR ⅜" DIA. _THEAD MACHINE SCREWS

	1st	2nd
GEAR RATIO	2.4:1	11:1
POWER RATIO	10.2:1	47:1
DRUM DIA.	119mm	4¾"
MAXIMUM DIA.	241mm	9½"
HEIGHT	254mm	10"

First, the winch drum must be removed. This is accomplished by one of several methods. Some winches have a snap ring that fits over the center spindle (around the handle socket); others have a screw inside the handle socket; while a third, more recent idea is to put a pair of push catches inside the drum socket. On almost all self-tailing winches the top part of the self-tailing mechanism unscrews, allowing the drum to be pulled off.

Once the drum has been removed, the gears and roller races are exposed. Always note how the various parts fit together so that you can put the winch back together. With the drum removed you can start to strip the winch. Most modern winches can be easily stripped from the top down. Older winches may have to be removed from the deck to get at the cogs in the bottom of the unit. If you have to unbolt your winches, be sure to use a good sealant when replacing them. Deck leak repairs are not part of this manual.

The experts place each part in a bowl of kerosene or paraffin to remove the grease. This grease may have reacted with salt water to become a lumpy mess and must be removed before the winch is reassembled. Check each component for cracks, shards of metal, and bent parts. Especially the pawls, springs, and roller bearings. On reel winches check the brake drum for cracks and wear. *Do not* place this drum in the kerosene.

All the pieces, except the drum, which should be wiped, should be cleaned and dried, coated lightly with the special winch greases supplied by the manufacturer, and reassembled. Try to avoid getting grease on the pawls and their springs; the grease may eventually combine with salt water and make the pawls stick.

DECK FITTINGS

Winches are the major movers of lines, sheets, and guys on a boat, but fairleads have to lead the lines to the winch, and once the line has been tensioned what happens to it? You can't simply let it go. It has to held tightly by a lock-off or a cleat.

Then there are the pieces that help keep you aboard the boat. Handrails and lifelines have their place on deck. Like the sail-handling lines, the anchor and its line need a stowage place. A place has to be found for the liferaft, a dinghy, possibly a pair of davits, a dodger, and scuppers, and lastly, people have to fit somewhere.

All this equipment must come from different manufacturers and be put in different places on the deck. Consequently, it takes a sailing juggler to figure out the logistics of designing a deck layout. Sound difficult? It is, but because of all the options, not because of the large number of variables. For instance, you can buy cam, jam, and clam cleats, brass, wood, nylon, steel, and aluminum cleats, and many different types of tracks and fairleads, all of which need to be analyzed to select the best for the job.

The Mainsheet Track

The mainsheet track runs across the cockpit or the cabintop. When it runs across the cockpit it generally chops the cockpit in two, making it uncomfortable to lie on the leeward side. Also, it generally interferes with the primary winch when running downwind.

We covered mainsheets in some detail in Chapter 3. Rather than repeat that information here, we'll look at other details. Where should the sheet be? Some of the options are (1) behind the aft end of the cockpit; (2) at the aft end of the cockpit; (3) in the middle of the cockpit; and (4) on the cabintop.

If positioned aft of the cockpit or in the afterpart of the cockpit, the boom should be high enough to pass over the head of anybody standing in the cockpit. This means a minimum of 6½ feet (approximately 2 meters) above the cockpit sole. Also, the mainsheet should not be led forward along the underside of the boom. In a jibe the loop of sheet hanging under the boom can catch around a crewman's neck. (While this is a method of reducing crew size, it is not recommended by most experts.)

So this option is restricted to a mainsheet that is trimmed by the helmsman (or a crewman sitting behind the helmsman), or one that is led forward inside the boom, which makes it a little more expensive than normal. It also requires a long boom or a center cockpit layout to get the mainsheet aft of the cockpit.

An aft cockpit boat with a long boom offers several advantages. (This option is opposite to "modern" thinking, but it is a viable idea, especially when the boat is small and the boom can be used as a boom tent over the cockpit.) The long boom is also useful if the boat is to have a dodger or dodger with curtains around the cockpit. It keeps the sail-handling items clear of the cockpit. If you opt for a long boom, the mast will be farther forward than usual, but it moves the mainsheet out of the cockpit and into a relatively "dead" area of the deck.

Putting the traveler in the middle of the cockpit breaks up the cockpit, as we saw earlier, but for the long-distance offshore sailor it has certain features that recommend it, the most important being that the mainsail can be trimmed from the safety of the cockpit. Also, the downward tension of the mainsheet almost directly opposes the upward tension in the leach of the sail. However, most people spend about 80 percent of their sailing time in the cockpit, and having the mainsheet in the middle of it can be annoying.

On many older IOR racing designs the mainsheet was still fitted at the end of the mainboom, but as the sail got smaller the boom became shorter and the mainsheet crept forward to the forward end of the cockpit. As usual, cruising boat design followed the racing trend. While this system has an advantage, in that the traveler structure makes a natural bridgedeck across the cockpit, which serves to stop water going below, it also has some drawbacks. First, it puts the mainsheet very close to the companionway hatch and causes difficulty if you have to go below when the boat is going to windward. Second, leading the sheet to a winch is very hard; many systems have been tried, but very few have been entirely successful.

For this reason, many production boat manufacturers have situated the mainsheet on the cabintop just forward of the companionway hatch. From a customer standpoint this feature has several advantages. First, it gets the mainsheet out of the cockpit. Second, it makes it possible to run the sheet lead forward and then back to a winch easily. And third, as long as the boom is positioned high enough, it is easy to fit a dodger or Bimini top. However, the disadvantage is lost efficiency in sheeting the mainsail and more work required to pull the sail in fully.

So there you have it. The mainsheet can be positioned in several places. Some are best for a particular purpose, others lose efficiency but make other parts of the boat more workable. Like everything else on a yacht, the mainsheet position and traveler efficiency are a necessary compromise that must be worked out to suit your type of sailing.

Headsail Sheet Tracks

How many times do you adjust your headsail sheet fairlead? Probably never, once it has been set, so why do you need a track? Why not simply put a padeye at each sheeting point? One reason is that a padeye and block at each point would probably be more expensive than a track with an adjustable car or fairlead. Another is that not all sails are made the same. A no. 3 from North would probably sheet in at a different place than would the same sail from Hood or Sobstad.

Having decided that a boat needs a track for headsails, we should decide where the track should be. Too far outboard and the boat will

FIGURE 5.12. *Genoa and staysail tracks should be positioned where they can make the sails work most efficiently. Usually the 150% LP line marks the aft end of the sail. At this point the track should be about 10 degrees from the centerline. The forward end of the track will end up about 7.5 degrees and staysail tracks will be about 6 degrees off the centerline.*

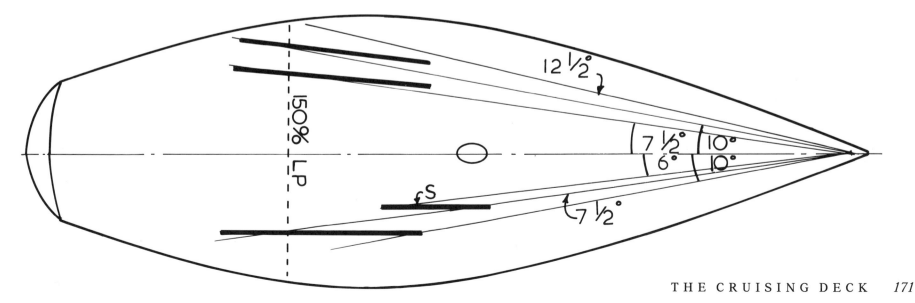

not sail to windward very well. Too far inboard and the headsail will backwind the main. Also, the track position should match the type of hull. For instance, it simply would not work to put a track in as close as possible to the centerline of a beamy, shallow-keeled cruising boat, whose hull form will not let the boat sail to windward like a 12 meter. This type of hull needs a track slightly farther outboard than usual. If the hull won't go to windward, why trim the sails to make it?

On the other hand a narrow meter type boat may have the genoa track set inboard of the rail even though the boat is very narrow. It has the ability to sail to windward, and the track position should reflect that ability.

The absolute minimum position a track should be set at is 7.5 degrees to the centerline, as in Figure 5.12. This position should only be used if you are designing a boat with certain characteristics:

1. Fairly narrow width, for instance, a cruising 6 meter.
2. A keel or hull that will work well to windward.
3. A reasonably short-footed sail on the headstay. The length on the foot should not be more than 130 percent J (the distance from the inner side of the headstay to the forward side of the mast). As J gets shorter, the position of the track can be moved inboard slightly. Some sails that are only 90 percent J are sheeted at a 6 degree angle, but that is not very common.

The more usual track position is near 10 degrees, but because cruisers don't need the last iota in performance, the mast staying base and spreader lengths can be slightly wider than usual and the headsail tracks slightly further outboard than usual, to about 12 degrees if desired. Note, also, that the chainplate position is often affected by the layout of the interior and that moving the chainplates in or out a small amount will affect the rig only slightly but could make the interior much more comfortable. A slightly wider angle has other advantages in that it will give better mast support and match the cruising hull a little better.

The length of the track is also of critical importance. Quite often a builder will use a short piece of track for economy, but when you as an owner want to increase your sail inventory, the track isn't long enough. This entails extra expense, as you have to purchase and fit either new track or a separate nonadjustable padeye.

Another problem is whose track to use. Most manufacturers make good track, and as long as it is installed properly it should do the job. However, I prefer to specify Harken track and jib cars because the cars slide so easily. I hate having to hammer at a car to move it under load. If Harken track is too expensive, then Nicro-fico has a wide range of tracks and cars.

A good boat will also have enough tracks to be able to set other sails when conditions warrant. A good sailor may set a staysail in reaching conditions, or he may have a track for a self-tacking headsail for sailing short-handed.

Cleats

Cleats hold lines, and there are many lines on every boat, but you shouldn't select the same type of cleat to hold every line. For instance, bow, stern, and mid-deck cleats should be of the traditional horned type. But lines used for the leach line or the even the sheets on smaller boats can be jam cleats.

What's the difference? A conventional horned cleat requires several turns to wrap the line around the winch, whereas a jam cleat holds the line as it is inserted into it.

By the way, many sailors put a half-hitch on every cleat when they tie it off. This is bad practice. Cleats are designed to hold lines without using a half-hitch. The hitch makes it hard to undo and can, if the load on the cleat is high enough, work itself tight so that the line has to be cut before it can be removed. If you have to get a line of the cleat in an emergency and it is seized tight you'll find yourself in real trouble. The only time I would use a half-hitch is when the boat is alongside the dock and I'm going to leave it for several weeks, and even then a properly made cleat would hold it without a half-hitch. Figure 5.13 shows the correct way to wrap a line around a cleat.

Conventional cleats should be properly sized. A rough guide is to divide the rope diameter in inches into sixteenths. The number of sixteenths gives the length of the cleat. For instance, a ½-inch (12-millimeter) line should have an 8-inch (200-millimeter) cleat (½ × 16 = 8). (For the metric, multiply the rope diameter by 16 and take the nearest-sized cleat. For example, a 20-millimeter rope will use a cleat of 20 × 16 = 320 millimeters.) Mooring cleats are a little more difficult to size because not everyone uses the same size mooring line. Figure 5.14 shows a graph of cleat size against waterline length taken from my earlier book, *Designed To Win*. This graph is applicable to most modern cruising yachts. Note that the bow cleats are one size larger than the stern cleats. This is to allow the boat to be towed using the bow cleats.

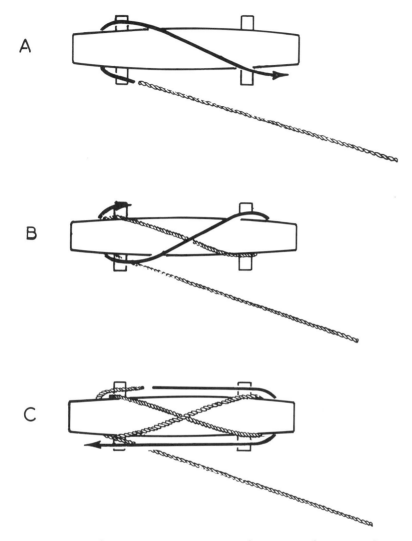

When deciding which cleats to use you should inspect the choices carefully. There should be no sharp edges, and all the corners should be carefully rounded.

Note, also, that the deck under the cleats should be reinforced and backing plates put behind every cleat. Mid-deck cleats are essential for putting spring lines on and should be positioned where they will not be tripped over by crew going forward.

While most of the cleats should be the conventional horned type, there should be room for cam or jam cleats. While these cleats are aimed at the racing end of the market, they can be used on a cruising boat for lines that are small and reasonably lightly loaded. If you intend to buy new jam cleats, try to purchase the metal type. A high load on a plastic cleat can result in the rope pulling through the cleat

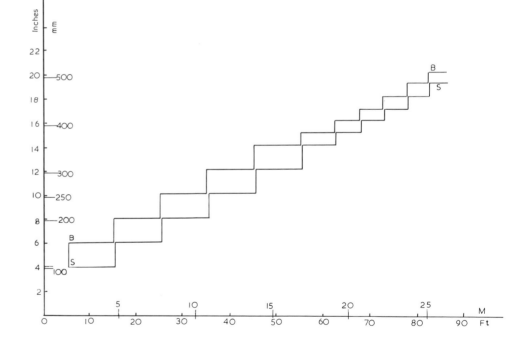

FIGURE 5.13. *The correct way to put a line on a cleat is* without *a halfhitch. In A the sheet is wrapped around the cleat, under the horn, and over the top. At B it is passed under the horn and back over the top. If you like you can add a second set of turns before wrapping the line around the bottom of the cleat. As long as the cleat and line are sized correctly, this will hold exactly the way cleats were designed to hold the line. Problems arise when the cleat is incorrectly sized for the line. When a halfhitch is wrapped around the cleat it can be pulled tight by the working end of the line and jam the entire thing completely.*

FIGURE 5.14. *A graph of cleat size against boat length. The upper line is for bow cleats, which are usually slightly larger to enable the boat to be towed. The lower line can be used for both middeck and stern cleats.*

FIGURE 5.15. *A bitt fitted in place of a cleat in the middeck area of an offshore yacht. Note how it is strongly through-bolted.*

post, they should be carried down through the deck to the hull proper and both the deck and the hull reinforced in way of them. A well-made set of bitts at the bow and at each corner of the transom can give character and individuality in this day of cloned cruisers as long as the rest of the boat is in character. Figure 5.15 shows how one manufacturer added character to his boat with bitts rather than cleats.

Mooring fairleads or chocks. Several types of fairlead can be used to lead the mooring line to the cleat or bitt. The most common are the Skene chock (in the United States) and the fully enclosed chock. Almost any type can be used as long as the edges are well rounded and chafe is minimized. If a mast line chafes through all you are likely to lose is a halyard, but if the mooring line chafes through you could lose your boat. When inspecting for potential chafe points, check the angle the mooring pennant will take when it leads to the mooring buoy. Often what looks fair ends up with a problem because the edge of deck just below the cleat bears on the mooring line.

Headsail fairleads. We have already looked at positioning the headsail lead and the T-tracks used. But the type of lead that can be used often varies tremendously, not only from builder to builder but often from boat to boat. My preference is for movable leads as supplied by Harken. However, most sailors won't want to use top-of-the-line gear and move the lead the way I do. These sailors would be content with a next best Nicro-fico or Lewmar system.

No matter which type you prefer, the track should have a fairlead car (sometimes called a slider), end stops, and at least two adjustable stops if the car doesn't have its own. It is also nice to have an extra stop or two that can take a shackle in case a lead should break or if a second sail is set.

At the back of the track is the genoa turning block (often called a foot block). Although some builders prefer not to fit a foot block, I believe it gives a better and more consistent lead to the winch. However, the block should be at least 18 inches away from the winch to prevent twists in the sheet binding in the block.

Once again, I prefer the double block, which gives a second option should the top or bottom sheave jam or foul. If you intend to set a spinnaker, then the top sheave in a double block can also be used for the spinnaker guy.

Lewmar and Penguin make a series of superb genoa blocks in both double and single units. Another option is the Harken Barbarossa block, which opens at the back to enable the sheet to be dropped in. This is a very nice feature if you need to change sheet leads quickly because they've been led wrongly.

and burning the jaws off. This is especially true when the line is slightly undersized. Cam cleats do have certain drawbacks. The springs inside can corrode, and they have a tendency to chew up the line. As long as you are aware of the drawbacks, you can use these cleats on your boat.

Many cruising boats have a *bitt* for the anchor line forward. Others have a set of bitts around the mast, the way old-time sailing ships did. For me, placing bitts around the mast smacks of fake tradition, somewhat like the plastic and chrome imitation pubs and bars in many ports. If you want bitts and pinrails around the mast, the boat should be designed to suit the character of the period. I hate to see bitts and pinrails next to a modern stainless steel winch. It doesn't quite carry off the part.

When a bitt or bitts are used as a bow mooring, anchor, or towing

Padeyes

It simply isn't possible to put an adjustable track and fairlead at every position on the boat where it is needed, so a padeye and removable block can be used. The padeye can be of the two- or four-bolt variety and must be through-bolted with a reinforcing plate behind it. I like the large selection of padeyes made by Nicro-fico and spec them for most jobs.

Padeyes can be used for a large number of items. The following is a short list:

· as a lead for the storm trisail/storm jib
· around the mast to clip extra blocks for halyards or reefing lines
· aft or on the cabintop to tie down the dinghy or liferaft
· on the quarter of the boat to sheet the reacher, spinnaker, or gennicker
· in the cockpit, or below deck, to hook lifelines
· on the bow to hook anchor retaining lines

In short, padeyes can be positioned anywhere on the deck to make any job easier. Just remember to reinforce behind the padeye in case it is used for a purpose you didn't envision.

Lock-offs, or Sheet Stoppers

In recent years the trend has been toward minimizing the number of winches on board and using a bank of sheet stoppers in front of the winch. This makes it possible to use several lines on the same winch. Here I like the Lewmar Spinlock units, which seem to hold the rope tight without chewing it up. They have special rope clutches for larger lines and sheet stoppers for smaller sheets.

Positioning the sheet stoppers is critical. They should be no less that 12 inches (300 millimeters) from the winch. Ideally 18 inches (450 millimeters) is better to give a fairer lead out of the stopper to the winch.

When using a sheet stopper make sure you have at least three or more turns on the winch before opening the stopper. Fewer turns could result in the rope sliding and your hand being pulled into the winch. Note also that stoppers should be used as a temporary solution. They are not for locking off a halyard and then setting sail across the Atlantic. A few hours is probably okay, but leaving the load on the lock-off for days at a time is not something I would recommend. Figure 5.16 shows a bank of sheet stoppers.

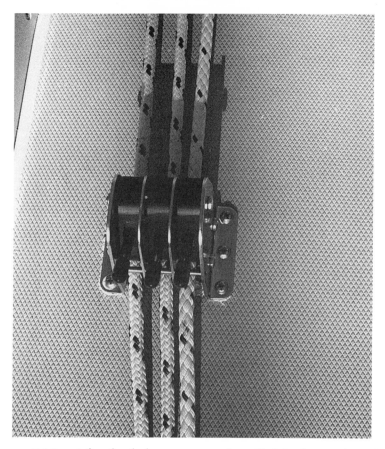

FIGURE 5.16. *A bank of sheet stoppers installed in front of a winch enables the winch to handle many lines.*

Handrails and Toerails

Sometimes you see a good-looking boat at a boat show and decide it's the boat you want to go sailing in. It isn't until you are out on sailing trials that you realize the boat has no handrails. To me, handrails—ideally along either side of the cabintop—are essential. But they are expensive to fabricate and hard to install and if not properly installed can cause deck leaks. Handrails on deck should be heavy enough to support the weight of a large crew but small enough to be gripped tightly by a hand. This means they will usually be 1–1¼ inches (25–30 millimeters) and will be bolted at intervals of not more than 12 inches (300 millimeters); 9–10 inches (225–250 millimeters) is the more usual bolting distance.

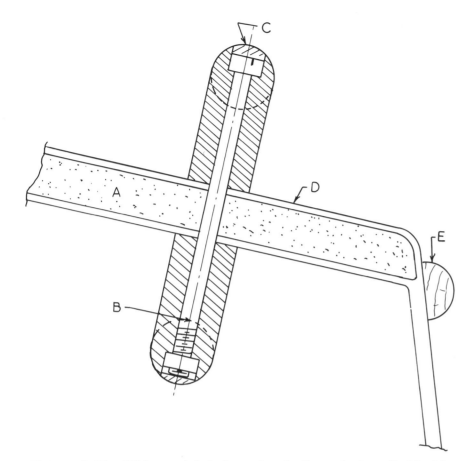

FIGURE 5.17. *With careful design a handrail can be installed inside and outside the boat in one operation. In this figure the interior and exterior rails are through-bolted. A is the deck core. B is the through-bolt, while C is the capping installed to hide the bolthole. On the side of the cabin is a piece of half-round capping E.*

When a handrail is properly built and installed it can be used for a number of purposes beside gripping. It can be a place around which to wrap sail ties when they are taken off the mainsail. Tucking a sail bag under it makes sure the bag won't blow away while you are working on deck. No doubt enterprising sailor will find other options, but be careful not to put too much load on the handrail. You could break it, and then it would have to be replaced.

With careful design, a handrail on the outside of the cabin can be matched to a grabrail inside and both rails bolted on using the same bolts, as shown in Figure 5.17.

Handrails, then, are an essential part of the deck layout and with a little ingenuity can serve many purposes. A similar comment can be made about toerails. Quite often, on a production boat, the toerail is designed as part of the hull-deck joint. The rail most often used is a perforated metal alloy rail bolted every 6 or 8 inches (150 or 200 millimeters). These rails serve a large variety of purposes. They can be used to hook snatch blocks into, to tie sail-handling lines on, to tie mooring lines and fenders to, and even as a place to hook the boarding ladder into. But be wary: several toerails use a machine-stamped hole, which has very sharp edges. These edges can easily cut through mooring and fender lines, leaving your boat without protection at the dock or, worse still, not even at the dock.

My preference is for a teak toerail with chock set in the rail and plenty of holes to allow water to drain off quickly. However, on some very high quality craft, holes in the toerail are simply not acceptable. They can leave streaks on the topside. Builders who do not want these marks to mar the beauty of their topsides put small drains just inside the rail and run the drain inside the hull and out just below the boot-top line. With three or more drains per side there can be six or eight extra holes in the hull just at the waterline. That is six or eight holes more than I like to have in the hull.

Hal Roth doesn't even like toerails. In his book (which all potential offshore cruisers should read) *After 50,000 Miles,* Hal describes how he removed the toerail and installed a small 4-inch (100-millimeter) high bulwark around the deck edge. Under the bulwark he left a 1-inch (25-millimeter) gap to allow water to drain. This is a very attractive alternative for the serious sailor, as the bulwark can easily be bolted to the stanchions and extra supports added midway between stanchions.

Compasses

Many people sail at night by staring at the compass and when its light is dimmed or goes out they are totally lost. The ideal way to sail at night is to pick a star somewhere in front of you and sail on it, checking your course on the compass. But that is an aside to our major purpose. We need a compass on a boat, and it needs to be *calibrated accurately.*

Compasses come in all shapes and forms. From the simple 6- or 7-inch (150- or 175-millimeter) Danforth or Ritchie on the steering pedestal to a 3-inch bulkhead-mounted unit. They all work best when there is no metal close by. We had one instance when the hook on a

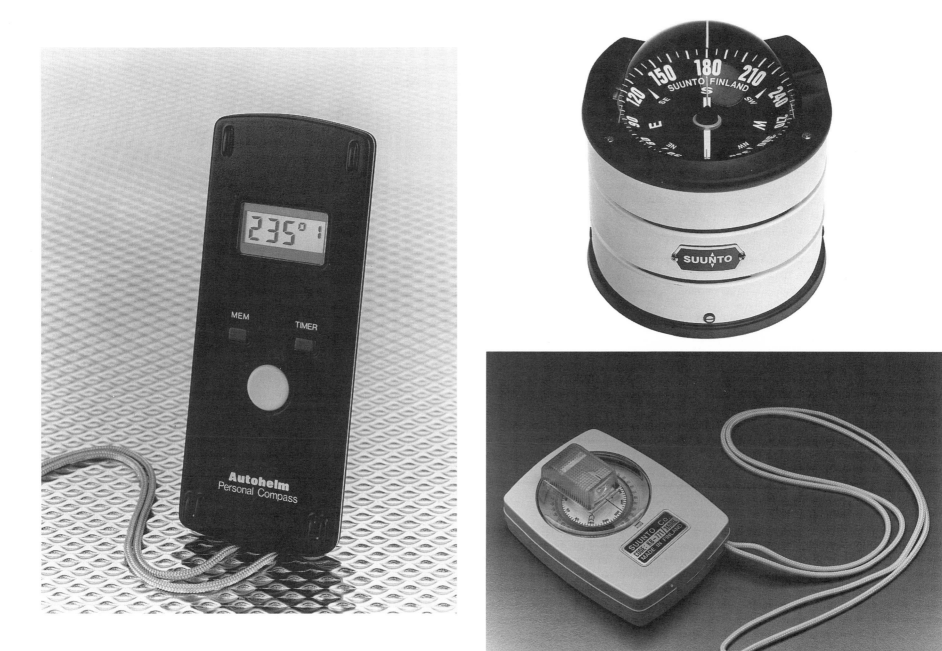

FIGURE 5.18. *A Suunto pedestal compass, the Suunto handheld, and the Autohelm hand-held compass. The Autohelm enables up to nine sights to be taken and recorded by pushing the button. (Photos courtesy of Suunto and Autohelm USA.)*

crew's harness threw the compass off. We sailed for several hours at about 15 degrees higher than we had intended until the watched was changed and the crewman moved away from the compass.

Most sailors like a large compass on the pedestal. The traditional favorites in the United States are the Danforth or Ritchie compasses. An equal or better unit is the Suunto compass made in Finland. These compasses have been around for many years and are only just being marketed in America.

The centerline compass should be directly in front of the wheel and easy to read. However, it should have a dimmable red light that the helmsman can reach. So many compass lights have to be adjusted by the navigator, who holds an unnecessary shouting match with the helmsman while the job is being done. My preference is for the compass to be a few feet ahead of the pedestal. But if it is installed on a convenient bulkhead you can bet somebody will stand between the helmsman and the compass. I also like two-wing compasses on the coamings. For these I generally specify the Suunto units. They seem to work well and are easily calibrated to match the pedestal compass.

Another compass that is of importance to the navigator when navigating close to shore is a personal compass. I thought the hockey puck was the ideal for this purpose, but I recently came across another one, the Autohelm compass. This one allows you to take a sight, record it in memory, and then take another sight, record that, and take another. When you go below you can recall the bearings at the push of a button. However, it does have some drawbacks. Apparently it uses a fluxgate compass, which is highly accurate but doesn't like to be heeled when taking a sight. Figure 5.18 show the various units.

Keeping the Crew Aboard

Yesterday's builders put a big solid bulwark around the boat for just that purpose. Boat builders today accomplish the same thing with a fence of wires around the deck. The wires are supported at either end by pulpits (or pushpits) and in the middle by stanchions. The pulpits are a handy item. They can be made to perform several tasks that could normally take several specially made pieces of gear.

The *bow pulpit* is usually 24 inches (610 millimeters) high. This comes directly from the racing rules, which have restrictions on lifeline heights. On a serious cruiser 27- or 30-inch (685- or 762-millimeter) pulpits and stanchions are a better height. My feeling is that the 24-inch (610-millimeter) posts are exactly the right height to catch you behind the knees and dump you over the side.

A bow pulpit can be used to hold the bow light. It can also have small ⅛-inch steel loops welded to it to hold the halyards when in port, which will stop the halyards banging on the mast. It can be designed to used as a seat for changing sails or watching porpoises gamboling in the bow wave. It can also have the headstay fitting integrated into it and can serve as a tie-down point for the anchor. Often, an anchor roller and trough can be integrated into the pulpit design. For the sailor who uses a spinnaker or running poles, it can have special fittings in which the poles are stored when not in use.

In short, pulpits can be used for many things other than simply to keep the crew aboard. The Freedom 25, for instance, uses its pulpit to support the spinnaker pole in a "shotgun" mounting. The pulpit's uses are limited only by the imagination of the user.

The *stern pulpit,* sometimes called a pushpit, can also be used for many other jobs. Life-ring holders can be built in, as can the flagpole socket, a barbeque grill socket, a stern light holder, and even the backstay chainplate. One use for the stern pulpit is as davits and a ladder for the dinghy. It has been used as a support for the mizzen sheet track on ketches or yawls and as part of the gangplank on boats moored stern to the dock.

The pulpit and aft stanchions should also be designed so that leecloths can easily be fitted around them. A cockpit snugly protected with leecloths can be a boon in inclement weather. The boat's name on the side of the leecloths also helps in identification should you happen to meet another vessel in the vastness of the ocean.

Finally, if you intend fitting a self-steering vane, then the pulpit can be designed to protect the vane and enable you to reach it for repairs or adjustment.

Pulpits don't have to be only at the bow and the stern. Some boats have them around the mast, or, where the headstay is set well inboard, there may be a pulpit around the headstay. A pulpit can be positioned anywhere where strong support is needed to perform work on deck. They can also be any height. For instance, if the pulpit were to be at the mast it could be 36 inches (almost 1 meter) high and carefully sited so that a crew working there could operate without being thrown around.

Stanchions can also do double duty in many cases. Leecloths can be tied to them; a small ring welded to them can make a handy place to stow the boathook or a place to which netting can be tied to prevent sails or children falling overboard. Here again, most builders use Offshore Racing Council (ORC) rules to position stanchions—not more than 7 feet apart and strongly through-bolted.

FIGURE 5.19. *The Lirakis harness is one of the best on the market. It comes in sizes for both adults and children. (Photos courtesy of Lirakis Inc.)*

Inboard lifelines (called jacklines in the United States) should have a place on all boats that go offshore. The line should be made up so that it can be easily connected to a padeye at the bow and at the stern. Ideally, a crew should be able to clip onto the lifeline before they leave the cockpit and go to the bow without unclipping.

In the cockpit strong points should be provided so that the crew can hook their harnesses into without having to tie their harness lines around the stanchions or pulpits.

Harnesses

Not only must there be lifeline fitted but the crew must wear a *harness* when the weather gets bad. Once again, the ORC has set minimum standards based on British Standard 4224-1975 and American Standard 2227-1978. These standards give specific details as to the webbing straps and materials. For instance, the main load-bearing webbing must be a minimum of 1½ inches (38 millimeters) wide, and any bracing straps should be no less than ¾ inches (15 millimeters) wide. It gives details of the safety line, securing buckles, and hooks and goes on to discuss the materials, from metal castings to sewing and splicing of the safety lines. Finally, it discusses various methods of testing the harness to ensure it conforms to the standard. If you are interested, a copy is available from the Offshore Racing Council in London or USYRU (United States Yacht Racing Union) in Newport, Rhode Island.

Now that the ORC has come out with standards, it is reasonable to assume that most manufacturers make their harnesses to that standard. The one most recommended and most used in the offshore racing fleet is the Lirakis harness, which according to their brochure exceeded the British safety standards and the ORC specifications. The secret of these harnesses is only just filtering through to the world of the cruising sailor, but they are the simplest and easiest-to-use harness in the industry. Figure 5.19 shows the Lirakis safety harness.

GETTING ABOARD

As freeboard becomes higher, so getting aboard becomes much harder. Transferring from the dinghy or the water into a boat is becoming a very large problem, and to alleviate it some form of steps or ladder must be provided.

One of the latest trends is to provide a large platform at the back of the boat and steps up the transom. While this does nothing for the aesthetics of the design, it makes it easy to get aboard. The aft step provides an area to swim from and a place to sit (with a harness on) when the boat is under sail. You can dangle your feet in the water and enjoy the sail. Some larger boats have taken this feature a step further and have an opening locker in the transom in which the dinghy is stowed. On the Hunter 54 this feature is a unique selling point, but it pushes the rudder post much farther forward than at the end of the waterline.

A ladder is another good idea for boarding. Usually the ladder is built into the stern pulpit and is made to be the same height as the stern rail. When it is down it is easy to use if you are stepping out of a dinghy. But on every one that I've used after swimming the ladder has not been deep enough in the water. I like to see a ladder designed so that at least two rungs, preferably more, are in the water when the ladder is down. That makes it easy to get aboard after swimming.

Quite often you will see a folding ladder hung from the rail to be used for boarding and disembarking. But this ladder has to be demounted and a place found to stow it. This problem was solved on one boat I worked on by putting steps in the hull, as shown in Figure 5.20. This made it easy to get aboard and did not require storage space.

Finally, another old standby that can be made to do double duty is the fender board. It can be used as a gangplank when required if lines are spliced into each corner and some form of fitting made to fix the board at the yacht end.

FIGURE 5.20. *Steps in the side of the hull can make it easy to get aboard a boat if the freeboard is high.*

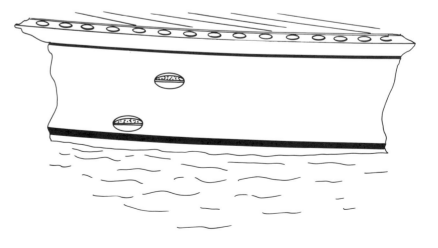

CARRYING A DINGHY

Most cruising sailors who venture away from the beaten track carry a dinghy to help them get ashore, although for the local cruiser this trend seems to be losing ground. In Europe, the inflatable dinghy, which can easily be stowed in a locker and inflated in minutes, is highly favored. American owners, on the other hand, appear to prefer a solid dinghy. However, this trend is slowly disappearing as prejudice against inflatables disappears.

What To Look for in a Dinghy

The attributes of a good solid dinghy are usually appreciated after the boat has been used for some time, but certain basic criteria should be looked for. It should be reasonably lightweight and have good freeboard, the ability to carry all the crew if needed, and a good fender rail that will not mar the topsides. It should be able to be powered by an outboard, by rowing, or even by sailing, and finally, it should have a strong towing eye situated low down on the bow.

Inflatables, on the other hand, have other advantages. Being rubber, they will not usually mar the topsides. They can stand some overloading without sinking, they can be carried either fully or partially inflated, and they can be used either partially or fully inflated. While partially inflated is not the best way to use the dinghy, in an emergency it is better than using a piece of a hard dinghy!

The inflatable has a large advantage in severe storm conditions because it can be deflated and stowed in a locker, while the hard dinghy may have to be cut away because of the extra windage it could cause.

Stowing the Dinghy

If storage space is at a premium, there is a decided advantage to having an inflatable, which can be stored in a locker measuring about 24 × 18 × 30 inches (.61 × .5 × .76 meters). On this boat the solid dinghy would have to be towed, which would mean extra drag on the boat and the possibility of losing the dinghy in inclement conditions.

Larger boats, up to 45 feet (13.7 meters), would probably find some form of deck stowage is the best method to carry a solid dinghy. The dinghy could be carried either upside down or upright. The way you choose should be governed by where you stow it. For instance, if the

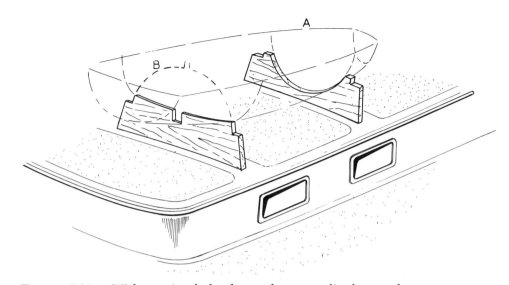

FIGURE 5.21. *With a pair of chocks as shown, a dinghy can be stowed either right side up as in A or upside down as in B. In B the gunwhales of the dinghy fit into the notches on the chocks.*

dinghy is to be stowed over the mid-deck hatch, under the main boom, then it would probably be best to stow it upside down. This would enable you to open the hatch in all but the worst weather. Note that if the dinghy is stowed on the main cabin it can be launched and retrieved by using the main halyard or the boom as a davit.

If your boat is not designed to carry a solid dinghy, it is a fairly easy job to fit chocks designed for the purpose. But before you do anything, make sure the dinghy will fit in the intended storage space. There may be enough deck space, but a sheet or vent may be in the way, and until you offer the dinghy to the space you may never notice until a lot of work has been done and much money spent. Figure 5.21 shows some chocks that can be used to position the dinghy either way up.

Larger yachts over 40 feet (15.2 meters) often have a dinghy that can be carried in davits on the stern. It is the rare yacht that carries a dinghy in midship davits anymore. Stern davits look efficient and can be made to do more than just carry the dinghy. However, stern davits do have some drawbacks. They put quite a bit of weight aft, especially if the outboard is stored on the dinghy. This extra weight contributes appreciably to the pitching moment of the yacht. The dinghy also has to be raised fairly high to avoid being swamped by the stern wave. But if you do intend to carry a hard dinghy, transom davits make it easy to launch and retrieve it. When they are coupled with a transom ladder or steps, using the dinghy becomes a real pleasure.

FIGURE 5.22. *The Nicro-fico solar vent keeps air inside the boat moving when nobody is aboard. This helps prevent mold and mildew from forming. (Photo courtesy of Nicro-fico Corporation.)*

VENTILATION

On one of my trips to Bermuda we encountered winds up to 65 knots. In those conditions the deck was awash with water. As most of the hatches had to be kept tightly closed, the dorade vents were the only way of getting fresh air below. But the small cowl that allowed the air to enter the dorade was so low that water was continually being deposited below via the dorade. This led to two conclusions about dorade vents. First, the drain holes must be large enough to drain off any water that finds its way into the vent box. Second, the scoop must be high enough off the deck so that green water doesn't continually wash into it. This means that a scoop height of about 18 inches (700 millimeters) is adequate.

Dorade vents are also vulnerable to catching sheets during a tack, especially if the vent is on the foredeck, so some form of guard must be fitted to avoid damage.

Other types of vents are the mushroom vent and the clamshell vent. Both can be used for offshore cruising, but both should be situated where they are unlikely to be covered with green water on a continuous basis. I especially like the Nicro-fico solar vent, which can operate whether anyone is aboard the boat or not. A small solar panel set in the middle of the vent keeps a fan turning. The fan can be used to exhaust stale air out of the boat on a continuous basis, keeping the interior fresh and free of mildew. Figure 5.22 shows a picture of this vent.

LIGHTING

Although this may seem to be a strange subject for a chapter on deck layout, it is, nonetheless, essential. A boat intended to sail at night needs navigation lights, compass lights, instrument lights, and spot or hand lights. It may also need lights to illuminate the deck or the sails if they have to be changed or adjusted.

Lights, then, are important, and the most important are the navigation lights, which must be visible for a certain distance, depending on the size of the boat. In calm water a tiny speck of light is easily visible for two miles, but when you put that light on a yacht, heel it 20 or 30 degrees, and put the boat in six- to eight-foot seas, it takes a big light to be easily seen. This is why many people are fitting tricolor lights at the masthead, which are visible for miles.

Before we go much further, let's look carefully at the International Regulations for the Prevention of Collisions at Sea (Colregs). The latest copy was published in May 1977. First they discuss the range of lights. Any sailing vessel under 12 meters (39 feet) long must carry a sidelight and a sternlight. The range of the sidelights is one mile and the stern light two miles. This size of craft may carry a combined light at the masthead, as in Figure 5.23. A boat over 12 meters may carry two all-around lights, a red one over a green, one above the other, as well as sidelights and a sternlight. In this case, however, the side and sternlight must be visible for at least two miles, and if a tricolor masthead light is used instead of a red over green, it, too, must be visible for at least two miles.

Sailing craft under 7 meters (23 feet) and boats being rowed shall, if practical, show the side and sternlights, but the boat can carry a white all-around light or a handheld torch if other lights are not fitted.

As to which type of light is the best, I have always specified Aqua Signal lights. I like their masthead units, and their bow units appear to be reasonably watertight. (I've yet to find a totally watertight bow light.)

The two-mile visibility requirement is said to have been met by fitting a 25-watt bulb in the light. But even this may not be enough if the light is not positioned properly. I have seen lights carefully placed behind the vertical center bar of the pulpit, running lights fastened to the shrouds and totally obscured by the headsail, and worst of all, in my opinion, a light built into a small aperture in the hull so that as soon as the boat heeled the light all but disappeared. Lights are not there to protect other ships from you but to protect you from other ships! Poor or nonexistent lights make it easy for you to be run down.

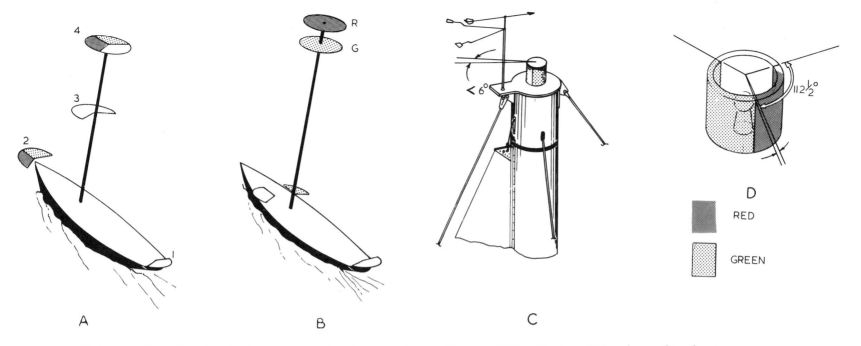

A B C D

A compass light, on the other hand, does not need to be seen by other boats, just by the helmsman and occasionally by other crewmen. It should have a dimmer switch so that its brightness can be controlled and a red bulb that allows the helmsman to look at it without destroying his night vision. The lights on the instruments should be red and dimmable for similar reasons.

For changing sails at night many experienced sailors prefer not to use deck lights but to use a hand light. They say the light can be directed where it is wanted. Most jobs can be done by the available light and feel anyway.

Other sailors prefer strong deck lights under the spreaders. I feel spreader lights have several disadvantages. They ruin the night vision of the entire on-deck crew. It takes 15–20 minutes to get full night vision back after they are turned off.

Secondly, the lights under the spreaders are vunerable to damage from the leach of the sail, and they tend to illuminate only the area around the base of the mast. If you bend over the sail, the sail is immediately cast into shadow, making a hand light essential anyway.

Having said that there are some deck lights that are very handy, I once saw a light that shone onto the tack of the sail from a deck locker just aft of the headstay. This makes it easy to unhook the sail or to see what the anchor line is doing in the middle of the night. Another light was situated in the cabintop and shone on the aft side of the mast. That

FIGURE 5.23. *Various lights for sailing boats.*

A The stern white sternlight at 1 and bow lights at 2 are the most conventional lights. When the boat is under power it should show a white light at 3. The tricolor masth light is an alternative.

B Larger craft can show red over green lights at the masthead.

C At the masthead any obstruction should not obscure more than 6 degrees of arc.

D The red and green sectors should fill 112.5 degrees of arc with not more than 2 degrees of confusion when changing from red to green.

way it didn't disturb the helmsman but helped the crew see the halyards at the mast.

If you are going to cruise extensively, an anchor light is essential. It is an all-around white light that is hung on a halyard in the foretriangle to show other boats you are anchored. In addition to that light at least three flashlights should always have fresh batteries. A hand-held spotlight is often handy for picking up buoys or rocks if you are groping your way into a strange harbor at night. There should also be plenty of spare bulbs and batteries aboard. While we are thinking on this line, there should also be on board spare bulbs for the compass, nav lights, and any other gear that requires a light at night.

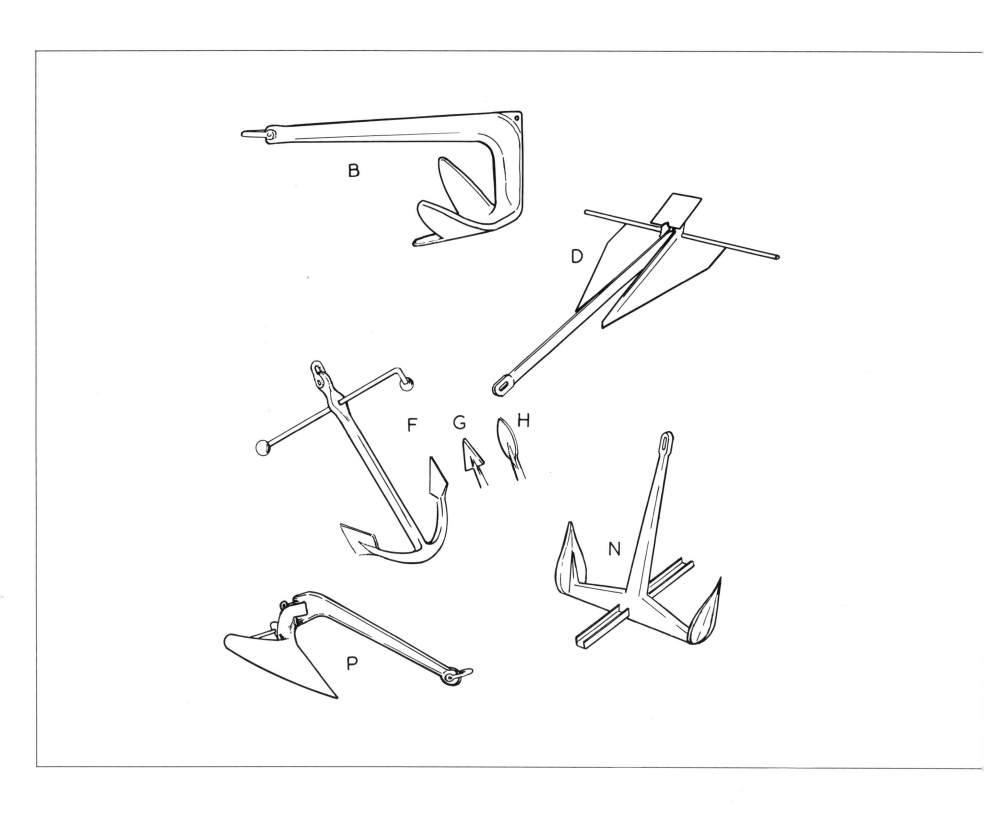

B

D

F   G   H

N

P

CHAPTER 6

Anchors:
Their Uses and Storage

The size of the anchor is a subject of great controversy. If you talk to one sailor, he'll tell you he's been using a 25-pound Danforth on his 50 footer for years. Another says his favorite is a 60-pound fisherman on the same size boat, without any problems. The only thing they'll all agree on is that the size and style of anchors vary, that anchor rodes vary in size, and that the amount of chain used, if any, will vary. So how do you select the best for your boat? To my knowledge no American insurance company provides a list of recommended anchor sizes. However, some classification societies, such as Lloyd's, do have anchor size information. Many manufacturers and magazines have published lists of anchor sizes; however, almost all of them advise increasing the weight if the anchor is to be used for long-term mooring. Unfortunately, there is no definite guide. First you must know the bottom, the type of boat, the type of anchor rode, and many other factors.

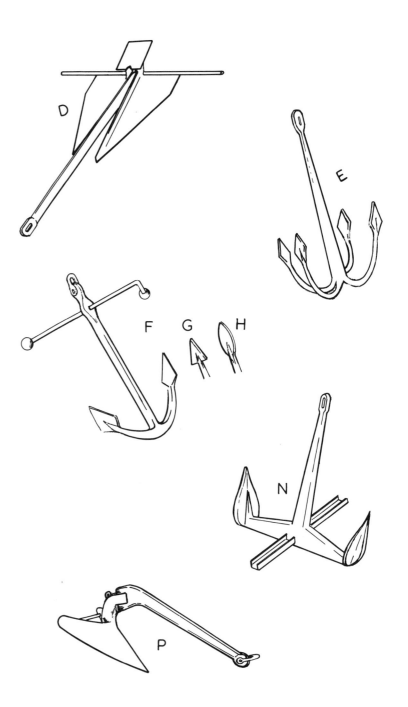
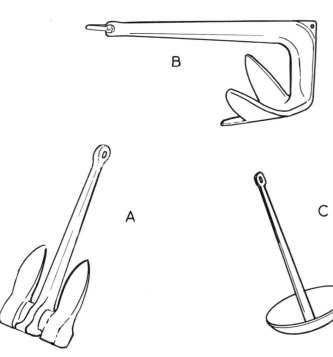

FIGURE 6.1: *Various anchors:*

A   *A U.S. navy anchor. A stockless type. Not often seen or used today.*

B   *A Bruce anchor. Another stockless type becoming very popular with yachtsmen.*

C   *A Mushroom anchor. Best for harbor use when it is silted in.*

D   *A Danforth anchor. A lightweight type. Very popular with the modern yachtsman. Easily stowed and used.*

E   *A simple grapnel. Sometimes called a rockpick.*

F   *The well-known fisherman (known in the United Kingdom as the Admiralty anchor). With triangular flukes it is called a yachtsman anchor. A Herreshoff anchor has diamond-shaped flukes, and a Nicholson anchor has spear-shaped flukes, probably to improve its holding power in rocks. As this was one of the most widely used types of anchor, there are many variations of fluke designed for specific applications.*

N   *A stock-in-head type, the Northill anchor. Not often seen or used today.*

P   *The well-known CQR anchor. Often called a plough after its digging-in action.*

But even before you drop the hook over the side, you should know the names of particular types of anchors. Often there are three or four different names for the same style of anchor. Figure 6.1 shows some different types of anchor. Then there's the problem of shackling the anchor to the chain or anchor rode (warp in Britain). Follow that by trying to get a shackled and moused anchor chain down the hawse hole, and you begin to see some of the problems associated with anchors and anchor handling.

THE FIRST ANCHORS

When we looked at our picture of the first sailor, we hypothesized how he got started. Eventually he had to stop sailing and moor his craft somewhere. No doubt, at first he hauled it up on the beach, but when he was over a lucrative fishing ground, he continually drifted away from it. This led to his finding a large rock and tying a rope around it. But the rope kept slipping off the rock, so he searched for a rock with a hole worn in it. This worked superbly until the wind got up and the anchor dragged.

Years later the first crude boat made from one log was expanded into boats made of several logs. However, it wasn't possible to scale the anchor up directly to suit the larger boat, and so one smart sailor in those far-off days had the bright idea of lashing a stick across the bottom of the rock to help the holding power. By experimentation over several hundreds of years they found that two spars lashed crosswise on the bottom of the rock did the best job of all of holding the boat in place. This type of anchor has been attributed to Indians, Tuscans, Chinese, Greeks, and Syrians. The truth of the matter is they probably visited each others' ports and saw the various anchor developments; as they were sailing home they figured a slightly better method of doing the same job and so improved the technique a little. When they returned to the port where they had first seen the idea, the locals saw the improvement and added their own touches. Like most early developments, this took hundreds or even thousands of years.

Then came the knowledge of metal casting and forging. The rock anchor gave way to metal anchors. Bronze, cast iron, and puddled and forged iron were all eventually tried. The waterfronts of most maritime nations are littered with the remains of various anchors lost by ships of earlier generations.

It wasn't until the expansion of maritime commerce that the anchor saw significant changes. Anchors had always been stowed on "cat-heads" in the forepart of the ship because it was so difficult to stow anywhere else. Anchors moved away from cathead stowage after the invention of the Martin close-stowing anchor. This development led to a closer look at various stockless-type anchors, and the "stockless" or "patent" anchor was patented in 1820 by Hawkins in England. Like many early experiments, this led to a flurry of development, resulting in the "wishbone" patent being granted in 1822 and the "swinging arm" type in about 1823. Both the wishbone and swinging arm types had moving parts, which gave them better holding power. After this bout of anchor design, inventors' minds turned to greater things, and the next improvement in anchor technology appeared over a century later, when Sir Geoffrey Taylor patented his "plough" or "secure" type. He had originally intended to call it the Secure anchor but decided that CQR would be easier for users to remember; consequently, this type is still known in many parts of the world as the CQR anchor. It is one of the most efficient anchors for use in mud or sandy bottoms and relies on the angle between the point and the blade of the plough to dig in quickly.

In 1939 the Danforth anchor was developed by R. D. Ogg and R. S. Danforth. This anchor was used extensively during World War II, when it gained a reputation for providing good holding power, light weight, and ease of digging in. On larger ships this anchor is also known as the Meon type.

In the late 1950s the Bruce anchor was developed for fishing vessels, later scaled up to be used on oil rigs, from which use it gained an enviable reputation. Today many boats are designed so that the Bruce anchor is self-stowing in the radius of the bow.

What are the options for today's sailor? Obviously he doesn't want to cart a basket full of rocks around to throw over the side as an anchor.

THE VARIOUS TYPES OF ANCHOR

If we use Lloyd's classification of anchors—"stockless," "stocked," and "high holding power"—we find certain types are both stockless and high holding power. So we'll add another criterion to distinguish them. The lightweight, high holding power types divide themselves from the stockless, heavyweight types quite nicely. But first we will need to define all the various parts of an anchor. Figure 6.2 illustrates the parts of the various types.

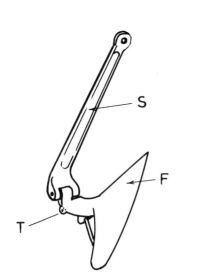

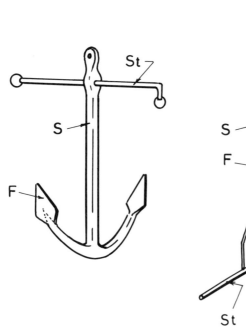

FIGURE 6.2. *The various parts of an anchor:*
S is the shank.
F are flukes.
St is the stock.
P is the tripping palm on the Danforth.
T is an eye for attaching the tripping line.

Anchors with Stocks

Probably the best-known anchor is the *fisherman* or admiralty type. This anchor relies on its weight to get it to the seabed and dig it into the mud. It has been around since the early days of anchors and has been made in many variations, some of which have taken the names of their manufacturers. For instance, the Herreshoff Manufacturing company made a fisherman with flukes shaped like a diamond, while the Nicholson anchor has more oval flukes. The Yachtsman anchor has triangular flukes, and other makers have spatulate flukes.

Yachtsman flukes, because they are triangular, have a tendency to catch the line behind the fluke and foul. Whereas diamond-shaped Herreshoff flukes allow a line to slide right off them. The finer flukes of the Nicholson are at their best on a rocky bottom or in weed, while the wider Herreshoff flukes are better in muddy or rock-strewn muddy bottoms. From this we can easily deduce why there are so many variations of flukes. Different fluke designs were intended to improve holding in different types of bottoms. No doubt, certain anchor types are much more popular in various areas because users have, by experiment, found the ideal match between anchor type and holding ground.

Most of the early fisherman types were made with a fixed stock and were difficult to stow, so later examples were made with a removable or folding stock. The one in most common use on the east coast of the United States is the Luke type, made by Paul Luke of Boothbay, Maine, which breaks down into three pieces—the stock, the shank, and the fluke arms—for stowage.

A different type of stocked anchor is the stock-in-head type. As its name implies, this type has the stock in the head of the anchor. The stock is set at 90 degrees to the flukes, which makes it hard to stow unless it is made to be collapsible. The Northill are examples of this anchor. While it has its drawbacks, it will apparently hold in many situations where the "lightweight" types cannot penetrate.

Stockless Types

Probably the best-known stockless types are the Danforth in America and the CQR in Britain. Both do an excellent job, but both are very different. The Danforth is a lightweight, high holding power anchor that relies on the dynamics of digging in to hold it on the bottom. It is said that the Danforth will "kite" as it is sinking. This could lead to it not being exactly where you want it to be when you are moored, but

I see this as a very minor problem. A larger problem becomes apparent on rocky or stony bottoms, where the anchor cannot dig in. This is where a fisherman comes to the fore. I've been told, but never experienced it, that a Danforth can also pick up a rock that will jam the flukes open, making it impossible to dig in. But, as I say, I've never experienced it in my extensive use of the anchor.

The Danforth is easy to stow—it is virtually flat—and when in a muddy or sandy bottom it works superbly. In the water, the flat tripping palms on the crown kick the points over. They then rest at an angle to the bottom. As soon as any strain comes on the anchor rode the points of the flukes dig in. More strain causes them to dig in further, and the anchor is very quickly buried deeply. To get it out, the pull can be reversed by using a tripping line, or if the pull is directed upward, the anchor will simply dig itself to the surface.

In an analysis of some tests I saw recently, several imitations were tested against the original Danforth. The results were surprising. Not only did the original dig in and stay there, but some of the imitations showed up very badly. One of them was so light it bounded along the bottom without digging in. So be careful when purchasing an anchor.

The CQR or plough anchor is probably the best-known and best-used anchor in the world today. It is one of the most efficient anchors in mud or sandy bottoms and relies on its weight and the angle between the point of the blade of the plough to dig in quickly. Its weight should be about the same as a Danforth for a given boat. Usually it is stowed in a roller on the bow, with the plough hanging over the bow. If it is stowed here it must be pinned securely in place. I've seen one jump off its roller and severely dent the underside of the pulpit as the boat rose to a sudden wave. Stowing it elsewhere on the boat is difficult because the anchor is reasonably heavy and not easily carried around.

A relative newcomer to the anchoring scene is the Bruce anchor. According to various articles I've read it was developed for fishing vessels who wanted a reasonably lightweight anchor with tremendous holding power. The anchor was made in two sizes, 50 kilograms (110 pounds) and 10 kilograms (22 pounds), but is available in many other sizes today. When the anchor proved successful, it was used in much larger sizes for oil rigs in the North Sea. After its success in this arduous area it was made in smaller sizes for yacht use.

The most unique aspect of this anchor is the shape of its flukes, which are reminiscent of a manta ray swimming through the water. It is this very shape that allows the hook to dig in very quickly and stabilize itself if the direction of pull is changed, when the tide

changes, for example. Also, the anchor has no moving parts; the solid one-piece casting eliminates mechanical problems. I have seen claims that the holding power is very high using a short scope. The figure given is up to 60 percent holding power at a 3 to 1 or even 2 to 1 scope. I would hesitate to recommend it until I tried it at such a short scope. They seem a little too short for me.

A similar type to the Danforth, the stockless, lightweight wishbone anchor was patented in America over 150 years ago. Like the Danforth, this anchor can also be jammed by rocks and weeds. But since the Danforth came on the market the wishbone anchor is rarely seen except for special applications.

The navy or stockless anchor is rarely seen on small boats. It is heavy. It is intended to be stowed in a hawsepipe, but it is reputed not to hold as well as its more modern counterparts. It was originally intended for use by the Royal Navy and was patented in 1821. For this reason it is often known as the navy or patent anchor. However, if you want to see one, some Royal Navy vessels still carry them.

The mushroom anchor: with the current overloading of any mooring grounds there's not mushroom for any more of them. (I couldn't resist the terrible pun.)

But space for permanent moorings is vanishing at an ever increasing rate, and this anchor is primarily used for permanent moorings. It is not very heavy and is best after it has been silted in for a few months or more. It does not penetrate well, but becomes very efficient after it has silted in thoroughly.

Probably the simplest stockless anchor of all is the grapnel type. Acknowledged to be ideal in rocky areas, it has several, usually four, tines sprouting from the bottom of the shaft.

Because it is often desired to position an anchor well away from the boat, a new Australian kiting design is intended to "kite" in the water to a desired position. Kiting is when the anchor generates some lift and rather than going straight down to the bottom, it glides toward the seabed. In some situations this feature is undesirable, but if you do not have a dinghy and cannot get the boat where you want it, the kiting feature may be useful.

A different anchor is the FOB hp type, shown in Figure 6.3. It looks to be a development of the Danforth type with sharper tines, which are expected to hold in weedy bottoms. The brochure also says that it will hold decently on a rocky bottom. I would have to check that before I recommended it.

The only type of anchor that does not sit on the bottom is the sea anchor. Every offshore yacht should have one on board. It is intended

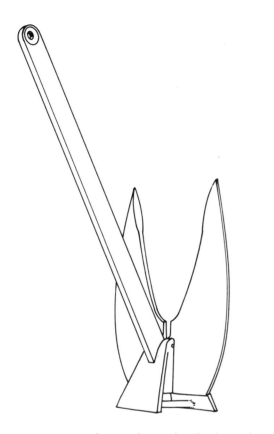

FIGURE 6.3. *An FOB hp anchor. This looks to be a development of the Danforth type anchor but according to the manufacturers brochure it will penentrate weedy bottoms and will hold decently in rocky bottoms. If these claims are true then it has a significant advantage over the tried and true Danforth.*

to slow the drift of a yacht to leeward in extreme conditions and to hold the bow of the boat at the best angle to the oncoming seas. Sea anchors look like canvas buckets with the bottom cut out and should be built with immense strength. Very often you hear of a boat setting a sea anchor only to have it destroy itself in a few minutes. The anchor has to hold the weight of the boat against the might of the sea. When you consider that the wind's power is squared every time its speed increases and the sea anchor is the only thing trying to stop the wind force, it has to be strong.

"I always use chain, and I want a locker that will hold 20 fathoms (36.5 meters)" was a request we had a few years ago from an owner. He wanted this in a 38-foot boat. After some questioning we found out that on his previous boat he'd used 2 fathoms (3.6 meters) of chain on the end of a 20-fathom nylon line without any problems, so why did he want so much chain now? His reply was that a more experienced friend said he should have all chain on his anchor line. We pointed out that 20 fathoms of ⅜-inch (approximately 10-millimeter) chain would weigh about 200 pounds (93 kilograms), which would be added to the weight of the three anchors he wanted to carry. All this weight would be close to the bow of the boat. Eventually he settled for nylon rode with some chain on the bottom of it.

Few sailors realize that chain is very heavy and modern cruising boats have become finer in the bow than ever before. This makes for a boat that will sail bow down if weight is added after the design is complete. If the design is a new one the weight can be taken into account, but it then becomes part of the design characteristics of the boat and is there for the life of the vessel. It will probably produce other undesirable characteristics, such as a boat that pitches and that will probably be wet in a head sea because of the extra weight in the bow.

The type of rode used should be carefully matched to the anchor, the holding ground, and the characteristics of the boat. For instance, you could be asking for disaster if you decide to use a plough on a jagged, coral bottom with a nylon line. The plough may catch and dig in. If it does, the line may survive being chafed against the coral, and if everything holds you may have to cut the anchor away because of it being impossible to unfoul it from the crevice in which it is wedged. In this case it would be better to use a fisherman or grapnel anchor with a length of chain and then the nylon rode.

Various tests have shown that the holding power of an anchor is reduced if the rode leads upward even a few degrees. For instance, a reduction of up to 25 percent of the holding power is possible if the rode is led upward at 5 degrees. The holding power can be reduced by up to 40 percent when the angle is increased to 10 degrees. It is a simple deduction that the best holding power is obtained when the shaft is parallel to the seabed.

Keeping the shaft parallel to the seabed means paying out plenty of scope (scope is the amount of cable let out) and using either an anchor weight or chain to hold the rode down on the seabed. This is where the anchor rode should be matched to the bottom characteristics. If you use solid chain, it will hang almost vertically from the bow, presuming no tide. Therefore you will have to back down on the line to get it to dig in. In this case a fairly short scope can be used and the chain will still lie on the ocean floor. A nylon rode with a length of chain between it and the anchor will help keep the anchor shaft on the seabed.

Note I've mentioned nylon anchor rode all through this discussion. It has a fair amount of stretchiness, which gives it good shock-absorbing capability. The open laid rope cable is the best type. Do not use polypropelene line, as it will want to float and would offer no catenary to the cable; in fact, it would try to lift the anchor off the seabed!

WHAT MAKES THE ANCHOR WORK?

It is an interesting combination of forces that makes an anchor operate successfully. It must be heavy enough to sink to the seabed without kiting or tangling with its own cable. More importantly, it should not foul the tripping line. Once on the bottom the anchor has to be aspected so that the flukes will dig in. On anchors like the Danforth, which lie flat on the seabed, this isn't normally a problem. The tripping palm ensures the flukes are accurately aligned to make it dig in.

The CQR and the Bruce anchor both lie on their sides and are dug in by dragging the anchors backward. Other types rely on the stock to trip the anchor to a position where the flukes can operate. As soon as the flukes have dug in the boat should be backed down hard enough to bury the hook sufficiently that a change in the direction of the pull—when the tide changes, for example—won't drag it out of the bed.

The power to dig the anchor in comes from backing the yacht down. The power to keep the anchor dug in comes from the various forces on the boat. They can be wind, tide, and wave action. Each contributes to the overall drag on the anchor, and the total is modified by the scope of the cable and the give in the nylon anchor rode. Plenty of scope will ensure the anchor is not subjected to sudden loads, which may lift it out of its nesting place.

HOW MUCH SCOPE?

A designer should have an idea of how much scope the owner likes to use because that will affect the amount of cable onboard. This, in turn, will govern the size of the cable locker and anchor storage. The amount of scope will depend on several factors:

1. The depth of water.
2. The type of anchor and cable.
3. The length of stay.
4. The type of bottom.
5. The proximity of dangers—rocks, other boats, or other obstructions.
6. The rise and fall of tide.
7. The weather.
8. The direction of tidal streams.
9. The hardness of the bottom.
10. The type of anchorage, open roadstead or protected harbor.

The prudent navigator will take all these points into account when he pays out the cable. So many variables are involved that to say you pay out 5 times the depth of water is an oversimplification of the problem. You could pay out 10 times the depth of water, but if your anchor is unsuitable for the bottom it won't hold unless it snags something. Let's look at each item in order and see how it affects the scope of the cable.

The Depth of Water

In general, the basic rule is to pay out five to seven times the depth of water.

The Type of Anchor and Cable

Here we'll assume that you have selected an anchor that is suitable for the bottom: a CQR, plough, Danforth, or Bruce for sand or mud bottoms; a fisherman or grapnel for rocky bottoms. The chain and nylon rode should also be suitable for the type of bottom. If these factors have been chosen correctly they shouldn't modify the basic length of scope. In addition to using a shorter scope, you should select an anchor that is suitable for the bottom and the duration of your stay. For example, a light anchor is quite adequate if you intend to anchor in a secluded cove for lunch, but for a longer stay or bad weather anchoring, a heavier hook will be needed.

The Length of Stay

If you intend to stay for only a short time and there will be somebody on deck keeping a weather eye open, then you should be able to get away with shorter scope. In general, the longer your stay, the longer the scope should be.

The Type of Bottom

The type of bottom could lead us to lengthen or shorten the scope. For instance, if we set an anchor on coral I would hesitate to have a long scope in case it chafed on another coral head. In this case, more chain and less line should be used. Another instance could be where the bottom is a very fluid type of mud. In this case the scope should be increased.

The Proximity of Dangers

The proximity of dangers will lead to modification of the length of scope. For instance, if we were anchored near a jetty and the tide changed it might sweep the boat within a few feet of the jetty. In this case we'd want to shorten the scope of the cable.

The Rise and Fall of Tide

If we let out the minimum scope and the tide comes in the scope will be below minimum. Therefore you should have an idea of how high, or low, the tide will be and pay out enough cable to ensure you have at least five times the depth of water at all states of the tide.

The Weather

In general, more scope in worse weather is better. The catenary of the cable will absorb many of the shock loads caused by high waves.

The Direction of Tidal Streams

The amount of scope is also dependent upon the direction of the tidal stream. But tidal streams can make the boat veer around unexpectedly if you have a lot of scope out. Also, eventually the direction of the stream will change and your boat will have to accommodate itself at the other end of its tether, which may be too near an obstruction for comfort.

The Hardness of the Bottom

The hardness of the bottom affects the type of anchor you can use and the amount of scope. For instance, you might use a CQR on a soft sandy bottom, but on a rocky bottom a fisherman would be your best bet.

The Type of Anchorage

In general, more scope should be paid out if you intend to moor offshore. Less scope can be used in sheltered waters.

PICKING THE RIGHT ANCHOR

The major influence on the holding power of the anchor is the hull of the boat, the amount of scope, and the wind strength. If we wanted to we could measure the frontal area of the boat and for any given wind strength make an estimate of the wind drag or windage of the boat. We could also estimate the tidal drag on the underwater part of the hull and on the anchor rode, and then estimate the increase in forces on the anchor rode due to the pitching of the boat. This should give us a reasonable estimate of the total drag on the anchor. Using this figure we could look up the holding power of various anchors and match an anchor to our estimated needs. Of course, we'd have to build in a factor of safety to end up with the final anchor size, or we can take the manufacturer's recommended size and go slightly larger or smaller depending on the type of sailing we will be doing.

ANCHOR STOWAGE

Anchors are big and heavy and a person trying to carry one around on a pitching and heaving deck risks damaging himself or the boat. So anchor-stowing techniques need to be simple, precise, and easy on the muscles. One very popular method is to stow the hook on the bow roller. Another, seen more often on production craft, is stowage in the anchor well. A large yacht may have a stockless anchor stowed in its own hawsepipe, or the hook can be stored on its own chocks on the foredeck. The least satisfactory way is to stow the anchor in the bottom of one of the sail bins, where it is usually covered with sails and hard to get at when needed.

Stowing the anchor on the bow roller fulfills all the criteria we mentioned earlier. But, too often, the end result is an unsafe, untidy, and sometimes dangerous situation. For this type of storage to work properly the anchor needs to be firmly fixed in place. First, the roller should be large enough to allow any shackles to pass over it easily. Note that if anchor chain is used without any nylon line, the roller should be made of metal. Then the flanges on either side of the roller should be high enough to allow a pin to be inserted to hold the anchor in place. On CQRs this pin can be passed directly through the anchor buoy lug, while on the Bruce anchor it should be in front of the shank.

I have seen Danforths stowed in this manner, but the result is very untidy. The Danforth is light enough to be stowed in its own well, which can be built into the boat against the side of the hull, or on its own chocks flat on the deck. Figure 6.4 shows a typical well detail. Other methods of stowing anchors are shown in Figures 6.5, 6.6, and 6.7.

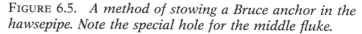

FIGURE 6.5. *A method of stowing a Bruce anchor in the hawsepipe. Note the special hole for the middle fluke.*

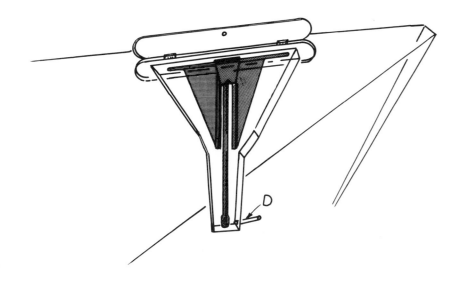

FIGURE 6.4. *It is easy to design a locker for the Danforth anchor right into the foredeck of the boat. However, the locker lid should be reasonably watertight and a drain should be provided.*

FIGURE 6.6. *Twin Danforths give this boat terrific holding power. But I would be happier with a Danforth and another type of anchor to give variation in holding possibilities.*

FIGURE 6.7. *Although this boat has two different anchors, neither of them is stowed well. Sailing off a large wave could displace the anchors and cause some damage.*

Getting a fisherman anchor aboard can often pose a problem. The stock sticks out at 90 degrees to the flukes, and the thing is usually unmanageable unless a davit is used to keep it clear of the boat. Figure 6.8 shows a simple removable davit. The davit holders are bolted to the bulwarks or cabin side, and a block and tackle is led from the davit to the gravity band on the anchor. Then it is a simple job to swing the hook aboard and break it down, ready for stowing. Another idea is to use a bowsprit/anchor handling platform, which can double as a cathead and keep the anchor away from the hull.

Plough, Bruce, and Danforth anchors are easily stowed in hawsepipes. Once the anchor is in position to be stored, it should be firmly secured. Either keeping tension on the chain or mousing the hook to a handy padeye is recommended. If chain is used for the last few feet of the rode, a devil's claw or chain stopper can be used to clamp the chain in place. Figure 6.9 shows a chain stopper. The devil's claw in Figure 6.10 can easily be fabricated for any size chain and adjusted with a bottlescrew or turnbuckle.

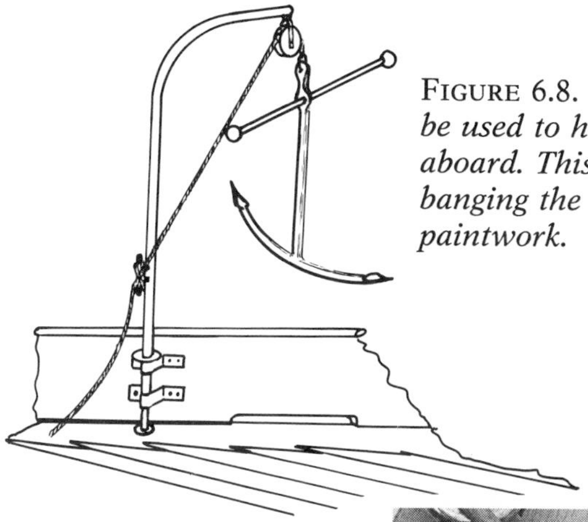

FIGURE 6.8. A removable davit can be used to haul a fisherman anchor aboard. This will stop it from banging the topsides and marring the paintwork.

The Anchor Well

On production cruisers, anchor wells are becoming very common. They do keep the foredeck tidy, but their use should be limited to boats that sail long distances offshore, unless certain requirements are met.

With water continually washing over the foredeck, some of it will find its way into the anchor well. For this reason the anchors and line should sit on a grating with large overside drains at the bottom of the well. I also think these wells should be kept as small as possible. It is nice to have the anchor windlass in the well and all the handling gear down there, but only if the boat is very large. Then the well can be made almost watertight and the equipment protected. Plus, the additional weight that far forward and high up does not affect performance too badly.

The stowage of items inside the well is also critical. It should be possible to tie the anchor down securely. There is nothing more disconcerting when sailing off a large wave than to see the anchor explode out of the well and disappear over the side because it was not tied down. Also, the use of the well should be limited to anchor-handling gear to ensure that the drain holes are not blocked.

Another useful item on the foredeck is a salt water washdown pump. With it the anchor and anchor rode can be washed off before being stowed. The washdown pump could also be switchable to be used as a fresh water washdown on the forward portion of the boat.

FIGURE 6.9. A chain stopper is a useful feature to have between the anchor and the windlass.

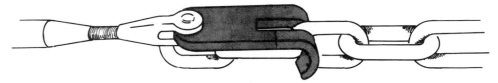

FIGURE 6.10. A simple devil's claw will serve to hold the anchor tightly if it is tensioned with a turnbuckle.

CAPSTANS AND WINDLASSES

The next useful item in the anchor-handling sequence is the windlass. Originally the term *windlass* was reserved for a horizontal shaft type and *capstan* for vertical shaft winches. But now the terms have become almost interchangeable. Capstans are a fairly recent development in the nautical world. They first appeared in the eighteenth century on old-time sailing ships. There they were positioned about two-thirds of the way aft along the gun deck. Very often the shaft of the capstan passed through two or three decks and was turned by men on each deck. Contrary to popular opinion, the capstan did not directly haul on the anchor cable. An endless line went around the cable and forward to the cable hawse. The cable was "nipped" to the endless line by "nippers," usually young boys who held their nipper until the cable was about to disappear down to the cable locker. This is where the British term *nipper* for a young boy comes from.

Today, if you want a capstan or windlass, you don't need a crew of a hundred or so men and a piper to turn it. Modern windlasses can be electrically, hydraulically, or manually operated. A windlass should have at least one chain gipsy and a drum, usually called a warping drum or barrel, for working cables. The larger windlasses usually have gipsies inboard of both port and starboard drums, and each drum can be driven independently of each other.

Most boats under 35 feet (10.6 meters) will use a manual windlass if they have one fitted. Almost all the manual windlasses are double-action types. That is, the drum or gipsy is driven on both strokes of the lever. Very few are single-action types.

Larger yachts usually have the engine and battery capacity to employ an electric or hydraulic windlass. To date my company has specified three types of windlass, and all our customers have been happy with our recommendations. The most impressive was a 25-year-old Ideal windlass from a boat on which we were supervising an overhaul. The windlass was a 32 volt model, the drum was corroded, and the paint was badly chipped. Ideal Windlass Company of East Greenwich, Rhode Island, converted the windlass to 12 volts, restored the drum, and repainted the entire unit at a total cost of $250. The windlass has worked perfectly since and should last another 25 years. I would recommend them to anybody.

Nilsson windlasses also have a good reputation. The catalog shows many different types and styles, and every sailor I've talked to says good things about them. The other manufacturer I like is Simpson Lawrence, but they are very expensive in the United States and I prefer to order direct from a European mail order house. There are several things to look for when selecting a windlass:

1. Size. The windlass should have a small footprint. Some of the smallest types are the vertical shaft capstans. Usually the motor is underdeck and all that is visible on deck is the capstan drum and push button.
2. Capacity. Not only should the windlass be capable of lifting the anchor, chain, and line, but it should be able to break the anchor out of reasonably firm ground. If the hook is wedged tightly, certain maneuvers can be performed with the boat to break it out.
3. Watertightness. The capstan or windlass should be watertight. If it isn't, the electric motor will soon corrode and stop working.
4. There should be a brake on the chain gipsy. This is to stop the chain from running away when the anchor hits bottom.
5. Check whether you want the through-deck hawse hole. It is standard on many windlasses, but it may not fit the interior design of your boat.
6. Check the maintenance schedule of the capstan or windlass. If you have to oil or grease it every time you use it, it may become more toil than it is worth.
7. Check the electrical requirements of the unit. Some work on 12 volts, other on 24 volts, and some on 110 or 240 volts. The amperage required should also be carefully checked. There is no point in selecting a windlass that runs your batteries flat every time you use it.
8. When checking electrical capacity, find out how much power it takes to stall the drum. The normal running power may be well within the capacity of the batteries, but the power to stall the unit could discharge batteries very quickly.
9. Match the windlass gipsy to the size chain you are using. A universal gipsy may not fit your chain, or, worse still, you may have to keep stopping to adjust the chain as it comes in.
10. Order a cover to protect the unit from salt spray.

Not many hydraulic windlasses are seen now. They do appear to be heavy, but with the trend toward higher pressure hydraulics it is probably only a matter of time before somebody designs a hydraulic windlass or capstan.

Locating the Windlass

Locating the windlass often poses problems. It should be far enough from the bow to allow working space around it. Pushing it aft will also move the weight back nearer to the center of gravity of the yacht and allow a chain stopper to be positioned between the windlass and the bow. It will also allow the anchor locker, with its attendant weight, to be positioned further aft. I recommend a minimum distance of at least 18 inches (approximately 450 millimeters) between the chain stopper and the windlass to allow the chain to be lifted off the gipsy or to remove overrides. Ideally, the anchor chain will end just before it gets to the windlass, so that changing from rode to chain is not required, but that is not always possible. The line should be washed as it comes aboard and fed into a cable locker for storage.

With anchor chains, shackles, and cables coming aboard over the bow roller and the windlass situated well aft, the movement of the chain along the deck is likely to produce some serious scratches and scuffs on the planking, as well as depositing a fair amount of sediment on deck. To avoid this chafing, strips should be used. They can be permanently or temporarily fastened to the deck and are used when the anchor or chain is coming aboard. Teak is prefered by some owners because it matches the deck material and is easily replaced. On other boats a brass or stainless steel strip is used.

To keep the area clean when hauling the anchor, small strips of teak can be positioned around the working area. They can be fixed or removable and are intended simply to aim the dirt toward the nearest scupper.

Anchors stowed in hawsepipes should have a means of tensioning the cable when the hook is stowed so that it cannot rattle. Chafe patches should also be fitted on the bow and anywhere the hook is likely to hit as it comes into the hawsepipe. These patches should be large enough so that the anchor will not damage the hull on its way into the hawsepipe.

STORING THE CABLE

This often presents a problem, especially on a small boat, which often does not have an anchor locker. The cable locker, where it is fitted, should be as far aft as possible. This, in itself, poses a problem of integration with the rest of the interior.

We solved this problem on a 37-foot (11.2-meter) sloop by sloping the hawsepipe aft, thereby keeping the chain resting on one side rather than banging against the sides as the boat pitches. The slope also served to move the locker aft, and by welding steps to the hawse we obtained a simple ladder for the foredeck hatch.

Page 148 shows a simple formula for calculating the volume that chain will take up. It is prudent to allow 10–15 percent more than the calculated value to ensure plenty of room. However, several other points should be kept in mind as well when designing the chain locker:

1. It should have a removable top to enable the crew to reach in and redistribute the chain.
2. It should have a grating at the bottom to allow the chain or line to drain.
3. A seal or cap should be provided to keep water out of the chain hawse. This may mean removing the chain from the anchor and tying it to the back of the cap with a short length of line. This is the only method of obtaining a watertight seal.
4. The chain will come aboard wet, so the locker should be able to be tightly sealed to prevent odor or dampness from spreading into the boat.
5. It is often useful to paint the chain or mark the line to show how much scope has been paid out.

Lockers are not the only place to stow anchor cable. On one small boat we kept the nylon anchor cable on an ordinary rope drum. When we anchored, a spare piece of dowel was pushed through the hole in the drum and the whole thing dropped into specially made hooks under the forehatch. The cable ran out easily, and when sufficient line had gone out it was made up on a foredeck cleat. A simple and effective storage device.

Anchor handling, then, is not simply a matter of buying the cheapest hook you can find. It is a matter for careful thought, selecting the anchor most suited to the area in which you intend to sail and the type of bottom where you normally anchor, picking the type of cable that will let the anchor do its job and, most importantly, paying out enough scope. But the job doesn't stop there. When the anchor is back aboard it must be cleaned and stowed and the line flaked and put away. After all, the very life of your boat and family could depend on that anchor, and careful consideration of all these points are essential if your boat is to be anchored securely (or should that read "CQR-ly"!).

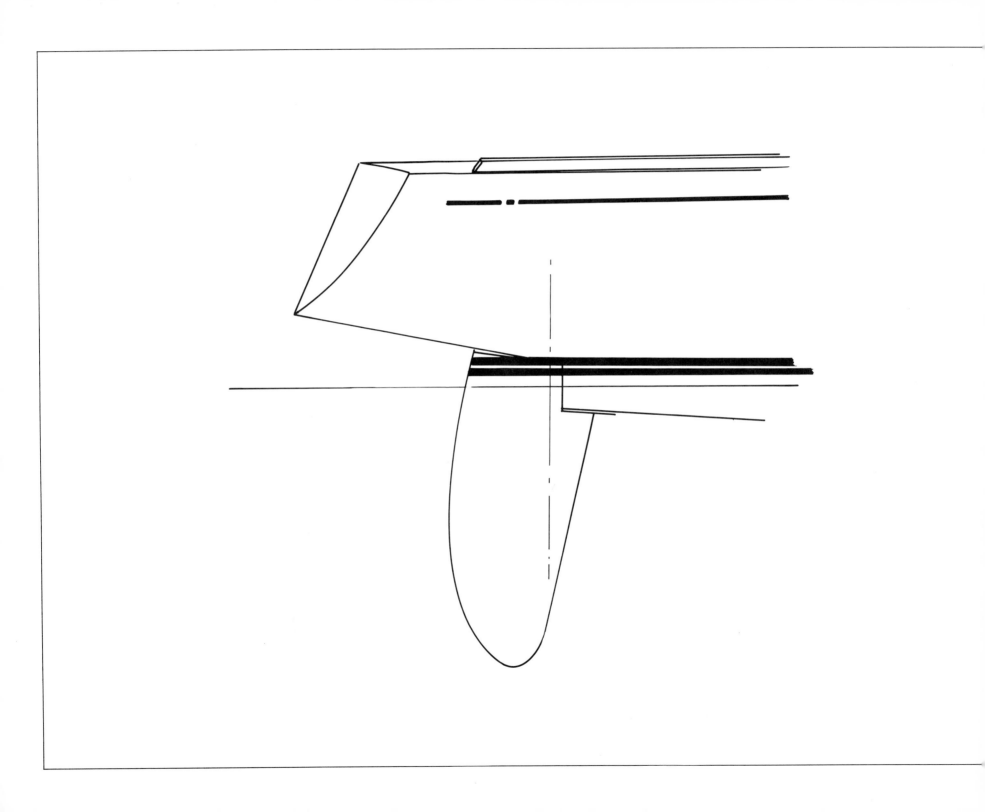

CHAPTER 7

A Sense of Direction

L ike the steering wheel on a car, a rudder is essential on a boat. Not only is the rudder essential, but so is some method of moving it. Rudders come in many shapes and sizes, and if you want to start an argument in any bar all you need do is ask a bunch of sailors what the best type of rudder is. Is it a balanced rudder, one with a skeg in front of it, or a rudder on the trailing edge of the keel? Should the rudder stock be raked aft or forward? How should the bottom/leading edge/trailing edge be shaped? These are all reasonably provocative questions.

IS A BALANCED RUDDER BEST?

This depends on what type of sailing you want. A balanced rudder gives the lightest and most sensitive steering. Sloping the blade aft will reduce the sensitivity somewhat and make the helm feel heavier. But a balanced

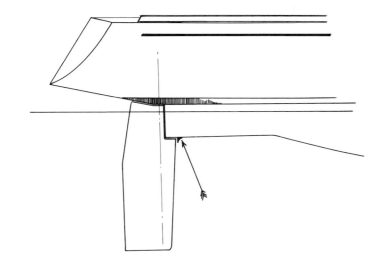

FIGURE 7.1. *A small pin in front of the rudder will usually stop seaweed, lobster and crab pot lines and other debris from jamming the rudder blade. The arrow shows the location of the pin.*

FIGURE 7.2. *A balanced rudder needs a bearing at deck level to stop it twisting in the boat. E is the squared-off stock for the emergency tiller. B is the top bearing. S is the rudder stock.*

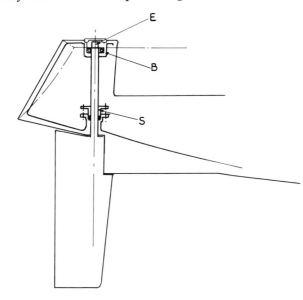

rudder will stall earlier than a rudder with a skeg in front of it, unless the rudder blade is made slightly thicker.

Another problem with balanced rudders is that they can get lines or weed fouled between the top of the rudder and the hull. Some cruisers install a small pin just in front of the leading edge of the blade to help deflect weeds and lobster pot lines, as in Figure 7.1. The stock for this type of rudder should also be designed slightly differently than for a keel- or skeg-hung rudder. Most of the strain on the stock is in the form of bending moment at the shaft-hull intersection. This means the stock should be designed to minimize bending rather than being supported at the top and bottom like a keel- or skeg-hung rudder would be. A balanced rudder stock should also have a deck-level bearing or a shaft from the bottom of the hull to the deck, as shown in Figure 7.2, to reduce twisting and racking loads on the bottom bearing and to keep the rudder straight in the boat.

Skegs are rarely seen on small boats (under 30 feet). On this size craft the skeg is usually so small that it is ineffective.

Because many of this type of rudder have sheared off at the bottom of the stock, the shaft should go all the way to the bottom of the rudder to minimize potential trouble. Figure 7.3 shows some of these features.

WHY IS A RUDDER WITH A SKEG BETTER FOR CRUISING CRAFT?

A skegged rudder is less sensitive than a balanced rudder, therefore, with a vane steering or an autopilot, it will be less work to keep the boat on course. The rudder blade is also well protected when it is operating behind a skeg. A third point in favor of a skeg is that the rudder stock is supported at both ends, reducing the need for a bearing at the deck and cutting down on any twisting or bending on the stock and blade.

But skegs should be solidly attached to the boat. There have been cases where the skeg has been damaged or ripped off and the boat has sunk. On a lesser level a flexible skeg may cause stiffness in the steering mechanism or even make the rudder lock up solid.

However, a major drawback with a skeg-hung rudder crops up when the propeller is situated just in front of the skeg. With a propeller close to the skeg, removal of the propeller shaft could be difficult or impossible unless special precautions are taken. Either the bottom half of the skeg must be made removable, or the shaft and engine must be situated a few degrees off center so that the shaft can be pulled out alongside the skeg. If this is not done and the shaft has to be removed by pulling the engine, the cost of replacing the shaft may be about four times the cost of pulling the shaft conventionally.

What About a Keel-Hung Rudder?

Keel-hung rudders lose a lot in sensitivity because they have to work in the turbulent flow immediately behind the keel. In other words, the rudder may have to be turned a few degrees to either side before the helmsman gets any feedback through the tiller.

However, a boat with a long keel has a high directional stability and, on the negative side, is often slow to come about so that the lack of sensitivity can make up for lack of attention on the part of the helmsman.

When the rudder is hung on the trailing edge of a fairly short keel, it is much nearer the boat's pivot point, and because the lever arm is shorter, it tends to be more effective than a rudder a long way aft.

Tank and computer tests have shown that the most efficient rudder style for control and small turning circle is a combination of a skeg and balanced blade positioned well aft. As you can see from Figure 7.4, the balanced part of the rudder is almost ideal for catching lobster pot lines and other waterborne debris.

Putting the Rudder on the Transom

This is the most common, cheapest, and simplest method of installing a rudder. It offers certain advantages and some disadvantages.

Its major advantage is the cost. Instead of a large, heavy stock, the rudder is mounted on two or more pintles. If you intend to sail offshore with this type of rudder, you should check the pintles carefully. They are probably the most common reason for rudder failure. Another advantage is ease of removal. Should you have a problem, pull the rudder off and repair it—unless the rudder has been pinned, then this advantage is gone. Yet another positive feature is the ease of mounting a vane on a transom-hung rudder.

On the negative side are the rudders that are damaged by the seawall when the boat is moored stern-to against a wall and the inherent weakness of a long, thin blade being held rigidly at one end and twisted, sometimes quite violently, at the other end. There is also a slight loss in efficiency when the rudder is placed at the transom. This is due to the loss of the end plate effect of the hull and some ventilation

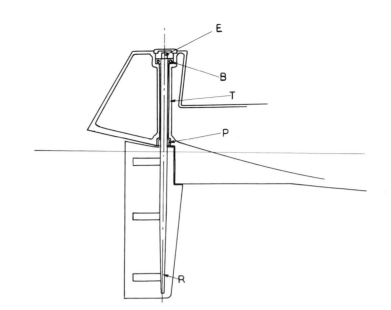

FIGURE 7.3. *The rudder shaft should go as far down the rudder blade as possible to stop any possibility of the rudder blade fracturing. Note also the tube (T) from the bottom of the hull to deck level. This eliminates the need for a stuffing box and makes it easy to install top (B) and bottom (P) bearings. E is the emergency steering fitting.*

FIGURE 7.4. *Carrying the skeg a little farther down the rudder gives the best of both worlds for the cruising yachtsman. He can have the benefits of a skeg rudder and a balanced rudder with very few of the drawbacks.*

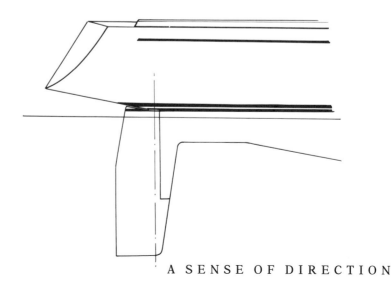

of the rudder blade unless special plates are fitted to reduce or eliminate ventilation.

When the Rudder Is Under the Hull

When the rudder is positioned under the hull some end plate effect is gained but at the additional expense of a stuffing box and inboard bearings. To improve rudder effectiveness, the gap between the top of the rudder blade and the hull should be as small as possible. Yet another place to improve rudder performance and stop fouling by lobster pots and water-borne debris is the rudder-skeg slot. Special care should be taken to reduce turbulence along this slot. Racing craft fit copper or mylar strips to reduce turbulence and increase efficiency.

Trim Tabs: Are They Useful?

This is an argument that can go on for a long time. On the one hand, a trim tab is an added complication and expense. Some designers say it is very hard to justify the extra cost and it is better to increase the rudder and keel size rather than add a tab. But, on the other hand,

FIGURE 7.5. *A parabolic-tipped rudder blade is said to make the boat steer better and reduce vortex drag.*

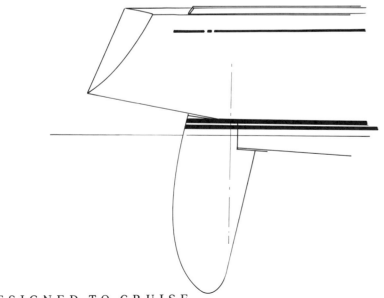

they can help windward performance somewhat and, more importantly, will serve as a spare rudder if the main rudder is damaged. My preference is not to have a trim tab.

However, since the 1983 America's Cup match, when the winged keel of *Australia II* gave the boat such an advantage, I have revised my opinion on trim tabs. If a winged keel is fitted, then a trim tab will increase the efficiency of that tab quite dramatically. In this case a tab is worth fitting.

Raking the Rudder Stock

Yet another perennial discussion is how much rake the rudder stock should have. All the experience I have as a designer and sailor, and all the test data I have seen, says that a stock that is almost vertical is best under the widest range of conditions. However, many designers slope the stock slightly to make it nearer 90 degrees to the hull surface. This reduces the gap between the rudder blade and the hull and still allows the blade to turn about 35 degrees either side of centerline without binding on the hull.

Raking the stock forward appears to increase drag. If the bottom of the stock is raked forward and the boat is heeled, water on the leeward side will be directed up the blade of the rudder. When this water gets to the hull it has nowhere to go and can only form a confused swirl, which increases drag and reduces speed.

The Shape of the Rudder Blade

Rudder blade shape varies tremendously from boat to boat. But there is quite a large amount of test data available to determine the most efficient shape and section. Unless practical reasons dictate otherwise, rudder blades should be as efficient as possible, regardless of whether a boat is intended for cruising or racing.

A typical example of this is the turning efficiency of a rudder with a parabolic tip, which is slightly better than one with a flat tip, as in Figure 7.5. The parabolic tip also reduces vortex drag and gives slightly better lift characteristics. However, because of its tapered curved shape it is more expensive to build.

A flat plate rudder, on the other hand, is inexpensive to build but is much less efficient than a rudder with the correct sectional shape.

The rudder should be as deep as possible. Most designers specify the depth as 70–95 percent of the draft, depending upon keel configuration. For example, on the fin-keel profile shown in Figure 7.6, the

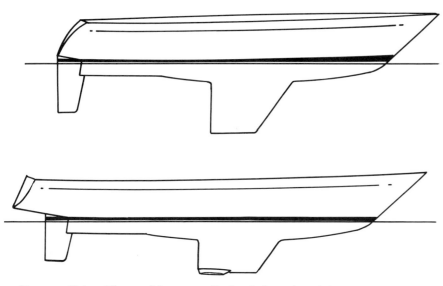

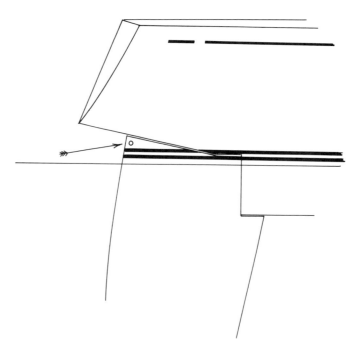

FIGURE 7.6. *The rudder on a fin-keeled yacht of fairly deep draft would normally be about 75–80% of the maximum draft. While the rudder on a centerboard or winged keel yacht may be as deep as 90% of the draft.*

rudder would be about 75 percent of the draft, while the centerboarder and long-keeled craft use about 95–98 percent. The leading edge of the skeg or rudder are best if they are parabolic, while the trailing edge should have a ¼-inch (6-millimeter) flat on it. As an additional safety feature it is worthwhile having a ½-inch (12-millimeter) hole drilled in the top of the trailing edge; then, should the stock break free of the blade, a line can secured to the blade, which will allow you some directional control to get you home. Figure 7.7 illustrates the detail.

STEERING GEAR

At the other end of the rudder is the steering gear. It, too, has many variations and styles of which the knowledgeable cruiser should be aware. From the simple tiller to a much more complex two-station hydraulic unit with trim tab controls, autopilot, and helm position indicators, the steering system is one of the major parts of the boat. It should be made as "breakproof" as possible, for without it it could be hard to get home.

FIGURE 7.7. *A small hole in the trailing edge of the rudder blade can be used to pass a line through should the rudder blade part from the stock when you are at sea.*

The Steerboard or Oar

The oar or steerboard (the term *starboard*—Old English *steoboard*, Middle English *sterboard*—is reputed to have been derived from the side of the boat on which the steerboard was placed) is not often seen today, having been replaced by more efficient rudders and tillers. But the idea is useful for an emergency: a steering board could be made up from a spinnaker pole and cabin sole board.

Tiller Steering

At one time tillers were the only known method of steering a boat. Even today they are one of the best known. The tiller may be attached to the top of the rudder blade in the case of a transom-mounted rudder, or it can be attached to the top of the stock. Yet another more unusual style is to put a tiller yoke on a mizzen mast or bitt and attach it to the stock with wires, as in Figure 7.8.

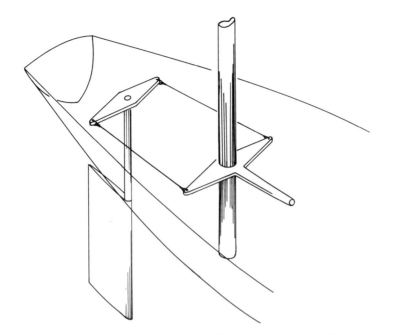

FIGURE 7.8. *If the mizzen mast is fitted where the helmsman would normally stand, a simple yoke can be made up to position the helmsman in front of the mizzen mast.*

FIGURE 7.9. *To eliminate the tiller sweeping the cockpit, a whipstaff could be used. When the arm is pushed to port the tiller turns to starboard. This makes it backward to the normal tiller.*

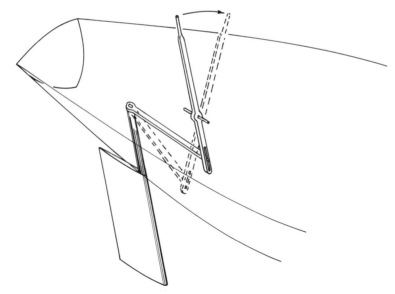

Tiller steering is certainly less complicated than a wheel, but a price must be paid for this simplicity: the sweeping of the cockpit with the tiller every time a boat is tacked or jibed. This effect can be minimized by careful placement of the crew and a minimum-length tiller, but it will still happen. However, on long offshore trips it is not that often that you tack or jibe, and usually the only crew that are on deck are busy with the sails. For instance, I can remember one trip to Bermuda when we tacked twice between Brenton Reef light tower and Kitchen Shoals buoy. A distance of over 600 miles. Another long-distance sailor tells of the time when he sailed trans-Atlantic and tacked twice, once in mid-Atlantic and once to enter the fairway!

Another limitation of tiller steering is that the helmsman must be well aft near the rudder unless the yoke feature is used. This means that the helm position must be well aft.

A Whipstaff

As sailing ships grew larger it became increasingly difficult for the helmsman, who had to stay aft near the tiller to see where the ship was going. One of the earliest mechanical linkages was devised to raise the man higher in the boat to enable him to see over the cargo or forecastle. The whipstaff, as it was known, fitted over the end of the tiller and operated in the *reverse* direction to the tiller. Figure 7.9 shows how it worked. This type of steering system can sometimes be seen on older harbor launches.

Wheel Steering

The next step in the control of ships was to connect the tiller to a wheel by means of cables and then to gear the turns of the wheel with tackles sited below docks. These systems became quite large, for instance, a 150-foot (46-meter) (on the gun deck) frigate built in 1812 weighing 1,000 tons (1,016 tonnes) had a 20-foot (6.1-meter) tiller with four-part tackles and a cable of 1-inch (25-millimeter) Manila rope connected to the wheel on the upper deck.

Wire and sprocket systems. Old-time steering systems have evolved into the modern types that use steel wires, quadrants, and steel or wooden steering wheels. Of all the steering systems in use, I specify the Edson system. They've been around since 1859 and have a pretty good idea how a boat steers. Their selection of equipment is very comprehensive, and whenever I've had a steering problem I've had nothing but courteous help from them.

The modern steering wheel offers several advantages over the tiller. The major plus is that it leaves much more room in the cockpit. Another is that it improves visibility for the helmsman. He can now sit well outboard and keep watch or steer without being limited to the tiller or tiller extension. Yet another major factor (which can often be used to mask a heavy helm) is the power that can be gained by using the right combination of quadrant, sprocket, and wheel diameter. Often a 28- or 36-inch (710- or 914-millimeter) wheel can be geared to have the power of a 10- or 12-foot (3- or 3.6-meter) long tiller. Against the advantages of the steering system must be balanced the additional complexity and expense, the extra friction, and the play in the wheel, which can reduce sensitivity.

The wheel steering system, often called pedestal or sprocket steering, uses a wire connected at one end to a quadrant bolted to the rudder stock. At the other end the cable is connected to a chain that runs over a sprocket at the top of the steering pedestal. The sprocket is keyed or bolted onto the same shaft as the steering wheel. Figure 7.10 shows a typical Edson system. Adjusting the size of the sprocket or the quadrant changes the gear ratio of the steering system and gives the helmsman more or less turns of the wheel to turn the rudder. This type of system enables the designer to place the wheel anywhere in the boat and still get good "feel" from the rudder—but, as with most things, moderation is best. If the wheel is too far from the quadrant the cables could stretch under load and jump off the sheaves. Because the system uses sheaves or pulleys to turn each corner, some space needs to be allowed for them when the boat is designed. Also, space should be allowed for the rudder quadrant, which means that there should be at least 18 inches (about .5 meter) around the rudder stock on boats up to 40 feet (12.2 meters) LOA. More space should be allowed on larger boats.

The pedestal is also a handy place for mounting the compass, engine controls, instruments—even a cockpit table can be attached to provide comfortable dining in the cockpit. However, if you decide to use pedestal steering you should have a guard around the compass to give the crew something to hold onto when they move aft. Many times I have seen a crewman grab the wheel or compass as the boat lurched, and once the compass came right off the pedestal! Figure 7.11 shows a typical guard.

Bulkhead-mounted steerers. Wheel steering need not be confined to a pedestal. The unit can be mounted on a bulkhead at the forward end of the cockpit. This offers certain advantages over the pedestal in that the helmsman can be placed under the dodger and can have a chart

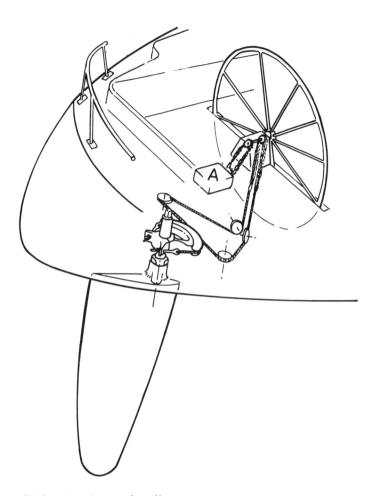

FIGURE 7.10. *A wire and pulley steering system. As the wheel is turned it turns the chain, which moves the quadrant. A is an autopilot. (Drawing by permission of Edson Corporation.)*

table immediately to hand. This can be taken to its logical conclusion and the helmsman's position put inside the boat, where he can steer the boat without getting wet! Using the wire and sprocket or pull-pull system it is a simple job to have an inside and cockpit steering position. But I would only recommend inside steering for a boat over 50 feet (15 meters) or on a craft specially designed for it.

Rack and pinion steering. When the wheel steering position is close to the top of the rudder stock, the cruising sailor might want to con-

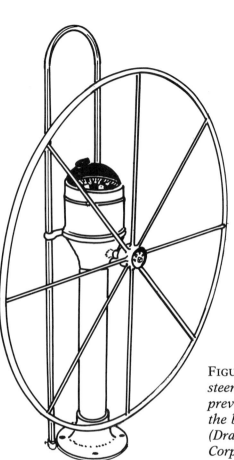

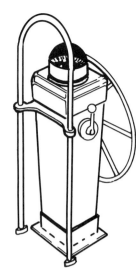

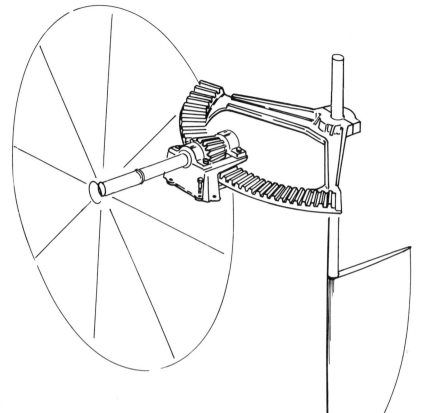

FIGURE 7.11. *Guards for pedestal steering units. Having a large guard prevents crew grasping the wheel as the boat lurches in a seaway. (Drawing by permission of Edson Corporation.)*

FIGURE 7.12. *Rack and pinion steering works well when the rudder is close to the steering wheel. (Drawing by permission of Edson Corporation.)*

sider a rack and pinion steering system. With this method the wheel can be positioned forward or aft of the rudder stock to get a powerful system with some feel. It is best for boats up to about 50 feet (15 meters) LOA that have a powerful helm, such as a catboat. Unfortunately, if the gears start to wear, some slop will creep into it. This slop can only be removed by replacing the gears, rather than tightening the wires, as in a cable system.

The advantage of the rack and pinion, though, is that it is a direct linkage, simple, easy to maintain, and very rugged. Figure 7.12 shows a typical system made by the Edson Corporation in the United States.

Worm gear steering is used for the older type of long-keeled cruising craft that have a lot of rake to the rudder post and a large amount of helm in any condition. This type of steering gear is often referred to

as nonreversing, in that the rudder cannot drive the steering wheel but the wheel can easily turn the rudder. Because of this lack of feedback this type of helm could be a boon for short-handed cruising. Its major disadvantage is that it takes a large number of turns to go from lock to lock and, at least on all the ones I have seen, requires copious amounts of grease to keep everything movable.

It works by having a worm drive on the steering wheel shaft. Turning the wheel and shaft drives a traversing nut up or down the worm. This nut is connected through a linkage to the rudder stock and turns as the nut moves. Figure 7.13 shows how this system works.

Linked steering. If you want to transmit power from one point to another, a rotating rod or bar will do so with very few losses. The drive shaft on your rear-wheel-drive car is a typical example. A similar method can be used to turn the rudder. The wheel turns a bevel gear, which turns a rod running down the inside of the pedestal. This rod turns another rod by means of a bevel gear. The second rod is connected to the quadrant with a rack and pinion.

A linkage of this type is very positive, and providing it is kept well lubricated, it will work well for years. But eventually the bevel gears and bearings wear and slop starts to appear. The cure for this wear is to replace the bevels and bearings.

Will Keene of Edson advises me that total replacement is not necessary with their system. They recognized that when a geared system is considered, approximately 30 percent of the gears get 80 percent of the wear. On your boat, as with your car, it is rare for you to use the extreme ends of travel in the steering system. Hence the majority of wear comes on the center teeth of the gears. Edson has redesigned its geared steering systems so that the center section of the gears is replaceable.

Push-pull or pull-pull steering. Most of us are familiar with the engine controls in the cockpit and how by operating the control we cause a greased wire to slide through a conduit. The Edson Corporation (and Teleflex Morse, among others) has used this technique to design a steering gear they call a pull-pull system. It comprises a chain that runs over a sprocket, as in the geared cable type, connected to two steel wires running through a plastic conduit. The wires turn a radial quadrant bolted to the rudder stock, similar to turning the outboard motor on a small launch. Figure 7.14 gives details. A similar system is the Teleflex Yacht Specialities system.

The system is good when the wheel is positioned a long way from the rudder stock and the conduit has to be snaked carefully behind furniture or other fittings. Care should be taken when installing this type of steering to ensure that any bends in the cable have as large a radius as possible. To ensure ease of operation the cable should be kept well greased. The manufacturer recommends that the system be checked before an offshore cruise and greased at least once per year. The cable should also be replaced every five years.

FIGURE 7.13. *Worm steering gear is slow but exerts a great force on the rudder blade. However, it does not have any feedback. (Drawing by permission of Edson Corporation.)*

FIGURE 7.14. *On a center cockpit boat it is not often possible to fit a wire steering unit. Therefore, a pull-pull system can be installed. In this figure the wire runs to the cabin sole and then enters a conduit, which guides it back to the rudder quadrant. C is the conduit. I are pulley idlers. W is the steering wire. (Drawing by permission of Edson Corporation.)*

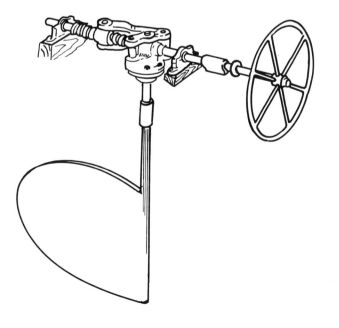

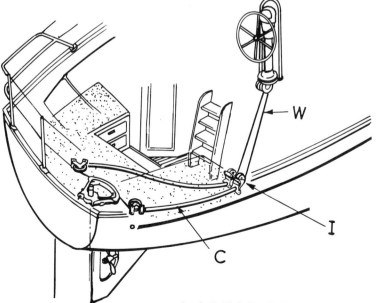

For me this is not a system for long-distance offshore sailing. The friction of the cable moving continually inside the conduit could cause wear and eventual binding of the steering. However, replacement should be as easy as pulling out the interior cable and replacing it with a new one.

Hydraulic and Electrical Steering

Many larger yachts and yachts with complex steering layouts often use hydraulic or electric steering because of the distance between the steering position and the rudder. Neither system has much feel and both are very expensive. In its simplest form the hydraulic unit consists of a hydraulic pump driven by the steering wheel. When the wheel is turned it forces oil along a line and into a cylinder. The oil causes the piston in the cylinder to move, pushing the single arm quadrant on the rudder stock in the desired direction. More sophisticated installations may use two or three steering stations with locks to allow only one position to be used at a time, an autopilot, and rudder angle indicator and a reservoir, all driving single or twin rudders.

Unless the boat is very big, I do not recommend hydraulic steering. It is very much like power steering on a large car: you aim the vehicle rather than steer it, and the only feedback you get is from the direction in which the front of the car or boat is going. Most hydraulic systems have little or no feedback and require a rudder angle indicator to tell the helmsman which direction he is about to go!

In the electrical system turning the wheel sends an electronic signal to a solenoid, which reacts to that signal by moving in or out and turning the rudder. This type of steering uses a lot of power, is prone to getting wet, and, in my opinion, has no place on a small boat.

We have looked briefly at some of the various types of steering gear available. But before selecting one type or another, certain other considerations should be reviewed.

Wheel Position

Where should the wheel be? A pedestal is an obvious answer, but would a bridgedeck carrying the mainsheet be better? Or could the wheel be bulkhead mounted so the helmsman could be sheltered behind a canopy?

These decisions are usually made during the design process and are often not referred to the owner unless the owner has specific requirements. For instance, the owner might ask that the helm position be under shelter. The designer then has a choice of putting it in the cabin, adding a pilot house, or situating the helmsman farther forward and putting a dodger over the cockpit. The selection he makes will depend on the type of boat being designed and its effect on the interior of the yacht.

Accessibility for Maintenance

Many boats have aft cabins or furniture around the steering position, which nobody wants to take apart every time a sheave needs oiling. So when a steering system is conceived the designer must ask himself, How can this part be repaired? Can a crewman install a new cable at sea? Can the whole system be maintained easily? If it cannot, then maintenance will be skimped and early failure could result.

Emergency Steering

The time to think about emergency steering is when the boat is on the drawing board. At this stage changes are inexpensive and any modifications to the other parts of the steering gear can easily be made. For instance, it may be preferable to install the emergency steering system in a seat, as in Figure 7.15, and have the emergency tiller on or under the seat rather than have a tiller bent to fit around the wheel.

FIGURE 7.15. *A is the usual position for the emergency tiller. B is an alternate position.*

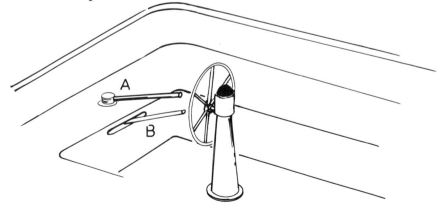

TABLE 7.1

Type of Steering System	Features	Disadvantages	Suitable Boat Systems
Wire Drive	Easy to maintain, easy to adjust, most common type can be fitted on pedestal or bulkhead. Good "feel." Gearing can be easily adjusted. More than one wheel or rudder easily incorporated.	Not suitable where steering pedestal is a long distance from the quadrant. Should have guards on all sheaves. Difficult to fit to vane steering.	Short-keeled cruiser, any boat where cockpit is aft. Best fitted on boat where sensitivity is needed.
Rack and Pinion	Easy to maintain. Moderate "feel."	Wheel must be near to rudder stock to fit this system. Will get sloppy as system wears. Fixed gear ratio.	Will fit most boats where a powerful control is needed.
Worm Gear	No "feel."	Will get sloppy as system wears. More parts to wear. Difficult to fit emergency steering.	Only suitable for fairly insensitive, long-keeled cruising boats.
Linked System	Good "feel." Can be mounted almost anywhere within range of rudder stock. Some systems can be adjusted to remove "slop."	Will get sloppy when worn.	Suitable for sensitive boats or short-keeled types.
Push-Pull System	Moderate "feel." Can be mounted anywhere in boat.	Cables need regular greasing.	Suited best for smaller boats that do not require much power to turn rudder.
Hydraulic	Can be installed anywhere on boat. Can have any numbers of steering positions, rudders, or autopilots. Very little feel.	Very heavy. Very expensive.	Large yachts 60–70 feet and up. Fishing boats and power yachts.
Electric	Can be installed anywhere on boat. Can have any numbers of steering positions, rudders, or autopilots. Very little feel. Electricity and seawater are not compatible.	Extra batteries are heavy. Expensive.	Large yachts. Power yachts. Fishing boats.

As we have just seen, there are many types of steering systems. The type selected should be based upon a number of factors:

1. Ease of maintenance.
2. Suitability for the boat.
3. Cost.
4. Amount of "feel" or feedback you desire.
5. Compatibility with the objectives of the boat.
6. Complexity; generally, the simpler it is the better it will work.

There are, of course, individual factors that may come into play. For instance, an owner who is a hydraulics engineer may be happier with a hydraulic system because he knows more about it than any other method. Don't simply take what is offered because that's the way it is. If possible, try them out and get the one that is best for you. Table 7.1 sums up the options. You could even go to the extent of consulting a steering company if you have any discussion on what is best. Companies like Edson provide a free design service to builders, designers, and owners.

VANE STEERING OR AN AUTOPILOT?

On long trips, some form of self-steering reduces the number of crew to feed, gives the helmsman time to read a book or catch up with maintenance chores, and adds more freedom to the job of sailing a boat. But there are a large number and different styles of vanes and autopilots for self-steering. So, which one is best?

Self-Steering with the Sails

When Joshua Slocum sailed around the world in 1806, he stayed on course by adjusting the trim of his sails and steering by hand only in extreme conditions. After sailing across the Atlantic he added a mizzen mast to make self-steering easier. Since that time many sailors have sailed long distances by trimming their sails to keep the boat on course. Most of them added a mizzen, and like many bright ideas it was developed by successive generations of sailors to become the modern vane steering system. The basic theory of the method is very simple and can be applied to any boat that is reasonably well balanced.

Using the Sails to Steer to Windward

Sailing to windward is the easiest point of sail to get the boat to steer itself. The sails should be sheeted in to their normal amount and the tiller adjusted until the boat is balanced. Once the boat is sailing itself, the helm can be lashed or pinned and the boat allowed to sail alone. Boats with a long keel that are moderately directionally stable will sail themselves fairly easily for long periods of time. Short-keeled craft and boats that pick up weather helm quickly as they heel, however, will tend to veer off course fairly quickly.

Offwind Sailing by Balancing the Sails

Slocum found spray could sail upwind by balancing the sails, but for sailing downwind it was necessary to sheet the flying jib in hard amidships and ease the mainsheet out as far as possible.

This was a very inefficient method of sailing the boat and would probably not work very well on the modern sloop. Therefore we should experiment to find other means of self-steering downwind.

The general principle is that simple. If the sail forces are kept forward of the drag forces the boat should sail downwind easily. Thus, using two almost equally sized genoas set in a twin groove luff system and no mainsail puts all the sail forces forward of the hull drag forces and works reasonably well. We used this method on one long downwind trip and simply tightened the brake on the helm. However, once the boat wandered off course, the only way of bringing it back was to unlock the brake and correct the steering with the helm.

On a reach the sails were sheeted so that the boat self-steered, but, again, this resulted in a loss of speed and the crew had to correct the helm whenever the boat wandered off course. In general, this type of self-steering enabled the helmsman to go below and get a cup of coffee but didn't allow him to leave the helm for prolonged periods.

It is apparent, then, that many boats can be self-steered at any wind angle provided the sails are adjusted correctly. However, trimming the sails to keep the boat on course will usually result in sailing at a slower speed than if the sails were trimmed properly. For this reason it may be well worthwhile to investigate either vane steering or an autopilot.

VANE STEERING

The boats that have been the easiest to steer themselves have usually been long-keeled ketches or yawls. The long keel gives the boat a built-in resistance to yaw, and the mizzen makes it easy to balance the sails to suit the course. (As we noted earlier, Joshua Slocum fitted spray with a mizzen.)

By observing the effect of this mizzen mast, early experimenters were able to link it to the rudder to gain some form of steering aid. (Thames barges, sailing all over the North Sea and the east coast of Britain, often had a mizzen on or near the rudder post to aid turning and steering.)

In early designs, vanes were often very large. Sir Francis Chichester often said about his vane on *Gipsy Moth* in 1960, that it was a small mizzen. This was because of the large amount of power needed to overcome friction and inertia and to turn the rudder. Since that time more powerful equipment has been built, vane size reduced, and self-steering efficiency thus increased.

There are three basic parts to any steering system: the vane, the rudder, and the linkage that ties the two together. All of these basic parts have various components depending upon the style and efficiency of the steering system.

The Various Types of Vane

When a boat is moving through the water there is a force acting on the rudder blade. This force can be broken down into three components: friction, rudder inertia, and water pressure. When the boat is moving slowly, the friction and inertia components comprise the largest percentage of resistance to turning. As boat speed increases so does the water pressure component. To self-steer the boat a vane has to overcome all the rudder forces.

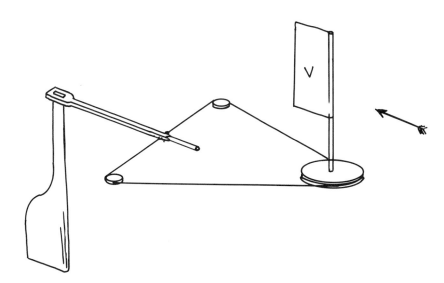

FIGURE 7.16. *The simplest form of vane steering is a vane connected directly to the tiller. When the wind turns the vane it turns the rudder and the boat slowly comes back on course. V is the vane, and the arrow shows the direction of the wind.*

When the boat is moving at a reasonable speed, a large vane will overcome the major force of water pressure and steer the boat. The problem arises when the boat is barely moving and large friction and inertia forces have to be overcome. To obtain enough force in this situation, a huge vane—which may be as large as a fair-sized mizzen—must be used, or a method of increasing the vane's power, such as a servo mechanism. While the sail could be reefed as the wind rises, a huge vane is not a practical proposition, and some other method of increasing the power must be used. The early experimenters first tried changing the angle of the vane's axis.

The simplest form of vane has been the *vertical axis type,* as shown in Figure 7.16. The power output depends primarily upon the size of the vane. Its major disadvantage is the amount of shaft rotation (the amount of movement available to move the tiller or wheel) it can produce. The shaft rotation can be increased by making the bottom drum larger and linking it to the rudder. However, a large force is required to turn the drum, which means a larger vane. Against this must be weighed the simplicity and relatively low cost. Raking the axis of the vane (tilting it aft or forward) for an *angled axis vane* increases the power slightly and also increases the sensitivity of the vane to changes in the wind angle and the yacht's heel angle. As the vane axis is angled, the power and shaft rotation decrease, although the resistance to yawing and oscillation increases.

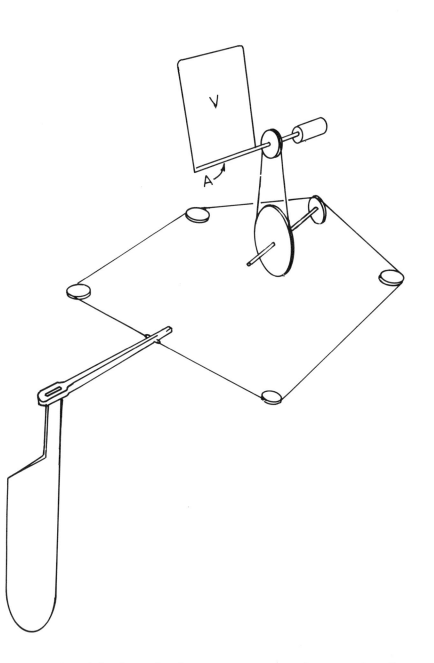

FIGURE 7.17. *A horizontal axis vane exerts more force on the tiller. As the vane is turned away from the wind it gets blown over further, creating more force to turn the tiller arm. A is the horizontal axis and V is the vane.*

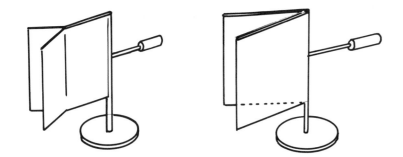

FIGURE 7.18. *A wedge or finned vane is more sensitive to wind direction.*

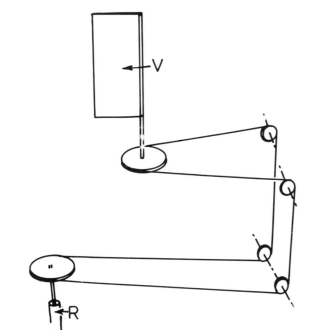

FIGURE 7.19. *If the vane is connected to a small trim tab on the rudder it can be made to turn the rudder to bring the boat back on course. Here the tab stock runs inside the hollow rudderstock. If the tab is turned to port by the vane, the rudder will turn to starboard to bring the boat back onto course. L is the tab linkage. T is the Tab. R is the hollow rudderstock, and V is the vane.*

In order to increase both the power and the shaft rotation—which means a smaller vane will do the same job as a vertical axis type—a *horizontal axis vane* should be used. As this type of vane moves away from the eye of the wind, the wind power blows it over, giving a large amount of shaft rotation, as shown in Figure 7.17. This increases its sensitivity and power, but when the system is not in use this movement is also the major disadvantage, necessitating removal of the vane.

A flat vane is somewhat insensitive to small changes in the wind angle. But it has been found that installing a *finned* or *wedge-shaped vane*, as in Figure 7.18, improves sensitivity, although at the expense of greater drag.

Trim Tabs and Servo Rudders

There are various methods for turning the boat when a vane is being used, the simplest of which is to link the vane directly to the tiller. This method usually only moves the tiller a small distance and takes a fairly long time to bring the boat back on course. It also takes a powerful vane to overcome the rudder forces. A better method is to utilize the water flowing past the boat to turn the rudder. This can be done either directly, by a trim tab, or indirectly, by a separate auxiliary servo rudder.

One of the least expensive methods of gaining more power to turn the rudder is to link the vane to a *trim tab* on the back of the rudder. Then, when the vane turns the trim tab it will turn the rudder. Figure 7.19 shows how this system works.

The trim tab has a disadvantage in that it is insensitive to small corrections. It has to turn enough to get out of the turbulence of the rudder and skeg—or, in the case of a long-keeled boat, the entire keel turbulence.

The other problem with this type of steering is that if the rudder is underwater the linkage can catch weeds and debris, which might damage or jam the trim tab, necessitating a trip over the side to clean it.

For a transom-hung rudder, this is a simple, inexpensive, and effective system, but an underwater rudder needs an expensive hollow rudder stock or tab control to be effective.

Hanging a rudder blade on a horizontal shaft creating a *separate pendulum servo rudder* translates the turning movement of the rudder into a rotational movement, as shown in Figure 7.20. When a vane is used to turn the rudder, the small amount of vane rotation is trans-

Table 7.2

Vane Type	Rudder Type	Linkage	Cost	Power	Sensitivity	Best-Suited Boat	Remarks
Vertical axis	Yachts Trim tab Trim tab Pendulum servo	Yoke lines or gears Mechanical or gears Mechanical Mechanical links and gearing	Low Moderate Moderately high High	Low Moderate Moderate Good	Acceptable Acceptable Acceptable Good	Smaller craft Transom-hung rudder Skeg rudder mounted under boat Medium and larger craft	
Horizontal axis[a]	Yachts Trim tab Trim tab Pendulum servo	Yoke lines or gears Mechanical or gears Mechanical Mechanical links and gearing	Moderate Moderate Moderately high Highest	Good—may have to be dampened Good Moderate Good	Moderate Moderate Moderate Good	Medium-sized craft, long-keeled, slow-to-react type. Transom-hung rudder Skeg rudder under the boat. Medium and larger boats	Most expensive and most sophisticated system.
Windmill[b]		Worm drive to tiller or linkage	Moderate	Good	Good	Any	
Autopilot	Any	Solenoid mechanical yoke lines.	High	Varies with type but generally good.	Good	Any	

[a]This type of vane is generally slightly more expensive and complicated than the vertical axis type.
[b]This system is still relatively undeveloped.

formed into a much more powerful action by the rotation of the rudder. This rudder action is strong enough for a small vane to drive a large main rudder.

Which vane is best for which rudder? Any vane can be fitted to any rudder or steering system, but some combinations are better than others. Table 7.2 shows which vanes are best for which boat and purpose.

Each system has good and bad points, and it is up to the individual or designer to decide which is the best for a particular boat.

A Vertical Vane Linked to the Rudder

One of the first of the modern vane systems was devised by Michael Henderson for *Mick the Miller*. I remember seeing the boat sailing in the Solent and wondering what the blade sticking up behind it was. As Figure 7.16 shows, this system was linked directly to the tiller, and as the vane turned so turned the rudder. As we saw earlier the disadvantage of such a system is that it requires a large vane to overcome friction and inertial forces for the gear to work. A derivative of this system is to use two meshing gear wheels, one on the vane, the other on the tiller. Thus, any movement of the vane is immediately transmitted to the tiller. The relative size of the wheels governs the sensitivity of the system.

According to the Amateur Yacht Research Society (AYRS), the vane for this system should be about four to six times the size of the rudder, and the rudder on a fin and skeg profile yacht should be about 4 percent of the lateral area.

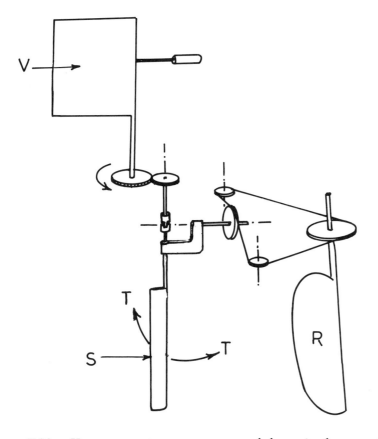

FIGURE 7.20. *Here a vane turns a servo pendulum. As the vane (V) turns, the pendulum (S) turns. This tends to kick the pendulum up out of the water in the direction T and exert a turning moment on the rudder (R).*

A Vane Linked to a Rudder Trim Tab

Because the vane was so large on earlier models, experimenters sought ways to make it smaller and to increase its power. One of the easiest ways of doing this was by making the vane turn a small trim tab.

In this case when the boat wanders off course the vane turns the tab—usually only a few degrees are required. The tab, working in the water, makes the rudder turn, bringing the boat back onto course.

One of the problems with this system is that large variations in course can result if the unit is not sized or set up properly. This happens when the main rudder turns in response to the trim tab movement, the trim tab turns still more. This will result in a meandering—sometimes quite a violently wandering—course. To remove this instability a linkage must be designed into the system.

A Vertical Vane Linked to a Pendulum Servo Blade

This system is more powerful than the two previous types but still suffers from the lack of sensitivity of the vertical vane systems.

A Horizontal Vane Linked to the Rudder

Although this system appears to be a good, inexpensive solution, the powerful movement of the horizontal vane can move the rudder excessively, leading to oversteering with quite rapid and erratic course corrections. With a suitably geared down linkage, however, quite good steering can be obtained.

A Horizontal Vane Linked to a Trim Tab

Again, step-down gearing is required if erratic course keeping is to be avoided. But the system loses a lot of the vane's superior sensitivity because the tab has to operate in the turbulent streamlines behind the rudder.

A Horizontal Vane with a Pendulum Servo Rudder

This is probably the finest, most accurate system available—but also the most expensive. The rudder should be a kick-up type to reduce damage from waves and floating debris. One of the drawbacks of this system is its complexity, which makes it tough to repair in the middle of the ocean.

A Windmill Steerer

There have been several proposals for a windmill system. The most obvious system is to use a windmill on edge to the wind, as in Figure 7.21; when the wind changes direction, the windwheel rotates until the system is aligned again. This is slow, but it could be a sensitive, powerful system at a fairly low cost and deserves a deeper look.

Are Wind Vanes Vanishing?

There used to be many different types of vane available. In fact, I once had a 3-inch-thick folder of information on the various vanes. But it appears that modern autopilots are gradually replacing vane steering. Technology is working its magic on the self-steering system, just as it is changing sail handling. Boats may never be the same again.

AUTOPILOTS

Vane self-steering is not the only form of self-steering. The electronics industry has given us autopilots, which maintain a constant course regardless of wind direction or velocity. The autopilot is set on a compass heading, and the machine automatically senses its own compass heading and course. When the boat goes off course, the unit applies the correct amount of rudder to bring the boat back onto the correct course. The autopilot can also work off the yacht's instrumentation. It can be set to steer a closehauled course using data from the apparent wind angle indicator.

Selecting an Autopilot

The choice of autopilot can be made two ways. If you are looking for the best and cost is not the principal consideration, then list all the features you think you need and do some comparison shopping. If cost is a consideration, a reasonably inexpensive, reliable unit can be purchased that will serve as a second pair of hands on the tiller. For five to eight times more you will get a higher degree of accuracy, greater torque output, programming ability, and the ability to link the unit to other instruments. The following items should be considered when shopping for an autopilot:

1. Cost. Does it do what you want at a price you can afford?
2. Sea conditions. In what sea conditions will you want the unit to steer the boat? A small inexpensive unit will probably have difficulty steering the boat in a heavy sea.
3. Power consumption. If the unit drains your batteries after an hour's use, you will either have to fit larger batteries or run the engine when the autopilot is running.
4. Loran or Satnav interface. If the unit can be programmed to change course, the chance of your forgetting to do so is eliminated.

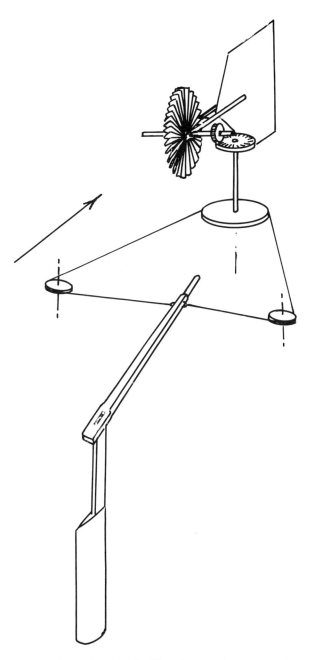

FIGURE 7.21. *When the windmill is kept edge on to the wind, friction in the system stops it turning. But when the wind shifts it will turn, making the rudder turn. While the idea is simple, many practical problems exist.*

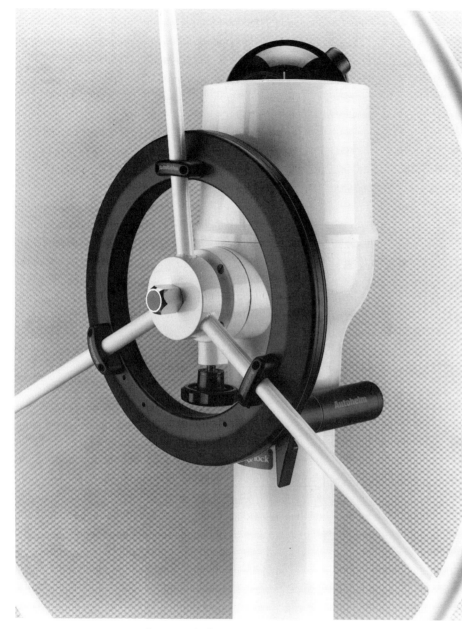

5. Get-you-home ability. Can it be installed separately from your steering, or is it a "bolt-on" that has to use the steering system to control the boat? In the former, the autopilot may have its own quadrant or tiller arm on the rudder stock and be totally independent of the normal steering system. Should the steering system break, then the autopilot can get you home. A less expensive system will use the boat's own steering gear to operate through, and if the gear fails it too is broken.
6. Service facilities. Where can the unit be serviced? Can you get worldwide service or only factory service? The latter is not much use when you are in Patagonia and need a part desperately.
7. Watertightness. In a system where the autopilot is set in the cockpit, it must be watertight. A few drops of salt water can play havoc with the electronics.
8. Force output. Make sure the autopilot is large enough to steer the boat. Too large a unit will simply drain the batteries, while too small a unit will be working overtime to control the boat, resulting in a meandering course and heavy battery drain.

The various parts of the autopilot are also important. One of the most important is the drive unit, which is attached to the steering system to apply rudder corrections. If the drive unit is not powerful enough, or rugged enough, poor performance and reliability will result.

The Drive Unit

Choice of drive unit depends upon the steering system. The most common choice is a linear drive attached to a small tiller arm mounted directly on the rudder stock above the quadrant or tiller. This method offers the safety of a backup steering system should the quadrant, linkage, or pedestal fail.

In the Cetrek system, rugged self-contained hydraulic linear drives are used as drive units. When the pilot is not in use, the hydraulic fluid bypasses the drive and develops a minimal load on the steering system. On a system with hydraulic steering, the hydraulic drive would simply be plugged into the hydraulic line.

Drive units by other manufacturers use a rotary gearbox with chain and sprockets to the steering system. However, this is being changed by a system from Autohelm, which is fastened directly to the steering wheel. As you can see from Figure 7.22, this unit is clean and very attractive and drives the steering wheel. As such it is easy to attach and remove and extremely rugged.

The Compass

For good course keeping an autopilot must have a responsive, accurate compass system that can operate at any angle of heel. All the latest use a "fluxgate" heading sensor. Although the technology has been around since World War II, it has only lately become small enough to be used aboard boats. The Fluxgate compass takes many thousands of readings every second. These readings are averaged and displayed on an electronic panel. Plus, the yacht's deviation can be programmed into the compass, and it automatically gives the correct reading for the helmsman to steer.

Basic Autopilot Controls

Most autopilots come in varying degrees of complexity. At the lowest end of the scale is the autofollowing type: the boat is steered onto a heading and the autopilot switched on and will then follow the course.

At the other end of the scale are the units that look like they would require a course of instruction on how to get the best out of the system. They have features that allow the crew to choose offcourse, distance, time, and watch alarms. They generally interface with other navigation equipment and usually, with input from the onboard log, can give you speed and averages. With all that, who needs more crew?

On sailing boats it is essential that the unit be controlled from the cockpit. Most of the Cetrek units have a small waterproof control unit that can be flush-mounted in the cockpit or mounted in a "pod" at the wheel. Other units have various methods of putting control in the hands of the helmsman. Some use a small control panel on a long wire. This allows the helmsman to move around the cockpit easily. On other systems the entire unit has to be mounted in the cockpit.

The autopilot should always be mounted within reach of the helm so that it can be disengaged in an emergency. After all, autopilots cannot see a tanker about to cut them in half.

Most pilots offer two basic controls, "rudder" and "response." The rudder control is adjusted to set the correct amount of rudder to be applied to maintain a good course without under- or oversteering. The response control adjusts the range of variation you want in the course. The ideal is to allow the boat to sail with minimal loading and power consumption. Once the boat goes beyond "normal" limits, the pilot should call for a correction. If you set too tight a variation, the pilot will be continually working to hold the boat on course and fighting

every wave. This is an easy way to run your battery flat very quickly.

In addition to the rudder and response controls, the pilot must have a system for putting the boat on the required course. The simplest is the autofollowing unit: the boat is steered onto a course and the unit engaged.

Slightly more complicated is the dialed-in course unit. In this system the course is dialed in while the unit is on. This method has some advantages in that the boat can easily be tacked by dialing the new course and letting the autopilot turn the boat while the lone crewman tends the sheets.

Additional Controls

At the top of the line the autopilot can take input from a variety of electronic devices. Many have interfaces that accept input from the Loran or Satnav units. Others can accept information from the wind instruments enabling it to sail a course to windward that will follow the wind shifts more accurately than most helmsmen. In effect, these developments in electronic course control have almost eliminated the future of windvane units.

The autopilot, then, is one of the most important pieces of equipment aboard most boats. With it a short-handed crew are relieved of the continual round-the-clock chore of steering. They can enjoy the cruise and take over the helm when they want to steer.

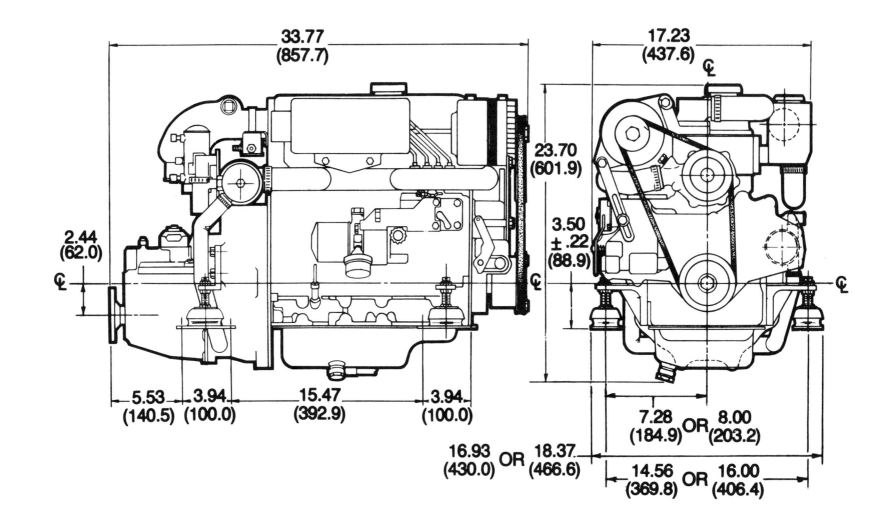

33.77
(857.7)

17.23
(437.6)

23.70
(601.9)

2.44
(62.0)

3.50
± .22
(88.9)

5.53   3.94
(140.5)   (100.0)

15.47
(392.9)

3.94
(100.0)

7.28   OR   8.00
(184.9)   (203.2)

16.93   OR   18.37
(430.0)   (466.6)

14.56   OR   16.00
(369.8)   (406.4)

CHAPTER 8

Powering the Yacht:
The Engine and the Generator

Almost every large boat built today has an engine. It's probably the most useful item on board. The engine does many things in addition to its primary job of moving the boat through the water. It drives the battery alternator and can be used to drive a bilge pump, refrigeration, and water pumps as well as giving you hot water via a heat exchanger.

Where more power for extras is required, on larger boats, an auxiliary generator can be used; on smaller craft the range of options is more limited. Solar cells, wind-powered generators, and water-powered generators can be either added in or designed into the boat. (See Chapter 10 for more on electrical power systems.) With a gas (petrol)- or diesel-powered generator many more extras are possible. Not only can electric motors be used to drive the various pumps and compressors, but stereos, TV, computers, air conditioning, hot water heaters, reverse-osmosis water makers, and even an electric stove in the galley are possible luxurious extras. In the following pages we'll look at the engine as a primary power source. Because a generator uses a similar engine to power the electrical motor, we'll include that in the discussion as well.

SELECTING AN ENGINE

What do you look for in an engine? Should it be quiet? Should it be diesel? Where should it be in the boat? Should it be an inboard, saildrive, or outboard? What type should it be and what horsepower should it have? All these are questions a designer asks himself when he is designing a new boat. First, the engine must be sized to power the boat and to have enough power left over to drive all the extras that are usually added. Second, the engine must have an adequate supply of air, fuel, and a method of dissipating the heat and exhaust gases. Third, it must be positioned where it is accessible for maintenance. Finally, it must be adequately muffled so that conversation is easy in the area around the engine.

Diesel or Gasoline

This is usually not an option on most boats. Only a few power boats are offered with gasoline engines these days. If you are wondering whether gasoline engines have an advantage, the answer is a qualified maybe. Each engine has points for it and points against. Table 8.1 lists them. As you can see, the gas engine has many items in its favor, but the volatility of the fuel scares many sailors away. Nowadays very few sailors want to sail on a boat that doesn't have a diesel engine.

Sizing the Engine

I've asked several designers how they select engine size, and the answers ranged from "experience" through "looking at similar-sized boats" to "calculating the horsepower required." We use a method of calculating the horsepower based on the wetted surface, displacement, LWL, required speed, and then we add in a factor for the front-end extras that can be bolted on to the engine. This gives us a shaft horsepower, and from that point we compare the required figure with the graphs given by manufacturers to select a suitable engine.

With the engine size estimated, the reduction gear ratio, prop size, and rpm can all be calculated. Sometimes this calculation will change the engine size, but usually the calculations are correct the first time.

TABLE 8.1   GASOLINE OR DIESEL ENGINE: WHICH IS BEST?

Engine	Advantages	Disadvantages
Gasoline	Reasonable engine cost	Fuel cost usually fairly high
	Lightweight engine	Higher fuel consumption than diesel
	Engine runs reasonably quietly	Requires more ventilation
		Carburetor operates poorly when boat is heeled
		Fuel fumes highly explosive
		Requires larger tanks to go as far as a diesel
		Has extensive electrical system that could corrode
Diesel	Fuel available everywhere and usually less expensive than gasoline	Engine heavier than gas engine, but modern turbo-charged diesels are becoming much lighter
	Much smaller safety hazard	Initial cost much higher
	Smaller diesel tanks required	Engine can be noisy

Care must be taken when calculating the propeller pitch and diameter. Our computer program requires information about the style, for example, feathering, fixed, or folding, the rpm, the maximum diameter that can be fitted, and a number of other features. It then estimates the pitch, the diameter, the tip speed of the blade, and whether that speed exceeds the cavitation limits for the propeller. (Cavitation is a form of boundary layer separation, rather like the stall that occurs when an airplane wing stalls and loses lift. It occurs when the propeller turns too fast and a cavity forms on the back of the blade. As the cavity or bubble collapses and reforms, it imposes severe shock loadings on the blade. Eventually these shocks erode the blade. During the advent of cavitation, thrust is reduced and performance drops dramatically.)

Many manufacturers prepare their own information on sizing the engine. Just looking over at the bookshelf I can see manuals from Cummings, Detroit Diesel Allison, Yanmar, Volvo, Lister, and Westerbeke. All these manufacturers have their own guides to engine installation, and most of the guides suggest how the engine should be sized.

Once you have decided on the required horsepower, then it's time to look at the manufacturer's graphs. Figure 8.1 shows one of these graphs. The curve shown is for an engine listed at 23 horsepower. These numbers are usually the output found at the testing facility at the plant and are often very optimistic, often not the output you are likely to obtain when the engine is installed.

That output is likely to be slightly lower, depending on how much equipment you want bolted onto the front of the engine. As a rough estimate I assume each item absorbs 2 or 3 horsepower. So if you had an alternator, a bilge pump, and a pressure water pump bolted onto the engine, you could lose up to 8–10 horsepower. This would make the 23 horsepower at the shaft of the engine appear as 13–15 horsepower.

Also, when looking at these charts you should realize that not every sailor likes to run his engine at full speed when under power. Most sailors will run at about 80–90 percent of maximum. From the chart we can see that 80 percent of 3400 rpm is only 2720 rpm, which gives a horsepower of only 16, subtract the additional 9 from that, and there is only 7 horsepower left with which to push the boat! Fortunately, this is only an example. If we were looking for an engine with 20–25 horsepower to push the boat we'd increase the engine size so that at 80 percent power and with all the bolt-ons there was a minimum of 20 horsepower. This would mean we would use an engine about 35–40 horsepower. But this example does serve to illustrate why many boats seem underpowered.

A few years ago we came across exactly this problem. An owner approached us about repowering his 40-foot boat. It had a 22-horsepower engine, and as long as the seas were flat the boat would power along nicely. But as soon as any waves got up there simply wasn't enough horsepower to push the boat into it and the crew had to sail everywhere, even into the marina in a raging gale. We repowered the boat with a 42-horsepower engine and a slightly larger propeller. The owner reported an amazing change in performance. The boat was easy to motor, the engine was quieter, and it could handle severe seas

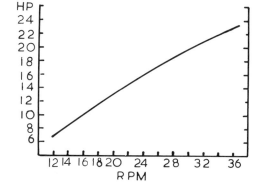

FIGURE 8.1. *A chart of engine rpm against horsepower for a 23 hp engine.*

without a problem. This is one instance where selection of the right engine by the original builder may have cost more initially but would have saved my client in the longer term.

Sizing the Generator

In selecting a generator, either a stand-alone unit or a smaller alternator attached to the main engine, we perform a different calculation. The generator is intended to provide enough electrical power to drive all the equipment on board. However, if we simply added up the total wattage of every item we would end up with a machine that was larger than the boat requires. It would also be much more expensive and would consume much more fuel. This would mean that we'd have to install larger fuel tanks and make the engine room larger.

So we make a different type of calculation, one that's a little more of an estimate. We first list every electrical item on the boat and then estimate how long it will be used in a 24-hour period. This is done for both sea conditions and port conditions. This gives us a total of watt-hours over a 24-hour period. When we divide that by 24 hours, we get a total wattage for the machine. Figure 10.1 shows the calculation sheet. Next we estimate the likely increase in power usage over the first year of the boat and obtain a figure that is added to the total above. We assume that this will represent 80–90 percent of the generator size. Now we look up the manufacturers' brochures to find a suitable generator. In the example you can see we selected a Westerbeke 7-kilowatt unit.

Once we have it sized, we have to find a space for the machine. Ideally it will be fitted in the engine compartment, where the sound-proofing, water cooling, fuel supply, and other requirements will be used for both the main engine and the generator engine.

ENGINE AND GENERATOR INSTALLATION

We are not going to discuss how the engine is physically installed in the boat; rather, we are going to look at the physical requirements of the engine and generator when they are installed in the engine room or compartment. Having said that, what do these engines need? Fuel is an obvious answer, but many more things must be considered if the installation is to be successful:

1. A fuel system.
2. A starting method.
3. A ventilation system.
4. A cooling system.
5. An exhaust system.
6. Engine and generator mountings.
7. Lubrication.
8. There will be an electrical system besides that provided by the generator.
9. Engine and generator instruments will have to be placed where they can be seen.
10. The engine may have various accessories.
11. Soundproofing will have to be provided for both machines.

All these points should be addressed if the engine is to work when it is called on.

The Fuel System

The fuel system consists of three parts: the tanks; the fuel lines or plumbing; and the filters and separators. The entire system is of critical importance to the continued good performance of all engines.

The tanks should be as near as possible on the same level or slightly above the engine and generator. The American Boat and Yacht Council recommends that tanks be resistant to deterioration by the fuel and that metals and alloys be compatible to minimize galvanic corrosion. Tank material should be a copper-based alloy, steel or aluminum. The most usual tank material in America is monel or stainless steel, both of which are relatively expensive. In Britain, the less expensive aluminum or steel is often used.

The type of material the boat is constructed of has some bearing on the type of tank material. For instance, an aluminum yacht would probably be built using a 5086 aluminum alloy; the tanks would probably be constructed out of the same material and built into the bilge of the boat. A fiberglass boat, on the other hand, may have aluminum or steel tanks, depending on the cost of the yacht. Galvanized steel tanks are not recommended because the zinc reacts with the fuel and can produce a sludge that will block the diesel's injectors.

The tanks should have baffles inside to keep the fuel from sloshing around, and they should have large removable plates on top so that the tank can get a thorough cleaning periodically. Ideally tank piping should all come from the top of the tank without any connections on the sides or bottom.

Tanks should be ventilated over the side, not into the bilge or any other part of the boat, and all connections from the tank to the engine should be pressure-tested to ensure fuel cannot seep out. Nothing is quite so debilitating to a crew as diesel fumes seeping into the accommodation. If there is the slightest queasiness aboard, the smell of fuel oil in the bilge will usually turn it into genuine seasickness.

The tanks should be strongly secured. Nobody wants a tank full of diesel oil breaking loose inside the boat. Usually furniture is built in around the tanks, fixing them firmly in place, but I was on one boat when the tanks appeared to be securely fastened by 2-by-3-inch timbers. When I looked in the bilge I found the timbers were simply resting on the tanks and were not even glassed in place! They were there just to keep the cabin sole on the top of the tank. They didn't even pass under joinery at either end. From what we could see the tank could be lifted straight out of the boat!

The tanks will require a fill line and a vent line, both of which are dealt with in the next section. There should also be a method of measuring the fuel in the tank. On a small boat that is usually done with a sounding stick. But as the size of the boat increases it becomes more difficult to check tank capacity with a stick, and a gauge or sight glass is used. The sight glass is set on the side of the tank and, to my mind, is always vulnerable to breakage. For that reason I prefer a gauge that can be read from the cockpit or bridge. The tanks can then be checked occasionally with a sounding stick, but most of the time the gauge could be relied on.

Piping should be sized to suit the engine or generator motor. Almost all engine manufacturers will provide a chart of piping sizes for their engine. According to ABYC, all fuel lines should be copper, nickel copper, or flexible piping, as long as they are electrolytically compatible with the tank material. At the engine end of the piping, it should have a section of flexible piping inserted to allow for engine vibration and hull flexing.

Each tank should have a vent line that goes from the tank to a vent somewhere on deck or over the side. The vent line should have a flame screen to prevent flames getting down to the fuel.

Rarely do people unfamiliar with engines know that a diesel engine requires a fuel return line. The fuel pump pumps far more oil than the injectors can use, and the extra fuel must be returned to the tank. So a fuel return must be correctly sized and installed.

As the fuel leaves the tank, it should pass through a *strainer* to remove any water and then through a *filter* to remove impurities. Not many of the smaller installations bother with a strainer, but almost everybody installs a fuel filter. Volvo engines have a strainer in the feed pump on the engine, but inspection of some of the other engine manuals reveals that some install a water trap on the motor and others specify that a water strainer be installed in the fuel line. A filter should be provided for both the main engine and generator fuel lines if they are not already fitted on the motor.

The filter is usually an item inserted in the fuel line, but again Volvo mounts it right on the engine. When it isn't mounted on the engine or as an extra safeguard a Racor filter can be installed in the fuel line. I think the Racor unit is currently the best available and best known. It has a clear glass cover, which allows you to see whether any impurities have collected, thus enabling you to make sure the filter is changed regularly.

The Engine Starting System

Larger diesel engines are started with compressed air, but the small size of engines in yachts dictates that they are, almost universally, started electrically. This means that an engine-starting battery should be provided. The battery should be large enough to crank the engine over many times before it is fully discharged. Usually most engine manufacturers will specify the minimum size of the engine-starting battery. On smaller engines—usually up to about 10–12 horsepower—provision should be made for the engine to be hand cranked. This means the designer will have to allow room at the front of the engine for a crank and the person to wind it.

Because the engine and generator are not often started at the same time, the battery intended for the main engine can be used to start the generator without a major increase in size or capacity. However, this arrangement is at best a compromise. It means that there is no backup to start the engine or generator should the battery go flat.

The main engine is also provided with an alternator, used to re-charge the battery when the engine is running. An alternator is used on the engine because it is smaller and lighter than a comparable DC generator. The AC power is rectified right at the alternator long before it ever gets to the battery. This does mean, however, that the alternator should never be disconnected from the battery while it is charging. Doing so will blow the rectifying diodes.

An auxiliary generator will probably have a circuit that feeds power to a transformer to step it down from 110 or 220 volts to 12 volts, and then the power is rectified before it charges the battery.

The Ventilation System

Diesel engines do need air. Air is mixed with the diesel fuel before combustion. On yachts it is assumed that the engine can draw enough air through the bilge to keep it going. But Roger Chrysler of the Volvo Penta (American) Corporation says that in an ideal situation all engines should have an air intake and an exhaust system fitted in the engine compartment. Diesels use a tremendous amount of air, and an air intake will help the engine run more efficiently and stay cooler, which will give it a longer life. The outgoing air serves to cool the engine and to ventilate any fumes out of the compartment. If fans are to be provided in the air ducts, they should be of the sparkless type so that any explosive fumes in the compartment are not ignited. (The fumes could come from the batteries being charged, when hydrogen is given off.)

The Engine Cooling System

Almost all diesel engines are cooled by sea water—sometimes called raw water—taken in through the bottom of the hull. This water then passes through a heat exchanger, where it absorbs heat from the engine cooling system and is then discharged back into the ocean. Ideally, raw water should never flow through the engine. When it does, rust, sand, scale, and mud can accumulate in the cooling system, requiring frequent cleaning. Usually, cleaning can be accomplished by the addition of chemicals to the raw water flow, followed by a good flushing. On smaller engines, the additional cost of the heat exchanger increases costs, and raw water is allowed to pass through the engine. In this case, an anode on the engine will prevent some corrosion.

The engine's cooling water system is totally enclosed and should be checked occasionally. The sea water system should be drawn into the boat via a through-hull on the bottom of the boat. Usually both the

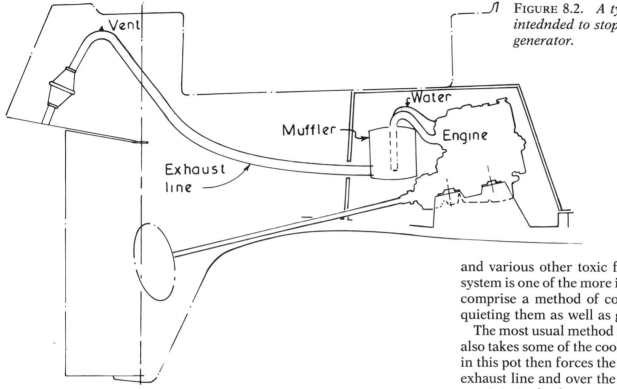

FIGURE 8.2. *A typical exhaust system. Note the vented loop intednded to stop water from flowing back into the engine or generator.*

generator engine and the main engine are fed from the same through-hull and filter. From there it should pass through a raw water strainer, which will filter out sand, seaweed, and other impurities. Then it passes into the heat exchanger on the engine. The heat exchanger is a fairly simple unit that allows the raw water to circulate around pipes holding the engine's cooling water. On some systems this water is then discharged into the exhaust line; on others it goes back over into the sea via another through-hull fitting. Some larger commercial craft have a heat exchanger mounted on the outside of the hull so that raw water never comes into the boat.

The Engine Exhaust System

If you've ever been in a compartment when the exhaust line has developed a leak, you'll know how uncomfortable it can be. Engine exhaust gases are very hot and contain a mixture of carbon monoxide and various other toxic fumes. For this reason the engine exhaust system is one of the more important parts of the installation. It should comprise a method of cooling the exhaust gases and some way of quieting them as well as getting them away from the boat.

The most usual method is to discharge the exhaust into a pot, which also takes some of the cooling water exhaust. The buildup of pressure in this pot then forces the exhaust gas-water mixture out through the exhaust line and over the side. However, great care should be taken to minimize back pressure in the exhaust line. High back pressure is one of the most common causes of poor engine performance. Figure 8.2 shows a typical detail. Note that the exhaust line has a vented loop just before it exits the boat. The loop is essential to stop water flowing back into the engine or generator, and the vent breaks the siphoning effect. Without it it is possible for water to be drawn back into the engine should the exhaust through-hull be immersed.

Engine Mounting

Engine beds, either metal beds bolted to the fiberglass foundations or solid foundations built into the hull on aluminum or glass boats, are where the engine is mounted. Once the engine is specified the designer need only look at the manufacturer's brochure to find the width of the engine mountings. With these known the engine beds can be designed. On a glass boat they may be made of solid plywood heavily glassed over, or simply molded into the interior pan. The mounting bolts are often glassed into the engine beds, leaving bolts sticking upward, on which the engine can be located. The theory behind this is that even if the nuts vibrate off the engine is held on the bed by gravity.

On a metal boat the engine beds are usually vertical plates with a large flange welded on top. In this case the bolts are passed downward through the flange in case the nuts drop off.

To minimize vibrations the engine should not be bolted directly to the engine beds, however. It should be mounted on resilient or soft mounts to allow it to vibrate and shift slightly without transmitting that vibration to the hull.

Engine Lubrication

While the smaller engines are unlike larger ship engines, which have to be lubricated almost constantly, there is still a need to check the oil and grease fittings. Unless the engine is in an easily accessible position, the owner will probably not bother to look at it from spring launch until the yard hauls the boat in the fall.

If taking the complete cover off the engine is difficult, a door or hatch should be provided to enable the dipstick to be checked. Ideally, of course, the entire engine box should be removable so that the engine can be checked visually for leaks and oil streaks, which might give early warning of potential problems. While the old style was to fit a custom-made drip tray under the engine, this is rarely done today, except on large custom yachts. Now, you are likely to see a molded fiberglass well under the engine to catch the fuel and oil that might drip from the engine. This well usually needs to be bailed into a bucket and the liquid disposed of carefully.

The stuffing box should also be in a position where it can be checked and tightened if required. All too often the stuffing box is set either under a foundation or so far aft that it is virtually invisible. In this case it is advisable to have a remote greasing unit fitted to ensure the stuffing box is adequately maintained.

The Engine Electrical System

If the engine is to work properly it will need an electrical system. The alternator has to charge the battery. The battery must have enough power to turn over the starter motor. There will also be an ignition circuit and an instrument circuit. With the exception of the instrument circuit each of these circuits must function properly to ensure the engine will work when it is needed. Several jobs must be performed during the season to ensure the electrical circuit stays in good shape:

1. Check the battery acid level with a hydrometer at least once per season. Also while you are checking the battery, check the terminals for tightness. The battery should sit in its own box and have its own vent fan to eliminate the hydrogen given off when it is being recharged. It is well to check the vent fan occasionally to ensure the ducting is connected and clear.
2. Check the belt tensions on the alternator at least once per season.
3. Check all the electrical terminals and grease them lightly at the beginning of the season. This will inhibit corrosion.
4. Once in a while take a look at the wiring to see that it is not resting on a hot surface or worn through with vibration.
5. Finally, when you have the cover off the engine or generator, take a look at the inside of the cover. Occasionally you might see a buildup of carbon deposits or oil, showing where the engine is leaking but not showing it on the block. Also you might find the soundproofing is deteriorating and needs to be redone. Little checks, when done often, can almost eliminate the larger problems caused by bad or nonexistent maintenance.

Engine and Generator Instruments

For the main engine most builders install the instrument panel given them by the engine manufacturer. It is adequate for most uses but usually has simple idiot lights rather than dials to tell you what is happening inside the engine. Unfortunately, by the time the idiot light comes on the problem has usually grown to major proportions. I prefer dials whenever possible because you can see instantly if an engine is overheating or if the oil pressure is dropping.

In order to monitor the dials the instruments must be somewhere within the helmsman's field of vision. Under the helmsman's seat, a spot that is rapidly gaining favor with some production builders, is the worst place for them.

Ideally, the engine instrument panel should be reasonably protected against the elements and in a place where it can be easily reached. The two are not mutually compatible on many boats, so a compromise must be found. I think the best compromise is to place the instrument panel in its own plexiglass-faced box high on the side of the cockpit. It can be read easily and is to hand in an emergency. If the panel is recessed it is unlikely to get damaged by the helmsman or crew working in the area.

The generator panel, on the other hand, needs to be carefully protected. On a boat with an aft helm station, the generator instrument panel is often near the main switchboard or in the navigation station. This too should have gauges rather than idiot lights. It usually has voltage and amperage meters, although they are often installed separately on the electrical panel.

If it is installed in the navigation area, near the electrical panel, it should be installed so that the navigator cannot inadvertently turn off switches or breakers. When the unit is installed outboard of the navigation seat the navigator will usually lean against the panel and damage it or other electrical equipment.

Engine Accessories

If you have only a main engine and no generator and decide you'd like hot water, there are two methods of heating water open to you. You can install a hot water heater that uses the cooling water system of the main engine, or you can go a slightly more circuitous route and install an electrically heated system with the heater driven off an alternator on the main engine and/or off the shore supply voltage.

The usual option is to use the waste water off the diesel engine and have an auxiliary heating coil that works off the shore supply system. As long as the heater is well insulated it will stay hot for some time.

You could also decide to install a hot water radiator to keep the boat warm. This, too, can be fed off the hot water outlet on the engine. Both of these systems use the engine cooling water to do their job.

You can also drive many attachments off the front end of the main engine. This is usually done by adding a pulley or two to the front end of the crankshaft. However, putting too much equipment on the front end can bend the crankshaft and cause an expensive engine repair. The extra pulley can be used to drive an array of devices; an extra alternator, bilge pump, hydraulic pump, refrigerator compressor, and pressure water pump are but a few of the options.

It is not usual to run any attachments off the front end of the generator. In this case you should use an electrically driven attachment and connect it up to the ship's wiring.

As you can see, the engine and generator are not equipment that enjoy neglect. To get the best from your motors you have to treat them well, and that means setting up a regular maintenance schedule. Spare parts such as fan belts, hoses, and a good tool kit should be kept handy. Most manufacturers supply a tool kit and a spare parts kit for their engines, and if you intend to venture far offshore it is advisable that you familiarize yourself with the basic troubleshooting operations on the engine and generator.

Soundproofing the Engine and Generator

Both the engine and generator make a tremendous amount of noise, and reducing the noise to an acceptable level takes careful soundproofing. First, engine vibration should be taken care of. This is usually accomplished by mounting the engine and generator on resilient or soft mountings, which are matched to the running speed of the crankshaft and mass of the engine.

Then the exhaust system will need quieting. This is done by muffling the line and using water-injected exhaust lines and, perhaps, running the exhaust out at the waterline. Often a second muffler such as an Elasto-muffle is added at the through-hull to add an additional layer of muffling.

Next, the generator can be purchased with its own soundproofing container. If you want the ultimate in quietness, this box is an essential.

Because engine noise can travel through the air intakes, the compartment should be ducted directly to the topsides and all holes into the compartment sealed. Then the engine compartment should be soundproofed. The best method of doing this is to glue a special material to the inside of the compartment. The material I have achieved best results with is a combination of lead and foam insulation. Generally the foam is about ¾ inch (18 millimeters) thick and then a layer of lead about ¹⁄₁₆ inch (1.5 millimeters). Finally a layer of foam about 1 inch (25 millimeters) thick is added to the lead and the whole thing faced with a washable vinyl. The lead-foam insulation comes assembled in a roll and is simply cut to fit the compartment and glued in place, or you can have the vendor install it.

THE PROPELLER

Feathering, fixed, or folding—those are your propeller options. Each has different characteristics, and your selection should be based on careful consideration of the best type for your boat. For instance, if your propeller is operating in an aperture, you may find that a three-bladed fixed prop will give you better performance because the blades are never completely blocked behind the deadwood as a two-bladed prop would be.

The Feathering Propeller

The feathering propeller will align its blades with the flow of water as the boat sails along. When the engine is kicked into gear the blades can either be manually cranked into position or will automatically take up the correct pitch because of the design of the prop. The best feathering propeller is the Max Prop. It is made in Italy and imported into this country. Available in two- and three-bladed versions, the prop works equally well both ahead and astern. If you find that the engine is overrevving with this prop, then it is relatively simple to reset the pitch and use all the engine power. Conversely, the pitch can be lowered if the engine isn't reaching its maximum power.

Another prop that can be feathered is the variable pitch Hundestat propeller. It uses a manual or hydraulic mechanism to adjust pitch under power to give best economy and powering speed. It has a very good reputation on larger boats, but I have never used one and am only going by its good reputation.

The Folding Propeller

The folding propeller's blades fold when the boat is under sail. In my experience a folding prop doesn't go as well astern as it goes ahead, but when the blades are folded it has less drag than the feathering prop. The only drawback to this prop is that, if the blades are not geared so that they both fold, it must be vertically centered to get the blades to fold properly.

However, if your shaft isn't marked there's a trick to this. The propeller is made so that the keyway is either at the top or bottom when the prop is centered. So all you have to do is check the position of the keyway. I know you can't see the keyway on the outboard end of the shaft, but the keyway on the engine coupling at the inboard end of the shaft is aligned with the outboard keyway, so you can use the inboard end to line up the prop if you don't have it marked.

In my estimation the best folding propeller around is the Martec, which we have specified for a number of boats. It works well, and I've always been able to get help from the factory when needed. But at low speeds a blade can flop open if the prop is not centered. While this is not much of a problem for the cruising sailor, it can be for the sailor looking for the best performance out of his boat. When using folding props, care must be taken to ensure both blades open under power. If only one blade opens, the subsequent vibrations can damage the prop or the strut or even tear the strut right out of the boat.

The Fixed Propeller

The fixed propeller is just as its name implies. The blades are fixed and it sticks out into the water stream whether the boat is powering or sailing. It has the highest drag of all types of sailing propeller, and the difference is clearly noticeable.

How Is the Propeller Selected?

The prop is usually sized by the architect, who will put the largest diameter possible on the boat. Larger props work more efficiently, but their size is limited by the available space. After all, a large prop is not that efficient if it causes vibration or undue noise. The pitch is governed by a number of factors that are incorporated into the propeller calculation: required boat speed, engine horsepower and rpms, size of the reduction gear, and type of propeller installation.

Most important is to select a propeller that will give the desired speed at the correct engine rpms and will not cavitate. Cavitation can cause prop erosion very quickly and is caused by selecting the wrong-sized propellor, one with too high a tip speed on the blades. The high speed causes the water literally to "boil" off the back of the blades. This boiling action is cavitation and pits and erodes the blades.

Propeller Installations

The most efficient propeller installation puts the prop revolving in clear water near the hull of the boat. However, on a sailing yacht it is difficult to position the prop in entirely clean water. There is usually a strut or boss in front of it. In extreme cases there may be a big lump of deadwood in front of the prop, but most designers are aware of the vibration caused and carefully fair in the deadwood.

The installation used most often is, to use IOR terminology, the *exposed shaft type.* That is, the shaft runs out of the hull through a strut. The boss of the propeller is located not more than one shaft diameter behind the strut; any further and the torque from the prop could bend the shaft. Care must be taken to ensure that the prop shaft can be withdrawn without removal of the rudder or engine. This is explained in the section on steering.

The *in aperture* installation is often fitted where it is desired to protect the prop from debris or ice. For instance, this type could be used on boats to be sailed in Arctic regions. It does not require a strut, as the prop is usually mounted directly behind the deadwood. The only problem with this installation is removing the propeller shaft. If the rudder and aperture are not carefully designed you could end up having to remove the engine in order to pull the shaft or change propellers.

The most usual installation next to the two above is the propeller on the *trailing edge of the keel*. In this type of fitting the prop is positioned directly behind the keel, and the keel is carefully faired to suit the installation. This is a simple, effective solution to the problem.

In all the propeller installations we've mentioned the prop is positioned close to a support, be it a strut or a keel, and that support usually has a bearing set in it, the cutlass bearing. It is important that every time the boat is hauled the cutlass bearing be checked for wear and play. I once sailed on a boat where the engine was misaligned and the bearing wore out in a few weeks. The problem was only noticed when the shaft started binding on the strut, and that was just before the strut broke, necessitating an expensive repair job.

The Propeller Shaft

The shaft is the connection between the engine and the propeller; without it the prop is useless. It should be stainless steel, monel, or bronze, depending on the other materials around it, and should be thick enough to prevent whipping. It should be supported by bearings or pillow blocks if its length is over 6 feet (2 meters). It is usually coupled to the engine with an engine coupling, but the latest trend is to use a special type of universal joint, which absorbs some of the vibration of the motor and allows for a slight misalignment.

Outboard Engines

An alternative to an inboard engine, with all its problems, is the outboard. It has certain advantages over the inboard, most significant of which is reduced installation cost. Consequently, you are likely to see smaller boats offered with an outboard as optional equipment. This only makes the boat appear inexpensive, however; the wise buyer will add in the price of the outboard when making the purchase.

With few exceptions, boats under 30 feet LOA use outboards. Where the outboard is stowed on the transom the transom will either have to be almost vertical or a bracket will be needed. In most cases a long shaft version will be needed to keep the outboard propeller in the water as the boat pitches. During racing or sailing, the outboard is often removed and placed below decks. This puts it in a position away from the transom, where its effect on pitching is reduced. However, if you intend to store the engine below deck, make sure that the fuel is turned off.

In some larger boats the outboard is installed in a designed-in well. In this case the shaft protrudes through the bottom of the boat. In some boats the outboard can be removed from the well and the opening replaced by a piece of false hull. In others it is difficult to remove and the shaft sticks into the water stream.

Strut Drives

Another system that appears to have found a niche in the sailboat market is the strut drive. Here the engine, reduction gear, and propeller are assembled in a complete package that is fitted onto a previously installed mounting in the boat. The mounting provides a seal around the strut. The only part of the unit that protrudes through the hull is the strut and propeller, making it cleaner than a simple outboard. The advantages of this system are that the unit is compact, shaft alignment problems are eliminated, and engines larger than outboards can be installed.

FIGURE 8.3. *When selecting an engine a large amount of time can be saved by using templates supplied by the engine manufacturers. A shows the Westerbeke 4.4BCD diesel generator unit; the Westerbeke 38B engine is shown on page 218. (Courtesy of Westerbeke Corporation). B shows the Volvo Penta 2002S Sail Drive unit. (Courtesy of the Volvo Penta of America Division of Volvo Penta Corporation).*

FIGURE 8.3A

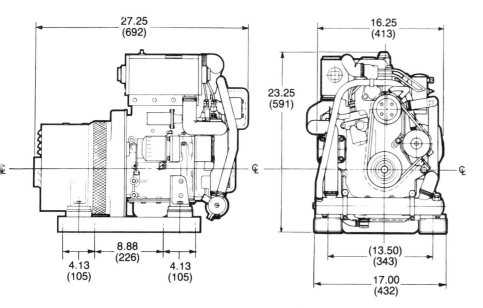

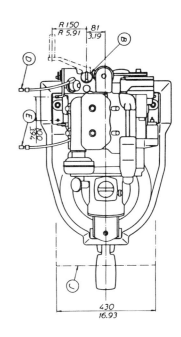

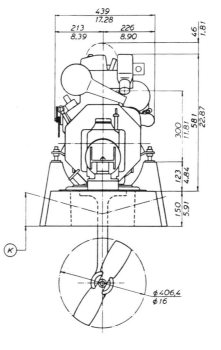

FIGURE 8.3B

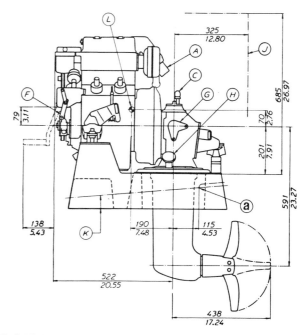

A = Exhaust elbow for
     hose I.D. 44/1.75
B = Oil filling
C = Oil dip stick, drive unit
D = Fuel connection for
     pipe 5/16″
E = Fuel return connection
     for pipe 5/16″

F = Speed control lever
G = Gear shift lever
H = Sea water cock
J = Min space when
     mounting drive unit
K = Lower edge to be cut
     acc. to hull form
L = Centre of gravity

a = Ref. point, see inst.-
     handbook publ no
     5122

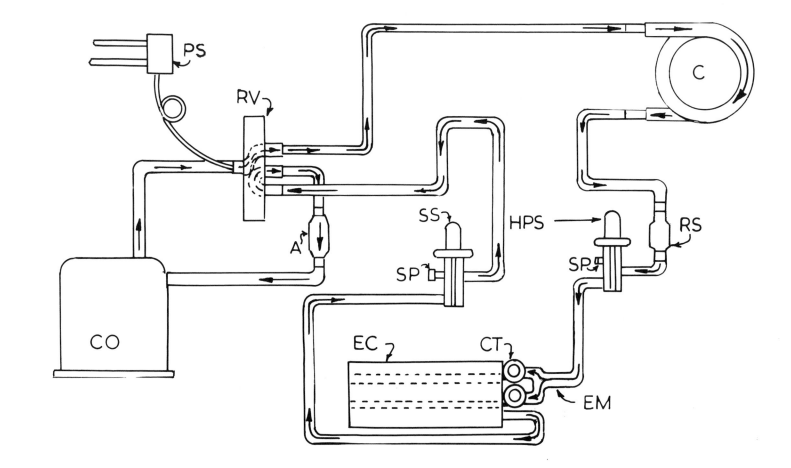

CHAPTER 9

Pumps, Compressors, and the Supporting Systems

It was only a few years ago that a well-equipped cruiser was lucky to have pressure fresh water. Nowadays, almost all cruisers over 35 feet have both hot and cold pressure water systems. Not only is pressure water included on larger vessels, but so may a freezer, a refrigerator, automatic bilge pumps, an anchor windlass, a watermaker, a microwave, and quite possibly air conditioning. However, there is a price for all these luxuries. The pumps and mechanical systems to support these items use a large amount of power and space. For instance, a small hot water heater might measure about 30 inches long and 12 inches in diameter (760 $\times$ 300 millimeters diameter), then the pump unit should be added in. This will take up another 6-by-12–inch space (150 $\times$ 300 millimeters), depending upon the pump. In terms of power, the same heater might use 100 watts of power, and the pump another 10–15 watts. Powering these items will require a generator or very large batteries and a method of keeping them charged. This power unit will also take up space. Because of the demands of space and power required to run these luxuries, they usually appear only on large yachts over about 40 feet. To my knowledge, the Pearson 37 (made in America) of 1988 vintage is the smallest production yacht that incorporates a generator to power a vast array of electrical items.

In spite of this, these luxuries are rapidly becoming essentials as owners treat their boats as second homes rather than vehicles in which to sail from one place to another, roughing it on the way. In the relevant chapters we've looked at the operator end, and in this chapter we'll deal with the mechanical end: how it works, how it is installed and maintained, and its range of functions.

PUMPS

It's appropriate that we look at pumps first because they are the most widely used. We've already mentioned the pressure fresh water pump. In addition, there are bilge pumps, both automatic and manual, sump pumps, salt water pumps, and pumps to supply water to the engine and generator.

The Pressure Fresh Water Pump

The pressure fresh water pump is almost an essential. Some sailors prefer a hand-operated unit because they say it saves water. But, in fact, for the prudent cruiser, both systems use about the same amount. If you need a certain amount of fresh water, you are going to use it whether it is hand pumped or pressure pumped.

When purchasing a fresh water pressure pump it is essential that the pump be self-priming. The way most of these pumps operate is to fill a "bladder" accumulator, which keeps the system pressurized. As the water is used, the bladder deflates until it trips a micro switch. Tripping that switch turns the pump on, and it refills the bladder. The pumps can be obtained with various-sized accumulators and should be sized to suit the expected water flow rate. In general, the larger the accumulator the fewer cycles the pump has to go through, reducing noise and wear on the pump.

The pumps I have been most impressed with are the Balmar pumps. They are built in Italy by Feit, who supply pumps to most of the best-known boat builders around the world. Another good unit is the Paragon pump. These pumps require a pressure storage tank for both the junior and senior pumps. At the time of writing I'm told the Paragon are slightly more expensive than the Balmar pumps.

The Salt Water Washdown Pump

A salt water washdown pump is not essential—a bucket of water will do just as well—but having a salt water washdown pump saves labor and effort. Usually these pumps are situated on the foredeck and with the aid of a short length of hose can be used to wash off the anchor and chain, wash the deck down, wash the afterdeck if you catch and gut a fish or two, and generally help keep the boat clean.

The unit is similar to the fresh water pump described previously. However, a strainer should be fitted at the intake end to ensure seaweed isn't sucked into the pump.

Bilge Pumps

Bilge pumps should be mandatory on every boat. Again, with no set standards for cruising boats, many manufacturers have turned to the ORC regulations to decide what to put aboard. The ORC regs insist that one pump be manually operable from the cockpit and one manually operable from inside the boat. That means every boat has to have two bilge pumps aboard that can be operated by hand. Many cruisers have a third or fourth pump driven by the engine or by an electric motor. The electric pump with its own float switch can be left on automatic and ensures that minor amounts of water are immediately pumped overside.

For a manual pump I have always specified Edson or the Henderson series. The Edson model 117 diaphragm pump will pump up to 30 gallons (113 liters) per minute. This model comes in aluminum or bronze and can pass small pieces of debris without clogging. This is a large pump, and, in general, the larger the pump the easier it is to use. Normally a pump of this size should be positioned under the cabin sole in every boat over 35 feet. A smaller pump, such as the Henderson Mk V, can be placed in the cockpit for pumping smaller amounts.

On smaller boats the Henderson Chimp could be used in both places. Both pumps should be readily accessible, not hidden under bunk cushions or in hatches.

The bilge line should go directly over the side via a vented loop. It is essential a vent be in the loop to prevent back-siphoning from the ocean into the bilge. Where more than one pump is installed, or the pumps have to empty several compartments, the lines are often led to a manifold, which can be switched from pump to pump or compartment to compartment and then overboard. This eliminates having many holes in the hull.

A boat, then, requires many pumps, all of which should be sized to suit the tanks and the requirements of the owner. In general, the larger the boat, the more likely it is to have a number of pumps for specific tasks.

Reverse Osmosis Desalination Systems (Watermakers)

Having discussed methods of disposing of the water we had better look at methods of making more. RO desalination systems work on the principle of forcing filtered sea water through a semi-permeable membrane. The filter reduces particle size to about 5 microns, and then the clean sea water is pressurised, sometimes as high as 800 psi, before it is forced through the membrane. On the fresh water side of the membrane the fresh water is then sterilized and piped to the tanks, while the residue is discarded back into the ocean. Only a small percentage of the fresh water is extracted, often less than 10 percent, and the remainder pumped overboard.

Watermakers come in a variety of sizes. Some will only make 100 gallons per day, others make 3500 gallons per day. The correct size for a yacht can be selected by analyzing the water needs of the boat for the day. The two major manufacturers of systems suitable for yachts are made by Sea Recovery systems and HRO systems. The HRO system claims to be the smallest and lightest desalinator yet developed, but I have never used one.

I have used a Sea Recovery system; however, the manufacturers say several points should be taken into account when sizing the system: (1) the vessel's present tankage; (2) The number of crew; and (3) daily usage in the past. You should add to this another item: the availability of space to install the unit.

Sea Recovery says that historically they upgrade 65 percent of their units within one year of purchase because concern for saving water is eliminated and consumption increases dramatically. In their experience daily usage for yachts under 50 feet is 10 gallons per day per person, which allows for showering and domestic chores but not flushing the head. They suggest that if you have a washing machine on board then add 40 gallons of water per load.

We had a watermaker on my last cruise to Bermuda, and it was amazing how often the crew showered and changed clothes, something they probably only did once or twice without a watermaker.

The calculation to size the machine is quite simple. Let's assume we have four people on board a 50-foot yacht:

$$\text{Water used} = 4 \text{ crew} \times 10 \text{ gallons} = 40 \text{ gallons}$$
$$\text{Washing machine} = 40 \text{ gallons}$$
$$\text{Washdown} = 20 \text{ gallons}$$
$$\text{Total} = 100 \text{ gallons per day}$$

If we assume the generator runs 6 hours per day, then

$$100 \div 6 = 16.67 \text{ gallons per hour}$$

The system rating would therefore be 16.6 gallons × 24 hours = 400 gallons per day.

This means that we would need a 400-gallon-per-day reverse osmosis desalination system. The one from Sea Recovery would be the SRC 400, and if we decided to put it in the engine room it would take up a space of 31 × 23 ⅛ × 18 ⅞ inches (787 × 587 × 480 millimeters) in its metal frame and would use up to 11 amps of 230 volt power. This power usage will have to be figured in when we look at how large a generator to install. (See Chapter 10: The Electrical System). Figure 9.1 shows the Sea Recovery R.O. System.

FIGURE 9.1. *The Sea Recovery Reverse Osmosis Watermaker. This compact system is designed specifically for yachts. (Photo courtesy of Sea Recovery Systems Inc.)*

The system should have certain options to get the best out of it. For instance, if you are going to be moored in a harbor where oil could be a problem, then an oil-water separator should be designed into your system. If oil reaches the membrane it will permanently destroy it. Where bacteria and micro-organisms are present, an ultraviolet sterilizer is recommended. Sea Recovery recommends this unit be installed where the system is to run in harbors, especially in tropical harbors. If this system is not installed, then the fresh water tanks should be treated with chlorine. Most of these options require the use of a booster pump to increase the water pressure.

Certain alarms should be included in the package. The low pressure alarm tells you if the filter is clogged, causing low pressure at the membrane. The vacuum pressure protection alarm shuts the system down if the filter clogs, preventing damage to the membrane and high pressure pump. A sound alarm alerts the user that the system is producing unsafe water. The unsafe or dirty water is directed back overboard, not into the tank. This alarm can be mounted on the bridge, in the cockpit, or anywhere else where the crew will hear it.

For the sailor who intends to sail across oceans and has enough generator capacity, the reverse osmosis desalination system (watermaker) has a lot to recommend it. No longer will you have to wait for a suitable rainstorm before you can shower or wash clothes. With this system the entire crew will be cleaner and much more hygienic.

In my observations of yachts all over the world, I have noticed that most cruisers without a watermaker have a water tankage of near or just over 5 percent of displacement (from the ratio: fresh water tankage (U.S. gallons) $\times 8 \times 100$/displacement in pounds). A cruiser that has the power to use the machine once per day can have a ratio as low as 3 percent, some even use 2 percent as a norm, but this seems to be getting a little low. If you want to make less water, or make it less often, then the tankage should remain about 5 percent.

AIR CONDITIONING

Air conditioning is being installed on more and more cruising yachts. It used to be that only boats over 70 feet had air conditioning, but now smaller and smaller vessels have air conditioning. I recently saw an air conditioning unit on a 40 footer, and I think it won't be long before the units are smaller and appearing on boats as small as 30 footers.

Air conditioning systems can be of several types:

1. A central compressor/condenser driving a cooling unit in each cabin.
2. A central compressor and cooling unit ducted to one or two cabins.
3. Several separate units, one in each cabin.

The most efficient is the central compressor driving remote units in each stateroom. This cuts down on power usage and gives you two or three adjustable outlets in different compartments.

On a smaller boat a central compressor/condenser and cooling unit hidden in a cabinet could be the least expensive option. It would only cool that stateroom, or by careful positioning and ducting it could be made to cool two compartments. However, trying to cool more than that can reduce efficiency quite dramatically.

Where the compartments are well separated, it could be more efficient to place separate units in each compartments. However, power usage will be quite high, and overside condensate drains would have to be provided for each unit.

The most efficient system is the central compressor driving a cooling unit in each cabin. This is the method used on many medium and large boats. The compressor's noise is well away from the cabin occupant, while the small cooling unit allows the temperature to be adjusted easily.

Air conditioning units do require that you have a generator on board in order to have sufficient power to drive the compressor and the remote units. The size of the air conditioning units must be included in the powering calculation to determine the size of the generator.

How does the air conditioning system work? A refrigerant, usually freon gas, is pumped through a compressor, which compresses the vapor into a hot gas. This gas flows through a condenser, where the heat is extracted from it by sea water and the gas changes back into a liquid form. From there the liquid freon passes through the cooling unit, where it cools the air that is passed over the coils. Here it changes into vapor and is piped back to the compressor, then the cycle starts all over again. When the summers are warm and winters cold, a reverse-cycle air conditioning unit can be used to warm the cabin in winter. That is, the air conditioning cycle runs backward to heat the cabin.

Sizing the System

The first item is to decide on the size of the system. This calculation should take into account several factors:

1. The amount of glass and the insulation value of the deck and hull material.
2. Whether the cabin is below deck level or exposed to the sun, as a pilot house is.
3. The volume of space to be cooled and the difference in temperature between the outside air and the desired cabin temperature.
4. Losses through leakage, for example, the loss of heat through open ports, people going in and out of the cabin.
5. The heat gained from equipment running in the cabin. Fans and other electrical items, such as a refrigerator or light bulbs, all give off heat when they are running.
6. Heat lost through the hull to the outside sea water. An insulated hull will lose less heat than a noninsulated hull.

The designer has to work out all these areas and volumes and then calculate the loss of cooling to determine the size of the unit. The size will be figured in BTUs (British thermal units) or kilowatts per hour

The next decision is to decide what type of unit should be installed. Should it be a central unit with ducts going to each compartment, or should it have a central compressor in the engine room with remote cooling units in the different compartments? The most common method is to install a compressor in the engine compartment and build remote coolers into lockers or under bunks.

Let's assume we have determined that we need a 12,000 BTU/hour unit. If we look at the manufacturer's catalog—this one is from Marine Development Corporation, which makes Cruisair air conditioners. We'll first need to pick a condensing unit. The WFA 12 unit seems to be the one we want. If we intend to install heating as well as air conditioning, we should specify the WFAH 12 unit. This unit has the refrigeration compressor, the refrigerant condenser, and all the associated electrical and mechanical components. It runs on 115 volts and uses 12 amps and adds another 1.4 kilowatts to the generator requirements, or, if the unit is fed from a shore supply, it will require a separate connection to the shore unit as well as the ship's shore supply connection. (See Chapter 10 for more on the electrical installation.) The condenser will require a sea water line to carry off the heat absorbed from the inside of the boat when it is cooled. So a sea water

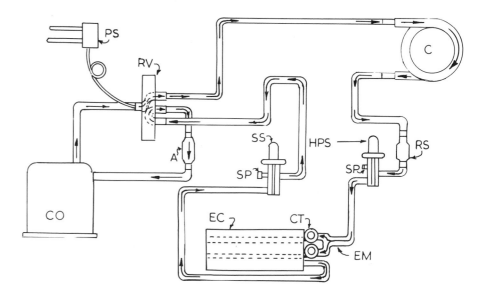

FIGURE 9.2. *The refrigerant flow/cooling cycle for the WFA12 air conditioning unit. (Photo courtesy of Marine Development Corporation.)*
   C—*Condensing coil.*
   PS—*Pressure switch.*
   RV—*Reversing valve.*
   A—*Accumulator.*
   SS—*Suction service valve.*
   SP—*Service port.*
   HPS—*High pressure service valve.*
   RS—*Receiver strainer.*
   CT—*Capillary tube.*
   EM—*Evaporator coil manifold.*
   EC—*Evaporator coil.*
   CO—*Compressor.*

pump must be provided. For the 12,000 BTU unit we selected we would need a PMJ250 sea water pump. This uses 0.9 amps, which must be added to the power consumed.

Having selected the condensing unit, we now have to decide where to put the cooling unit. If we are going to cool one large open space, then we would select a single 12,000 BTU unit and install it in a locker somewhere in the cabin. If a large locker is not available, then two

FIGURE 9.3. *Marine Development Corporation's WFA12 air conditioning unit. (Photo courtesy of Marine Development Corporation.)*

REFRIGERATORS AND FREEZERS

In the section on interior design we looked at the requirements for the icebox or freezer cabinet. In this section we will look at how the system works and what is required in the way of compressors/condensers, cooling water, and electrical consumption. There are three main types of refrigeration: (1) the thermo electric system; (2) the absorption system; and (3) the mechanical system.

The *thermo electric system* is used for the small portable ice chests that must be plugged in and kept running to work efficiently. They work by applying electricity to two dissimilar metals. One of the metals gets hot, the other cold. Heat flows from one to the other and cools the box as it moves. This is known as the Peltier effect.

The *absorption system* is rarely seen today. It requires a pilot light, and, as we saw earlier, it can cause a major explosion when combined with a gasoline engine. It works by using a heating source to vaporize ammonia. The heating source can be propane or other, but the efficiency of the unit drops off quickly as the boat heels and the unit is tipped away from the vertical. When the ammonia is vaporized it flows into coils in the icebox and the icebox cools the ammonia, causing it to condense. When it has condensed it is pumped back to the flame and revaporized. The flame should ignite automatically as the box heats up and therefore will require a pilot light.

This poses certain problems, in that the pilot light may not stay lit as the boat bounces around on the ocean. It is also inefficient when the ambient air temperature is very high, and, of course, the heat source will add to the temperature inside the boat.

The most common system is the *mechanical system,* which works in a similar manner to the air conditioning unit. It uses a compressor to compress the freon vapor into a hot gas. From there it is pumped through the condenser (heat exchanger), where the freon condenses back into a liquid. This liquid passes through the icebox, where it absorbs heat from the chamber by boiling or vaporizing. At this point the cycle starts all over again.

Rather than passing the freon through a cooling unit, as is done with an air conditioning unit, the freon passes through holding plates that contain a mixture of sodium chloride, water, and alcohol. This mixture is specially formulated so that it has a low freezing point and does not expand or contract.

At the other end of the unit is the compressor/condenser unit, which is usually placed in the engine compartment or in a locker by

smaller units could be selected and installed on either side of the compartment. If several compartments are to be cooled, then a much smaller unit—dependent upon the size of each compartment—can be installed in each compartment. Each cooling unit is connected to the condenser by insulated refrigerant lines. Note also that a condensate drain must be provided, which can be fed overboard at the cooling unit or at the condenser. Figure 9.2 shows the refrigerant flow cooling cycle, and Figure 9.3 shows a self-contained air conditioning unit for yachts.

the freezer if space allows. The refrigerant (freon) is moved between the working parts in insulated piping.

The compressor/condenser unit must either be run off the main engine or coupled to its own electrical motor. Usually the electric motor option is chosen because it is easier to keep the batteries topped up than to run the main engine every time the refrigerator needs cooling.

If we intend to have both air conditioning and a refrigerator-freezer, then we will have two compressor/condenser units in the engine compartment. With the addition of batteries, bilge pumps, and other equipment, we are rapidly filling the engine compartment. However, there is much more equipment that may be required in this space. We should look at heating systems, ventilation, and fire control systems.

HEATING SYSTEMS

In tropical areas the boat needs to be cooled, but in more northerly ports an efficient heater can make the difference between an enjoyable springtime cruise and a miserable cold one.

Heating systems come in many shapes and styles. If your boat is set up for air conditioning, usually it is a simple matter to install a reverse-cycle heating system. If you do not have this option, various forms of space heaters, stoves, and electrical systems can be used.

Reverse-Cycle Heating

As its name implies, the reverse-cycle unit is simply a cooling unit running backward. Instead of taking the heat out of the interior of the boat and getting rid of it by heating the circulating sea water, it takes heat from the sea water and uses it to heat the inside of the yacht. It is best used where the sea water is warm enough to have some heat that can be extracted. This means that the efficiency of such a system is dependent upon the difference in temperature between sea water and the interior temperature of the boat.

Space Heaters

These heaters heat the air and distribute it around the boat. The best I've used is the Espar unit. It can be installed in the engine compartment and the hot air ducted to any part of the vessel. It runs on diesel

fuel, and I've heard some complaints of being able to smell the diesel; however, I've never experienced them. The unit itself is quite compact and can be installed quite easily.

Sizing the heater can be of critical importance. Too large a unit could turn the interior into a sauna, while too small wouldn't do the job properly. Like air conditioning, the calculation is based upon several features:

1. The insulation value of the hull.
2. The size of the space to be heated.
3. The difference in temperature between the inside and outside air.
4. Leakage between the inside and outside, including the number of times the hatches or ports are opened.

FIGURE 9.4. *The Balmar cabin heater. (Photo courtesy of Balmar.)*

Cabin Heaters

In spite of having the option of reverse-cycle air conditioning and space heaters, there are those of us who still prefer to go below and see a warm stove mounted on the bulkhead. To be able to walk over to it and warm your hands or other parts is one of the pleasures of cold weather sailing.

Several manufacturers produce bulkhead-mounted cabin heaters fueled by diesel. If the boat will sail in cold water most of its life, then these stoves can be installed with their own tiled fireplace around them, when they become a major feature of the interior layout.

This type of stove should have an air intake line, usually from a dorade vent, and an air exhaust line going to its own flue on deck. If this is not installed then it is possible for carbon dioxide to build up and asphyxiate the occupants.

Another option is catalytic heaters, either electric or gas-powered. The electric version consumes quite a lot of power, but if you are using the boat alongside then it is a viable plug-in option. They do tend to produce a buildup of water vapor inside the boat, however, which causes problems if it is allowed to freeze and thaw.

Balmar/Dickinson has a range of stoves in stainless or brass to match the interior of the boat. These stoves can be obtained with electric air intakes, flu vent kits, and a draft-assist fan to ensure the stove works under all conditions. Figure 9.4 shows the Balmar cabin heater.

FIRE PREVENTION SYSTEMS

Obviously, the fire extinguisher is the most common method of extinguishing fires. But there are many other factors that should be taken into account before locating extinguishers. A booklet available from the National Fire Protection Association, Batterymarch Park, Quincy, Massachusetts, looks at the various factors that cause fires and discusses how they can be minimized or eliminated.

But the average sailor who already has a boat usually doesn't want to make expensive changes; he wants to add a few fire extinguishers and go sailing. There are many types of extinguisher available. Water being the most common. But water does not do a good job on many chemicals and can be a hazard when used on electrical fires. For chemical fires a foam or powder extinguisher is recommended, and many electrical fires are best controlled with a carbon dioxide or halon extinguisher. A fire blanket is also a good standby for all fires. The type of extinguisher, then, should suit the type of fire. On a boat, the most usual fires are galley stove fires and engine room fires.

The best extinguisher for a galley fire depends upon the type of fuel used. If you have an LPG or CNG system, an alcohol (methylated spirits) fire is best fought with a halon extinguisher. Although a chemical powder extinguisher can do almost as good a job, the powder tends to result in a much higher cleanup cost. Coal or wood fires can usually be extinguished with water.

In America, Coast Guard regulations ensure that most boats with an engine have at least one extinguisher aboard, but it often pays to have several placed strategically around the boat. For instance, suppose you were on deck and had a smoky fire in the galley. If your extinguisher were in the galley you'd have to go below, grope your way through the smoke, and try to put out the fire. In this instance an extinguisher just inside the companionway door would enable you to attack the fire without going below.

Engine room fires are a different proposition. First, they are usually in an enclosed space, and, contrary to popular belief, most engine room fires are caused by the electrical wiring rather than fuel. Don Harrington of Fireboy Systems in Grand Rapids, Michigan, says that people tend to be very cautious about the fire potential of fuel but neglect to inspect their wiring, which chafes and eventually causes a short circuit and potentially a fire. In the larger engine room these fires are best fought with a permanently installed and fully automatic system. Fireboy Systems makes an automatic halon unit that can be installed in the engine room. The unit uses a fusible link that is melted by low temperature. A link melting sets off the system before the fire has had time to gain a major hold.

Fire prevention is, then, a serious matter. It doesn't take much to start a fire, but a good extinguishing system will quickly bring it under control. If you own a boat, why not take a look at your firefighting arrangements and upgrade them if necessary?

Without all the smaller pumps and compressors the modern boat would be that much simpler, but the levels of luxury to which many cruisers have become accustomed would not be possible. However, if you have several units aboard, it is well to set up a maintenance schedule and make sure everything is kept in good shape. After all, what is the use of a pump that will not work?

FIGURE 9.5. *A fire extinguisher is essential in or near the engine compartment. Here a Fireboy unit is positioned at the aft end of a large yacht's engine room. Note that it is securely fastened and can be lifted out of the brackets easily. (Photo courtesy of Fireboy Systems Inc.)*

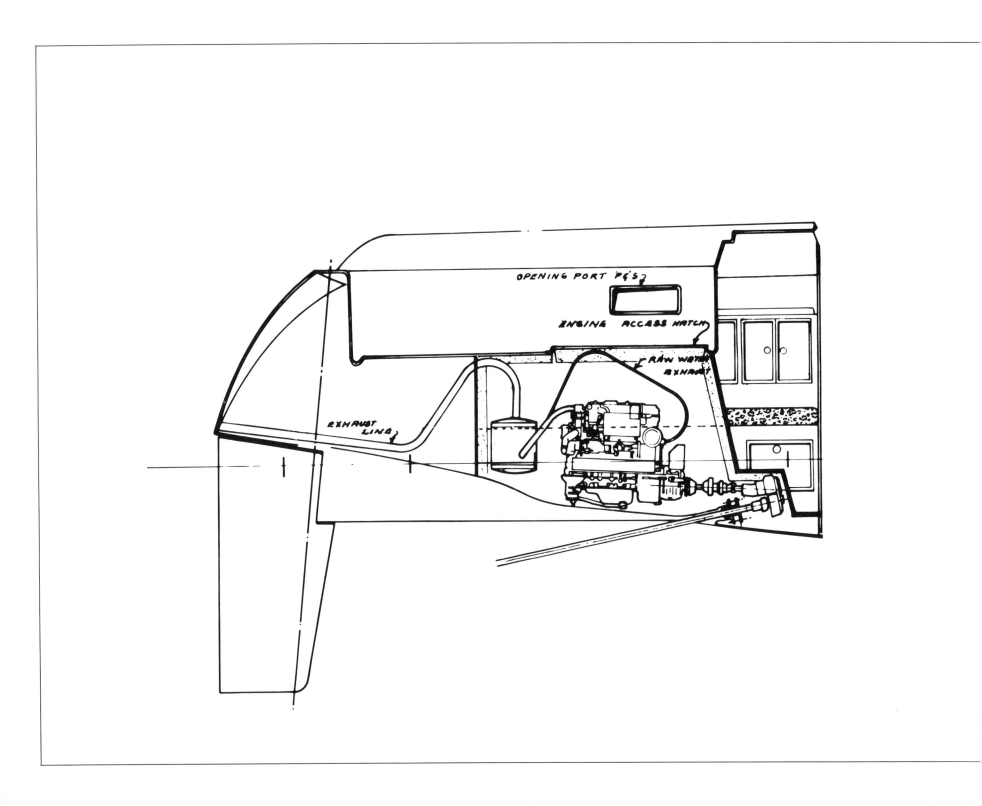

OPENING PORT PC'S?

ENGINE ACCESS HATCH

RAW WATER
EXHAUST

EXHAUST
LINE?

CHAPTER **10**

The Electrical System

Once a cruising boat owner was satisfied with a single battery, which started the engine and powered a light or two inside the boat. Today very few owners would accept that simple a system. The modern offshore sailor, while he may still yearn for simplicity, is almost bound to have radios, lights, Loran or Satnav, and a host of other electrical items aboard. These all use power, which has to come from the batteries.

The batteries have to be kept charged, which means an alternator, generator, or some other system has to be available. As it is difficult, if not impossible, to connect the electrical items directly to the battery, a switchboard must be installed with its own meters and breakers to monitor the system. If the system is large, several subboards must be incorporated. They have to be connected with a mass of correctly sized wires, all of which should be properly color-coded. The electrical system sounds like a mass of discordant pieces, but

FIGURE 10.1. *The Ferris generator mounted on the mizzen mast. This unit has had its blades removed to stop it revolving in port.*

it shouldn't be. In the following pages we'll look at the modern yacht's electrical system and its component parts.

GENERATING ELECTRICAL POWER

There are many ways of generating electrical power, from the fully fledged generator giving up to 10 kilowatts to the small solar cell that provides just enough output to run a small ventilation fan. They all have their place on board.

Solar Cells

Solar cells have an output dependent upon the number of cells and the amount of sunlight available. Part of the beauty of solar cells is that they can be positioned almost anywhere on the boat. The transom is a common place on larger craft, while on other boats they can be positioned on hatches or on cabintops—anywhere the cells won't get walked on regularly.

Solar cells are panels of photovoltaic cells that convert sunlight into electrical power. A small panel measuring about 18 × 12 inches (457 × 305 millimeters) will output about .75 amp at 12 volts under peak operating conditions. Enough to keep your battery charged. A larger system measuring about 36 × 16 inches (914 × 406 millimeters) can put out up to 2.5 amps at 12 volts. These panels can be connected in parallel to raise the output.

They are best thought of as a backup system to keep the batteries charged and to keep some of the electronic instruments running. They should not be used when high power drain is needed.

Wind Generators

Wind generators are becoming more common. I've seen several lately, and the Neptune Supreme from Hamilton Ferris Co. is a well-known design. It can be mounted in the rigging when it uses the wind as a primary energy source, or with a conversion kit the system can be mounted on the transom. In this mode it tows a propeller through the water generating power as the boat moves. The unit weighs 20–25 pounds (9–11 kilograms) depending on whether it is rigging mounted or water powered. Its output will vary depending on wind strength and boat speed. Under ideal conditions you could get over 10 amps of power.

Another unit is the Balmar CS120, which can generate up to 12 amps. The only warning when using a wind generator is to make sure it is positioned high enough so that the whirling blade is well away from anyone walking underneath. If you have a mizzen mast on the boat, that would be the ideal place to mount one of these generators. Figure 10.1 shows a Ferris generator with its blades removed for safety, and Figure 10.2 shows the Balmar CS120.

On the other hand, if you are worried about the blades and can't get them high enough, you should look at the water-powered Ferris unit. However, this too has a drawback: at higher speeds the spinner can jump out of the water. Some manufacturers recommend a diving plane to keep the spinner deep in the water. I have also heard of the spinners being eaten by large curious fish.

Portable Generators

We did one five-day offshore trip with a portable Yamaha generator tied on the afterdeck. It sat there waiting to be used. When power was needed we simply took the leads from the generator to the battery, making sure to connect them up correctly, and walked back to the generator. A quick yank on the starting cord and the little machine coughed into life and charged the batteries. Yamaha, Yanmar, Honda, and others make small air-cooled generators that are ideal for boats. You can get a Balmar 100 that puts out 100 amps to charge your batteries, or a larger model, up to 3 kilowatts. The size you need on board, however, will depend on the time it takes to recharge your batteries and to do all the other things you may want to do. For instance, you might want to cool the icebox or refrigerator or pump the bilge. With a small generator this would have to be done after the battery is charged. A larger unit would enable you to do both things at once, but the machine is larger and heavier, uses more fuel, and is much more difficult to protect in inclement weather. (These machines should never be operated below deck. The exhaust in such an enclosed space could kill you.)

Permanently Installed Generators

One of the most common methods of obtaining extra power is the water-cooled, permanently installed generator. It can vary in size from 2 kilowatts to 32 kilowatts. These gensets allow you to operate all the extra equipment you may want to have installed.

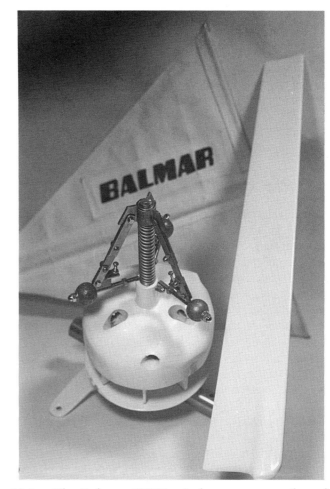

FIGURE 10.2. *The Balmar CS120 wind generator ready to be installed. (Photo courtesy of Balmar.)*

They can be purchased with either gas or diesel motors, and it makes sense to order the diesel version if you have diesel for the main engine. The major manufacturers of gensets are Kohler, Onan, and Westerbeke. In my office we have specified Westerbeke most often and have found the company to be particularly helpful. I've heard good reports about the other sets but have never used them.

The first thing to remember with a genset is that it can be twice as dangerous as the main engine. At the one end there is the diesel engine, which is hot and noisy and spitting out carbon monoxide, and at the other end is an electrical motor putting out up to 240 volts. Both can kill you!

Nevertheless, they are worth having aboard. The output from the generator allows many extras that would not otherwise be possible.

Alternator Running off the Main Engine

Almost all boats powered by an engine have an alternator or generator belt driven by the main engine. This alternator is usually installed by the engine manufacturer or installer and ranges from about 30 amps to 190 amps on the larger ones. On smaller engines the alternator is used principally for battery charging. In this case, the alternating current is changed to DC by rectifying diodes installed directly on the machine. The presence of the rectifying diodes indicates that the operator must use care when operating this alternator. If the alternator is run in an open circuit or in a short circuit, the diodes can be destroyed. In an open circuit situation the alternator output voltage increases until it simply blows the diodes. In a short circuit situation (when the alternator is connected up backward), the diodes try to conduct the battery current against the alternator current and blow. So you will have to be careful if you decide to install a new alternator.

The larger units that can be fitted on more powerful engines often put out 190–200 amps at either 12 or 24 volts. This size machine should be used if you have a high power drain and an engine large enough to support it. It would not be used simply for battery charging unless you had a huge bank of batteries and a commensurate power drain. You might run shipboard lights, pumps, and other devices while charging the batteries, or you might install extra batteries to run a power inverter and use a large alternator to recharge the batteries quickly. Another point to be aware of is that a large alternator can also be expected to absorb up to 5 horsepower from the engine.

Power Inverters

Although the principle has been around for a long time, it is only recently that inverters have become popular on boats. Inverters convert battery power to alternating current and step up the voltage from 12, 24, 32, or 48 volts to 110 or 230 volts AC. The power output varies according to the load but can be as high as 2,600 watts, depending upon the machine and the manufacturer. They are used when the load is high but of short duration or a low load over a longer time period. They have an efficiency rating of over 90 percent and are ideal for driving a television, computer, microwave, and some tools. As an example, if a generator is turned on to power a television set or computer, the interference, even with suppressors, is quite high. With an inverter that interference is virtually eliminated. However, inverters do have drawbacks: they will not power air conditioning or watermakers. The power drain is too high for too long.

The Balmar inverter, model no. 2012, can produce up to 2000 watts at 117 volts. However, it does have a price. The battery drain is reasonably high; typically 9.25 amps from the battery for every 100 watts used at 110 volts. But when the unit is on standby it only uses .03 amp. Thus the inverter is at its best when the load is cyclic; for example, when lights are turned off and on. The inverter only uses power from the battery when it is called for, whereas a generator keeps running and generating power whether the power is used or not.

To run an inverter you will need heavy duty batteries and a method of recharging them quickly. Balmar recommends deep cycle batteries with a high output generator and Powercharger unit. If you have all these items the advantage of the inverter is freedom from the vibration, exhaust smoke, and noise of a generator.

Generator Selection

After you've decided that your new boat will have a generator aboard, your first job is to pick the correct size. To do this we perform the calculation outlined in Table 10.1. Note how an estimate of harbor and sea usage is obtained before the unit is selected. In this case we have determined that we'll need a 6-kilowatt generator.

If we take into account fuel consumption, weight, and output, we find the generator load is about 4,300 watts. Adding 15 percent to 20 percent (a figure used because it is anticipated that the owner will add more electrical items), we find that we need about 5 kilowatts of power. By inspecting manufacturer catalogs, we find that Westerbeke makes a 4.4- and a 7.7-kilowatt unit. The 4.4-kilowatt unit weighs 410 pounds (186 kilograms), and the 7.7-kilowatt unit weighs 520 pounds. Because the weight difference is small, the designer would probably call the owner for his opinion. Now we have to decide how it will be fitted in the boat, how fuel and water are going to reach it, and how the sound will be reduced. The latter question is easy: we can use the

				Generator Load			
				in Port		at Sea	
Item	No.	HP	Connected watts	Load Factor		Load Factor	Watts

TABLE 10.1 GENERATOR LOAD ANALYSIS (110 VOLT SYSTEM)

Item	No.	HP	Connected watts	in Port Load Factor		at Sea Load Factor	Watts
Refrigerator compressor	1	—	350	—	—	1.0	350
Refrigerator compressor	1	—	350	—	—	.5	175
Anchor windlass	1	2	1,500	.5	750	—	—
Fresh water pressure pump	2	¼	200	.2	40	.2	40
Engine compartment blowers	2	¼	200	.6	240	1.0	400
Galley stove	1	—	4,000	.4	1,600	.4	1,600
12 volt charging	1	—	800	1	800	1.0	800
Searchlight	1	—	250	.1	25	—	—
Coffeemaker	2	—	600	.4	240	.2	120
Toaster	1	—	700	.2	140	.1	70
Heater	1	—	400	.3	120	.1	40
Lights	10	—	700	.5	350	.5	350
			(10,050)		(4,305)		(3,945)

The total connected wattage is 10,050 watts; however, this is not a good figure to use to size the generator. The wattage of each item is modified by the load factor. (A load factor of 1 would mean the item is in use 24 hours per day.) From this calculation we find that the power required will be 4,305 watts, or 4.3 kilowatts. if we add 10–15 percent as a factor to compensate for the additional items that will be added at a later date, we should be looking for a 5.5- or 6-kilowatt generator.

Westerbeke sound guard enclosure. This makes the unit physically larger, but it reduces the decibel count to a tolerable level.

Fuel oil can easily be supplied from the main tanks, and the cooling water supply will come from a Y valve on the engine intake. Sometimes the manufacturer will specify a separate cooling water intake with its own filter. The designer should be aware of that and call it out in the specs.

Shore Supply

At one time or another we've all noticed the long yellow shore supply cables snaking their way down the dock and onto a large boat. A single cable can usually supply all the power needed, but a larger cruiser with air conditioning often has two cables.

The cables are rated according to their carrying capacity and are usually obtained in 15-, 20-, 30- or 50-amp sizes. Marinco is probably the best-known supplier.

When buying a shore supply cable look for the following features (cables are generally supplied by the marinas in Britain, so you won't have to buy them there):

1. The cables should have covers and sealing collars for use in a wet environment.
2. Make sure the cable is not cut or damaged. A visual inspection will find most cuts and nicks.
3. The better cables have a threaded cap or locking blades to ensure that they cannot fall out of the shore supply socket. You will also want to have an adapter or two handy to ensure the cable plug and the socket match.
4. If possible, get a moisture-resistant system.
5. Make sure the cable will fit the power inlet on the boat.

The power inlet is another essential part of the shore supply line. It should be fully watertight when closed and easy to reach. The connectors should again be of the locking type to ensure they are not pulled out as the boat surges in the tide.

The position of the inlet is also critical. Too low and sea water washing down the boat could flood it. Too high and the cable will make a loop that could cause trips and falls. The inlet should be rated for at least the power of the cable, but as cables can be increased in power-carrying capacity simply by inserting a heavier cable, the ideal inlet will have a minimum 50-amp rating.

These, then, are the basic methods of supplying power to the yacht. They all have their strong and weak points, and when used carefully there is no reason not to have plenty of electrical power available at any time.

Having supplied the power to the onboard electrical grid, we must spread it throughout the boat to drive fans, lights, batteries, and electronic equipment. But first we have to protect the yacht electrically from surges and spikes in the shore supply and shoreside electronic or electrical interference.

When we have power aboard its voltage must be changed to charge batteries. It will need to be rectified to convert AC to DC for battery charging. Then it will have to pass through the switchboard and circuit breakers and to outlets before it can be used.

THE ISOLATION TRANSFORMER

I once heard of a new aluminum boat tied to a steel piling bulkhead. The boat was connected to the shore with an electrical cable. Unfortunately, the yacht's wiring had a ground fault somewhere in the system. Power came from the shore supply line to the boat, into the boat's electrical system, and through the fault directly to the hull. Because sea water is such a good conductor of electricity, the return path was from the hull to the steel bulkhead. This flow turned the boat into one side of a gigantic battery and the steel bulkhead into the other side with the sea water acting as the electrolyte. In a few days the hull was severely weakened and in one or two places corrosion actually started small leaks. On a fiberglass boat electrolytic corrosion can corrode the propeller, shaft, and strut and eventually attack the through-hulls. For this reason an isolation transformer is an essential on all boats, not just alloy ones.

When the shore supply is fed to the boat, it should go directly to the primary winding of an isolation transformer. The isolation transformer is often part of the battery-charging transformer. The reason for the isolation transformer is to eliminate any possibility of electrolysis. For this same reason the ground-carrying parts of the system should have a ground fault interruption breaker. This will effectively provide an electrical break between the shore supply and the boat.

The American Boat and Yacht Council has several pages in their manual of ABYC standards and recommended practices on the installation of isolation transformers, and their advice should be heeded.

BATTERY-CHARGING TRANSFORMERS

The name *Constavolt* is almost generic for marine chargers, and I have to admit we've rarely looked beyond the La Marche Constavolt. The units are almost never noticed by the owner until something goes wrong. They just sit on the bulkhead humming quietly to themselves and doing a perfect job. If only every other fitting performed in the same way!

The battery charger is sized according to the required current output, which is based upon the size and capacity of the batteries. The Constavolt units can be provided with options to allow you to charge just one battery or several banks of batteries. It is connected into the electrical system usually at a point where it can be fed by any of the power supply options.

Most chargers charge the batteries at a high initial rate, which tapers off as the battery reaches its fully charged voltage. It can also sense when the battery is being drawn down faster than usual and will increase the charge rate to compensate. When the unit is charging a bank of batteries, it senses which batteries need more power and ensures that the entire bank is charged to full capacity.

Battery chargers and isolation transformers both consist of many windings of copper wire. For this reason both are heavy. A typical isolation transformer can weigh in the region of 150–350 pounds (68–160 kilograms), while a battery charger can weigh between 30 and 140 pounds (14 and 64 kilograms). You may think that the ideal place for them is in the bilge, but any water getting into the units will render them useless, that is, if it doesn't cause a short circuit and a fire. So both units should be positioned high on the side of the yacht in the engine room where the chances of water ingress are minimized.

THE BATTERY ISOLATION SWITCH

When you leave the boat it's nice to know that the batteries are isolated from the electrical system. Or should the engine-starting battery be totally run down, you can switch over to the house batteries to start the main engine or generator. A battery isolation switch can give you this peace of mind and should be installed between the battery and the breaker panel. One of the best-known switches in this field is the Guest. Depending on which model you desire, you can isolate the batteries, or switch one or both banks on separately or together. In general the heavy duty model, designed for high amperage service, should be specified if you intend switching between engine-starting batteries. Note also that the engine-cranking amperage should be lower than the switch amperage rating.

THE BATTERY

In order to start the boat's engines, generators, or pumps, some form of "energy store" is required. On large ships this "store" is compressed air, but on a yacht it has to be a battery. On very small boats it is the operator. For instance, to start an outboard the energy store is the person who pulls the starting cord. The battery, then, is the core of the entire electrical and mechanical system on board. As many of us have experienced, a dead battery ensures that lights don't work, the engine cannot be started, and the expensive electronic instruments simply look attractive in their plastic and chrome cases.

A battery is composed of cells, and each cell contains two dissimilar metals and an electrolyte. The metals used in a battery can be almost any kind positioned far apart on the galvanic scale. Table 10.2 lists the metals on the galvanic scale. However, various other factors, such as economics, preclude picking any two metals off the scale. If we picked platinum and magnesium we'd have a battery that worked, but it would be incredibly expensive to produce in any size. Consequently the standard battery has either lead plates or nickel and cadmium plates.

The Lead Acid Battery

As the name implies, the cells of this battery are made of two different types of lead and an acidic electrolyte. The plates are usually a lead frame filled with a mixture of red lead or litharge and soft lead immersed in sulphuric acid. Charging the battery converts the positive plate into lead peroxide and the negative plate to lead, while hydrogen is given off. On the discharging cycle lead peroxide gradually gives up oxygen, which combines with the hydrogen of the electrolyte to form water, and the lead combines with the sulphur to form lead sulphate. As a boat owner you are concerned with the hydrogen given off during charging. If it is allowed to accumulate inside the boat it could cause an explosion. To eliminate the threat of explosion a sparkless fan should be specified to vent the battery box or compart-

TABLE 10.2   THE GALVANIC SCALE FOR METALS MOST OFTEN USED ON BOATS

Metal	Voltage Difference
Titanium	passive
Type 316 stainless steel	passive
Type 304 stainless steel	passive
Nickel (passive)	.15 volts
Silicon bronze (Everdur)	.19 volts
Monel	.20 volts
Copper (and copper paint)	.25 volts
Red and yellow brass	.26 volts
Manganese bronze	.28–.36 volts depending on alloys
Tin	.44 volts
Lead	.56 volts
Cast iron	.70 volts
Wrought iron	.70 volts
Mild steel	.71 volts
Aluminum	.72 volts
Galvanized iron	1.00 volts
Zinc	1.10 volts

Current flows from zinc to gold, and corrosion will occur at the zinc end of the scale if the two metals are connected together electrically and immersed in sea water.

Where there is a difference in voltage of more than .2 volts, corrosion is likely to occur.

ment when batteries are being charged. Before the days of "maintenance-free" batteries, an owner always had to add water to the battery as the hydrogen boiled off, lowering the level of electrolyte. Modern batteries are totally sealed and need no maintenance other than ensuring the terminals are kept clean and erosion free. They don't spill acid and are smaller, making them ideal for use on boats.

The Alkaline Cell

Alkaline cells use nickel hydroxide and cadmium as their positive and negative plates and use an alkaline solution of potassium hydroxide in distilled water as the electrolyte. They have certain advantages over lead acid batteries:

1. They are more robust.
2. They have a longer life.
3. They will stay inactive longer without discharging.
4. Overcharging will not damage the plates and ruin the battery.

Their disadvantages are:

1. Lower voltage per cell.
2. Greater initial cost.
3. Higher internal resistence between plates.

When an alkaline cell is discharging, the negative plate material (cadmium) is oxidized while the positive plate material becomes an oxide.

In general, lead acid batteries are used aboard all boats except for some of the smaller craft, which may have an alkaline cell or two aboard.

Sizing the Battery

How does a builder know how large a battery should be installed on board? Especially when electrical and electronic equipment is multiplying at such a great rate. The only way to determine battery capacity correctly is to perform an electrical load analysis. Table 10.3 shows a typical calculation. Each item of electrical equipment is listed, together with the number of them on board and the amperage or horsepower. The next column shows the hours per day the item is likely to be in use under normal conditions. Multiplying the hours per day and the wattage yields the total watt-hours. Adding up the list gives the total watt-hours the system is in use per day, in this case, 2293.2 watt-hours. Now, if we divide this number by the voltage, in this case 12 volts, we get the ampere hours the system uses in one day. Thus 2293.2/12 = 191.1 ampere hours per day. Now we know that the battery will be drained of almost 200 ampere-hours (AH) per day. The ship's battery, then, must be at least that size to run all the equipment.

TABLE 10.3   12 VOLT SYSTEM FOR A 49' KETCH

Item	Number	Watts Per Unit		Connected Watts	Batteries Hours in Use Per Day	Watt Hours
Dome Lights	8	.58A		55.68	3×6 Hrs=	125.28
					1×1 Hr.=	6.96
Bunk Lights	6	20W		120.00	120×.75Hrs=	90.00
Step Light	4	.24A		11.52	11.52×8Hrs=	92.16
Chart						
Table Light	1	6W		6.0	6×5 Hrs=	30.00
Locker Lights	5	.9A		54.0	54×0.5 Hr=	27.00
Floor ER Lights	2	0.7A		16.8	16.8×1 Hr=	16.8
Anchor Windlass	1	10.5A to 80A	.5	900W max	—	—
Auto Pilot	1	2A Cruise				
		3A Rough		96W max	30W×12 Hrs=	360.00
		8A Peak				
Foghorn compressor	1	5.2W	.2	5.2	5.2×.25 Hrs=	1.3
ER Blower Fans	2	60W		120	120×.25 Hrs=	30.00
Freezer Compressor	1	20A		240W	—	—
F.W. Pressure System	1	0.6A		7.2W	7.2×4.5 Hrs=	32.4
Radar-Decca 090	1	120W		120W	120×1 Hrs=	120
Nav Lights Bow	1	25W		50W	50×9 Hrs=	450
Stern	1	25W				
Masthead Light	1	25W		25W	25×9 Hrs=	225
SSB	1	Tx 6A		72W	12×10 Hrs=	120
Radio Tel		RX 1A			72×1 Hr.=	7.2
VHF	1	TX 7A		84W	6×10 Hrs=	60
		RX 0.5A			84×.1 Hr.=	8.4
Loran C	1	25W		25W	25×14 Hrs=	350.00
Wind Instruments	4	.35A		4.2W	4.2×24 Hrs.=	100.8
Bilge Pump	1	.75A	.25	9W	9×1 Hr.=	.9
Electrasan (W.E.unit)	2	.2A		4.8W	4.8×6 Hrs=	28.8
Sump Tank Pump	1	—	.25	180W	180×.05 Hrs=	9.0
Signal Lamp	1	60W		60W	60×.02 Hrs.=	1.2
TOTAL:				2266.4		2293.2

There are 2266.4 watts connected to this system, however, most of the time equipment will be turned off. To make the calculation, we figure out the hours per day the equipment will be in use and multiply that by the wattage. This gives us a total of watt-hours per day the batteries need to supply. Dividing watt-hours by the voltage gives us the battery ampere hours required. In this case it is 2293.2 ÷ 12 = 191 ampere hours. Therefore, a 200 AH battery will do the job if we intend to charge the battery every day. If we intend to charge it once every three days we would have to increase the battery size by 3 × 200 = 600 AH.

*Set breaker at 80 amps. Run when engine is running
**Run when engine on, but run before starting engine
Run engine when cooling freezer.

This assumes no reserve and that the battery will be charged every day. If we want reserves, we should add in another 50 percent and for every day the battery is to operate without recharging we should add 100 percent of its capacity. So if we didn't intend to recharge the batteries for a week we would have to provide 7×200 AH = 1400 AH. A large bank of batteries for any boat!

Engine-Starting Batteries

The system we just described was intended to run only the yacht's equipment. To start the engine we need to add an additional battery. This process is slightly easier in that a telephone call to the engine manufacturer will usually get the desired information. Table 10.4 lists engine manufacturers' recommended sizes. From this list we can see that for the Perkins 4-230 engine a battery of between 170 and 200 AH is required for best performance.

The generator battery size should be specified in the same manner, although most moderately sized gensets use a battery of about 100 AH. All three battery banks can be charged off the same source of supply, which should be set up to keep them all fully charged no matter whether shore supply, generator, or engine-powered alternator is being used.

TABLE 10.4 STARTING BATTERY SIZES FOR VARIOUS ENGINES		
Engine	Starting Battery Size (Ampere Hours)	Horsepower
Westerbeke 21	90–125	21
Westerbeke 44	125–140	44
Westerbeke 52	150–170	52
Farymann 24	88	24
Farymann 32	100	32
Volvo 2001, 2002, 2003	80 min.	9, 18, 28
Volvo MD 17D	110	36
Volvo MD 22	110	57
Perkins 4-108	125	42
Perkins 4-230	200	56

THE MAIN BREAKER PANEL

The electrical power has to be split up and fed around the boat. This is the job of the breaker board or panel (distribution panel in Britain). But it also does much more than hold the electrical circuit breakers. It may have voltmeters, ammeters, charging meters, and shore supply monitors. It can also have both 110-volt and 12-volt breakers, and 12-, 24-, 32-, or 48-volt breakers, a switch to lock off shore supply when the yacht is running on its own power, ground fault lights, and the generator controls, including stop and start buttons. A good electrical panel will have each circuit listed and an indication of whether the breaker is made or not. The largest panels can be several feet long and include a wiring diagram for every circuit; the smallest fit in a locker near the nav table.

Here on the east coast of the United States the most commonly used breaker panels are manufactured by Bass Products. These panels may be custom designed by a company like Bass or designed specifically for the boat by the yard's own shop. The AC-DC meters and all breakers should be clearly labeled, as should the ship-shore selector switch and LED circuit indicator lights on any panel, whether it is installed by the yard or by an electrician.

Where there are subcircuits a secondary panel could be inserted into the system. These secondary panels can be wired for any function. For instance, an owner may want a separate panel for the electronic equipment in the navigation area. In this case the panel may have 8 or 10 breakers on it, each labeled for an item of electronic equipment. While this is more common in a larger system, there is no reason why it could not be installed in a smaller boat.

Another panel could be installed in the cockpit to enable the helmsman to turn on lights without leaving the wheel. In this case the panel would have to be waterproof. Bass makes a panel for exactly this purpose.

The breakers for electrical panels should all be marine-rated and be large enough for the equipment on the circuit. In general, all breakers should be double-pole (stopping the circuit from being back-fed when the breaker is off) and fully floating (that is, the circuit wired with a positive line and a negative line and a separate ground or earth going to all the ground terminals on the instrument casings).

WIRING

The electrical wiring must be of a large enough diameter to run the electrical equipment attached to that wiring. If the wiring is too small it might overheat if a high current is passed along it, or the voltage might drop to levels where it cannot power the equipment. If there is a single common fault with marine electrical systems it is the use of wiring that is one or two sizes too small for the amperage and distance. The diameter of the wiring is directly proportional to the voltage drop along that wire, so that if too small a diameter wire is used an excessive voltage drop could be recorded. This would mean that a fan which is supposed to run at 12 volts may only have 10 volts reaching it if too small a diameter wire is used. In consequence the fan would run slowly or not at all.

The ABYC and Lloyd's recommend that every electrical conductor have some method of identifying its purpose. The ideal method of doing that is to color-code the wires. For instance, all ground wires should be green. The ABYC recommends that the following colors be required for direct current electrical systems:

Color	Use
Green	Bonding
White or black	Return, negative main
Red	Positive mains, particularly unfused systems

They also recommend a marine wiring color code for DC systems under 50 volts. Lloyd's has similar requirements for color-coding conductors. The ABYC also gives current ratings for various sizes of conductors for AC and DC systems. For more information I recommend joining ABYC, whose address is in the back of this book.

INTERIOR LIGHTING

There is such a large variety of interior lights that it is difficult to specify particular lights or positions for those lights. However, there are certain principles we can use to give us the best interior lighting. For instance, we know that each bunk needs a light. It should be a relatively high-powered light to enable the occupant to read at night, but not too highly powered that it causes a massive battery drain if it is inadvertently left on overnight.

For this use I would recommend a swivel light that can be adjusted by the person in the bunk. Bass makes several suitable types. A normal light would be the regular Endura light, but if you wanted high-intensity light you could select Super Endura lights, which use a reflector bulb to give you up to four times the brightness with only half the power drain.

Overhead lights should be provided in passageways. This can either be a fluorescent Trimlite or a simple dome light. The fluorescent gives a harsher light but draws less power than the incandescent dome light. Usually fluorescent lights are kept for use in areas that require a lot of light without regard for aesthetics, say, in a sail bin, or in a large locker where plenty of shadowless light is needed. But you should be aware that fluorescent lights can cause interference with radios and other electronic equipment. For this reason they should not be used in or close to the navigation area.

Steps should be illuminated so that no one slips down them. The best way of doing that is to use a steplight built into the step. If this uses a red bulb then it could be left on during a watch change and not affect the ongoing watch's night vision.

Night vision is the reason why many yachts are fitted with a special dome light. This light has two bulbs, one red the other white. It is a simple job to use the toggle switch to operate either the red or white light.

The other place where particular attention should be paid to lighting is in any work areas and in the navigation area. If we want to work in the kitchen we need plenty of light. Overhead lights give some, but a small fluorescent behind a valence either under or in front of the cabinets will give light right where it is needed, on the countertops. If you have a favorite space to work when you are on a trip, then you may need special light to illuminate it. A case that comes to mind is operating a navigation computer. A light directly behind the computer will reflect off the screen, whereas a light directly in front of the machine will be in the operator's eyes. So the positioning of lighting for this compartment should be figured out carefully.

A similar problem is encountered in the rest of the navigation area. Charts should be illuminated without disturbing the other crew, who may be asleep nearby, and without making it hard to read the instruments. In this case a Flex-lite could be the answer.

The choice of lights, then, is a matter of relatively major importance to the sailor who intends to live on his boat for some length of time.

A poorly situated light can turn a comfortable daytime layout into an area impossible to use at night. Only by thinking carefully about how the compartment is going to be used when it is illuminated will the lighting be suitable.

LAYING OUT THE ELECTRICAL SYSTEM

The designer has given you a blueprint of the interior of your boat and asked you to lay out where you want the lights. At first it seems like a daunting task. But if you carefully go through the drawing you will find the areas that need light. The first places for lighting are the steps—the companionway steps and all areas where the sole level changes. These will have red step lights fitted.

We'll want to illuminate general areas with overhead dome lights. These can be marked in on the drawing.

Next we'll need bunk lights. We'll put one in the corner of each bunk. They should be fitted where the occupant climbing in and out of the bunk won't hit them. They should also be high enough so that a person rolling over in his sleep will not hit them. Usually this means each bunk light is high on the inside corner of the bunk.

Now we have the general areas covered and we can get down to lighting specific compartments or areas. In the navigation station should have a Flex-lite and a red/white overhead dome light. There should also be a small light inside the navigation table. With these lights the navigator will have plenty of light, and a crewman writing up the log will have adequate red lights.

With specific lights positioned in each compartment or area we end up with a drawing that looks like Figure 10.3. Now we know exactly how many lights we'll need and where they should be. From here we can start laying out a wiring diragram. We'll first have to decide which lights we want to put on each circuit. In general, wiring is laid out to minimize cable; we don't wander back and forth across the boat laying cable.

THE WIRING DIAGRAM

At this stage the wiring diagram is a simple schematic. It shows each light and its type. Now we can add in the other machinery. Some authorities recommend that lighting and power circuits not be mixed; others don't seem to worry about it. I prefer to keep them separate. Battery sizes can be accurately determined by recalculating their loads. The design of the boat is now becoming more accurate as the equipment and loads are accurately determined.

At this point the wiring diagram is starting to become fairly com-

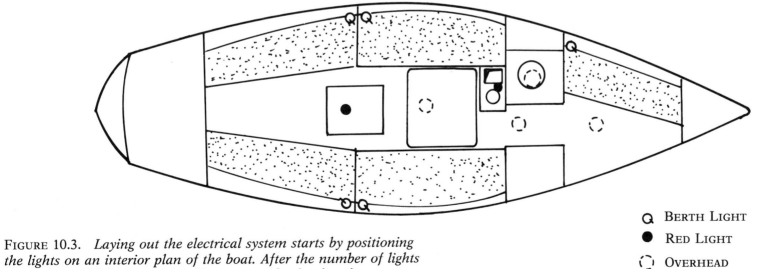

FIGURE 10.3. *Laying out the electrical system starts by positioning the lights on an interior plan of the boat. After the number of lights has been established, a wiring diagram can be developed.*

ℚ BERTH LIGHT
● RED LIGHT
◌ OVERHEAD

plex, and the designer should check manufacturers' brochures and data to ensure that any special electrical requirements are being met. Gradually, a complete wiring diagram will be made and checked. At this point it should be referred to the owner to ensure that all intended equipment is included.

Having produced a wiring diagram, some designers develop a harness drawing to show the electrician how the harness is to be made. However, most designers leave the details of the harness to the man on the job, who usually has enough experience to figure out the best wiring path for the boat. On production boats, where the harness is installed in the overhead before the deck is put on, a harness drawing would be needed. Many production boats install the harness in a conduit to make it easier to rewire or work. In this case the conduit is simply a plastic tube of a suitable diameter, or width if square conduit is used, through which the wiring is run. This is especially useful when the wiring run is long and straight. Corners, bends, and joints are negotiated by installing premade units that fit directly onto the conduit. These enable the electrician to pull wiring through the conduit without ripping it apart. When the wiring is installed the unit is covered or capped to ensure it stays clean and as moisture proof as possible.

The engine room wiring is often much more complex than the rest of the boat and will take into account the engine room layout as well as the particular circuitry of each piece of equipment. For instance, a water heater may require a 12-volt and 110-volt supply. This will need to be included on the wiring diagram before it goes to the builder. Often it will mean that the designer will have to get wiring diagrams for all the equipment in the engine room before the diagram can be finished.

On the wiring diagram, each piece of equipment should be clearly marked. Its fuses or breakers should be shown, and the wire size should also be clearly detailed. A finished wiring diagram is usually quite a work of art and enables a competent electrician to trace any wire or piece of equipment on board.

GALVANIC OR ELECTROLYTIC CORROSION

There are one or two problem areas with electrical wiring. The first is where metals far apart on the galvanic scale are used in the hull, and the second is when electrical leakage occurs. As we mentioned earlier, if we select two metals far apart on the galvanic scale and place them in contact with sea water we can create a battery *if the metals have a path by which the electrodes can move around the circuit.*

The ship's wiring can inadvertently aid this process. It can provide the instrument that connects the two pieces of metal, turning it into a battery. For this reason we have to be very careful to ensure all parts of the wiring system are "fully floating."

In galvanic corrosion the different metals cause electrical current, which causes the corrosion. All that need be done to ensure there is no electrolytic corrosion in a boat is to make sure the current flows around the circuit without any leaks. Leaks can be caused by chafed wiring, knicks and cuts in wires, a poorly insulated conductor, improperly installed electrical or electronic accessories, and a number of other items. By keeping your wiring in good order electrolytic corrosion can easily be prevented.

CATHODIC PROTECTION

Boat builders and owners can virtually eliminate galvanic corrosion by bonding together dissimilar metals that protrude outside the hull. Items such as the propeller, rudder stock, metal through-hull fittings, and the strut should be bonded together using a heavy duty conductor such as a number 8 gauge wire or heavier or by a 1-by-1/8-inch copper flat bar. The wire or bar should also be connected to a sacrificial anode—usually made of zinc. The current that flows around the circuit corrodes the zinc without harming the other metal parts of the boat. Sacrificial anodes should be replaced every year for maximum protection. Note that the zinc works best when it is exposed to sea water. It should not be painted with antifouling.

LIGHTNING PROTECTION

What do you do if you are out on your boat in a thunderstorm? I've heard many suggestions, from taking the mast down to trailing wires over the side. I was once on a boat where the owner decided to trail wires over the side. He fastened two crocodile clips to the shrouds. Connected to the crocodile clips were two pieces of ordinary house wiring, which were trailed in the water beside the boat. As the house wiring is rated for about 250 volts and a lightning strike is likely to produce thousands of volts his precautions were totally inadequate.

Lightning protection is simply a method of providing an outlet for the voltage generated by a lightning strike on the mast or rigging. In its simplest form it is a small aerial at the top of the mast connected to a copper cable running down the mast and into the water.

However, it is not the cable that causes the problems, it's the connections. When many thousands of volts try to get across a poorly made connection they generate heat. That heat is often enough to blow apart a soldered joint. So all joints should be strongly bolted. If you have a metal mast, then it should be bonded to a keel bolt to give the current a direct path into the water. Note also that any cable used to conduct lightning away from the boat should be as straight as possible, with no kinks or sharp turns.

Lightning connectors should take the shortest path to the water. For instance, taking a thick cable down the mast and to the keel bolt is probably inadequate. The ideal system has a copper plate recessed into the bottom of the hull. The cable is connected directly to that plate. The whole thing should be installed in such a way that should lightning strike and the plate be destroyed the boat would still be watertight and would not be in danger of sinking. Therein lies the problem: it is very difficult to come up with an adequate method to protect the boat sufficiently.

For that reason, most owners simply carry some heavy wires with crocodile clips on one end and large copper plates on the other. If a thunderstorm is around the wires are clipped to the shrouds and the plates lowered into the water. This does provide some measure of safety, but it is not foolproof.

GROUNDING SYSTEMS

With a fully floating system the electrical current should flow around the circuit and back to its starting point without touching a ground or earth line. However, should a fault occur in an instrument and the case or chassis of that instrument become charged electrically, the only path to ground could be through the person touching that case or chassis. For this reason it is essential that all cases, chassis, switches, panels, sacrificial anodes, and lights have a separate ground line. Then, if a short occurs, the ground line will complete the circuit without electrocuting the operator. Most ground lines are connected to all metallic objects throughout the boat and bonded to a keel bolt or to the engine mount so that a short circuit will be harmless. Note, however, that a short circuit can cause electrolytic corrosion. So it pays to check the grounding circuit occasionally.

The yacht's electrical circuitry is not that complex, but a few rules need to be followed when designing and wiring the boat. For that reason it is best that a complete wiring diagram be developed and that all cables be large enough to carry the needed current and voltage. Care should also be taken to allow for future expansion, which will almost certainly be required.

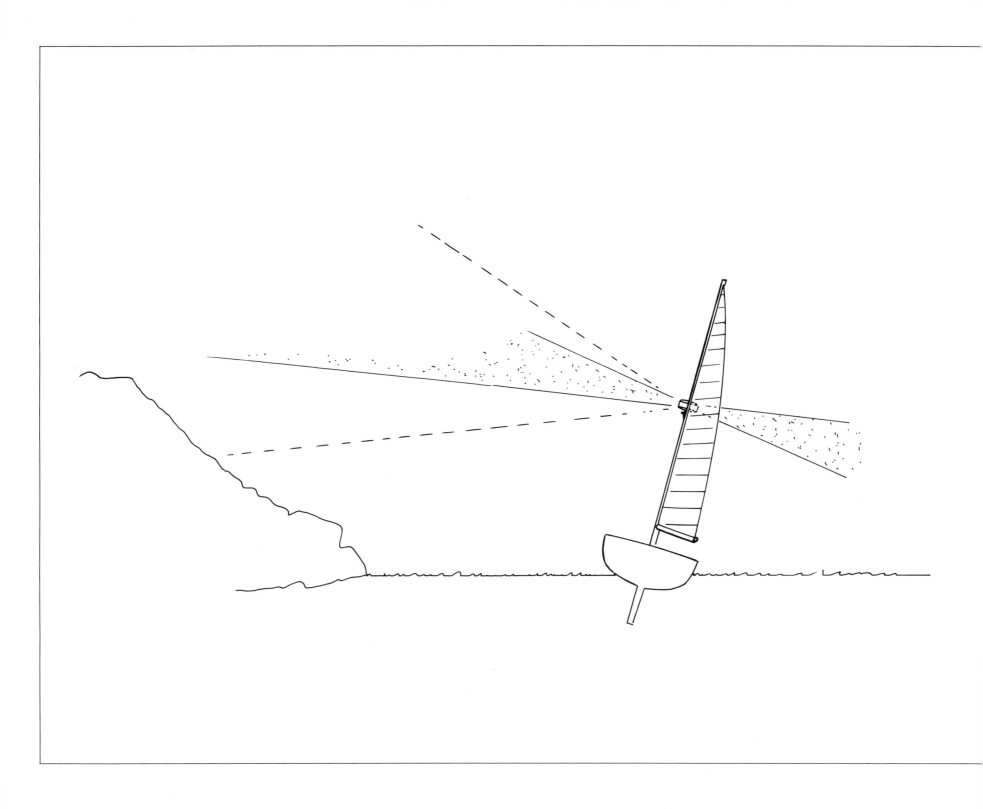

CHAPTER *11*

Electronics

It's December 15th and your wife has just told you she has bought the wind instruments you've always wanted for Christmas. You are excited but wonder, has she bought the right ones? Can you take them back if they are not what you need? Who will install them? There are so many different types of electronic instruments available today that even experts find it confusing to decide which they want and which are just gimmicks.

Once again the right choice comes down to the type of sailing you do and what your budget can stand. If you are cruising around in a sheltered lake or bay you won't require radar. However, you'll probably need something to measure depth. But do you want to measure the depth in front of the boat? Under it? To the side of the boat? If you are a fisherman you might choose the latest side-scan sonar system. A yachtsman might want a reasonably simple system that tells him the depth under the boat. However, this usually tells you when you are aground after the boat is on the mud. A system that looks in front of the boat may be the best. But if it is installed incorrectly it too might be useless, or even worse it might give you a false sense of confidence.

Selecting the right electronics, installing them correctly, and using them properly are the topics of this chapter. While I recommend gear that I've used and trust, you may find a less expensive or better item that will do the job.

MEASURING THE DEPTH

Do you know how deep the water is under your boat? Chances are you have a depth sounder on board and a glance at it will tell exactly how much water you are sailing in. But is the depth sounder calibrated to the depth of water under the keel or the depth of water under the unit? If it's the latter you could find yourself aground because the keel span has not been accounted for.

An echo sounder works by sending a pulse of high frequency sound down to the seabed. That sound wave is reflected off the ocean floor and back up to the unit. By measuring the elapsed time for the pulse to make the round trip the depth is measured. The depth readout can be digital, flashing, or written onto graph paper. The better units enable you to ascertain what type of bottom you are sailing over, and some can also tell you if you are sailing over a school of fish. However, these are not generally found on a sailing yacht.

The type of unit found on a sailboat is likely to be a digital unit that sounds an alarm when the depth of water is below a preset minimum. The digital readout is precise and easy to read and can be very reassuring.

Many smaller yachts have a flasher type of unit. This can be hard to read in daylight, and unless you are experienced in its use it can give a reading that needs some interpretation. But when you are experienced, it can tell you more than the digital readout. For instance, it may show a solid band when you are sailing over a hard, level bottom. But if the bottom changes to soft mud or becomes uneven then the display can become irregular, giving you a wide band of readings. Without experience at interpreting what is below the boat you should proceed with some caution in shallower areas.

To make the display easy to read in daylight it should be positioned where the helmsman and the navigator can both see it and, if possible, where the dial or readout is in shadow. Often these points are incompatible. Some sailors like to put the readout on a panel in the hatch-way, where it can be swung away when not in use. Other like to have it on the aft face of the bulkhead. If this is the position you choose, make sure it is high enough to be seen if somebody decides to sit in the cockpit.

The latest depth sounders have voice synthesizers, which talk to you as you are sailing into shallower water. With these units you don't have to be constantly looking at the screen; you simply listen. I expect we'll see more and more talking depth sounders on the market in the next few years.

When the unit is installed the transducer should, ideally, be on centerline just forward of the keel, but not so close that the keel will interfere with the signals. However, in a heavy sea you might find that the boat is bouncing around so much that air is getting washed around the transducer and a false reading is obtained. For this reason some people prefer to position two units either side of the keel and use a mercury switch to automatically switch between transducers. This position also allows the transducers to be sloped slightly outward to improve the return when the boat is heeled.

One of the problems with an echosounder on a sailing boat is getting a consistent reading when the boat is heeled. The width of the pulse varies with the manufacturer and might be 15–30 degrees either side of vertical. On the narrower widths it is sometimes so narrow that its return is missed by the transducer head. On a digital unit the unit usually averages the signal and ignores the missed return, but a flashing unit can give a false reading somewhere on the dial. If this happens more than once the person watching the flasher could be deceived into thinking the water depth had changed.

BOAT SPEED INDICATOR AND LOG

The next instrument you will want is the boat speed indicator and log. Boat speed is of primary importance for keeping a good log. It not only tells you the speed of the boat in any given situation but enables the crew to get a reasonably accurate feel for how fast they think they have been sailing over the last hour or two. When the crew record the average speed in the log it allows the navigator to complete a DR plot.

To obtain a boat speed reading you need a sensor below the hull. It should be positioned in a region of clean water flow where air entrapment will not interfere with the sensor. This usually means the paddle wheel will be situated at some distance out from the centerline, just forward of the keel. Some systems use a paddle wheel; others use a hairlike needle. The B&G sonic speed system is unique in that it uses two sensors that beam a sound signal from one to the other. It measures the doppler shift of the sound signal as the boat travels through the water.

The log is usually part of the boat speed package and records the distance traveled by the boat over a certain time. Some logs record the total distance traveled by the boat and the distance traveled since the log was reset. Others simply record the distance traveled.

WIND INSTRUMENTS

After the depth sounder and boat speed indicators, the next electronic item you are likely to purchase will be wind instruments. But whose should you buy? Where should they go? Where should the display be positioned? And what are the options?

For the truly serious sailor who wants the very best there are only two choices: Ockam or Brookes and Gatehouse. Both systems can be purchased in modules and expanded as finances allow. Both systems have a remarkable array of features. Less expensive and less expansive units are made by IMI, Rochester, VDO, Datamarine, and many others. While most of these names are well known and produce a good product, you should evaluate any system carefully and talk to previous users before plunking down your cash.

Both the B&G and Ockam units have a central processor (CPU) to which many inputs can be attached. (Don't make the mistake of calling the wind instrument CPU a computer. It isn't. A computer has a CPU inside it as well.) For instance, the three most useful functions are boat speed, wind speed and wind angle. To find these functions you need the CPU, a masthead indicator, and a boat speed sensor. If you are happy with just these functions, then many instrument manufacturers make a unit that gives you these functions in one package. Rochester, IMI, and Seafarer all make systems of this size. Let's look at the basic units and then at all the extras that can be obtained, together with the other electronic gear that is needed to interface with the CPU.

Wind angle tells you where the wind is coming from relative to the boat. Normally the apparent wind angle is displayed in degrees from the centerline of the boat at the bow. But both the Ockam system and B&G have programming in the CPU that enables them to calculate the magnetic wind direction. Note that no tidal correction is applied to this calculated wind direction. However, Ockam does have software that will make an allowance for it. (If we wanted to get highly specific, we would say that apparent wind speed, apparent wind angle, and boat speed can be read from the instruments. From these inputs the CPU can calculate boat relative to true wind speed and true wind angle, and then the software can subtract a correction to get earth relative wind speed and direction.) This earth relative wind speed is the wind direction you would see if you were standing on the shore and appears as the number of degrees from magnetic north. Magnetic, sometimes called true, wind direction is useful for telling the navigator where the wind is likely to be coming from after a tack. For this reason it is more useful to the racing sailor. ("Magnetic wind direction" is used here because the commonly used term *true wind* is not strictly correct. If the wind were to be taken from true north, deviation would have to be added [or subtracted] from the magnetic north reading. Note also that the direction of the wind relative to the boat is known as wind angle, while the wind direction refers to geographical wind direction.)

Wind speed is an important function. If you are carrying a sail that is only supposed to be set in winds lower than 10 knots, then the wind speed indicator will tell you more accurately than simply sniffing the breeze. Wind speed can be displayed as apparent or true wind speed. Instrument-calculated true wind speed is a function of boat speed,

FIGURE 11.1 *The wind triangle with Va* representing apparent wind, *Vt* true wind, *Vs* boat speed, and *β* leeway angle.

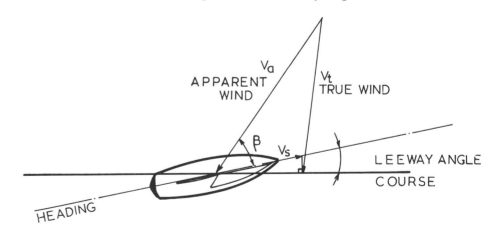

apparent wind speed, leeway, apparent wind angle, heel angle, and upwash (the distortion in airflow when air is washed upward over the sails when the boat is heeled) calculated by the CPU. True wind speed is a function of boat speed, wind speed, leeway, and wind direction and is calculated by the CPU. It can be thought of as the wind speed you would feel if you were standing perfectly still. Apparent wind speed is the direction the wind is coming from when you are standing on the boat and it is moving through the water. Figure 11.1 shows the wind speed triangle.

These functions combined with depth are all the cruiser really needs. In fact B&G has combined all these features into a system called the Hydra 330, a package that has all the monitors and displays built in and ready to go.

The few functions mentioned above are all that is needed to go sailing almost anywhere, provided you are a good navigator and don't like to rely on electronics to do most of the work for you. If you are like me and love to use all the extra gizmos and gadgets, there is a large range of extra features that will save you work and effort.

Other functions can be added to the basic system:

1. *Heading:* That is, the actual heading being sailed by the yacht. This is used when calculating leeway. (This requires the compass unit.)
2. *Leeway:* How much the boat is sliding sideways as it is being sailed to windward. Both heading and leeway are most useful when you are trying to get the best performance out of the boat and in the calculation of true wind angle and speed.
3. *Heel angle:* Most of us use a simple inclinometer, but this function calculates it electronically.
4. *Time:* The elapsed time function is useful for setting the log, recording log entries and watch changes, etc.
5. *Rudder and (if fitted) trim tab angles:* With hydraulic steering this is an essential. It is not so important with wire or pull-pull steering systems.
6. *VMG:* Best speed to windward. This is a racing function, but it can also be used to settle the "who's the best helmsman" argument.

The functions outlined above can be made without adding extra equipment to the system. But if you add a Loran, Decca, or Satnav and interface it with the instrument CPU, then many more options are available:

1. *Current set and drift:* This function tells you what the tide is doing to you.
2. *Waypoint range and bearing:* How far it is to the waypoint and what the bearing is. For instance, suppose you were sailing to Bermuda and put in the waypoint for North Breaker buoy. The range and bearing indicator would show you how far you are away from it and its bearing at any time during the trip.
3. *Back range and bearing:* A function similar to waypoint range and bearing except that it tells you where you are in relation to the place you just left.

With all these functions, who needs more? But there are many more. Most are oriented toward racing and are of little use for the average cruising sailor.

NAVIGATION SYSTEMS

It used to be that you found your way across the ocean by sailing south until you reached the desired latitude and then made your way east or west until you hit land. Today navigations systems are much more sophisticated.

For some the idea of navigating consists of looking for a yacht that has a Loran or Decca antenna, powering over, and asking them where your destination is. Fortunately these people don't go very far offshore. Offshore cruisers, on the other hand, have to know where they are. This means they have to be able to use the plethora of instrumentation available and when out of sight of any electronic system they should be able to use a sextant. In the following pages we'll briefly review what is available, its range, and its accuracy.

Loran

The word comes from *LO*ng *RA*nge *N*avigation system. It was originally set up as Loran A during World War II and in the early 1970s was changed to Loran C. It is a pulsed wave in the 100 khz range that gives reasonably accurate fixes over a fairly long distance: 1,000–1,200 nautical miles is a reasonable range for the ground wave, and at night the sky wave can double the distance, but accuracy will vary with the distance from the transmitting stations.

The system operates in a chain of a master and up to five slave stations that send timed pulsed waves. The receiver measures the difference in signal travel time from itself to the master and a slave station. This gives it a line of position (LOP). LOPs are digitally displayed on the face of the receiver.

Loran does have some drawbacks, however. Loran is only now being installed around the world. A new system is being installed around the coast of China. Chains are in place in many parts of the Northern Hemisphere, and the system is continually being updated and improved.

The system is accurate to within 200 feet (approximately 60 meters), but there are some areas that give variability in position. Apparently, if the signal passes over land and water several times it can be deflected slightly. In the Bahamas and much of the Caribbean, for instance, Loran is notoriously poor. Manmade interference and atmospheric noise can also reduce the signal's accuracy.

Repeatability is very good, however. Once you have passed a buoy and have recorded the LOPs, then Loran can bring you back almost exactly to that point.

To use the Loran readout requires a special chart that has LOPs overlayed on it. However, most modern receivers have a latitude and longitude readout, which makes it easy to plot lat and long on a conventional chart.

Installing Loran is easy, but certain rules should be observed when positioning the Loran antenna. In general, the entire length of the antenna should be clear of any metal obstructions, which could alter the pattern or shield the signal. Another item that must be observed carefully is the method of grounding the set. Improper grounding can result in the ground lead becoming part of the antenna, which will distort the signal.

Most experts, when they install the set, mount it in its specified position and get it completely hooked up. Then they move the antenna around until the reception is the best it can be. Other antennae or receivers can complicate reception, so great care should be taken to get the antenna positioned correctly.

Decca

Decca is used principally in European waters, although there are stations in Australia, the east coast of America, India, South Africa, and Japan. Like Loran it is a hyperbolic navigation system and is very accurate, usually to within 100 yards (91 meters). It is said to be more accurate than Loran and that no special chart is needed. This has changed since the early days, when special Decca charts were required with the hyperbolic curves overprinted on them. However, while Loran can have accuracy problems at long range, Decca has a much shorter range (about 250 miles under good conditions).

Omega

Omega provides several advantages that Decca and Loran cannot, but its accuracy is poorer, therefore it should be used in conjunction with Decca or Loran. It is another hyperbolic system but uses very low frequency (VLF) signals, which give it a range in excess of 5,000 miles. Because Omega has such a long range, very few transmitting stations are required, making the system available virtually worldwide. It can be used under all weather conditions and has the same accuracy under day- or nighttime conditions.

Satnav

Since the United States put satellites into space, the potential for a highly accurate satellite navigation system has existed. The system as it now stands uses a number of satellites in orbit above the earth. As the satellite passes over a ground station its exact orbital position is computed by means of measuring the doppler-shift between the signals. These position figures are then sent back to the satellite for transmission to ships on the surface of the earth. A yacht passing within line of sight of the satellite receives the signal and processes it. The result is the yacht's position displayed as latitude, longitude, and Greenwich Mean Time. Because the system uses satellites that revolve around the earth, it is available worldwide.

But as the satellites can only be used when they are visible to the receiver it would take several of them to keep a steady fix going. Unfortunately, there are only a few satellites, and time between signals may vary considerably. This is unfortunate, but when the system is used in conjunction with Loran, position accuracy can be increased dramatically.

Global Positioning System (GPS)

A system already planned and ready to be deployed and which will replace all current navigation systems is GPS. It has several advantages over Loran and most of the other systems in use today. The plans call for a number of satellites orbiting every 12 hours. There would be 21 satellites, with 18 of them giving continuous worldwide coverage.

Accuracy is reputed to be within a few feet if the government will allow the technology to be used. But the government wants civilian users to have a slightly less accurate system, which will give positioning to within 600 feet (about 180 meters). However, it probably won't be available to the recreational sailor for many more years.

Omni

The Federal Aviation Administration (FAA) has a line of stations that continuously broadcast a signal that is unaffected by atmospheric conditions. Each Omni station has a distinct frequency, and the receiver locks into the range line. The Omni receiver simply indicates any deviation from the range line.

It is mostly used for aviation and rarely seen on yachts. It is available worldwide, but for a boat its range is usually limited to 50–60 miles.

Radio Direction Finding

RDF is probably the oldest electronic method of finding your way around the ocean. The shore station broadcasts a signal, usually in the form of a letter of Morse code, on various frequencies. The RDF unit on the boat receives that signal, and by turning the antenna the operator can zero in on the station. This will give a line to that transmitter. If this exercise is done for two other stations, then a triangle will usually be obtained, inside which is the boat's position.

The RDF range is usually about 50–80 miles (80–128 kilometers). However, bearing errors can creep in if certain features are not corrected when the unit is installed:

1. Wire lifelines that completely circle the boat can cause errors of 2 or 3 degrees. The lifelines should have insulated connectors or be tied with line to eliminate that problem. You should try to avoid all continuous loops of metal anywhere on the boat.
2. Fluorescent lights and some other electrical items can distort the bearing.
3. Metal boats block the signal from the receiver. The direction finder aerial should be at least 30 inches (.75 meters) above the highest point of the boat.
4. When taking bearings, keep the aerial away from large pieces of metal—winches, mast, steering gear, etc.

COMMUNICATIONS DEVICES

You have just sighted land after a seven-day trip and want to alert your wife or girlfriend to meet you at the dock. How do you get in touch? The days of signal flags are long gone. But you have a SSB and VHF radio on board. So you simply pick up the handset on the SSB and phone the marine operator. Usually they will put you through to your wife in a few minutes. Such are the wonders of modern communication.

Single Sideband Radio

Otherwise known as HF-SSB or high frequency single sideband, this transmission operates in the 1.6–18 MHz range. It can be used worldwide when the conditions are right. Unlike VHF radio, which is line-of-sight, SSB can use ground waves and is reflected off the ionosphere during optimum conditions, usually during daylight hours, when sunlight is strongest. However, because the SSB transmission is reflected off the sky wave and VHF transmissions are line-of-sight, there is often a gap between the two. This gap can vary between 50 and 150 miles (85–250 kilometers).

A typical SSB has a number of channels, usually 24–30, which operate in simplex or duplex mode. That is, in the simplex mode, transmission and reception are on the same frequency. In the duplex mode transmission is on one frequency and reception on another.

The antenna for a SSB unit can be very hard to install correctly. Most installers will use a dipole vertical antenna, which may be as long as 15 feet.

For emergencies the 2182 frequency is used. Many units have a switch or button that will automatically tune into 2182. Transmission modes can be voice, Morse code, fax, or telex.

Very High Frequency Radio

A VHF radio is used for line-of-sight communication, generally about 50–75 miles (80–120 kilometers). VHF sets can be obtained with as many as 55 channels, not all of which are usable by a yachtsman. Most units come ready to install and require only a small antenna. They are most favored by boats that will stay reasonably close to shore.

In an emergency, channel 16 is monitored by the Coast Guard.

However, it should be reserved for this use; too often somebody holds a conversation on channel 16 rather than switching to another channel.

RADAR

Almost all of us have seen warships heading out to sea with their radar antenna rotating. Some ships have huge dishes, which can see over the horizon; others have smaller units, which revolve in quick speedy circles. For yachtsmen the choice is much simpler. The range of most radars for yachts is usually between 20 and 50 miles (32–80 kilometers). The practical limit is even lower and depends upon the height your radar scanner is above the water. On average most sets are about 20–25 feet (6–8 meters) off the water. This gives them a practical range of only 5–6 miles (8–10 kilometers). However, when most freighters are moving at 12–15 knots, you still have about 20 minutes to take avoiding action.

Another item that limits the range of radar is the heel angle of the yacht. If the boat is heeled and the vertical beam width of the set is fairly narrow, then you are not going to get very good resolution. Figure 11.2 shows why. So when buying a radar set, it pays to ask what the vertical beam width is.

FIGURE 11.2. *The vertical band width of the radar is important for a sailing yacht. If it is too narrow it may not "see" land when the boat is heeled. However, too wide a band width may lead to too much "clutter" on the screen.*

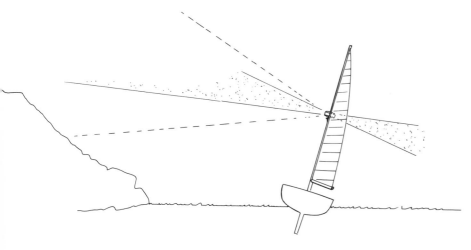

Radar operates by sending a short, high frequency pulse of radio waves toward the horizon. Any metallic object will reflect some of that energy back to the scanner. The scanner then sends this signal to the radar unit, where it is amplified and displayed on the radar screen. The screen display tells the operator what is around him.

RACONS AND ANTICOLLISION ALARMS

Because the radar sends out a radio signal, it is possible for an alarm to receive that signal and alert the operator. Racon beacons are triggered by the radar pulse from a ship and send a coded signal to the radar set. This signal appears as a distinct trace on the screen. However, Racons are expensive and are not generally available for yachts. Usually they are used for fixed structures or buoys.

Yacht owners can obtain a simple alarm system that sets off a buzzer when the radar pulse from another ship is sensed. They usually only display the direction from which the radar signal is coming. But they can alert the crew, which can turn on their own radar and find the ship in time to take avoiding action if it is required.

Another device is the Combi Macro Compass, from IMI. When this unit is set to "Rx," it can be used to find a transmitting radar set. If a radar is found, an LED on the compass flashes to alert the operator. By pushing the button on the unit, a bearing to the radar is obtained.

ELECTRONIC COMPASSES

If you are intending to use an autopilot, it is almost imperative that you use an electronic compass. The latest units are much more sensitive than the magnetic card compass.

The latest word in miniaturized compass technology is the "flux gate" compass. The term describes a compass with no moving parts. The compass uses a flux gate to measure the strength of the magnetic force field lines around the earth. It is extremely accurate and has some advantages over the more common magnetic card compass. The major advantage is that the sensing unit can be placed in the bilge, or anywhere else on the boat where it is away from large masses of metal and magnetic influences. The display, as on many electronic instruments today, is usually shown on a liquid crystal display (LCD). The compass should be thought of more as a backup to the magnetic card unit rather than the primary unit. It is best when used in conjunction with other electronics, when its accuracy and speed can interface with wind instruments to give almost instantaneaous readouts.

EPIRB

As part of the search and rescue system known as SARSAT-COSPAS, the EPIRB can save your life. The EPIRB (emergency position indicating radio beacon) works in a similar fashion to the Satnav system. Once the EPIRB is activated, a satellite passing overhead picks up the signal and relays it to a ground station. The ground station alerts the Coast Guard, which sends a rescue unit.

EPIRB are small, often hand-held size, and are perfectly watertight. They are activated by being switched on after a sinking or capsize and keep transmitting their signal until the batteries wear out.

It is best to leave the unit on once it has been switched on to give the rescue party a beacon to find. There was a case a few months ago of a sailor who kept turning the unit off after a few hours of transmission to conserve the batteries. It took far longer to find him because every time the Coast Guard thought they had a fix he'd turn the unit off and they had to wait until it was turned on again.

FIGURE 11.3B

FIGURE 11.3. *Instruments can be integrated into groups to perform several functions. In A the Vigil C100 Loran and Vigil US 32 radar give position and proximity to land or to other vessels. In B the Autohelm ST-7000 Autopilot and electronic instruments work together to steer the boat to windward or on a predetermined course. (Photos Courtesy of Autohelm USA.)*

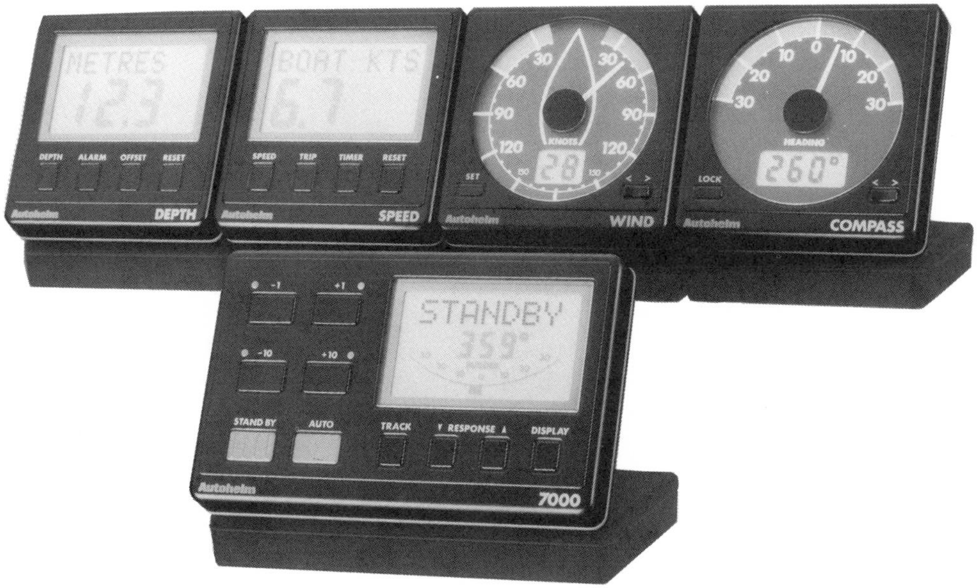

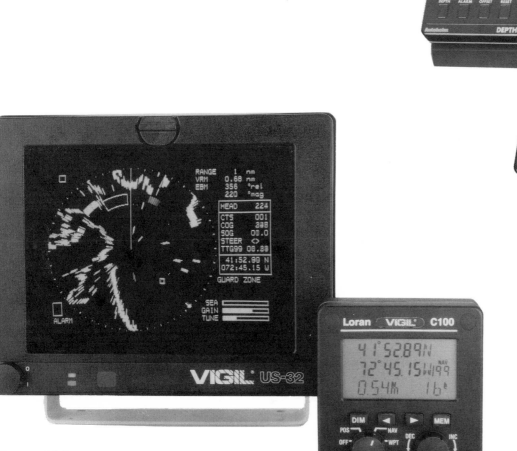

FIGURE 11.3A

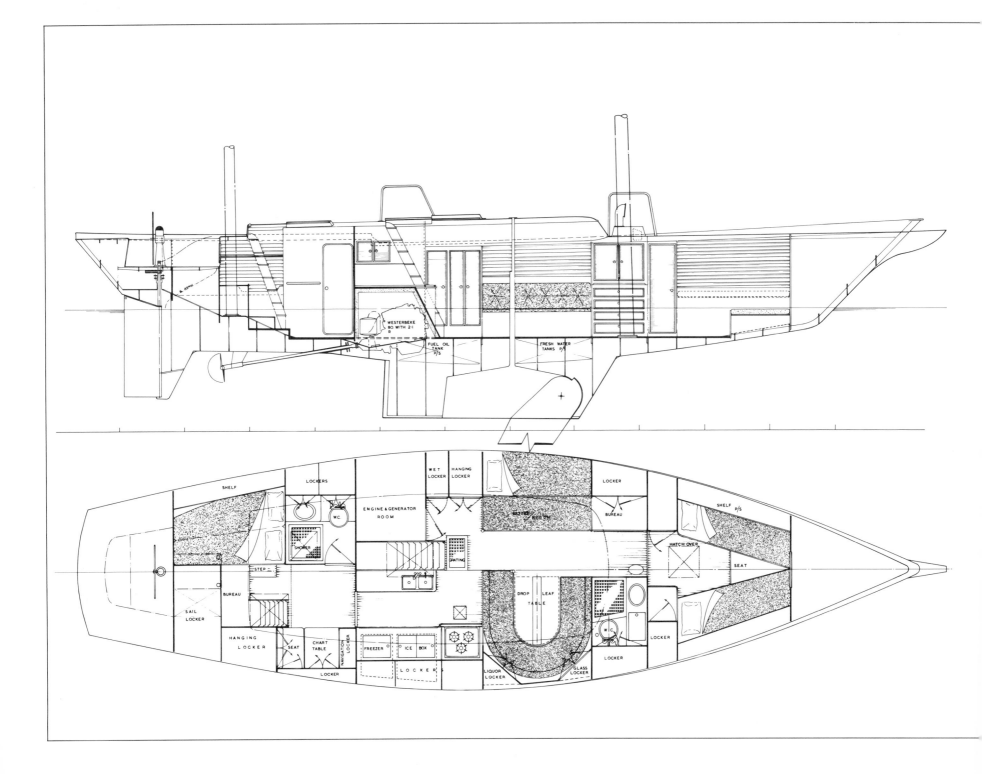

CHAPTER 12

The Push-Button Boat

With the trend toward larger boats and easier operation of those boats, it won't be long before boats could become totally push-button. I see old-time sailormen throwing up their hands in horror. But look where the technology is going. We now have hydraulic winches, hydraulic reefing systems, hydraulic sail furling systems, and electronic systems that sense where the wind is coming from and the wind strength. It may not happen right away (although I know two vessels are being built in America that use most of the technology outlined here), but sometime soon somebody will put together a complete "push-button" package.

Let's look at what's available and see where it can go. We've already mentioned hydraulic winches and reefing systems. We also looked at automatic pilots. Now let's suppose we put them together with a top quality electronics package.

In the boat of the future, suppose we want to leave the mooring. We turn the key and push the button that starts the engine. Then, without leaving our comfortable seat at the helm station we check around for other boats. None are close, so we push the button to raise the anchor. Jets of water spray down the hawsepipe to clean the chain as it comes aboard. The anchor line drops automatically into the anchor well until the hook is pulled tightly into the hawsepipe. The tension on the anchor line tells the windlass the hook is in, and it automatically drops the chainlock.

Wind direction and speed are sensed by the masthead unit. This communicates with the electronic navigation package to find out where the boat is relevant to the mooring, the course desired, and the destination. The electronic chart system displays the chart for the area on the screen and shows the boat's position. It highlights areas too shallow for the boat in red and will set off an alarm if the boat closes nearer than 100 feet (about 30 meters). If the crew want to override the system, they have the opportunity at any time, but they decide that the waypoints they put in earlier are sufficient. Now it's up to the computer to get them there.

The Loran, or GPS (global positioning system), interface checks with the chart and the wind instruments. They decide the course is dead upwind. So the central computer tells the boat to sail as close to the wind as possible and kicks in the wind vane to interface with the autopilot. The computer then unrolls the mainsail and sheets it to a predetermined sheet tension. At this point the computer announces that the sail is sheeted fully home and uses a camera mounted on the mast to check the shape of the mainsail. It compares the shape of black tapes sewn on the sail with the shapes in the computer's memory banks and notes that the sail is a little full for the conditions and tensions the outhaul to flatten the lower part of the sail.

It follows that step by unrolling the genoa and sheeting it in until the predetermined sheet tension is found. The camera on the mast swings around and checks the genoa shape, matching that against the shape already stored in the yacht's computer. It decides to move the sheet lead forward slightly. With a whirr of the hydraulics the lead moves forward. Now the boat is brought onto the optimum course. The heel angle indicator is asked if the boat is heeled properly; the answer comes back affirmative. The boat sails on its best heading toward the distant destination.

Let's say the wind increases and swings through a 50 degree change. As it increases the heel angle indicator picks up the increased heel. It tells the computer, which asks the sheet tension meters what the load

is. The load on the sheets and halyards has risen appreciably. So the computer asks the autopilot whether the helm load has increased. It has, so the decision is made—by the computer—to reef the mainsail.

It transmits the order and the mainsail is automatically reefed on the roller furling gear inside the mast. The load on the helm lightens up, but the boat is still heeled too far. So the computer decides to reef the genoa, again by furling it. The genoa sheet lead is automatically moved forward to suit the smaller genoa. When that is done the heel angle comes back to acceptable values. The sheet load meters are also checked, and they too have come back to acceptable levels.

Now the computer has decided the other tack is the favored route to the island, so it decides to tack the boat. In its best computer voice it tells the crew that the boat will be tacked in one minute. One minute later the computer says "Lee ho" and puts the helm over. The sails are automatically sheeted in on the other tack and checked by the mast camera, and the boat heads toward its destination on a close reach. The sails are eased out to conform with the new heading. The sheet lead is moved forward hydraulically until the top of the genoa stops luffing. The mainsail is eased out on the sheet, and some twist is put in by easing the vang slightly. The boat speed and course are compared with the polar diagram stored in the computer's memory banks. The speed is not quite what it should be so the computer goes through a check of all the onboard systems.

It finds that the backstay tension has backed off from the value it was originally set at. So it turns on the printer and makes a note to the crew to check the hydraulic backstay valve. This fault is automatically added to the log when it is printed every half an hour. Meanwhile it tensions the backstay a little more.

The log is much longer than we are normally used to. The computer monitors outputs from all the electronic and hydraulic systems and records them. It even goes to the extent of automatically receiving the weatherfax map and checking it against the local atmospheric pressure before calling the navigator's attention to a possible course change to take advantage of the better weather conditions on the other side of the high.

If the course were to be across the Gulf Stream, the computer would receive the latest stream update via facsimile, together with any eddies and meanders. It would then check the ocean temperature and compare that to the boat's position and the Gulf Stream chart before analyzing the course to take advantage of the vagaries of the Gulf Stream and then plotting the best speed and course to the boat's destination.

During all these evolutions the Satnav has been checking the boat's position and is backed up by the Loran. A radar detector has been checking the horizon for any radar emissions, and the depth sounder has been checking ahead and to the side of the boat for shallow water. A distant ship is picked up on radar and its course plotted. The computer decides that it will pass within the half-mile alert circle and warns the crew by speaking to them. The two crew, meanwhile, have selected dinner from the menu displayed on the computer screen, put it in the microwave, read a book, and reeled in the fishing line on the transom.

Should they get bored, they can play the computer at chess, or any other video game, call up the latest HBO movie, or simply relax on deck and enjoy the sail, knowing that the computer will alert them if any problem arises.

The central computer has not only been monitoring all the sailing events but has been recording water use, the state of the batteries, the temperature in the freezer, the air conditioning temperature, and the amount of fuel and stores on board. When the water level reaches a predetermined low, it will turn on the reverse osmosis watermaker and generate some more.

If the batteries are low, it will check the time of day, check whether the crew is awake, and decide whether power use will climb or fall before making the decision to start the second generator.

The fuel and oil levels of the generator and main engine are carefully monitored when they are in use, and rather than simply lighting idiot lights, it will generate a readout as part of the log every half an hour. If a problem occurs it will perform diagnostic testing before telling the crew what the problem is, where it is, and pointing them to the correct page in the computer-generated manual for repair.

In fact, every item of equipment is monitored by the computer; should anything fail, it will perform a diagnostic test. The results of the test will be printed out along with the parts required for repair and the manual for repair.

Sound far-fetched? All the technology to do the above is here now. Then the joy or drudgery of sailing will be gone. No more will the helmsman get wet standing his lonely tricks at the helm. No more will the crew be exhausted and leave it too late to get the final reef in. The computer will either tell them when to change sail or do it all for them.

That is until a wave soaks the computer systems. Then the lonesome sailor will have to know how to get home. He (or she) then has two options. The first is to tear the computer boards out and replace them with the spares that the yacht is required to carry by its insurance carrier, or if he belongs to the manufacturer's repair network and has the latest in radios aboard, he could call up the central equipment manufacturer, who, with the company helicopter, will fly out to the beleagured yacht. A trained technician will jump from the chopper into the ocean alongside with all the spare parts. The yacht's tender will pick him up and he will climb aboard, remove a few circuit boards, insert new ones, and get the system back up to speed. Once the job has been done the repairman will climb back into the dinghy and motor clear of the yacht's rigging. From this position he will be winched aboard the helicopter and whisked back to land.

This probably sounds like science fiction, but the push-button boat is here. Hydraulic reefing systems are now small enough to be used on 45 footers or large enough for boats well over a 100 meters (320 feet). It won't be much longer before they are small enough for 30 footers, and when that happens they will have reached the largest part of the sailing market. Marry the hydraulic reefing systems to hydraulically driven winches and you have the beginnings of the system I outlined above. Most boats have electronics aboard already. How long will it be before the electronics are integrated with a central computer? It is already happening in the racing fleet, although the racers are using the electronics package to find the last iota of boat speed. In the cruising fleet the central computer can be used for many other things, from checking the course to monitoring the sails and the rig loads.

This scenario will be expensive, but in a few years it will be here. In the twenty-first century we'll look back at those brave sailors who sailed long distances and wonder how they did it without all the modern navigation systems.

Possibly, in some far-off time, a child will look at a sextant in a museum and wonder how it works. Next to it, a copy of HO 208 will be displayed and the child will wonder why all those tables are in a book rather than in the powerful computer he has on his wrist. Such is the price of progress.

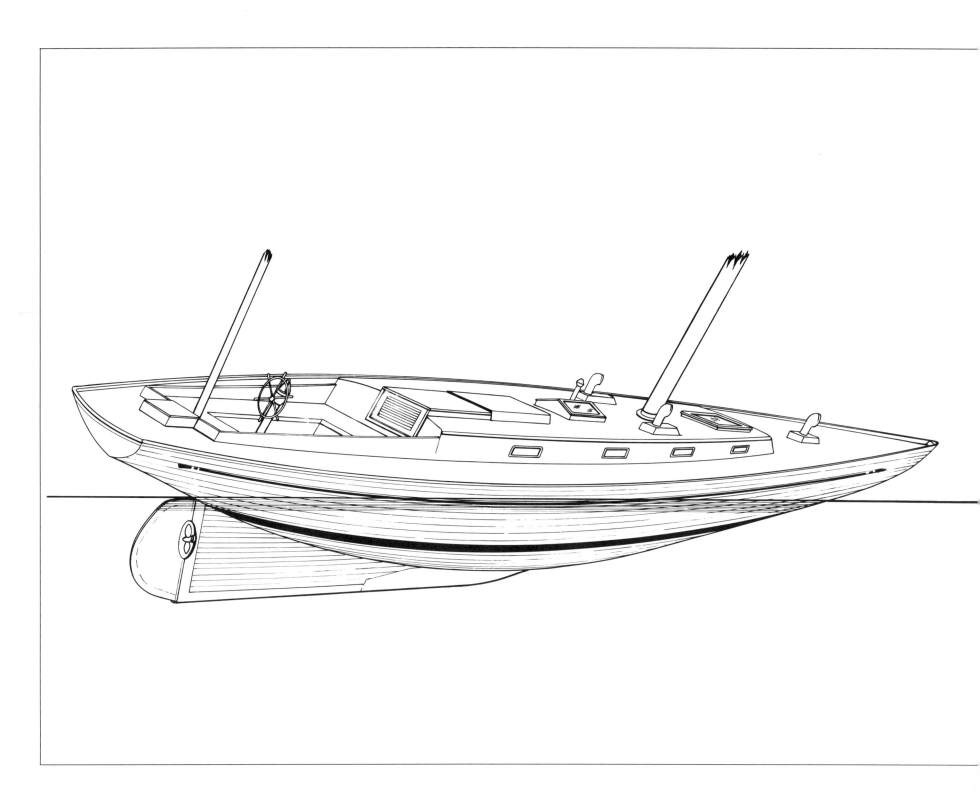

CHAPTER 13
Having a New Boat Designed for You

Almost every sailor who owns his own boat buys a production boat first. After owning a few boats, he formulates the outline of his ideal boat. The fantasy continues every time he is drifting along with the side of the helmsman's cockpit digging into his side. It grows stronger as the genoa sheet lead hangs up on the forehatch, as it has done every time he's tacked the boat.

Finally, he puts that boat on the market. The day it's sold he's incredibly happy. The financial drain is gone; now he can look forward to weekends away from the boatyard. Weekends, when he'll have time to do something other than work on the boat. The euphoria lasts for about six weeks before our sailor is prowling into brokerage offices and around marinas looking for the elusive dream.

He cannot find what he is looking for, and one day he starts talking to a builder. The builder is looking for work and persuades the sailor to visit his shop to see the latest sleek craft ready to be launched. After a long look through the new boat, the sailor wants to talk costs and describe his fantasy.

COSTS

Costs can vary dramatically. If you are a handyman and have the time to build your own boat, it can cost half as much as a production boat. However, this also assumes that your time is free. If you want the latest and fanciest yacht available, then the cost could be 50 percent more than the cost of a production boat. But there are many ways to get your dream, not all of them incredibly expensive. Here are some of them.

STOCK PLANS

Many designers have plans of various boats available. The plans may be of boats designed years ago or plans specially designed to be sold as stock, or often, plans for a boat that never got built. They can usually be bought reasonably inexpensively. For instance, almost all the plans in this book are from a brochure of plans designed by Roger Marshall Inc., 44 Ft. Wetherill Rd., Jamestown, RI 02835. Your own improvements or additions can be designed into them. If necessary I will advise on changes or on the practicability of your ideas. This is just one example; in the back of many sailing magazines you'll find the names of many designers who develop stock plans.

DEVELOPING A NEW DESIGN

Developing a new design can be expensive, depending on the designer and the amount of detail you want in the new boat. In general it takes two to three months for one man to design a new boat from scratch. This time has shortened slightly with the advent of computers, but usually the designer uses the computer to give you a better picture of the boat's performance potential rather than a less expensive boat. He also has more time to work with you to develop a better boat than he could when all the drawings were hand drawn.

If you intend having a new boat designed from scratch to suit your requirements, figure a design cost 5–10 percent of the total cost of the boat. The percentage is largely dependent upon the amount of detail work and supervision involved. If you want every item detailed out before construction starts, then the cost may be higher than that quoted. Usually the designer will give you an approximate cost and bill you on an hourly rate for the time involved.

Having obtained a design, the next step is to build it or get it built. In the next section we'll look at the two extremes: building a boat yourself from scratch, and having the boat built so that your only job is breaking the Champagne bottle over the bow and stepping aboard.

BUILDING IT YOURSELF

Consider the sailor who wants to build a boat for himself. He would like to keep the costs down and to get sailing fairly quickly. The first step is to write to all the companies that sell stock plans and to designers who specialize in stock plans. If this is the method you intend to adopt, be sure that you give approximate parameters such as LOA, LWL, beam, maximum acceptable draft, approximate displacement, and the type of material you intend to build in. Any other information you can give the designer will enable him to respond more specifically to your requirements. Many design offices have a wide range of plans available and don't want to spend time selecting a bunch of drawings defined by vague parameters. For instance, we recently had an inquiry for a boat with a beam of not more than 12 feet. This was the only requirement and probably came from a person who's building shed doors were only 12 feet wide. However, it was the only specified requirement and told us that the person had not really thought about the boat they wanted. Using the one parameter given we could have sent him every design under 40 feet (12 meters) and a few larger boats. Needless to say, it would be very expensive for the small design office to reply to every inquiry of this type.

The available stock plans can vary from highly detailed to simple sketches, depending on whether the boat was built by an experienced builder or by a builder who needed every detail laid out. They are usually available at a fraction of the cost of a new design. However, any extra development work will usually be charged at the designer's or architect's normal fee.

Having selected and ordered the stock plans the owner-builder then has to find a place to build the craft. To some extent the building will depend upon the type of construction. For instance, if you intend to use fiberglass construction with thermo-setting resins, the temperature and humidity should really be controlled. This means the building should have exhaust fans as well some form of humidity control. A WEST or DuraKore hull laminate may not be quite so critical, but the bonds will be stronger if the moisture content in the wood, and the humidity in the air, are low.

Costs of materials will vary, sometimes quite dramatically. It usually pays to purchase in the largest quantities you can afford and to pay cash. Most lumber companies will give better prices if they are paid immediately in cash. Another idea one amateur builder had was to set up a boat-building company, which gave him access to OEM (original equipment manufacturers) prices. This often resulted in a 30–50 percent discount over retail prices.

The next stage is building the hull. For one person working alone it will take two to three weeks of full-time work to loft the boat out. Allow another eight weeks for cutting frames and starting the setup. Then you need to finish the plug and start on the hull. The hull portion represents about 25 percent of the boat, and as the time required to build a 40-foot boat can be over 12,000 hours, you can get some idea of the size of the job you have taken on.

However, there are faster ways to get your ideal. You can often purchase a fiberglass ready-made hull at a reasonable price. This will save you about 1,500–3,000 hours, depending on the size of the hull. Should you decide that you really want to build your own hull, then the first step is to set up a strongback, loft the hull, and start cutting frames.

Setting up a Strongback

Setting up a strongback is a relatively simple job. The strongback is the grid on which the entire hull is to be constructed. Therefore, it wants to be perfectly aligned and very strong. Usually they are made out of 2 × 10–inch (50 × 250–millimeter) or heavier lumber. When the frame has been made it is trued up so that the top surface is absolutely horizontal. At this point experienced builders apply a mix of resin and microballoons about every 3 or 4 feet (1 or 1.25 meters) around the base to anchor the frame firmly to the floor.

Lofting the Lines

Lofting the lines—rescaling the drawing from the scale at which the designer drew it to full size—is probably the most difficult job an amateur builder will face. This has to be done very accurately and carefully. It helps to understand the way the designer drew the lines and the terminology used.

The designer will provide a set of lines and a table of offsets. The first step is to lay out a very accurate grid, which will comprise

1. The waterlines, usually spaced 1 inch (250 millimeters) apart.
2. The buttocks—spacing will vary depending on the whim of the designer.
3. The station lines—most designers use 10 stations over the waterline length of the boat.

This grid will give you the layout for all the fore and aft lines of the vessel. Usually the grid is quite compressed, in that the base line is laid down first, followed by the waterlines. The stations are added. Now the buttocks can be laid out in black. Next the waterlines can be laid over the top of the buttocks in red. Finally, the diagonals can be laid over the top of the whole thing in green.

Concurrent with the longitudinal lines you should lay out the body plan. This should be done on a separate loft floor alongside the main hull and will have buttocks, waterlines, and diagonals laid out on it.

Taking the table of offsets all you need to do now is mark out each waterline, diagonal, buttock, or section and join up the dots. It is best to lay them out and join them one at a time. Usually some fairing will be required to ensure the boat is smooth in three dimensions.

Setting up the Frames

Having laid out the sections, temporary frames will have to be fabricated. These are usually made at each section. The hull thickness is subtracted from the lofted section, and the new section minus the hull thickness is transferred to a wooden form. After marking, the wooden form is cut to the shape of the frame. These forms are accurately set up and trued up on the strongback.

At this point the edges of the frames are still parallel to the centerline of the boat. To make the hull fit properly, the frame edges will have to be beveled so that a batten laid on several frames is fair. This is not difficult to do and is made easier by careful fairing with long battens.

Once the frames are set up on the strongback, the method of building the hull varies with the material. At this point it advisable to have a nearby advisor who is experienced in the tricks of using the material. Any questions can be referred to him.

Building a boat is not a fast job if done properly. Constructing the hull of a 40-foot boat can take 2,200–3,000, hours depending on the skill of the workers. From starting work to launching the boat can take 8,000–12,000 hours, depending on complexity. The hull comprises about 25–30 percent of the materials and time. That's how much you can save if you purchase a ready-made hull and deck.

For an amateur builder working in his spare time, devoting, say, 35 hours per week to the project, building your own boat can take about four years! But even with a low labor rate the saving in real money can be in the thousands of dollars. A word of warning though: skimping on materials could lead to a boat totally unsuitable for the sailing you want to do. Also, it is as expensive to build an ugly boat as it is to build a good-looking boat. The good-looking boat will have a much higher resale value when the time comes to move up to a bigger vessel. This will enable you to recoup a large part of your initial investment. Maybe you could even make a profit!

A CUSTOM DESIGN

If you are the type that bends a nail at first swipe, then building your own boat is not for you. But you can still have a design at a reasonable price. In this case, the first step is to approach a competent designer or naval architect. Make an appointment and have a list of your requirements ready. In my office I have an owner's questionnaire that I send to prospective clients. This helps the owner and me pinpoint the type of design most suitable for his needs.

Preliminary Design Work

After this initial flurry of letters we generally meet and a set of preliminary drawings is commissioned. Their cost varies between $500 and $2,000, depending on how specific the owner's requirements are.

The preliminary plans comprise a sail plan and exterior profile, an interior layout, an interior profile, and occasionally a preliminary deck plan. The idea is to give the owner some idea of the layout of the boat and to have something that can be used for bid plans as well as being a basis for the weight and other preliminary calculations that will need to be made.

Bid Plans

When the owner approves these plans, a bid package is made up. The bid package will contain

1. All the preliminary plans.
2. A few sections showing the approximate construction or a construction plan of similar yachts.
3. A set of written specifications detailing every piece of equipment expected to be in the new boat. These specifications are developed from previous boats and can often run to 40 or more pages in length.
4. A covering letter laying out the owner's requirements and asking the builder to submit a bid to build the boat.

When the bids are received from the builders we sit and analyze them. They can vary tremendously, and some builders accidently "forget" to include some items. This makes their bid seem low, and the forgotten items get added in as extras, increasing the final cost.

Bid plans can vary tremendously. For instance, on a recent design we received bids on, the top price was 50 percent higher than the lowest bid! The lowest three bids were comparable to the cost of a production boat, while the highest bid was about 35 percent higher.

At this stage we try to take the client around to meet each of the builders and to inspect examples of their latest work. Some builders may bid low but their work is good and their labor rate is low; others may bid high and still do poor work. We look for good, high quality work at a reasonable cost.

When the builder has been selected, the client will contract for a building slot and commission the design. The cost of a custom design can be roughly approximated to the cost of the boat. It usually runs between 5 and 10 percent of the total cost of the boat, depending on how much detail work and supervision is required. When the boat is under construction we like to inspect it regularly, charging the time and expenses to the owner.

What does the owner get for his money? In general—and this depends on the designer—the owner will get complete plans to build the boat. The number and complexity of the drawings will vary from design to design, but here's what we usually supply for a boat about 40 feet LOA:

1. Lines plan
2. Offsets
3. Keel and rudder drawings
4. Interior arrangements
5. Joiner sections
6. Sail plan

7. Deck plan
8. Deck geometry and reinforcement plan
9. Construction plan
10. Construction sections
11. Various smaller construction detail plans
12. Engine room layout

Additional plans may be provided depending on the builder and owner:

13. Electrical schematic
14. Electrical wiring diagram
15. Plumbing diagram
16. Mast arrangement
17. Rigging plan
18. Detail plans of various parts of the boat

These plans remain the property and copyright of the designer, and the owner buys the right to build one boat from them. They are usually marked that they should be returned to the designer after use, but in practice this is rarely done unless the boat is a top secret design.

Once the boat is built and launched, the yard, designer, and owner take it out on sea trials to ensure everything works and that it powers and sails the way it was designed. When everything is working properly, it is handed over to the owner.

Occasionally, a design is not quite what it seems to be. It may float down by the bow, or it may not power as fast as it should. These problems do occur with a new boat and have to be solved. Usually the designer will put in time, as will the yard, to get everything right, at no extra cost to the owner. However, this should not be construed as endorsing poor workmanship on anybody's part. A boat is a complex object and errors can be made.

However, it is possible to have a custom design built to your requirements for not too much more than a good production craft. Occasionally the cost may be even less than a production boat. Many people who compare production and custom designs assume that the cost of custom design is going to be much higher than a similar production boat. It is not generally realized that a large percentage of the cost of a production boat goes into the marketing and advertising of that product, a cost most production builders have to maintain. With a custom boat a much higher proportion of the overall cost goes into the boat rather than into overhead.

In purchasing a boat designed to your exact requirements you have more boat, it is designed exactly to suit your requirements, and it is made of the materials you choose. However, the decision to go custom needs careful thought and a good project manager.

Suggested Additional Reading

DESIGN

Cruising Catamarans. Newbury, England: Amateur Yacht Research Society, 1977.

Gutelle, Pierre. *The Design of Sailing Yachts.* Lymington, England: Nautical, 1984.

Kinney, Francis. *Skene's Elements of Yacht Design.* New York: Dodd, Mead, 1981.

WOODEN BOATS

The Gougeon Brothers on Yacht Construction. Bay City, Mich.: Gougeon Brothers, 1979.

Jurd, K.H.C. *Yacht Construction.* St. Albans, England: Adlard Coles, 1970.

Steward, Robert. *Boatbuilding Manual.* Camden, Me.: International Marine, 1980.

Wood Handbook: Wood as an Engineering Material. U.S.D.A. Agricultural Handbook. Washington, D.C.: Government Printing Office, 1974.

FIBERGLASS BOATS

duPlessis, Hugo. *Fiberglass Boats.* St. Albans, England: Adlard Coles, 1973.

Hart, Chris, et al. *Klegecell Composite Structures.* Grapevine, Tex.: North American Klegecell, 1980.

Johannsen, Tom. *Airex Construction.* Buffalo, N.Y.: Chemacryl, 1973.

Owens Corning Fiberglass also publishes numerous booklets on marine uses of fiberglass. See your local dealer for details.

METAL BOATS

Nicolson, Ian. *Small Steel Craft.* St. Albans, England: Adlard Coles, 1971.

Pratt, Mike. *Own a Steel Boat.* Camden, Me: International Marine, 1979.

FERRO-CEMENT BOATS

Bingham, Bruce. *Ferro-Cement.* New York: Cornell Maritime Press, 1974.

OTHER USEFUL BOOKS

Bamford, Don. *Anchoring.* Newport, R.I.: Seven Seas Press, 1985.

GENERAL

Dashew, Steve and Linda. *The Circumnavigators Handbook.* New York: Norton, 1983.

Fletcher, Mike, and Bob Ross. *Tuning a Racing Yacht.* New ed. New York: Norton, 1975.

Howard-Williams, Jeremy. *Sails.* New York: John de Graff, 1983.

Marine Electrical Systems. Maidenhead, England: Lucas Marine, 1982.

Marshall, Roger. *Designed To Win.* New York: Norton, 1979.

Marshall, Roger. *A Sailor's Guide to Production Sailboats.* New York: Hearst Marine Books, 1985.

Nixon, W. M. *The Sailing Cruiser.* New York: Dodd, Mead, 1977.

Roth, Hal. *After 50,000 Miles.* New York: Norton, 1977.

Street, Donald. *The Ocean Sailing Yacht.* 2 vols. New York: Norton, 1973.

Index

shroud end fittings on, 109–10
wire or rod, 109
starting system of engine, 223
stay length in scope amount, 192
stays, 108, 109
staysail, 89–91, 94, 95, 101
staysail schooner, 91, 93
staysail tracks, 171
steam-bent frames, 57
steel boat building, 53, 54, 76–80
steerboard, 203
steering, 30, 199–217
  autopilot for, 213, 215–17
  balanced rudder for, 199–200, 201
  rudder with skeg for, 200–203
  stern shape influence on, 28
  vane, 210–15
  vane vs. autopilot, 209–10
steering gear, 203–9
  emergency, 201, 208–9
  hydraulic and electrical, 208, 209
  maintenance accessibility of, 208
  selecting of, 209
  steerboard or oar, 203
  tiller, 203–4
  wheel, 204–8
  wheel, position of, 208
  whipstaff, 204
stem piece, wooden, 57
steplights, 250
steps for getting aboard, 180
stern pulpit, 178
stern shapes:
  steering affected by, 28
  variety of, 25–26
stock, rudder, 202
stock-in-head anchor, 186, 188
stockless anchors, 187, 188–91
stock plans and designed boats, 270
stocks, anchors with, 188
storage areas, 145–49
  bilge as, 148
  under bunks as, 148–49
  chain lockers as, 148
  cockpit lockers as, 147
  foul weather gear lockers as, 147

galley, designing of, 130, 131–32
  hanging lockers as, 147
  lazarette as, 132, 145–47
  lockers as, 131, 138–39, 147–49, 150, 159,
    160–62, 163, 193, 197
  see also stowage
stoves, 120–27, 131
  alcohol (methylated spirits), 121–22, 123,
    124, 125, 238
  choosing best type of, 123–5
  compressed natural gas (CNG), 121, 123,
    124, 238
  diesel, 122, 123, 124, 125
  electric, 123, 124, 125, 126
  gasoline, 125
  gimbaled, 124, 127
  heating, 238
  kerosene (paraffin), 122–23, 124
  microwave vs., 123, 124
  propane, butane, or liquified petroleum gas
    (LPG), 121, 123, 124, 125, 238
  pros and cons of, 125
  safety features of, 125–27
  wood or coal, 123, 124, 125, 238
stowage:
  anchor, 148, 192–95
  anchor cable, 197
  book, 144
  chart, 143
  dinghy, 181
  flag, sextant, foghorn, and larger tools,
    144
  sail, 159, 160–62, 163
  small tool, 143
  see also storage areas
strainers, fuel, 223
strip planking, 59
strongback, setting up of, 271
strut drives, 228
stuffing box, 225
S2 glass reinforcement, 63, 64, 71, 73, 74
support systems, 233–38
  air conditioning as, 234–36
  fire prevention, 238
  heating as, 237–38
  refrigerator-freezer as, 236–37

reverse osmosis desalination (watermaker)
  as, 233–34
swage fitting, 110
switch, battery isolation, 246–47
swivel lights, 250

tables, 150
  chart, 141–43, 144, 153
  dining, 136
tacking, self-, equipment, 102–3, 164–65
tackles, 166
tangs, 104, 105–7
tanks, fuel, 222
Taylor, Sir Geoffrey, 187
teak, 55, 62, 80, 149, 160, 176, 197
thermo electric refrigeration, 236
Thomas W. Lawson, 91
tidal streams, direction of, in scope amount,
  192
tide:
  readout of, 258
  rise and fall of, in scope amount, 192
tiller steering, 203–4
time elapsed readout, 258
toerails, 160, 161, 175–76
tools, 52, 54, 67, 75
  large, stowage for, 144
  small, stowage for, 143
topping lift, 114
topsails, 94, 97, 101
total draft, 24
tracks:
  headsail sheet, 171–72, 174
  mainsail, 107
  mainsheet, 48, 165, 170–71
  self-tacking, 102–3, 164–65
transformers:
  battery-charging, 246
  isolation, 246
transom, 28, 45
  rudder on, 201–2
trim, hull interior, 149–50
  fabrics in, 149
  use of color in, 150
  wood finishes in, 149–50
trim, sail, 162–65